The Classical Animated Documentary and Its Contemporary Evolution

The Classical Animated Documentary and Its Contemporary Evolution

Cristina Formenti

BLOOMSBURY ACADEMIC
NEW YORK • LONDON • OXFORD • NEW DELHI • SYDNEY

BLOOMSBURY ACADEMIC
Bloomsbury Publishing Inc
1385 Broadway, New York, NY 10018, USA
50 Bedford Square, London, WC1B 3DP, UK
29 Earlsfort Terrace, Dublin 2, Ireland

BLOOMSBURY, BLOOMSBURY ACADEMIC and the Diana logo are trademarks of
Bloomsbury Publishing Plc

First published in the United States of America 2022
Paperback edition published 2023

Copyright © Cristina Formenti, 2022

For legal purposes the Acknowledgments on p. x constitute an extension
of this copyright page.

Cover design: Eleanor Rose
Cover image: A still from *Fresh Laid Plans* (1951), Dir. George Gordon,
John Sutherland Productions

All rights reserved. No part of this publication may be reproduced or transmitted
in any form or by any means, electronic or mechanical, including photocopying,
recording, or any information storage or retrieval system, without prior
permission in writing from the publishers.

Bloomsbury Publishing Inc does not have any control over, or responsibility for, any
third-party websites referred to or in this book. All internet addresses given in
this book were correct at the time of going to press. The author and publisher regret
any inconvenience caused if addresses have changed or sites have ceased
to exist, but can accept no responsibility for any such changes.

Library of Congress Cataloging-in-Publication Data
Names: Formenti, Cristina, author.
Title: The classical animated documentary and its contemporary evolution /
by Cristina Formenti.
Description: New York, NY: Bloomsbury Academic, 2022. | Includes bibliographical
references and index. | Summary: "Addresses the evolutions undergone by the animated
documentary throughout the decades, in order to re-position it within a broader historical
and theoretical context"–Provided by publisher.
Identifiers: LCCN 2021048049 (print) | LCCN 2021048050 (ebook) | ISBN 9781501346460
(hardback) | ISBN 9781501346484 (epub) | ISBN 9781501346477 (pdf)
Subjects: LCSH: Documentary films–History and criticism. | Animated films–
History and criticism.
Classification: LCC PN1995.9.D6 F686 2022 (print) | LCC PN1995.9.D6 (ebook) |
DDC 791.43/3409–dc23/eng/20220112
LC record available at https://lccn.loc.gov/2021048049
LC ebook record available at https://lccn.loc.gov/2021048050

ISBN: HB: 978-1-5013-4646-0
PB: 978-1-5013-7610-8
ePDF: 978-1-5013-4647-7
ebook: 978-1-5013-4648-4

Typeset by Deanta Global Publishing Services, Chennai, India

To find out more about our authors and books visit www.bloomsbury.com and
sign up for our newsletters.

CONTENTS

Figures vii
Acknowledgments x
Abbreviations xii

Introduction 1

PART I   Theoretical and Historical Issues 11

  1 Reality's Two Animated Faces 13

  2 The Sincerest Form of Docudrama 34

  3 A New Periodization for an Old Form 49

PART II   The Rise and Affirmation of an Audiovisual Form 75

  4 The Age of the Origins, 1909–39 77

  5 The Classical Age, 1940–85 94

  6 The United States 123

  7 Great Britain 162

  8 Canada 185

  9 Italy 203

PART III The Contemporary Production, 1986 and Beyond 225

  10 Private Truths and Inner Realities 227

  11 The Persistence of the Classical Animated Documentary 246

Toward a Post-Animated Documentary Age? 259

References 266
Index 301

FIGURES

1.1 Blood cells as represented in *Blood Transfusion* 18
1.2 Blood cells as represented in *Defense against Invasion* 18
1.3 Frame from *The Battle of the North Sea* offering a legend of the symbols employed in the film 19
1.4 A shot from "The Dance of the Lemons" scene in *Waiting for Superman* 20
1.5 An example of the data visualization-driven animation from *Waiting for Superman* 21
1.6 An example of the employment of the pointer stick from *How the Telephone Talks* 26
1.7 Giordano Bruno flying through the Cosmos in *Cosmos—A Spacetime Odyssey* 29
2.1 A shot of a recorder from *Irinka & Sandrinka* 38
3.1 In *Look Who's Driving*, Charlie's thoughts are made visible using a comic book-like approach 68
3.2 In *Man Alive!*, the worries of Ed Parmelee are visualized through thought bubbles 68
3.3 One of the strips created using frames from UPA's *Look Who's Driving* and published in the newspaper *The San Saba News and Star* 69
4.1 A shot of the fly too cute for being envisioned as an enemy that stars in *The Fly* 82
4.2 In *Diseases Spread*'s coda, the personification of disease acts in front of a map of Japan 84
4.3 The personified gasoline drop protagonist of *Down the Gasoline Trail* 90
4.4 A frame from *Down the Gasoline Trail* in which Chevrolet's logo is well visible 91
5.1 In *The Traitor Within,* the cells forming our body are represented as assembly line workers in coveralls 102
5.2 In *Magic Lab*, pepsin is portrayed as a worker involved in maneuvering a crane 103
5.3 The everyman protagonist of *A Great Problem* 104
5.4 A red blood cell as personified in *Blood* 116

FIGURES

6.1 An advertisement of John Sutherland Productions that well synthetizes the studio's tendency to adapt its "style" to the needs of the client 146
6.2 The personification of a fuel oil molecule in *Gasoline's Amazing Molecules* 146
6.3 A shot revealing how the shape of *Gasoline's Amazing Molecules'* personified fuel oil molecule is devised from its habitual scientific graphic visualization 147
6.4 The personification of the atom in *A Is for Atom* 147
6.5 Air, fuel, and ignition as portrayed in *The ABC of Internal Combustion Engines* and its "sequels" 148
6.6 An example of brand placement in the animated visuals of *Good Wrinkles* 150
6.7 Planet Earth as represented in *Food Will Win the War* 155
6.8 Sleepy yawning while working in *The Winged Scourge* 156
7.1 A shot of a Bank Giro Credit paper slip by Barclays from *The Curious History of Money* 170
7.2 A frame from *Pan-tele-tron* wherein there are some cameras with the Philips logo 170
7.3 A shot from *Refining* wherein the animated voice-of-authority is inserted in a live-action background 176
7.4 A military motor vehicle moving away from a landscape devastated by the conflict in *The Moving Spirit* 182
7.5 The military motor vehicle transformed into an automobile for civilian use after entering a landscape wherein peace has been restored in *The Moving Spirit* 183
8.1 A frame from *Teeth Are to Keep* showing a piece of cutlery next to the heads of Roger and his family members 191
8.2 A frame from *Teeth Are to Keep* showing a toothbrush next to the heads of Roger and his family members 192
8.3 A sun shining over the sea as represented in *Energy and Matter* employing a childlike graphic style 195
8.4 The school of fishes that stands for its category in *Fish Spoilage Control* 196
8.5 The army of spoilage bacteria from *Fish Spoilage Control* 197
8.6 The faceless and nameless animated human protagonist characters of *Population Expansion* 197
9.1 The *Koch bacilli* as depicted in *Public Threat n. 1* 206
9.2 Nitrogen, phosphorus, potassium, and calcium as represented in *How to Feed Plants* 211
9.3 Nitrogen, phosphorus, potassium, and calcium as represented in *Fertilizers* 211
9.4 In *Baby Story*, Bozzetto represents the ovum as a prosperous Rapunzel-like queen trapped in an egg 213

FIGURES

9.5	Two sketched couples dressed in clothes from the eighteenth century that are shown in the act of dancing in a scene of *Adventure in the Cell* 218
9.6	The pyramidal cells responsible for our voluntary movements as represented in *Anatomy of Motion* 219
9.7	The representation of the human brain in *Hemo the Magnificent* 219
10.1	In *Ryan*, red spikes come out of Larkin's head when he talks about how limiting lack of money can be 230
10.2	The animated figure deprived of elements that could connote it as female or male associated with the testimonials of Bill, Samuel, Steve, and Camille in *Sleepless* 243

ACKNOWLEDGMENTS

Before being a book, this project was a doctoral thesis that I researched and developed at the Department of Cultural Heritage and Environment of the University of Milan. First and foremost, I thus wish to thank Raffaele De Berti, a caring mentor who not only has provided me with constant encouragement throughout the years of the Ph.D and beyond but has also left me free to pursue this research despite not being as much a fan of animation as he is of documentary.

A special thank-you goes also to Michael Renov, who has generously offered me his mentorship. I am particularly grateful for a conversation we had over lunch at the Visible Evidence conference in New Delhi that has ended up being pivotal for determining the focus of my research, and consequently the shape of this book. At a time in which I was still very much concentrating on the contemporary animated documentary production, he asked me a question that made me realize I should have been "more audacious" and ventured out of the contemporaneity-focused debate on the form to explore, instead, the still uncharted path of its history. I hope this book will prove to him a satisfactory answer to that thought-provoking question.

Special thanks are due also to Andrea Mariani and Luigi Boledi for having shared with me materials that have proven particularly useful for the chapter devoted to the classical Italian documentary as well as to Giaime Alonge, Elena Dagrada, Arild Fetveit, Oliver Gaycken, Mauro Giori, Ohad Landesman, Laura Rascaroli, and Malin Walberg for their encouragement and feedback at different stages of the project. I am also grateful for having had the chance to share and discuss chunks of my research with Nichola Dobson, Nea Ehrlich, Christopher Holliday, Annabelle Honess Roe, Misha Mihailova, Chris Pallant, Sheila Sofian, Gail Vanston, Paul Ward, Brian Winston, and the many other scholars who are part of the Society for Animation Studies and Visible Evidence communities.

The research for this book has been conducted in many archives and libraries throughout the world, where I have received invaluable help in accessing materials key to it. In particular, I wish to thank, for their precious assistance, Libby Wertin at the Margaret Herrick Library, Claudia Giordani at the Film Archive of the Cineteca di Bologna, Antonella Angelini at the

Bibliomediateca Mario Gromo, Frédéric Martel Savard at the National Film Board of Canada, and archivist Stephen Tollervey and librarians Sarah Currants, Ian O'Sullivan, and Peter Todd at the BFI.

I also wish to thank Katie Gallof and Erin Duffy at Bloomsbury Academic for their support and attention throughout the editorial process.

Finally, I must thank my parents, Mario and Mariapia, who have been extremely supportive, providing me with their love and even some "unofficial grants," Filippo for his invaluable IT help, and Clara, Margherita, Stella, and all the other friends who have endured my constant talking about this project for years without ever complaining for it.

I would like to dedicate this book to the memory of my grandmother, Mariuccia, who would have been eager to see it printed. Until shortly before passing away, she helped me stay on track with writing by constantly asking when she would have been able to hold the book in her hands.

ABBREVIATIONS

BBC	British Broadcasting Company
BFI	British Film Institute
BP	The British Petroleum Company
CBS	Columbia Broadcasting System
C.C.C.	Catholic Cinematographic Center
CGI	computer-generated imagery
CHC	Community Health Council
CIDA	Canadian International Development Agency
COI	Central Office of Information
ECPA	Établissement de conception et de production audiovisuelle des armées
EDF	Électricité de France
FMPU	First Motion Picture Unit
GPO	General Post Office
ICI	Imperial Chemical Industries
INCOM	Industria Corto Metraggio
ISOTYPE	International System of Typographic Picture Education
MGM	Metro-Goldwyn-Mayer
MOI	Ministry of Information
NFB	National Film Board of Canada
NHS	National Health Service
OCIAA	Office of the Coordinator of Inter-American Affairs

ABBREVIATIONS

OPEC	Organizzazione Pagot & Company
SBS	Special Broadcasting Service
UPA	United Productions of America
VR	virtual reality
WHO	World Health Organization

Introduction

As Donald Crafton (2013, 297) highlights in *Shadow of a Mouse*, although "performing the unreal ... has been animation's stock-in-trade for most of its existence," this medium has not exclusively been used to recount magic kingdoms and enchanted imaginary realms. Animated films have also been frequently employed "as authorities about what is real" (Crafton 2013, 297).[1] Indeed, next to the more renowned fiction production, we can also find a rich array of animated titles tackling an aspect of the social world, whose first examples date back to the early days of this medium (see Torre 2017, 172).

Among these animations that deal with the real are also the so-called animated documentaries. That is to say, animated works that, in narrating an aspect of our world, employ animation's fictional language and mode of representation. Therefore, in order to qualify as an animated documentary, an audiovisual text has to result from the blending of factual content with a fictional form. It instead does not have to be made using a specific animation technique, nor does it necessarily have to be entirely in animation. It can also be just partly animated. However, its portion in animation has to be substantial and integral to the narration. Gunnar Strøm goes as far as to argue that, in order for a film to be deemed an animated documentary, at least 50 percent of it has to be in animation (Strøm 2003, 49). In my view, aprioristically establishing a fixed percentage could end up proving restrictive. Also, adopting just this criterion would reduce the classification of partly animated fact-based films to a merely quantitative matter. I thus believe it proves vital to consider, next to the quantitative aspect, also the role that the animated sequences have in the audiovisual work they are part of. In consideration of the foregoing discussion, I would suggest that for a partially animated film to be defined an animated documentary, its portion in animation must make up a significant part of the film and "be integrated to the extent that the meaning of the film would become incoherent were it to somehow be removed" (Honess Roe 2013, 4), as it occurs for instance in the features *Chicago 10: Speak Your Peace* (2007, dir. Brett Morgen) and *Dead Reckoning: Champlain in America* (2009, dir. Marc Hall). Titles like *Bowling for Columbine* (2002, dir. Michael Moore) and *Waiting for Superman* (2010, dir. Davis Guggenheim) that contain just brief and sporadic animated interjections would instead not qualify as animated documentaries, even if animation's fictional language and mode of representation are employed in them (see Chapter 1). In the same way, a film that in talking about the real employs only (or in any case predominantly) what in Chapter 1 I will show to be animation's nonfictional graphic vocabulary and mode of visual exposition does not classify as an animated documentary, even when it is entirely in animation.

The focus of this book is precisely the animated documentary, a form that commenced being scholarly investigated in the late 1990s. In particular, two 1997 articles kickstarted the development of an academic discourse around it: "If Truth Be Told, Can 'Toons Tell It? Documentary and Animation," written by Sybil DelGaudio for the journal *Film/History*, and "The Beautiful Village and the True Village: A Consideration of Animation and the Documentary Aesthetic," authored by Paul Wells for a special issue on animation of *Art and Design* (see, respectively, Del Gaudio 1997; Wells 1997). However, it was not until the early to mid-2000s that the scholarship on this form started effectively building up. The paper "Animation: Documentary's Imaginary Signifier," given by Michael Renov at the Visible Evidence X conference, most likely springboarded this new and more consistent wave of scholarly literature on the animated documentary.[2] Indeed, at the end of it, he encouraged documentary scholars to "forge alliances with the world of animation and animation studies and thus develop a more collaborative and well-rounded understanding of and appreciation for this dynamic and increasingly prevalent cinematic form" (Renov 2002). Made in a period wherein the production of animated documentaries was undergoing a new peak, this invitation has propelled a progressively greater scholarly attention to the form (e.g., see Strøm 2003; Patrick 2004; Ward 2005, 82–99). This, in turn, has led, first, to the publication, in 2011, of a special issue of *Animation: An Interdisciplinary Journal* devoted to the animated documentary (see Skoller 2011) and, in 2012, of *Animated Realism. A Behind-the-Scenes Look at the Animated Documentary Genre*, a collection of interviews with leading makers of this typology of animations (see Kriger 2012), and, subsequently, in 2013, to the appearance of the first English-language monograph addressing the form: Annabelle Honess Roe's *Animated Documentary* (see Honess Roe 2013).[3] The publication of this book, paired with constant growth in the number of animated documentaries produced (and especially of feature-length ones), has fueled a further, still ongoing wave of scholarly contributions on this form both within animation and documentary studies (e.g., see Wells 2016; Sung 2017; Conde Aldana 2018; Ajanovic-Ajan 2019), the most full-bodied installments of which are the anthology *Drawn from Reality. Issues and Themes in Animated Documentary Cinema* (see Murray and Ehrlich 2019) and the monograph *Animating Truth. Documentary and Visual Culture in the 21st Century* (see Ehrlich 2021).

Although it is just a little more than two decades since it began receiving scholarly attention, the animated documentary can thus count today on a vibrant and growing body of literature. There is, however, an aspect of it that remains largely disregarded: its history.

The Animated Documentary and the Progressive Jettisoning of Its History

Before long, the most important work of any given moment slips into the fold of history. Contemporary now, historical soon. This may appear to be a natural process of temporal progression: things happen, priorities change, new work arrives before us and demands attention. But it is not quite so natural as it may first appear. Of all the things we experience in a given day, only a handful of these things remain actively remembered weeks, months, and sometimes years later. . . . Much emerges, much disappears. (Nichols 2016, xvi)

As Nichols suggests, it is inevitable that, with the march of time, a part of the titles produced in a given period ends up being wiped out from our collective memory in order to make space for new ones. Scholars are crucial agents in this slow but inescapable selection process. The greater or lesser attention they pay toward a film contributes to determining whether in the long run it will make its way in history books or it will end up buried under the dust of oblivion.

What the animated documentary has been subject to is, however, more than the inexorable, physiological selection process described by Nichols, since to be progressively whipped out has been its history as a whole. Indeed, in the very first essays on the form, among the examples discussed were mostly works created before the 1980s (see Del Gaudio 1997; Wells 1997). Nevertheless, the more the body of literature on the animated documentary has grown, the more the attention has come to focus almost exclusively on the works created during the last three decades (with disproportionate attention being paid to *Waltz with Bashir* [*Vals Im Bashir*, 2008, dir. Ari Folman]).[4] Earlier titles, instead, are hardly given any consideration. Filed away into the precursor folder, they tend to be briefly mentioned only when the need is felt to acknowledge that the ones produced today root in a longstanding tradition of employing the medium of animation also to address the real. Consequently, the vast majority of animated documentary's existing historical accounts come down to no more than a few paragraphs offered within literature otherwise focused on exploring this form's present-day production (e.g., see Ward 2005, 83–4; Honess Roe 2013, 9–13; Kraemer 2015, 57–9).

Unquestionably, the many contributions resulting from looking at post-1980s animated documentaries have been important, because they have had the merit of building up a discourse around a form that had been neglected for far too long. Nevertheless, the progressive lesser attention given to its history has determined for the animated documentary to come to be widely understood as a strictly contemporary form, born out of the removal from the image of "the responsibility for determining documentary value," which "the digital destruction of photography's evidential pretentions" has prompted (Winston 2013, 26, 24). As a matter of fact, scholarly, it is as such that the animated documentary is predominantly theorized today. For instance, in the chart illustrating the evolutions undergone by documentary filmmaking throughout the decades that he offers as part of his introduction to *The Documentary Film Book*, Brian Winston places the animated documentary among the purely "post-Griersonian, post-1990" practices (Winston 2013, 25). Likewise, in his monograph *Animation-Process, Cognition and Actuality*, Dan Torre writes that it was "[p]articularly beginning in the 1990s" that animated documentaries started to emerge (Torre 2017, 172). More recently, in her book-length study *Animating Truth*, Nea Ehrlich even goes as far as to argue that the use of "animation to portray 'the real'" would be the result of a cultural shift that occurred in the twenty-first century (Ehrlich 2021, 2). According to her, it would have been only after the release of *Waltz with Bashir* in 2008 that the animated documentary "has proliferated widely" (Ehrlich 2021, 2).

The position of Annabelle Honess Roe, who is the author of highly influential scholarship on the form, is slightly different but always in line with the idea that the animated documentary is a product of contemporary times. Indeed, she recognizes at least that animation has long been used in nonfiction contexts. However, she also argues that, with the exclusion of *The Sinking of the Lusitania* (1918, dir. Winsor McCay), all nonfiction animations produced before the mid-1980s are to be envisioned just as a "pre-history of animated documentary" (Honess Roe 2016, 45). In other words, she conceptualizes historical examples of reality-centered animations as works that have created the conditions for the emergence of the animated documentary as a full-blown form in the contemporaneity, but that cannot be ascribed to it.

The Classical Animated Documentary and Its Contemporary Evolution stems from the belief that it has become urgent to return to the animated documentary its historical dimension before it becomes too difficult to eradicate the already widespread misconception of it being a form without a past. In particular, the book focuses on those neglected forty-five years of its history, spanning from 1940 to the mid-1980s, during which the animated documentary first reached its maturity, in order to show how the contemporary production, often greeted as innovation, is instead just the most recent evolution of a longstanding form.

The reader should, however, not expect a traditional history of the animated documentary, but rather a treatise of the form wherein the historical and theoretical discourse are woven together. Indeed, precisely since up to now this form has been conceptualized mostly by taking as a referent the contemporary production and its specificities, some of the conclusions reached within the existing literature no longer prove valid for the form as a whole once we acknowledge its past. Therefore, rather than merely tracing the growth and evolution of the animated documentary across the decades, it is necessary to rethink it from a theoretical viewpoint as well.

Moreover, through the examples chosen, *The Classical Animated Documentary and Its Contemporary Evolution* tries to return the variety of styles and production techniques employed in making these films as well as the geographic breadth of this form. Indeed, a transnational perspective is here adopted. Still, more considerable attention is devoted to the works from countries like the United States, Great Britain, and Canada, which between the 1940s and the mid-1980s were leading producers of this typology of audiovisual works. In fact, providing a comprehensive global history of the animated documentary is beyond the scope of this book. Hopefully, however, by making apparent the importance of considering the historical dimension of the animated documentary, this volume will prompt in-depth inquiries into the many national productions that, due to space constraints, could not be covered here.

Structure of the Book

The Classical Animated Documentary and Its Contemporary Evolution is composed of three parts. The first one, "Theoretical and Historical Issues," questions a series of widely accepted ideas on the animated documentary so as to reconceptualize this form, also in the face of its history. Each chapter adds up to the broad definition of the animated documentary given here, contributing to refining and detailing it. In particular, Chapter 1 sets the ground for identifying what an animated documentary is and what it is not by trying to understand if animation effectively has just a single mode of visual representation. It is shown that if, as it has been done up to now, we look at the animated works addressing our world from the perspective of realism, we cannot but conclude that this medium has only one, inherently fictional mode of visual representation. If we look at factuality-related animations under the lens of what Bill Nichols (1994, 47) refers to as "discourses of sobriety," we can instead identify both a fictional and a nonfictional mode of representing reality through animation: respectively, the fabled and the sober animation.

After having highlighted that animated documentaries are characterized by an exclusive or at least predominant employment of the fabled animation, Chapter 2 questions the current widespread classification of these audiovisual works as full-fledged documentaries equitable to live-action ones. It is demonstrated that it would be more appropriate to place the animated documentary in animation's docufiction territory. More precisely, considering the many similarities it bears with the docudrama but also the difference it entertains with it, the chapter proposes to redefine the animated documentary as the sincerest form of docudrama.

Chapter 3, instead, at first, disproves the shared idea for which the animated documentary would be a form that has come to take shape as such solely after 1985. Indeed, it is outlined how already between the 1940s and the mid-1980s makers, producers, and critics employed the expression "animated documentary" or its synonyms "cartoon documentary" and "documentary cartoon" to single out educational, scientific, and public service animated works that, in order to illustrate aspects of our world, combined entertaining and imaginative animated visuals with an informational voice-of-God commentary. Subsequently, the chapter proposes a new treble periodization of the animated documentary. More specifically, it depicts how we can divide its history into the following three macro periods: (1) an age of the origins, ranging from 1909 to 1939; (2) a classical epoch, going from 1940 to 1985; (3) a contemporary era, which started in 1986 and is still ongoing. In so doing, the reasons why the animated documentary endured an evolution precisely in the moments in time identified are explained, showing how such shifts are strongly interconnected to changes that the documentary itself has undergone.

The second part of the book, "The Rise and Affirmation of an Audiovisual Form," constitutes the core of it, since, with the exclusion of Chapter 4, it focuses on the animated documentary's classical era. More precisely, Chapter 4 briefly looks at how several films that were made between 1909 and 1939 anticipated the traits bound to become characteristic of this form and, in hindsight, can thus be considered early examples of it, even if they are not informed by a shared approach and originally were not referred to as animated documentaries. Chapter 5 provides, instead, a general overview of the classical animated documentary, illustrating the traits shared by the numerous works created in this period. It also depicts how such era of this form's history can further be divided into: (1) a short phase of affirmation running from 1940 to 1945, (2) a more extended consolidation phase going from 1946 to 1967, and (3) a phase of gradual transition toward the contemporary approach spanning from 1968 to 1985.

The following chapters focus each on the production of one of the three nations that have had a leading role in the establishment and development of the classical animated documentary's canons: the United States (Chapter 6), Great Britain (Chapter 7), and Canada (Chapter 8). In particular, after addressing more generally these countries' animated documentary production, each chapter spotlights a studio whose work has been highly influential both at a national and international level, namely, the Walt Disney Studios, the Halas & Batchelor Cartoon Films studio, and the animation department of the National Film Board of Canada, respectively.

The second part of the book then ends with a chapter on the classical Italian animated documentary. This is not to suggest that Italy was the only non-English-speaking country to engage in the production of animated documentaries in this period nor that it was necessarily the chief one. On the contrary, many leading animators and animation studios from other non-English-speaking countries have experimented with this form as well. For instance, in the Netherlands, Joop Geesink's studio Dollywood, which was specialized in stop-motion animation, next to fictional titles, has also produced several animated documentaries. Among them are, for instance, *The Story of Light* (1954, dir. Joop Geesink) and *Light and Mankind* (1954, dir. Willem Van Otterloo) on the development of lighting or *Getting Warmer* (1963, dir. Henk Kabos) on the evolution of heating across the decades. Similarly, in Czechoslovakia, titles such as *How Man Learned to Fly* (*Jak se člověk naučil létat*, 1958, dir. Jiří Brdečka), which offers a thong-in-cheek history of aviation, and *The Creation of the World* (*Stvoření světa*, 1958, dir. Eduard Hofman), a feature co-produced with France that can be considered an example of a religious animated documentary, have seen the light.

The reason why I have chosen to devote Chapter 9 to Italy is that an animation industry has been absent in this country for long and the small number of titles produced using this medium was the result of individual efforts. Nevertheless, a consistent number of animated documentaries were produced here as well during the time frame in question. Looking at the production of this country thus makes it apparent both how widespread the animated documentary was in this period and how influential the American model has been outside of the US borders. In particular, similar to what is the case for the previous three chapters, also in this one, while providing an overview of the overall national production, special attention is paid to the rich corpus of animated documentaries created between the late 1950s and the early 1970s by the animation division of the studio Corona Cinematografica, and the presence of similarities to the coeval US production is illustrated.

The third and final part, "The Contemporary Production, 1986 and Beyond," shows how the animated documentary production of today does not represent a complete otherness from the classical one but rather its evolution. More precisely, Chapter 10 focuses on those animated documentaries depicting personal traumas, states of mind, and other inner processes of specific individuals that constitute the bulk of this form's contemporary production. Indeed, obviously, due to its very nature (see Chapter 1), an animation can never aim to be purportedly objective in the same way as a live-action work is. In fact, because of its genesis, any animation is intrinsically characterized by subjectivity. However, classical animated documentaries have strived for lending viewers a somewhat impression of objectivity by adopting (and adapting) what Bill Nichols ([2001] 2017, 22) refers to as the "expository mode" of documentary representation. Indeed, the latter, as Jane Roscoe and Craig Hight (2001, 18) point out, "presents the filmmaker as an objective outsider" and suggests to viewers that the film they are watching is "value-free and objective." As Chapter 10 will show, starting from 1986 the animated documentary has, instead, increasingly come to embrace, and put at its core, the subjective. In other words, it has mirrored the changes that have been occurring within the documentary proper in post-modern times after the existence of what Linda Williams (1993, 12) calls the "paradox of the intrusive manipulation of documentary truth" (i.e., the paradox for which, whatever the approach adopted, documentary truth is anyhow "subject to manipulation and construction by docu-auteurs who, whether on camera . . . or behind, are forcefully calling the shots") has become blatant. Chapter 10, however, examines these contemporary animated documentaries imbued with subjectivity to show how, unlike what could seem at first glance, they bear many similarities with the works of this form's classical age. Chapter 11 further proves the existence of a continuity between the pre- and the post-1985 animated documentary production by illustrating how titles developed according to the approach characteristic of this form's classical era have kept being produced even after the mid-1980s, albeit in smaller numbers and mainly for television.

The concluding chapter examines some relatively recent online interactive animated documentaries (also known as animated i-docs). More precisely, it focuses on three titles, *The Next Day* (2011, dir. Jason Gilmore), *Invisible Picture Show* (2013, dir. Tim Travers Hawkins), and *Last Hijack Interactive* (2014, dir. Tommy Pallotta and Femke Wolting), wherein we register a shift from what typically occurs in an animated documentary in terms of the treatment of the animated visuals. Indeed, in these works, the animation is reduced to a visual filler, leaving the sole sound to shoulder the task of advancing the narration. Given this peculiarity, it is asked if such works may constitute the first germs of a slowly rising post-animated documentary era.

Notes on the Text

Chapter 2 is a revised version of the previously published article "The Sincerest Form of Docudrama: Re-framing the Animated Documentary," *Studies in Documentary Film* 8(2) (2014), 103–15. Some sections of Chapter 9 have previously appeared in "Note sul documentario animato italiano e il suo periodo delle origini," *Immagine. Note di storia del cinema* 15 (2017), 65–83, and "Dal neorealismo al documentario animato scientifico: le animazioni 'realiste' di Gibba," *Cabiria* 44 (2014), 4–19.

Notes

1 For the purpose of this book, the term "film" will be used in a broad acceptation. It will be employed to identify not just the titles created for the big screen but rather any audiovisual work regardless of its medium of destination.
2 The key role of Renov in the development of an academic discourse around the animated documentary has been underlined also by Strøm: "Scholarship in this relatively new field appeared at the SAS conference in the late 1990s, later entering the academic documentary scene supported by scholars like Michael Renov" (Strøm 2015, 92).
3 Honess Roe's book has, however, not been the absolute first monograph on the animated documentary. A year earlier an Italian-language book on this form by Lawrence Thomas Martinelli had appeared (see Martinelli 2012).
4 If compared to the amount of scholarship addressing the animated documentary in general, the one on Folman's feature appears to be almost excessive in quantitative terms. Indeed, a non-exhaustive list of scholarly writing focusing on *Waltz with Bashir* would include: Mansfield 2010; Yosef 2010; Stewart 2010; Landesman and Bendor 2011; Mengoni 2011; Peaslee 2011; Schlunke 2011; Atkinson and Cooper 2012; Kohn and Weissbrod 2012; Viljoen 2013; Viljoen 2014; Kroustallis 2014; Kraemer 2015; Rastegar 2015, 185–204; Perrett 2016; Ekinici 2017; Miller 2017; Kunert-Graf 2018; Murray 2019.

PART I

Theoretical and Historical Issues

1

Reality's Two Animated Faces

In a long-neglected article on animated documentary written in 1955 for the *Health Education Journal*, Walt Disney argues that through animation it is possible to "discount the truth with excessive laughter as well as with the boredom of ponderous belabored soberness" (Disney 1955, 74). With these words, the father of Mickey Mouse seems to suggest that form-wise, when employing this medium to represent the real, an animator is faced with two possible approaches: a fictional and a nonfictional one. Still, whether this is effectively the case or not is an issue that the existing scholarly literature addressing reality-related animation disregards. It has always been taken for granted that, since "even at its most mimetic (e.g., *Final Fantasy: The Spirits Within* [2001]) animation just does not correspond to the real in the same way as live-action" (Ward 2008), this medium can have just a sole, inherently fictional mode of visual representation. As a consequence, it has been assumed that content alone should make up the criterion by which to distinguish nonfiction animations from fictional ones. This, in turn, has brought to sidestep what I believe should instead have been the first questions to tackle: Is the one showcased by animated documentaries truly the only possible way in which reality can be depicted through animation? Does animation, unlike live-action, effectively lack a nonfictional mode of visual representation?

Undeniably, if looked at under that same lens of realism we use to assess the proximity of live-action audiovisual products to the actual physical world, any animated work dealing with reality-related topics will appear intrinsically fictional in form. In point of fact, notwithstanding that "realism has long been a topic of debate within media studies, as the term is marked by both a variety of definitions and assumed ideological impact" (Mittell 2001, 22), as spectators we tend to partake a shared conception of what a cinematic representation should look like in order to be deemed true-to-life. In particular, for viewers to consider realistic a filmic image presented to them in a nonfiction context, they have to be able to identify a mimetic correspondence between it and its real-life referent. Indeed, even though it has largely been proven how easy it is nowadays to alter a photographic image, the presence of an indexical linkage between a filmic representation and its factual model is still considered "a seemingly irrefutable guarantee of authenticity" (Nichols 1991, 150). Yet, when animation is used to portray true-life occurrences, at the level of visuals, the resulting films can hold with their real-world referents either an iconic or a symbolic relationship, but hardly an indexical one. Indeed, due to this medium's intrinsically fabricated nature, the ontology of an animated movie resembles more that of a painting or a sculpture than that of a photograph.[1] To put it as André Bazin would have, albeit most animation techniques—similarly to what occurs in the case of photography—foresee at some point the employment of a camera's "impassive mechanical process" (Bazin 1967, 14),[2] this medium—like the aforementioned plastic arts—remains strongly "based on the presence of man" (13). As a consequence, regardless of its subject matter, an animation is always an artificial creation in fee to that same "inescapable subjectivity" which "casts a shadow of doubt" over painted images (12). In other words, also when an animated work illustrates a fragment of reality, what the viewer sees unfold on screen is far from being an objective record of the factual events it depicts. Rather, it is a *creative* (and often *imaginative*) *interpretation* of a real-life occurrence that cannot but reflect its author's point of view.

It thus comes as no surprise that, as far as this medium is concerned, what is understood as realism is instead a form of "over-illusionism" (Wells 1998, 27). Indeed, the yardstick against which to evaluate the degree of realism of an animated film has long been identified in the "hyper-realism" of Walt Disney Studios' movies (25). Hence, as Stephen Rowley (2005, 68) observes, conventionally this medium's benchmark for realism is filmic works that not only showcase a style for animating movement based on exaggeration (as is the squash and stretch) but also "abound in magical acts (the Queen's transformation in *Snow White*, boys turning into donkeys in *Pinocchio*), animation of usually inanimate objects (Pinocchio himself, and the living mountain, flowers, and broomsticks in *Fantasia*), animals being able to speak (*Dumbo* and *Bambi*), and decidedly unreal bodies (an elephant that can fly with its ears in *Dumbo*)." Therefore, what can be deemed realistic for animation is quite far from that mimetic correspondence to a real-life model whose presence we as viewers consider indispensable in order to accept a live-action product as a documentary. Not casually, when explaining where the various typologies of films would fall on the mimesis/abstraction continuum that she theorizes as the best possible instrument to assess the degree of realism of any audiovisual product, Maureen Furniss ([1998] 2007, 6) suggests that the placement of a title like *Snow White and the Seven Dwarfs* (1937, dir. David Hand) would be approximately toward the middle of this scale, but nearer to the side of abstraction. She explains this allotment by showing how, if on the one hand this feature "has a relative naturalistic look" and some of its protagonists are "based on human models," on the other hand "its characters and landscapes can be described as caricatures, or abstractions of reality, to some extent" (Furniss [1998] 2007, 6).

One could argue that the technological advancements of the last two decades have made it possible to obtain animated films far more respondent to our general conception of realism than *Snow White and the Seven Dwarfs* and the other features produced at the Walt Disney Studios in the classical era. Undoubtedly, today, through CGI animation it is possible to create audiovisual works that showcase a higher degree of mimesis. In particular, exploiting the *mo-cap* system, from the early 2000s onward films like, for instance, *Final Fantasy: The Spirits Within* (2001, dir. Hironobu Sakaguchi and Motonori Sakakibara), *The Polar Express* (2004, dir. Robert Zemeckis), and *The Adventures of Tintin: Secret of the Unicorn* (2011, dir. Steven Spielberg), whose protagonists are incredibly realistic, animated human characters, have been produced. Still, as Annabelle Honess Roe (2013, 83) points out, "somewhat paradoxically, viewers find talking cars less troubling than very photorealistic computer-generated animated humans." Indeed, the latter characters tend to cause the so-called uncanny valley effect. That is, they provoke in spectators a sense of unease, which is elicited precisely by their strong likeness to real-life human beings. More specifically, animation cannot reach photography's mimetic correspondence to its model, since it is "essentially based on stylization and abstraction to some degree, even in its most apparently photo-realistic form" (Wells [1996] 2011, 232). Thus, however realistic a human-like character is, it cannot fully be so. Also, due to this breach, the employment of photorealistic animation, instead of favoring a greater empathy toward the protagonists of the film, generates uncanny feelings in viewers.[3]

In short, regardless of the yardstick by which we choose to assess an animated film's degree of realism, we will always end up reaching Paul Ward's conclusion that "animation's essential 'abstraction' tends to make the viewer aware that s/he is watching something other than a mimetic recording of an external reality. Any realism obtained in these films is to do with generic/narrative conventions and verisimilitude rather than any sense of the film actually resembling the world we live in" (Ward 2008). Therefore, as Ward points out in another essay, "even the most 'realistic' animation . . . will be watched *as* animation, rather than as a 'recording' of an actual pro-filmic world. That is, despite any truth claims made, or real-world situations and relationships shown, the 'animatedness' will still be an overriding feature of the film for the viewers as they watch the film" (Ward 2005, 89, original emphasis). Hence, if we look at animation from the viewpoint of realism, the scholars who have given for granted that, to establish whether a film created using this medium pertains to the fiction or the nonfiction realm, we should look only at its content appear to be entirely justified. Indeed, no matter what graphic language and mode of representation are employed, an animation will never be able to respond to our idea of what realism is within a factual audiovisual context.

Beyond Realism: Animation and the Discourses of Sobriety

Nevertheless, if we take into account all the animations dealing with reality-related topics created throughout the history of this medium, we will notice two opposed macro tendencies as far as the graphic vocabulary employed and the representational strategies utilized are concerned. More precisely, we will be able to isolate, on the one hand, filmic texts wherein, in order to illustrate a fragment of our world, is made use of all the "graphic and narrational anarchy" enabled by animation itself (Wells 1998, 23); on the other hand, audiovisual works in which a schematic and diagrammatic animation that draws its visual vocabulary mostly on a symbolism developed as part of a precise scientific graphic language (such as that of cartography, of medical illustration, of technical drawing, and so on) is employed to the same end. Examples of these two approaches in animating reality are, for instance, respectively *Blood Transfusion* (1941, dir. Hans M. Nieter) and *Defense against Invasion* (1943, dir. Jack King). Both these shorts are partially animated films, primarily didactic in intent, that have seen the light in the early 1940s and address a factual topic that falls within the realm of medicine. In particular, the former provides an account of the blood transfusion process and its history, whereas the latter illustrates the operating principles of a vaccine. Nevertheless, as far as their visuals are concerned, the representational strategies deployed in these two films could not be more diverse. The animated segments of *Defense against Invasion*—which was produced by the Walt Disney Studios for the Office of the Coordinator of Inter-American Affairs—"abound in striking and imaginative visuals" (Kaufman 2009, 144). They showcase the same narrative devices used by the company to give life to their fictional works, such as anthropomorphism, synecdoche, dramatization, visual metaphors, and so on. Indeed, in this case, the agenda pursued has been that of creating a film that is able, at the same time, to inform and entertain.[4]

On the contrary, in *Blood Transfusion*, which was produced by Paul Rotha Productions Ltd. on commission of the Ministry of Information, a diagrammatic graphic language known as Isotype is used. The latter was initially developed by sociologist Otto Neurath and his wife Marie to translate quantitative information and statistics into universally understandable pictographs, so as "to promote social and scientific planning to the general public" (Boon 2008, 128). In creating this picture language, as they have more than once underlined, Mr. and Mrs. Neurath have built on the idea of designing a graphic system whose "essential quality" was to be that of conveying "factual knowledge" without utilizing "emotional means" (Neurath in Burke 2013, 14). Thus, the Isotype complied well with Rotha's idea for which, when employed in visual education, graphic symbols had to be clear and neutral. Indeed, in a 1946 article titled "The Film and Other Visual Techniques in Education," he writes: "If a symbol is designed to convey a meaning, which is its only reason for existence, the act of conveyance must be near instantaneous as the relation between the eye and the mind permits" (Rotha 1946, 142). Subsequently, he adds: "The neutrality of symbols is also of significance. If facts and information are to be presented without bias, as map-makers should present their atlases, the symbols used in charts and films should have no negative or positive associations. The aim is to provide information for free discussion from any point of view and perhaps for very different arguments" (Rotha 1946, 142).

Therefore, it does not surprise that in 1941 Rotha started with the Neuraths a longlasting collaboration, of which *Blood Transfusion* is only one of the many outputs (see Burke 2013, 366–89). Nor does it astonish that this cooperation brought the Isotype language to be put to use for creating nonfiction animations, referring to which Marie herself has written:

> People who have seen *The world of plenty* [sic] or *Blood transfusion* may have noticed that the Isotype diagrams used in them are somewhat different from other diagrams used in films. For instance the little man figures never make funny faces to provoke a laugh. . . . We think out: which is the point that has to be brought home, and then we try to do so in such a way that everybody will grasp it. We avoid distracting the attention from the more important issues. (Neurath 1946)

In short, unlike noted for *Defense against Invasion*, the agenda with which the animated segments of *Blood Transfusion* were created was not that of amusing viewers while instructing them, but instead of conveying blunt facts in a clear and essential way through a visual language developed according to a scientific methodology.

A concrete example of the differences existing between these two films in terms of graphic language and representational strategies employed is offered by the way in which blood cells are pictured in them. In Neither's short, they are visualized as black dots that float in a grayish liquid (which stands for plasma) and flow within two thick black lines that represent the outlines of a blood vessel (see Figure 1.1). In King's film, instead, they are

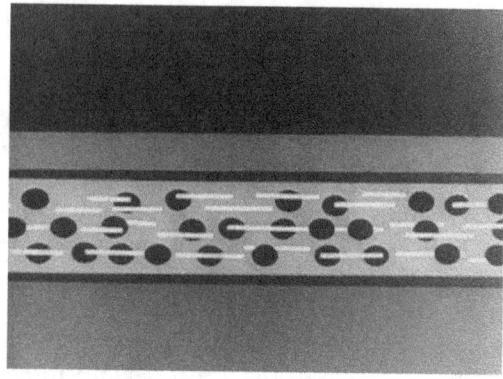

FIGURE 1.1 *Blood cells as represented in* Blood Transfusion.

FIGURE 1.2 *Blood cells as represented in* Defense against Invasion.

portrayed as red blob-like workers with a white hardhat, who walk around the streets of a modern city that stands for our body (see Figure 1.2).[5]

Another pair of films that well exemplifies how, throughout the history of this medium, two different approaches have been employed in animating our world could be *The Sinking of the Lusitania* and *The Battle of the North Sea* (1918). Aside from the year of completion, these films have in common the fact of each depicting a specific episode of the First World War, respectively the 1915 sinking of the British passenger liner Lusitania and the naval combat fought between the British Royal Navy and the Imperial German Navy from May 31 to June 1, 1916, near the coast of Denmark's Jutland peninsula. Nevertheless, also in this case, when it comes to the mode of visual representation and the graphic vocabulary displayed, the two films diverge considerably. Although more moderately than in *Defense against Invasion*, *The Sinking of the Lusitania* makes use of fictional representational strategies such as visual metaphors or synecdoche.[6] In addition, the factual events in it recounted are dramatized by employing "a variety of dramatic 'cinematic' angles and compelling perspective and subjective shots throughout" (Canemaker 1987, 154), so as to foster an emotional response in the viewer.[7]

Instead, *The Battle of the North Sea* uses only aerial shots, with the effect of creating a distance between the spectator and the events recounted. Furthermore, the visual language in it employed is dry, schematic, and reliant on a symbolism more or less scientifically developed. Indeed, the film alternates succinct intertitles exposing the bald facts related to the battle of Jutland and animated maps illustrating the maneuvers executed by the fleets involved in the combat. More specifically, thanks to the employment of the stop-motion technique, oblong paper cut-outs, more or less big in respect to the dimension of the actual ships they stand for, move over one-dimensional, elemental backgrounds created drawing from the graphic vocabulary of cartography. Therefore, preexisting pictographs proper of a specific scientific visual language are blended with symbols created on purpose, of which, however, a legend is provided in the film's second intertitle (see Figure 1.3). Additionally, these purposely made-up symbols also seem to have been developed following a "scientific" methodology. That is, the pieces of cardboard representing the various vessels seem to have been cut out proportionally to the importance and dimension of their real-life counterpart. Moreover, as noted for *Blood Transfusion*'s animations, *The Battle of the North Sea* also is shaped by a merely informational agenda,

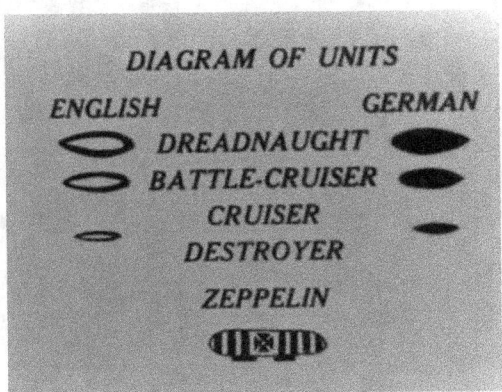

FIGURE 1.3 *Frame from* The Battle of the North Sea *offering a legend of the symbols employed in the film.*

a fact that its opening intertitle makes clear when stating: "Animated from data contained in British and German reports, official and non official."

From the examples provided up to now, it may seem that instances of the coexistence of two opposite approaches in animating reality are identifiable just in the cinematic production of the past. On the contrary, they can be tracked down even in strictly contemporary audiovisual works. A case in point is Davis Guggenheim's feature *Waiting for Superman*, wherein these two modes of animating reality exist side by side. Indeed, in this otherwise live-action documentary dealing with the shortcomings of the US school system, we can find animated sequences wherein the factual events recounted are dramatized, and this medium's fictional devices are exploited. An example in this sense is the segment wherein animation is deployed to explain how a praxis—that in Milwaukee is referred to as "The Dance of the Lemons"—exists whereby principals exchange yearly their worst teacher with the less qualitative one of another school in the hope that the one they will get will be better than the one dismissed. This is translated literally into pictographs by showing an animated actor impersonating a principal who waltzes out of his school building and toward that of a neighbor institution with a lemon-headed man (representing his worst teacher) (see Figure 1.4). Once he reaches this second building, he throws his dance partner into it, causing some cracks in its external walls, metaphorically conveying the idea that, due to the presence of this new teacher, the school's quality has decreased.

FIGURE 1.4 *A shot from "The Dance of the Lemons" scene in* Waiting for Superman.

However, throughout *Waiting for Superman,* animated segments wherein aspects of the factual issue at stake (like the rates with which incompetent tenured teachers are fired or the percentage of students who score poorly) are conveyed through a diagrammatic graphic language are also present (e.g., see Figure 1.5). These animations are accompanied by captions indicating the source from where the data in them illustrated were taken. In other words, they are footnoted in a similar way to what occurs for scholarly literature, a fact that identifies them as driven purely by the intent of visualizing data, rather than informing entertainingly, as is instead the case of a scene such as that of the Dance of the Lemons.

In light of all the foregoing, a question cannot but arise: What if Disney was right after all? What if animation has always had both a fictional and a factual mode of visual representation and we have never spotted the latter simply because that of realism is not the right perspective from which to seek it? Indeed, we too often forget that, as Wells (1998, 6) recalls, animation is "a distinctive form that works in entirely different ways from live-action cinema" and that, consequently, what proves to be the best criterion for isolating the latter's nonfictionality may not be suitable in the case of the former.

It is inadvertently always Disney to indicate to us where to look in order to identify a more adequate parameter, when in his aforementioned article, he states that through animation, reality can be accounted both in an entertaining and in a *sober* way. Although unknowingly, the father of Mickey Mouse is here suggesting to us that, rather than from the viewpoint of realism, it might be more profitable to consider animation in terms of

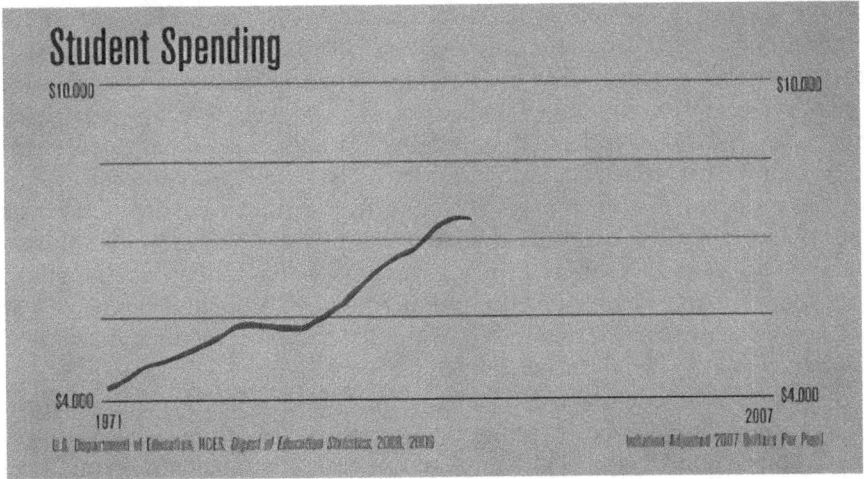

FIGURE 1.5 *An example of the data visualization-driven animation from* Waiting for Superman.

that "sobriety" identified by Bill Nichols as a peculiar trait of nonfiction. In his 1991 monograph *Representing Reality*, referring to live-action documentaries, Nichols writes:

> Documentary film has a kinship with those other nonfictional systems that together make up what we call the discourse of sobriety. Science, economics, politics, foreign policy, education, religion, welfare—these systems assume they have instrumental power; they can and should alter the world itself, they can affect action and entail consequences. Their discourse has an air of sobriety since it is seldom receptive to "make believe" characters, events, or entire worlds (unless they serve as pragmatically useful simulations of the real one). (Nichols 1991, 3)

Three years later, in the book *Blurred Boundaries*, Nichols specifies that one of the characteristics that serves to distinguish the modes of representation of documentaries from those of fiction films is precisely the fact that the former adhere "to the principles of rhetoric that govern the discourses of sobriety" (Nichols 1994, 47). He adds: "Such discourses attempt to represent the state of affairs in the historical or natural world itself rather than offer openly imaginative representations of it. Their sobriety allows such discourses to count narrative technique among their rhetorical strategies but with little stress on *complex* narrative form or on the construction of imaginary worlds" (Nichols 1994, 47, original emphasis). If we look in this light at the titles mentioned up to now, we can notice that what distinguishes the animations of *Blood Transfusion* and *The Battle of the North Sea* from those of *Defense against Invasion* and *The Sinking of the Lusitania* as well as what differentiates *Waiting for Superman*'s second typology of animated interjections from those of the first kind is precisely the fact that, while the latter ones have a tie with the discourses of sobriety only at content level, the former hold a relationship with it also at the level of form. Indeed, they employ a graphic vocabulary developed in a (somewhat) scientific context and a "serious," non-entertainment-driven mode of exposition, whose main trait is that of being schematic and diagrammatic. Therefore, the adoption of the perspective of sobriety enables to state that animation also has its nonfiction visual language and mode of representation: the one deprived of frills and connected at some level with science that is traceable, for instance, in films like *Blood Transfusion* and *The Battle of the North Sea*.

One could contend that the identification of animation's nonfictional form in a schematic mode of representation and its juxtaposition with one that is made "attractive" by the deployment of a series of fictional and imaginative narrative strategies represents somehow a return to that longstanding bias for which beauty and truth are irreconcilable. As Michael Renov has pointed out referring to live-action nonfiction films, "the creation of beautiful forms and documentary's task of historical representation" are not incompatible (Renov 1993, 24), since "the aesthetic function can never be wholly divorced from the didactic one insofar as the aim remains 'pleasurable learning'" (35). He adds: "That a work undertaking some manner of historical documentation renders that representation in a challenging or innovative manner should in no way disqualify it as nonfiction because the question of expressivity is, in all events, a matter of degree" (Renov 1993, 35). Still, first, I am here not advancing that animated films like *The Sinking of the Lusitania* and *Defense against Invasion* are less true in content, because they exhibit imaginative visuals and anarchic narrational strategies. I am merely suggesting that, in them, reality is portrayed through a fictional form. Second, not casually, in theorizing precisely on the employment of animation to address factuality-related topics, eleven years apart one from the other both Paul Wells and Craig Hight have referred to the sober visual language deployed by films like *Blood Transfusion* and *The Battle of the North Sea* as a veridictive mark, thus unconsciously consubstantiating the idea of it being recognizable as this medium's nonfictional mode of representation. More precisely, in his essay "The Beautiful and the True Village: A Consideration of Animation and the Documentary Aesthetic," Wells describes "the use of schematic or diagrammatic modes of pictorial information" as a convention that, at the same time, enables to expose in a clear way the knowledge conveyed and to augment "the supposed 'authority' invested in the data" (Wells 1997, 41). Analogously, in his article "Primetime Digital Documentary Animation: The Photographic and Graphic within Play," among others, Hight elaborates on the digitally animated segments of the History Channel series *Line of Fire* (2002), wherein the battles each episode recounts are visualized schematically by drawing upon conventions of cartography and vexillology. In so doing, he writes: "The digital battle map ... is typically used to reinforce the certainty of the historical narrative that such documentaries construct" (Hight 2008, 15). Hence, he also recognizes this schematic and dry typology of animation as a marker of factuality, a fact that further supports the idea of it being identifiable as animation's nonfictional visual language and mode of representation.

In sum, what emerges is that, similarly to what happens for live-action, also for animation a nonfictional and a fictional manner of recounting factual occurrences are identifiable. As we have seen, they both can be tracked down in entirely animated works as well as in factual products' animated interjections, they can coexist in the same film (as the case of *Waiting for Superman* shows), and one is not the evolution of the other, but rather they have been (and still are) present in parallel across the history of cinema. Only, in order to spot these two modes of representation—that I propose to call the sober and the fabled animation respectively—it is necessary to stop looking at this medium in terms of realism and adopt the perspective of sobriety instead.

Now that we have determined this, let us see in greater detail what the main traits of these two manners of visual representation are and how they have been used throughout time.

The Sober Animation

When in 1909 Émile Cohl decided to employ the medium of animation to recount a factual occurrence rather than a fictional story (as he had done up to that moment), he opted for a dry and diagrammatic visual language, developed according to a defined methodology, that positioned the viewer as a distant observer. Indeed, although this film, entitled *The Battle of Austerlitz* (*La bataille d'Austerlitz*), is now lost, we know that it retraced through a series of animated maps the various phases of the 1805 battle that saw Napoleon defeat the troops of Tsar Alexander I and Holy Roman Emperor Francis II. Moreover, from a detailed article published in the magazine *The Nickelodeon* a few months after the film's completion, we learn that

> The technical data were taken from the works of Commandant Colin, known for his special studies of the battles of the First Empire. His indications have been scrupulously observed in cutting out squares of cardboard proportional in size to the importance of the body of troops represented, and in placing them on the map in the different positions corresponding to their real movements over the ground. Finally, to take account of the elapsed time, a clock-dial has been placed in a corner of the map, and its hands are seen to move during the progress of the battle...
>
> The film was made by placing the black cards representing the allied armies and the white ones representing the French army in the different positions occupied by them, and at the same time moving the hands on the clock-dial. (Gardette 1909, 119)

The same article also explains that the point of view herein adopted was a distant one, similar to that "an observer... placed at a very great height, say in an airship" could have had of the battle (Gardette 1909, 119).

Following in the footprints of Cohl, in the subsequent decade numerous other films similarly illustrating key battles through a succession of animated maps and explanatory intertitles were created, among which are the already mentioned *The Battle of the North Sea* or Frank Percy Smith's *Kineto War Maps* (1914–16) series.[8] However, *The Battle of Austerlitz* gave rise to more than just the map-film genre. It introduced the mode of portraying reality that has become this medium's nonfictional form of visual representation: the sober animation. In fact, in the 1910s, the schematic and diagrammatic approach to the depiction of our world exhibited by Cohl's film was not employed just to represent war-related occurrences. On the contrary, to the same period dates, for instance, *Animated Mathematics* (*Mathematische Trickfilme*, 1912),[9] a German series made up of over twenty-five hand-drawn animated films illustrating mathematical theories. Conceived by math teacher Ludwig Münch as a tool for making abstract concepts, such as the Pythagorean Theorem, more easily comprehensible to his students, these black-and-white animated films showcase a succession of simple and clear line drawings, all crafted using the visual vocabulary of geometry. Thus, although here the symbols proper of cartography give way to those of mathematics, the same dry, expository, and schematic approach that characterized *The Battle of Austerlitz* is deployed.

Similarly, in the post–First World War, John Randolph Bray's studio has used sober animation to explain the operating principles of technological objects or human body organs. Indeed, between the late 1910s and the early 1920s the Bray Studios have produced several animated films—among which are *How the Telephone Talks* (1919), *How You See* (1920, dir. Jack Leventhal), *Action of the Human Heart* (1920, dir. Francis Lyle Goldman), and *How We Hear* (1920, dir. Francis Lyle Goldman)—that, regardless of the subject addressed or of who authored them, all alternate short, explicative intertitles and essential, diagrammatic animations crafted by exploiting the graphic vocabulary either of medical illustrations or of technical drawing, depending on whether the mechanics depicted are those of a body part or an object.[10] In addition, these animated films are characterized by plain white backgrounds that, to put it as Roger Odin (2004, 197), prevent the viewer from building a space, a world. Also, labels comparable to image captions appear here and there over the animations to ensure the concepts illustrated come across clearly. Thus, overall, these dry animated works bear a strong likeness to a lecture. In particular, a clear correlation with the latter is established through the presence on screen, from time to time, of a pointer stick directing the spectator's attention toward a set part of the image (e.g., see Figure 1.6). Indeed, as Mihaela Mihailova (2019, 33–4) underlines, "the pointer stick . . . functions as a widely recognizable stand-in for an invisible instructor, clarifying concepts and guiding viewer attention from beyond the frame."

In short, the dry expository form of visual representation used by Cohl in *The Battle of Austerlitz* soon became the dominant mode for describing the real through animation. And, with the passing of decades, although the fabled animation has progressively been preferred when having to create entirely animated films dealing with our world, the sober one has not been dismissed. The finest example of its employment in the classical era is probably Walt Disney Studios' *Four Methods of Flush Riveting* (1942, dir. James Algar), which not casually has been described as "a dry animated lecture" with a look "akin to textbook diagrams put into simple motion" (Honess Roe 2011, 16). Indeed, in this short produced on commission

FIGURE 1.6 *An example of the employment of the pointer stick from* How the Telephone Talks.

of Lockheed Aircraft Corporation, sound-wise a didactic voice-of-God commentary explains the four different methods a riveter can use to bind together aluminum sheets. Meanwhile, visually the various procedures outlined are illustrated through simple diagrams that are almost exclusively in the tones of gray, move on a plain blue background, and are created using the graphic vocabulary of technical drawing.

However, sober animation has not been employed just in several entirely animated films. Throughout the years it has also been used to craft, for otherwise live-action documentaries, countless animated interjections that are didactic in nature and aimed at illustrating data or complex concepts regarding the real. And, in contemporary times, as Honess Roe (2013, 9) points out, "the use of animated maps, charts, graphs and diagrams in mainstream formats ranging from television news to theatrical documentary . . . has become so commonplace to the point of being inconspicuous."

In short, since that first employment made by Cohl in *The Battle of Austerlitz* in 1909, the sober animation has continued being used to elucidate aspects of our world, coming to acquire a well-defined set of traits. In particular, it has three main characteristics. The first consists in the employment of a graphic vocabulary for the most part borrowed from a branch of scientific visualization or, at least, developed following a somewhat scientific methodology, as we have seen to be, for instance, the case of *The Battle of the North Sea* or *Blood Transfusion*. Hence, whereas the shots of a live-action documentary showcase an indexical correlation with the fragments of reality in them portrayed, those of the nonfiction works made using this typology of animation hold with their factual referents only an arbitrary relationship, forasmuch as pictographs created building "on accepted frames of reference in science that often are no longer challenged or revisited" (Pauwels 2006, xv) are mostly deployed in them. Still, as Luc Pauwels recalls, "visual representations are not to be considered mere *add-ons* or ways to popularize complex reasoning; they are an essential part of scientific discourse" (vii). Therefore, precisely in light of its use of such graphic vocabulary, this animated language ends up having with the discourses of sobriety an even deeper linkage than the one that the nonfictional visual language of live-action holds with it.

Sober animation's second trait is the implementation of a dry mode of visual representation. Indeed, the agenda underlying the creation of these animations is that of illustrating to the viewing public data and information regarding the real in a straightforward and clear-cut way, without any frill. In other words, they are thought to fulfill a similar role to that carried out by a textbook diagram or by the drawing a teacher may do on a board in order to clarify a complex concept to his or her students. Hence, for the purpose of adhering to this agenda, a schematic and diagrammatic visual approach is employed, leaving the task of lecturing the audience to the intertitles or to a voice-of-God narrator. Moreover, the backgrounds for the animations tend to be plain, or at least one-dimensional, and devoid of any unessential element that could provide a distraction from what is being elucidated or undermine the clarity of the information conveyed.

The dry and essential character of sober animation's representational approach is also at the bottom of its third trait, which entails blocking the viewer from putting in place those operations that Roger Odin refers to as the "construction of a diegesis" and the *"mise en phase"* (Odin 1995, 228). In point of fact, the sober animation not only envisages the spectators as students to impart a lesson to, positioning them as passive receivers, but also prevents them from both building a world (i.e., a diegesis) and getting involved affectively with what they are offered to watch.[11] That is to say, it inhibits viewers from following their instinct of activating a fictionalizing reading by blocking some of the latter's core operations, leaving them with no other option but to approach what they are viewing as a discourse and not as a story. This result is achieved, first of all, through the schematic and diagrammatic character inherent to this mode of visual representation itself, which not only allows to construct just "spaces of signs" that, despite recalling our world, do not pertain to a world but also inhibits viewers from empathizing with what they see unfold on screen. This outcome, however, is obtained also through other devices, such as plain, one-dimensional backgrounds, the adoption of an aerial or frontal, seemingly objective point of view, and the deployment of animated arrows that, like the pointer used by a teacher to direct the attention of her or his class toward an element present on the board, draw the attention of the audience toward the part of the filmic image where what the intertitles or the narrator are talking about in that set moment is represented.

Hence, sober animation mobilizes the operation essential for a film to be read as nonfiction, namely the placement of the viewer "in the position of a *real* Addressee, i.e., an Addressee having to take seriously, in reality, what he is offered to watch" (230). It also enhances the "degree of 'documentarity'" of the film in which it is employed (229), guiding the spectator to adopt a "documentarizing reading" in a more unambiguous way than what many live-action nonfiction works do, a fact that further supports the idea of sober animation being animation's nonfictional mode of representation.

The Fabled Animation

In the same year in France Cohl completed *The Battle of Austerlitz*, in Great Britain Frank Percy Smith finalized *To Demonstrate How Spiders Fly* (1909), a stop-motion film that illustrates how spiders can utilize their threads as "parachutes." In particular, here Smith used a mechanical model of a spider to enact how such arthropods lift their legs after having thrown their silk to allow themselves to be dragged in the air, and subsequently execute a series of mid-air acrobatic maneuvers in order to descend. Hence, a single animated actor has been employed to stage (not without comedic effects) a practice that is carried out daily in real-life by a whole species. As a consequence, unlike observed for the films using the sober animation, *To Demonstrate How Spiders Fly* constructs a diegesis, complies with the rules of narrative structuration, and entertains viewers while instructing them. Smith's film can thus be recognized as a first example of the employment of what I have proposed to term the fabled animation.

Originally, it was rarer for animators to choose to employ this second mode of representation when dealing with factual subjects. Nonetheless, as *To Demonstrate How Spiders Fly* and *The Sinking of the Lusitania* prove, we can find examples of its adoption to create (almost) entirely animated works also in the early days of this medium's history. For a sizable use of such visual language, we have, however, to wait for the late 1930s, a period starting from which it has increasingly been employed in the creation of reality-related animated films. Also, the fabled animation has progressively come to be more and more used to create animated segments of otherwise live-action documentaries. Indeed, we already have examples of fabled animation, for instance, in the renowned sequence of a camera positioning itself on its tripod and then walking away of *Man with a Movie Camera* (*Chelovek s kino-apparatom*, 1929, dir. Dziga Vertov) or in the animated segment resurrecting the long-extinguished mammoth of *Letter from Siberia* (*Lettre de Sibérie*, 1958, dir. Chris Marker). Still, today the animated interjections recurring to this mode of visual representation have become countless because animated segments of this kind are increasingly used in place of live-action reenactments. The fact that such a shift has occurred is particularly evident by looking at the television series *Cosmos*. In Carl Segan's popular 1980 series *Cosmos—A Personal Voyage*, live-action reconstructions were employed to narrate the historical occurrences that had taken place before the advent of cinema. In the 2014 re-boot of the program, *Cosmos—A Spacetime Odyssey*, animation (and more precisely the fabled animation) has instead been used to this same end. As a consequence, for instance, in the first episode of the series, a cartoon character embodies the Dominican friar and astrologer Giordano Bruno, and the happenings he has been the protagonist of are dramatized without refraining from exploiting animation's omnipotence, to the point that we can even literally see the character fly through the cosmos (see Figure 1.7).

Generally speaking, fabled animation's main trait is that of employing fiction animation's same visual vocabulary and narrative devices in order to obtain accounts of reality that are at the same time informative and amusing. As John Halas and Roger Manvell point out in their textbook *The Technique of Film Animation*, "cartoons can make entertainment out of the presentation of facts, figures, systems and ideas" (Halas and Manvell [1959] 1976, 116). That is, the "facts of life" that "would normally be repellent or boring or unintelligible or at least uncomfortable for the average citizen to absorb during his leisure" can be conveyed "painlessly" through animation (133). Achieving such a result is the agenda underlying the fabled animation, and simultaneously it is through the deployment of the latter that this outcome is attained, forasmuch as such mode of representation draws on

FIGURE 1.7 *Giordano Bruno flying through the Cosmos in* Cosmos—A Spacetime Odyssey.

the same visual language and narrative tools employed in fiction animated movies. Indeed, it fully exploits the graphic freedom, the aptitude to "go places live-action cannot" (Canemaker in Artis [2007] 2014, 238), and the "magical" representational devices peculiar to the medium of animation, among which its capability "to make literal what can be, normally, only figurative, its power of exaggeration in order to present ideas with impact, its ability to project a thought until it obtains an entirely new and, in a curious way, more truthful aspect" (Halas 1956, 6). In concrete, this employment of fiction animation's same graphic vocabulary and narrative devices translates as follows:

1. One or more animated figures, which can be regarded as full-fledged actors—only made of shapes and colors instead of flesh and blood—or, like Donald Crafton (2013, 17) would say, as actual performers that "just happen to be animated," are utilized to enact the factual events recounted. In so doing, either a dramatization of the real-life occurrences told is operated or, more rarely, a comedic quality is bestowed to the narration. Hence, whichever the case, emotional response from the audience is elicited.

2. Full usage is made of those "magic" narrative devices that Wells (1998) identifies as distinctive of animation, such as metamorphosis, synecdoche, metaphor, symbolism, condensation, associative relations, and penetration (i.e., "the ability to evoke the internal space and portray the invisible"). For instance, a metaphor used by the voice-of-God narrator will be literally translated into pictographs or an otherwise non-filmable internal state described by an interviewee will be turned into appealing visuals.

3. Not only anthropomorphism and zoomorphism may be employed but also laws of gravity may be defied, having, for example, human-like characters spread their arms and fly.

4. The ability of color "to create *any* effect, whether it be dramatic, somber, joyous or otherwise" and to "emit a feeling that can affect viewers" may be exploited (Furniss [1998] 2007, 73, original emphasis). For instance, non-naturalistic colors may be used at a dramatic hand, to convey an emotion or generate one in the viewer.

5. Characters are immersed in two-dimensional (or even tridimensional) backgrounds.

Therefore, the fabled animation not only is characterized by a lack of sobriety at the level of visuals but also fosters those operations of construction of a diegesis, narrativization, and *mise en phase* that the sober animation instead blocks. This, however, does not imply that the audience will read the films employing such mode of representation as fictional works. In effect, Odin highlights that, technically, as long as the audience is invited "to construct an Enunciator who functions as a *real* origin" (Odin 1995, 229, original emphasis), any audiovisual work can be read as a documentary. Only, if the above-mentioned operations are not obstructed, the spectators will perceive the film in question as marked by a low degree of documentarity.

Nevertheless, the reason why I believe "fabled" to be the most appropriate term to identify such mode of representation is that its other key trait is that it invites the viewer to put in place not a documentarizing reading but rather precisely what Odin (2004, 89) refers to as the "fabled reading." The French scholar theorizes the latter as foreseeing the construction of "an Enunciator who functions as a real origin that places the spectator in the position of a real Addressee and tries to norm his behaviors" (93, my translation). Still, Odin explains the fabled reading as a "midway" reading between the documentarizing and fictionalizing reading. On the one hand, he shows how this regime of communication mobilizes the same operations that constitute the process of fictionalization but organizes them differently. On the other hand, he illustrates how, similarly to the documentarizing regime, the fabled one offers viewers a discourse and urges them to construct an Enunciator who functions as a real origin. However, it positions the spectator as an "Us real Addressee," and not as an "I real Addressee," like the process of documentarization would instead do (Odin 2004, 93). Indeed, a fabled regime of communication is put in place when the peculiar vicissitudes of one or more specific figures are watched as a more general discourse on a determinate issue affecting our world. Its distinctive trait is, thus, a "generalizing discursive process" that is activated through the deployment of an array of devices imbued with fictionality, which simultaneously favor such universalization but do not prevent the viewer from being involved affectively by what is recounted. Among them, Odin mentions the synecdoche, the metamorphosis, the stereotypy, symbolism, and "the drawn image" (which enables the production of a schematic representation, less detailed than a photographic one) (90–3),[12] all representational tools that are proper of animation's fictional mode of representation and, as a consequence, of the fabled animation.

Actually, the medium of animation itself already potentially fosters the activation of a fabled reading, since, like Halas and Manvell have underscored, "where live action particularises, animation generalizes, and in the process makes what it seeks to explain universal" (Halas and Manvell [1959] 1976, 134). Additionally, a less detailed representation than that allowed by photography is almost always achievable through such a medium. In effect, not only is this the case for any animation created using the techniques of drawing and rotoscoping, but it can also be for those crafted utilizing CGI. Examples are the shorts *Paperman* (2012, dir. John Kahrs) and *La Luna* (2011, dir. Enrico Casarosa), which Helen Haswell shows to be the result of the "application of hand-drawn and organic techniques within a digitally animated environment, to create an aesthetic that evokes nostalgia for traditional animation" (Haswell 2014, 10). Moreover, as Odin argues, the same effect of a greater sketchiness than that of live-action photography is not obtainable just through a drawn image (or one that resembles it). On the contrary, it is achievable through any animation technique foreseeing the fabrication of an image, like for instance puppetry animation. However, if the generalization is at the heart of this medium in many ways, it is only when the more fictional visual language of animation, with its narrative tools promoting a universalization of the events recounted, is utilized to narrate the factual that the viewer is concretely brought to put in place a fabled reading, rather than a fictionalizing one. Indeed, on the other occasions, the spectator would not be prompted to build an Enunciator who functions as a real origin, a fact that we have instead seen to be a requirement for the activation of this regime of communication. Simplifying, we could thus say that a film (or a segment of a film) employing the fabled animation works in a more similar way to Aesop's fables than to a live-action documentary. Like these ancient Greek tales, it uses means of fiction to impart to a group of people a teaching that applies to reality. The only difference is that, while Aesop's fables avail themselves of fiction both at the level of form and content, the former does so only at the level of form, requiring the viewer to consider its content instead as factual.

Notes

1. This remains true also in the case in which a technique such as rotoscoping that foresees a somewhat indexical link to reality is employed. Indeed, the presence of the body of the factual model underneath the animated one tends to provoke in the viewer uncanny feelings, since as Johanna Bouldin (2004, 13) depicts, "this cadaverous persistence of the original body insinuates a kind of ontological ambiguity and uncertainty into the animated body."

2. There are, however, also techniques, such as the draw-on-film animation, that do not foresee the use of a camera in order to create the film.

3. For a comprehensive account of the uncanny valley, see Tinwell (2015).

4. For a treatise of *Defense against Invasion*, see Kaufman (2009, 143–5).

5. The existence of a profound difference between the representational approach employed by Disney and the one that informed Neurath's work is underlined by the latter himself in a letter to Wolfgang Foges written in 1942. Here Neurath stresses that, whereas Disney's agenda was that of entertaining the viewer while educating him, his intention was instead to purely provide the spectator with "some *educational information*" (Neurath in Burke 2013, 370, original emphasis).

6. For instance, after the *Lusitania* navigates past the Statue of Liberty, we see a curtain progressively closing, metaphorically suggesting the passing of time (see Canemaker 1987, 154).

7 For an in-depth analysis of *The Sinking of the Lusitania*, see Chapter 4.
8 For a treatise of the *Kineto War Map* series, see Low (1950, 171–2).
9 Thierry Lefebvre (2005, 569) dates this series as far back as 1903. Yet, he does not provide any explanation regarding this choice. I thus believe more appropriate to adopt, instead, the 1912 dating proposed by Oliver Gaycken (2014a, 72), both because it appears more coherent in respect to the history of animation and because it coincides with what is indicated by the Deutsches Institut für Animations film.
10 The intertitles of these films were so concise that in many cases the explicative text was just enclosed in small rectangles and superimposed on part of the drawings.
11 It is important to note that, if the viewer cannot construct a world, then the operation of "narrativization" is blocked, "since the two actantial structures that constitute narrativization require an imaginary world in which to function" (Buckland 2000, 92).
12 The other processes Odin specifically cites are the "image-suitcase" (i.e., an image that carries both a purely iconic signifier and an iconic-kinetic one that refer to two distinct but interconnected meanings), the "transition through linguistics" (namely a usage of pictographs that favors a process of non-individualization), and the "refusal of words" (thanks to which the characters, and thus the occurrences recounted through them, rid themselves of any specific cultural-linguistic context) (Odin 2004, 90–2, my translation).

2

The Sincerest Form of Docudrama

Ever since the late 1990s, when they first started to attract theoretical attention, animated documentaries have been scholarly classified as documentary films, as they use animation to narrate fragments of the actual world rather than of an imaginary world. What is more, often, they have been fitted into one of Bill Nichols' (1991, 1994) documentary modes of representation. Just to make a few examples, in the essay published in *Film/History* in 1997, Sybil Del Gaudio argues that animated documentaries should be considered as examples of the "reflexive" mode (Del Gaudio 1997, 192), whereas six years later, on the pages of *Animation Journal*, Gunnar Strøm classes part of these works as "performative" documentaries (Strøm 2003, 52).[1] Most recently, Pascal Lefèvre (2019, 23–8) has argued that, depending on the traits they showcase, these animated works can fit either in the "poetic," "expository," "participatory," or "performative" mode, or even in more than one at the same time.

As suggested by Jonathan Rozenkrantz (2011), this tendency to invoke "Nichols' typology . . . in the discourse of animated documentary" probably rests at the same time on the desire of validating such films as full-fledged documentaries and on the conviction that this legitimation can be achieved simply by shoehorning them into one or more of these categories. However, I believe that, if a necessity of justifying the animated documentary's allotment within the documentary realm is felt, it is because these audiovisual texts hold only a tenuous relationship with it. The expression "animated documentary" has always been employed in conjunction with audiovisual texts that, in illustrating an aspect of our world, make use of the fabled animation and not to those utilizing the sober one.[2] In other words, it has not been used to identify those filmic and televisual works that mobilize a documentarizing reading by drawing on animation's nonfictional language, but rather those that invite the viewer to put in place a fabled reading through employing this medium's fictional mode of representation.

In point of fact, as we will see more in detail in Chapter 3, although, scholarly, the animated documentary started receiving proper attention only in the late 1990s, amid animation producers, film critics, distributors, and even the Academy of Motion Picture Arts and Sciences, the term "animated documentary" commenced circulating already in the 1940s. Back then it was used to single out expository films that, in order to instruct viewers on an issue regarding their everyday, combine entertaining and imaginative animated visuals with an informational voice-of-God commentary. Indeed, works such as, for instance, *The Winged Scourge* (1943, dir. Bill Roberts), *Brotherhood of Man* (1945, dir. Robert Cannon), and *Charley in New Town* (1946, dir. John Halas and Joy Batchelor) and the other shorts featuring the character of the everyman Charley that were produced by the Halas & Batchelor Cartoon Films studio for COI in the late 1940s were referred to as animated documentaries in this period.[3] For long, this has been the typology of animated works designed with the expression "animated documentary." As a matter of fact, when in 1997 the first scholarly contributions on the relationships between animation and documentary appeared, among the titles discussed as examples of animated documentaries were expository animated films that employed the fabled animation to illustrate a fragment of our world. Indeed, to be considered in these initial scholarly works are titles like the short *Camouflage* (1944, dir. Frank Thomas), wherein a talking, anthropomorphic chameleon teaches a group of US aviators how to conceal their planes effectively (see Del Gaudio 1997), or the series *I'm No Fool. . .* (1955–6) and *You and Your. . .* (1955–7), starring animated actor Jiminy Cricket (see Wells 1997).

Very soon, the attention of scholars has, however, shifted toward the more contemporary production.[4] The expression "animated documentary" was thus started to be used mostly in conjunction with works that provide (first-person) accounts of real-life experiences of specific, existing individuals, such as *Silence* (1998, dir. Orly Yadin and Sylvie Bringas) on Holocaust survivor Tana Ross or *Snack and Drink* (1999, dir. Bob Sabiston) on autistic boy Rayan Power. In particular, nowadays the animated documentary par excellence tends to be identified in *Waltz with Bashir*, a feature film recounting its director's attempt to recover his lost memories of fighting in the 1982 Lebanon War. Therefore, whereas the typology of titles referred to as animated documentaries has changed in various respects, to be talked about in these terms are still audiovisual works that reenact and dramatize factual-based events exploiting animation's fictional mode of representation. Indeed, in these films also non-naturalistic colors can be used to convey a feeling or an emotion for dramatic purposes, as in *Waltz with Bashir*; objects can come to life, like it happens to a set of beverage dispensers provided with hands, arms, and eyes in *Snack and Drink*; or an image can morph into another, as it occurs extensively in *Silence*, where, for instance, a live-action baby transmutes into a white skeleton-like animated figure, children transform in cockroaches, and a man acquires the semblance of a rat. Moreover, since many of the works that have been referred to as animated documentaries after 1985 are animated memoirs and memory is a mental faculty that "includes events and experiences that took place factually, and events and experiences that did not," content-wise these works may weave together "the real and the imagined, the actual and the fantastic" (Landesman and Bendor 2011, 3).

In sum, the expression "animated documentary" has always been used to single out animated works wherein real-life events are *reenacted* for the camera by "fabricated" actors, be they novice performers or well-known animated stars, as the cases of *The Winged Scourge* and the series *I'm No Fool . . .* and *You and Your . . .* show it used to occur from time to time in the past. In other words, the term "animated documentary" has always been employed to identify audiovisual works that, on the one hand, like Paul Ward (2005, 8) shows to be proper of documentaries, make "assertions or truth claims about the real world or real people in that world (including the real world of history)," but, on the other hand, they

1. intrinsically rely on reenactment (see Fore 2011, 278);
2. are "locked into a tenuous relation with the world" they represent, "a relation expressed in the mixing of 'realistic' themes with fantastic forms" (Landesman and Bendor 2011, 2);
3. share with historical fiction the problem of finding themselves "with a body too many," whose presence alone "testifies to a gap between the text and the life to which it refers" and "reduces representation to simulation" (Nichols 1991, 249). In fact, in animated documentaries, this breach is even more evident than it is in historical fictions, because the bodies in question not only have a different materiality from real-life ones (as they are made of shapes and colors and not of flesh and blood) but also frequently do not even resemble by far their factual counterpart, since it is not uncommon for film directors to opt for a non-mimetic style.

One could argue that some of the titles that throughout history have been identified as animated documentaries contain also a small quantity of sober animation, which, as seen in Chapter 1, is one of those veridictive marks that a film needs to exhibit in order to be perceived as a documentary (e.g., see Roscoe and Hight 2001, 15). More precisely, it is the veridictive mark par excellence when it comes to an animated work. However, veridictive marks have to be *consistently* present in order to induce viewers to read a film as a documentary, and this is never the case in the audiovisual works that have been and are today referred to as animated documentaries. In point of fact, when sober animation can be identified in them, it is present in a percentage minimal or anyhow significantly inferior to that of the fabled animation displayed. Therefore, its presence within animated documentaries is never sufficiently substantive to induce the viewer to read these films as full-fledged documentaries.

Factual Sounds with a Wink

Since image-wise animated documentaries do not hold a direct relationship with the physical world, in order to endorse the rightness of classing them as full-fledged documentaries, there is the tendency to draw attention to the fact that sound-wise they bestow instead great proximity to live-action documentaries. In effect, since its advent, sound has carried out much of the burden of authenticating as factual what in them is recounted. Only, over time, how this has been done has changed, following the evolution that the documentary itself has undergone. In the past, similar to what was commonplace in the coeval live-action nonfiction production, an informative and didactic voice-of-God commentary characterized most animated documentaries.[5] This disembodied voiceover narration, which was introduced in the 1930s, is a major feature of expository documentaries that has soon come to be associated with "ultimate wisdom" and "impartial truth" (Nichols [2001] 2017, 124), and consequently has become a synonym of authenticity to the ears of viewers. Therefore, its presence within past animated documentaries has acted as their primary marker of veridiction.

Expository animated documentaries whose "soundtracks' voiceovers . . . are vessels of both information and authentication" are being produced even today, as is, for instance, the case of the series *Walking with Dinosaurs* (1999, dir. Tim Haines and Jasper James) and *Planet Dinosaur* (2011, dir. Nigel Paterson) (Honess Roe 2013, 50). Yet, from the mid-1980s onwards, the bulk of this form's production has become interview-driven animated works that provide an account of traumatic life experiences or subjective states of mind of specific individuals. This evolution can once again be seen as determined by the transformations that the live-action documentary has endured. Indeed, since it carries "the evidential weight of a legal testimony," the interview has come to be increasingly employed in the live-action nonfiction production to the point of having now become "one of the recognizable markers of documentary on film and television" (Honess Roe 2013, 75). Also, this relatively recent change undergone by the animated documentary has possibly enhanced the proximity of these works' soundtracks to those of live-action documentaries. Indeed, since they are now frequently composed by audio recordings of real-life interviews, "animated documentaries often retain the same oral/aural link with reality as conventional documentaries" (27). This fact—which tends to be underlined in the films themselves by having shots of a recording device in

FIGURE 2.1 *A shot of a recorder from* Irinka & Sandrinka.

action, such as a microphone or a recorder (e.g., see Figure 2.1)—has brought many to view the soundtrack of these works as the component that would unquestionably make an animated documentary a full-fledged documentary. For instance, Brian Winston writes that "it is the act of witnessing expressed in the soundtrack that makes these cartoons documentaries" (Winston 2008, 282). Analogously, when, in making *The Beloved Ones* (2007), filmmaker Samantha Moore was faced with the impossibility of using the recordings of the interviews she had conducted and had to replace them with a rereading of the testimonies by actors, she feared "that the documentary status of the film would be compromised by this jettisoning of original sound" (Moore 2013).

However, it is essential to remember that an animated documentary is an *audiovisual* product. Hence these films' soundtracks cannot be considered per se. They must be taken into account in connection with the visuals that accompany them, since, as Michel Chion (1994, xxvi) has convincingly demonstrated, "we never see the same thing when we also hear; we don't hear the same thing when we see as well." Indeed, "the image ... makes us hear sound differently than if the sound were ringing out in the dark" (21). In other words, when related to visuals, sound acquires a meaning that by itself it would not have: "Depending on the dramatic and visual context, a single sound can convey very diverse things. . . . The same sound can convincingly serve as the sound effect for a crushed watermelon in a comedy or for a head blown to smithereens in a war film. The same noise will be joyful in one context, intolerable in another" (22–3). Equally, I argue, the documentary value of a factual soundtrack can be enhanced or diminished by the visuals to which it is combined and by how it relates to them.

The clearest example in this sense is offered by Nick Park's *Creature Comforts* (2003–11). In each episode of this clay animation television series produced by Aardman Animations, recordings of real people's interviews, wherein the interviewees are asked to talk about an aspect of their own life (e.g., living conditions, working life, habits, and so on), are used to voice Plasticine anthropomorphic animals. Therefore, for instance, in the episode "Working Animals" (2003, dir. Richard Goleszowski), a red ant sitting on a slice of bread recounts: "I have worked in a hotel. . . . And I would be there at night. I would work at the desk and help in the kitchen. But, I would also clean the toilets. Why not? I like different roles. It just means I can channel the madness in different areas." Likewise, in "The Beach" (2003, dir. Richard Goleszowski), a pig leaning on the enclosure of a piggery with a mud stain on its ear declares that "he" would not swim in the sea, because in it there are "too many germs . . . , too many things that can make you ill and bad." By embodying these bits of interviews in animal characters with human-like features, Aardman's animators lessen the documentary value of such declarations in favor of a comical effect. That is, if these same *vox populi* statements were to be broadcast on radio, the resulting program could undoubtedly be considered a documentary. However, as soon as we insert them in a visual and dramatic context that drastically differs from that in which they were originally recorded (as it happens in *Creature Comforts*), the overall effect for the viewer is no longer that of dealing with documentary material, and this occurs despite the fact that such interviews entertain an indexical relationship with reality.

One could contend that this is an extreme case since these recordings are used to a comedic end because the series is intended mainly as an entertainment product. As a matter of fact, *Creature Comforts* is not even an animated documentary but rather an animated mockumentary (see Wells 1997, 42–3). Nevertheless, for every animated documentary that recurs to a factual soundtrack, it is similarly true that through its visuals "the animators . . . construct an 'imaginative interpretation of what is heard.' In other words, they construct 'a world' that will metaphorically emphasize (or ironically undermine) what the viewer is hearing on the soundtrack" (Ward 2006, 122). Indeed, the animations associated with these factual soundtracks are not merely illustrative of the interview situation during which they were recorded. On the contrary, they tend to dramatize the content of the interviews. Also, the audio recordings of real-life testimonies around which these films are usually built are mostly made either into the lines of the animated actors standing for the people who originally pronounced those words or into a first-person voiceover narration that guides the viewing public through the story. The former is, for instance, what occurs in *Ryan* (2004, dir. Chris Landreth), where the declarations of Ryan himself and of other real-life people who have been asked to talk about him become the words proffered by the onscreen animated characters representing these persons. The latter is instead the case of *Seeking Refuge* (2012, dir. Andy Glynne), a series of five films created for BBC, each illustrating the traumatic story of a child who, obliged to flee his or her country of origin, has sought refuge in the UK. In these shorts, the recordings of the interviews are transformed into a voiceover narration that blends characteristics of two kinds of voiceover narrations proper of fiction films: the voiceover during a flashback and the interior monologue. More precisely, the voiceover narration in which such aural testimonies are made works "to affirm the homogeneity and dominance of diegetic space" (Doane 1980, 42) and does not remain disembodied. That is, it can be yoked to the body of an onscreen character and, in a similar way to what is the case for an interior monologue (see 41), it tends to be represented simultaneously to such body. However, it does not become an extension of it, since typically, as is characteristic of the voiceover during a flashback, this voiceover tends to effect "a temporal dislocation of the voice with respect to the body" of the animated actor standing for the real-life interviewee (Doane 1980, 41). Indeed, through skillful editing, the recollections of the child at the center of each *Seeking Refuge* film are transmuted into a first-person narrator that conducts us through the visual dramatization of his or her own relatively recent past.

Moreover, we can even find cases of contemporary animated documentaries wherein declarations by the same real-life interviewee not only keep shifting between being a voiceover narration and the lines of an animated actor but also are embodied in multiple onscreen characters. This occurs, for example, in the shorts of the *StoryCorps* series animated by the Rauch Brothers when, during its aural recollections, the interviewee quotes a direct speech. As a matter of example, we can consider *The Road Home* (2013). Here, the audio memoir of Eddie Lanier, a homeless with a history of alcoholism who found a friend in a passerby, is animated. In this short, Eddie's declarations are mostly made into a first-person voiceover narration. However, from time to time, when he recalls something that somebody has told him or a conversation he has had, his words are embodied in the animated actors standing in for the person who proffered those words. As a consequence, only in the first sequence of *The Road Home*, the same male voice of a now old Eddie is already made into the lines of three different characters: first, a passerby woman, then, the protagonist's father, and, finally, a fourteen-year-old Eddie.

In brief, even though the aural recordings that form the soundtracks of contemporary animated documentaries bear an indexical link to our world, their "eccentric" employment somehow weakens the overall documentary value of these films' sound component. And, this fictionalization of the soundtrack is typical of the animated documentary in general and not just of the form's current production. As we will see more in depth in Chapter 5, the voice-of-God commentary of classical animated documentaries also becomes eccentric from time to time. That is, it occasionally loses that "radical otherness with respect to the diegesis," which Doane (1980, 42) shows to be the distinguishing trait of the nonfiction film's voiceover commentary. Indeed, the voice-of-God should be characterized by detachment, neutrality, disinterestedness, and omniscience (see Nichols [2001] 2017, 123). Also, it should speak "without mediation to the audience, bypassing the 'characters' and establishing a complicity between itself and the spectator," and it should come from an unspecified place outside the diegesis (Doane 1980, 42). Doane adds: "It is precisely because the voice is not localizable, because it cannot be yoked to a body, that it is capable of interpreting the image, producing its truth" (Doane 1980, 42). Yet, here and there in classical animated documentaries this authority and apparent objectivity of the voice-of-God are diminished by having the latter temporally fall short of one of these characteristics. This can be done in a variety of ways,[6] among which is, for instance, having the protagonists of the film interact with the voice-of-God as if it was not just the viewer who could hear the commentary but they also could. A case in point is *Man Alive!* (1952, dir. William T. Hurtz). This UPA short sponsored by the American Cancer Society illustrates the importance of seeking medical care immediately when experiencing cancer symptoms by telling the exemplar story of the everyman Ed Parmelee,[7] who refuses to recognize that his stomach problem may be a severe issue. Toward the middle of the film, all of a sudden, the voice-of-God narrator starts addressing directly the protagonist of the short and says: "Just a minute Ed. You are being difficult, you know?" The character, who at that moment is taking a shower, pops his head out of the shower's curtains, and replies: "I am being difficult?" It starts as such a dialog between him and the voiceover that reduces the latter more to a voice-off, precisely because this disembodied voice comes to be acknowledged within the diegesis. As a consequence, the voice-of-God narration temporally falls short of its documentary character.

In sum, generally speaking, while on a purely aural level the soundtracks of animated documentaries undeniably showcase great proximity to those of documentaries, they, however, end up being "fictionalized," and thus see their veridictive character diminished through how they interrelate with the animated visuals.

The Animated Documentary and Its Likenesses to Docudrama

In light of all the foregoing, rather than undertaking the slippery and ruinous route of attempting to prove that these animated works equate to live-action documentaries on all counts by stretching through the roof Grierson's (1933, 8) definition of documentary as "a creative treatment of actuality,"[8] would it not be more appropriate to allocate the animated documentary in the docufiction territory? In particular, considering that it retells factual occurrences through fictional modes of delivery, I believe it should best be defined as a form of docudrama.

In the introduction to the volume *Docufictions*, Gary Rhodes and John Springer (2006) describe docudramas as those films that combine documentary content with a fictional form. Later on, the two scholars specify that a docudrama is "a fabricate *recreation* of actual people or events" in which "the devices of fictional narrative are used to render more vivid the conflict and drama of the 'real' subject" (Rhodes and Springer 2006, 5–6). If we compare this definition to what was previously outlined for the animated documentary, it immediately surfaces a clear alikeness, at least at a broad level, between these two typologies of audiovisual works.

However, animated documentary and docudrama do not share only the fact of reenacting real-life occurrences through fictional and dramatic structures. They have numerous other similar elements as well. First of all, like docudramas, animated documentaries, "distinct from conventional documentaries, ... replace indexical, 'unstaged' images with a quasi-indexical narrative" (Lipkin 2002, 1–2). Nevertheless, at the same time, both these typologies of audiovisual works ask viewers to consider them as truthful portrayals of the events that they depict, despite their reliance on fictional narrative strategies and aesthetics. In other words, the filmmakers of both forms request the audience to view their films as if they were documentaries (see respectively Roscoe and Hight 2001, 45; Honess Roe 2013). Indeed, in illustrating the relationship that docudrama entertains with fiction and nonfiction, Derek Paget first writes: "The docudrama ... inevitably points more insistently towards its origins in the real world than other kinds of drama" (Paget [1998] 2011, 8). He subsequently adds:

> the docudrama seeks to overlay the Stanislavskian emotional equivalence of "As If" with a documentary-indexical "See This!." The relation to reality claimed in the solely dramatic "as if" through equivalence and parallel, is present in docudrama through reconstruction/re-enactment (these words/actions, in this place). At the same time viewers will usually be aware that the events dramatized really happened; they exist, as it were, in parallel to acted ones. (9; see also Roscoe and Hight 2001, 45)

More specifically, docudramas claim this direct relationship to factual occurrences mostly either through captions or through declarations by the voiceover but can do so also by having the actual protagonist(s) of the events depicted briefly appear onscreen or by displaying a small amount of documentary material (see Paget [1998] 2011, 97–105). Similarly, animated documentaries are reconstructions of real-life events that point to the factuality of the occurrences in them reenacted and ask viewers to approach them as veridical accounts of the events they narrate, even if, in illustrating them, aesthetics and modes of representation proper of this medium's fictional production are used. They can claim a direct link to reality through both textual elements and paratexts (e.g., publicity, marketing materials, and filmmakers' interviews).⁹ In particular, the primary way in which the factuality of what is illustrated in a classical animated documentary is pointed out is through indicating in the titles that a scientific consultant was availed of in the making of the film or, more rarely, by having he or she appear onscreen. This is what occurs, for instance, in *Our Mr. Sun* (1956, dir. Frank Capra), where the professor of the University of Southern California Dr. Frank C. Baxter appears in the role of Dr. Research. In contemporary animated documentaries, instead, the most widespread way of pointing to a direct link of the film with our world is by underlining that the film's soundtrack is factual through the aforesaid shots of a recording device in action. However, in several cases, this direct reference to real-life events is even claimed in the same way as in docudramas, namely through a caption or a declaration by the voiceover narrator that connects the narrative to its factual referent. As a matter of example, *Chicago 10*—which uses animation to reenact the *Chicago 8* trial in order to overcome the lack of live-action footage of the proceedings—opens with a caption pointing out that the film is an *adaptation* from the trial's court transcripts. As such, it is thus established immediately that what is illustrated is based on factual data while, at the same time, underlining that what the viewer is about to see is a dramatization of what happened. Moreover, this caption is followed by a second one that, as it often happens in docudramas too (see Paget [1998] 2011, 99ff.), places the film historically, by saying: "1968. The Vietnam war has been raging for over three years. In that time nineteen thousand two hundred seventy-two Americans have been killed and countless more wounded." Analogously, *The Green Wave* (2010, dir. Ali Samadi Ahadi)—which reenacts what occurred in Iran on the occasion of the 2009 presidential election—begins with some animated shots of Teheran accompanied by a voiceover narrator that explains: "In 2009 Iranian suffered from unparalleled depression. Journalists and dissidents were imprisoned, and all foreign media expelled from the country. All the stories told in the following animations are authentic excerpts from Internet blogs written by courageous people within Iran, who dared to tell the world what was happening to them."

One could argue that *Chicago 10* and *The Green Wave* pertain more likely to the documentary realm than to that of docudrama because they contain various shots which bear an indexical link to reality since in them the animation is combined with archival footage and photographs related to the facts narrated. However, as anticipated, also in docudramas, we can find a limited presence of archival footage or aesthetics proper of documentary filmmaking. As Leslie Woodhead outlines in an essay published in the volume *Why Docudrama?*, docudramas' claims of portraying events that have a real-life referent "are often heightened by the deliberate deployment of techniques and mannerism derived from factual documentary" (Woodhead 1999, 108).

Consequently, the presence of documentary aesthetics and materials is not in contradiction with *Chicago 10* and *The Green Wave*, which are possibly considered docudramas. On the contrary, one should view it as an additional trait that animated documentary and docudrama share. Indeed, as Paget illustrates, the "use of *documentary material* is an important and distinctive convention of . . . docudrama" employed to authenticate it "as part-documentary" (Paget [1998] 2011, 105, original emphasis). Moreover, in this perspective, also the presence of some sober animation that, as we have seen, can be identified in several animated documentaries does not make them any less alike to docudramas.

Second, animated documentaries and docudramas also share the same kind of subjects. Steven Lipkin, Derek Paget, and Jane Roscoe outline that docudramas tend to do one or more of the following: "re-tell events from national/international histories, either reviewing or celebrating these events; . . . re-present the careers of significant national/international figures, for broadly similar purposes as the above; . . . portray issues of concerns to national/international communities, in order to provoke discussion about them" (Lipkin, Paget, and Roscoe 2006, 14). Equally, we have animated documentaries such as *The Sinking of the Lusitania*, *The Romance of Transportation in Canada* (1952, dir. Colin Low), and *Chicago 10* that retell historical events or retrace the history of something with either a celebratory (as in the case of Low's film) or a revisionist aim (as in McCay's and Morgen's films). We also have animated documentaries like *The Invisible Moustache of Raoul Dufy* (1955, dir. Aurelius Battaglia), *Ryan*, and *McLaren's Negatives* (2006, dir. Marie-Josée Saint-Pierre) that re-present the life of significant figures.[10] Finally, we have many titles such as, for example, *The Winged Scourge*, *Children of the Sun* (1960, dir. Faith and John Hubley), *It's Like That* (2003, dir. Southern Ladies Animation Group), and *Little Voices* (*Pequeñas voces*, 2010, dir. Jairo Eduardo Carrillo and Oscar Andrade) which portray issues of concerns, in their respective times, to specific communities. In particular, the first three films enlighten on malaria, world hunger, and Australian detention centers for asylum seekers respectively. The purpose of *Little Voices*, instead, is to "inform the wider public . . . about the situation of children caught up in the Colombian conflict" (Conde Aldana 2018, 53).

Additionally, Lipkin, Paget, and Roscoe (2006, 14) point out that in more recent times docudramas have "increasingly focused upon 'ordinary citizens,' thrust into the news through special (and often traumatic) experiences." Plus, Jane Feuer refers to a part of the docudrama production as "trauma drama" (Feuer as quoted in Lipkin, Paget, and Roscoe 2006, 18), a definition that perfectly suits also contemporary animated documentaries such as *Silence*, *Waltz with Bashir*, and the many other titles which equally are "post-traumatic films" that deal with distressing memories (Morag 2013, 132).

Furthermore, as well as docudramas, many animated documentaries tend "towards person-centered . . . 'social dramas'" (Lipkin, Paget, and

Roscoe 2006, 16). That is, they also tend to recount the experiences of specific individuals in order to shed light on a social issue felt as relevant. This, before the mid-1980s, was achieved by telling the exemplary story of an everyman, as in *Man Alive!*, or in any case of one or more figures incarnating an entire category of people, as in *Children of the Sun*, which sensitizes around world hunger by counterposing a healthy and an undernourished child who stand respectively for all rich and poor kids. Today, instead, animated documentaries shed light on "social problems ... and difficult 'human' issues" precisely by narrating the experiences of one or more real-life persons (Paget [1998] 2011, 9), as it occurs for instance in the aforementioned *It's Like That* or in *Centrefold* (2012, dir. Ellie Land), which, in order to raise awareness around female genital cosmetic surgery, recounts the personal struggles of three women who have undergone labiaplasty.

Even the reasons why it is chosen to narrate real-life occurrences in animation form are basically identical to those identifiable at the roots of docudramas. As Ward (2005, 34) highlights, a filmmaker decides typically to make a docudrama rather than a documentary when "either there is no 'direct' record of the events that can simply be drawn into the documentary context ... or there are issues around anonymity or other problems with access that mean that reconstruction is one of the only options available." Analogously, the principal motives why an animated documentary is opted for are: to compensate for the lack of live-action footage on that set real-life occurrence or fact (whether it be because it is unfilmed or unfilmable), to protect the identity of the subject by granting him or her anonymity, and to convey subjective conscious experiences or emotions (see Honess Roe 2013; Glynne 2013, 75; Martinelli 2012, 34).

Finally, the docudrama and the animated documentary partake the same reflexivity toward the documentary. That is, by depicting factual events through fictional narrative structures and aesthetics, even if not necessarily self-consciously, they both call attention to the limitations of the documentary discourse in portraying reality. In other words, as Del Gaudio (1997, 192) suggested about the animated documentary, both these hybrid forms pass comment on the documentary, underlining the impossibility for a live-action camera to document some aspects of reality, such as our inner processes.

A Matter of Sincerity

While docudrama and animated documentary bear many similarities, there is, however, an essential difference between them. The former is liable to the criticism of "potentially misleading the viewing public" (Roscoe and Hight 2001, 42) because the viewer could mistake it for an actual documentary. It is thus necessary to signpost it being a mixture of fact and fiction (and not an exact depiction of the real-life occurrence it retells), through those same captions that are used to anchor it to the actual world (see Woodhead 1999, 109; Paget 2000, 198–201). The animated documentary, instead, cannot be confused for a documentary, since, as Paul Wells notes, animation is "a medium which is informed by self-evident principles of construction . . . as . . . it does not use the camera to 'record' reality but artificially creates and records its own" (Wells 1998, 25). As Sheila Sofian puts it, "[o]ne could argue, therefore, that the use of animation is in some ways more transparent, more 'honest' than the use of live action in that it does not conceal the filmmaker's control over the media. Since the filmmaker's hand is plainly visible, the viewer is presented with an obvious construct: there is no disguising the filmmaker's manipulation of the imagery" (Sofian 2019, 221–2). In fact, behind the choice of telling an aspect of the real through animation, there may be the precise desire of that work's director to signpost the frailty of the truths presented. It has been the case for Keith Maitland when making his feature animated documentary *Tower* (2016) on the 1966 shooting at the University of Texas at Austin. Indeed, he has declared that he has chosen to employ rotoscope animation because "[i]n *Tower* people are recalling 50-years old memories, which are fallible, and this style acknowledges that" thanks to its "dreamlike quality" (Maitland in Miller 2018).

Undeniably, one could contend that a CGI animated documentary as Tim Haines' *Walking with Dinosaurs*, wherein a highly photorealist style is employed and the voice-of-God narrator treats the images shown "as if they were actual natural history footage filmed in the usual way" (Honess Roe 2013, 51), can likewise be accused of deceiving viewers, as it has effectively occurred (see Midgley 1999, 9). However, in the vast majority of cases, even when in CGI, animated documentaries leave no doubt to spectators that what they are seeing "isn't a recording of an actual referent, but an iconic representation of a possible one" (Rozenkrantz 2011). In fact, most animated documentaries are characterized by a non-mimetic animation, a fact that emphasizes their images' fictive status. In brief, customarily, when watching an animated documentary, the viewing public cannot but be aware that the film proposed has been "built, rendered and fashioned (or, to use another term—performed) by the unseen hands of the animator" (Ward 2011, 298–9).

Hence, since animation's presence alone is a flagrant declaration of these audiovisual texts' constructedness and audience members can hardly be tricked on the ontological status of the images presented, animated documentaries inherently overcome those ethical issues that live-action docudramas instead raise. Given this, I propose to redefine the animated documentary not just as a form of docudrama but as the sincerest form of docudrama. With this, however, I do not want to suggest that animated documentaries are in all respects as live-action docudramas, because this would mean perpetuating the mistake of not acknowledging animation as a medium of its own with characteristics and rules that differ from those of live-action. What I propose is, instead, to recognize that animation also has its docufiction realm inhabited by several different forms resulting from the hybridization of fiction and nonfiction elements,[11] and that one of these forms is what we have come to call the animated documentary, which, more precisely, should be envisioned as this medium's counterpart to the live-action docudrama.

Notes

1. For a more detailed account of the various representational modes in which these films have been fitted throughout the last two decades, see Honess Roe (2013, 17–22).
2. As it is shown in Chapter 3, the same is valid also for the variants of this label "cartoon documentary" and "documentary cartoon."
3. Regarding the dating of the films forming the so-called Charley series, there seems to not be a consensus among scholars. For instance, Roger Manvell (1980, 13) dates them all between 1946 and 1947. According to Vivian Halas and Paul Wells (2006), these shorts were created in 1947. John Southall (1999, 81), instead, suggests that they were produced between March 1948 and January 1950. In light of this confusion, the years I provide here refer to the first release of these films, which can be identified with certainty. More precisely, I have extracted them from a scrutiny of the magazine *Documentary News Letter*, in which the new titles distributed in British cinemas were indicated monthly.
4. Already in his 1997 essay, Wells mentions also works like the series *Blind Justice* (1987) and the *Abductees* (1995, dir. Paul Vester) in discussing the shapes that the animated documentary can take (see Wells 1997, 43–5).
5. A small number of this period's animated documentaries is, instead, characterized by what Nichols ([2001] 2017, 53) defines a "'voice-of-authority' commentary." For a treatise of this variant, see Chapter 5.
6. For a complete overview of the ways in which the otherness of the voice-of-God commentary can be diminished in classical animated documentaries, see Chapter 5.
7. Curiously, the name chosen for the character is that of an actual UPA employee, the animator Edward (Ted) Parmelee. For an account of his work, see Lenburg (2006, 277); Abraham (2012).
8. As Derek Paget argues, "Grierson's defining phrase 'the creative treatment of actuality' . . . has often been misquoted. . . . More than once 'creative' has become 'imaginative'" (Paget [1998] 2011, 171).
9. On paratextual authentication in animated documentaries, see Honess Roe (2013, 65–7).

10 In particular, Battaglia's film represents the life of a French painter that had recently died, while the other two are about renowned animators.
11 Similar to what Rhodes and Springer (2006, 4–9) suggest, I am here intending docufiction as a middle ground between fiction and nonfiction populated by several different hybrid forms derived from the crossbreeding of fiction and documentary, among which are mockumentary and docudrama.

3

A New Periodization for an Old Form

According to Annabelle Honess Roe, aside from obviously having to talk about the social world and be "recorded or created frame by frame," an audiovisual text has to comply also with a third condition in order to be deemed an animated documentary: it must have "been presented as a documentary by its producers and/or received as a documentary by audiences, festivals or critics" (Honess Roe 2013, 4). Based on this last criterion, she reaches two conclusions that have come to model the current understanding of this typology of audiovisual works. The first is that the animated documentary would be fundamentally just a contemporary form, since, according to her, "[i]t was not until the 1980s and 90s that filmmakers began making short films that combined animation and documentary and calling them 'animated documentaries'" (Honess Roe 2016, 45). The second—which likely builds on a partition of the typologies of nonfiction works into "documentary and nondocumentary" that Bill Nichols ([2001] 2017, 104–5) offers in his *Introduction to Documentary*[1]—is that all "advertising, scientific, educational and public service films" in animation would necessarily fall outside the animated documentary category "because they are neither intended nor received as documentaries" (Honess Roe 2013, 4).

Still, even if in assessing the boundaries and the coming into being of this form we adopt Honess Roe's same yardstick, the animated documentary proves to have a history that not only goes farther back in time than the 1980s but also is interwoven with advertising, scientific, educational, and public service cinema—like, by the way, the history of documentary itself (e.g., see McLane [2005] 2012). A look at the "inseparable" paratexts of the nonfiction animations created before the 1980s discloses it.[2] Indeed, commencing from the 1940s, many have been the audiovisual works referred to in reviews and newspaper adverts precisely with the expression "animated documentary," or its once more popular synonyms "cartoon documentary" and "documentary cartoon." For instance, in 1944 on the *Detroit Free Press*, Walt Disney Studios' partly animated feature film *Victory through Air Power* (1943, dir. Henry C. Potter, Clyde Geronimi, Jack Kinney, and James Algar)—based on the namesake best-selling book by Major Alexander P. de Seversky, explaining the importance of air control in modern warfare—was advertised as a "documentary cartoon."[3] In 1945, another Walt Disney Studios production was, instead, referred to as a "cartoon documentary" in a review of *The Film Daily*. The animated film in question is *Something You Didn't Eat* (1945a, dir. James Algar), a short sponsored by the US Department of Agriculture that instructs American housewives on how to use the seven primary food groups essential to proper nutrition ("Something You Didn't Eat" 1945b, 11). The same label was also employed in an article that appeared on May 12, 1948, in *Variety* with regard to UPA's *Brotherhood of Man*, a short on tolerance sponsored by the United Automobile Workers, wherein the message that no significant biological dissimilarities exist between men of different races is conveyed through having a voice-of-God narrator prove this to an animated actor impersonating the average white man ("Pictures" 1948, 17).

In the June 14, 1952, issue of *The New York Age*, columnist Edward Murrain (1952, 21) described *More Than Meets the Eye* (1952, dir. Bill Hurtz)—a short aimed at "selling" the relevance of radio advertising in a period wherein television is establishing itself as the leading broadcast medium (Abraham 2012, 99)—as "a remarkable *animated documentary* film, produced for CBS Radio by United Productions of America." Similarly, on March 19, 1953, *The Daily Courier* defined *Man Alive!*—another sponsored UPA production that is, in essence, a public service film ("Junior Aides" 1953, 4)—as "a documentary cartoon on cancer." In the early 1950s, critic Bernard Orna (1954, 29) presents to the readers of *Films and Filming* Halas & Batchelor Cartoon Films studio's *Power to Fly* (1954, dir. Bob Privett) as "one of a series of documentary cartoons" sponsored by the Anglo-Iranian Oil Company. Analogously, when in September 1956 Walt Disney Studios' animated dramatization of the history of the domestic cat, *The Great Cat Family*, was first televised, basically every US newspaper described it in words such as "an all-animated cartoon documentary tracing the ancient origins of the common cat 4,000 years ago and the cat's importance in the world of literature" (e.g., "Great Cat Family" 1956, 5; Jenkins 1956, 15). In 1958, on the *Independent Press-Telegram* the label "cartoon documentary" was employed in conjunction with *The Story of Oil* (1955, dir. Les Clark), an animated short produced by the Walt Disney Studios for the Richfield Oil Corporation that at the time used to be screened as part of *The World Beneath Us*, a free attraction that for some years was offered in the Tomorrowland section of Disneyland. *The Story of Oil* was described as "a Walt Disney animated *cartoon-documentary* film in Technicolor" (Karns 1958, A.14) with a subtle advertising agenda that exploits in full the fabled animation. Indeed, not only, by exploiting the narrative device of condensation, *The Story of Oil* synthesizes in five minutes the three-billion-year geological history of Earth but also, as highlighted on the pages of *Business Screen Magazine*, it does so "[i]n humorous but believable fantasy" ("Story of Oil" 1955, 6A). In fact, for instance, we see its protagonist, the animated character Prof. Rich Field, crop "up as a stone age man, riding a bright red horse or perched on the forehead of a robin's-egg-blue mastodon" ("Story of Oil" 1955, 6A).

A year later, in 1959, *The Daily Republican* used the expression "cartoon documentary" with regard to yet another Walt Disney Studios work: *Man in Flight* (1957, dir. Hamilton Luske), which, recycling some of *Victory through Air Power*'s animated sequences, traces the development of aviation from Wright Brothers' first experimental airplanes to the contemporary jet ("Walt Disney Free" 1959, 6).

On April 5, 1960, *The San Francisco Examiner* employed the label "animated documentary" to describe *Rhapsody of Steel* (1959, dir. Carl Urbano), a short produced by John Sutherland for US Steel that narrates the history of metal from prehistoric times to the present days with the intent of promoting steel ("Clay Ready" 1960, 4). Likewise, in March 1964, in announcing the broadcast on Channel 12 of Frank Capra's *Hemo the Magnificent* (1957, dir. Frank Capra), wherein hosts Richard Carlson and Dr. Frank Baxter dialog with an animated personification of blood, *The News Journal*'s television listings presented it as "an animated documentary on blood circulation" ("Channel 12" 1964, 23). Equally, a month later, *St. Claude Daily Times* referred to Walt Disney Studios' short *Toot, Whistle, Plunk and Boom* (1953, dir. Ward Kimball and Charles August Nichols), whose leading character is an anthropomorphic talking howl, as "an animated documentary dealing with the evolution of music" (Gill 1964, 10).

Many more examples could be brought. Nevertheless, I believe that the ones provided here suffice to make apparent how at least among film critics the understanding of animated documentary as a class of audiovisual works started to make inroads in the 1940s. In a similar manner to what Rick Altman shows to be commonplace for nascent film genres (see Altman 1999, 30–48), the two terms indicating the main "characteristics" blended to generate this form (i.e., "documentary" and "cartoon"/"animation") could alternatively act as the noun serving as host or the hosted adjective. Yet, the resulting labels were used to identify the same typology of reality-related animations. More precisely, these expressions were employed to single out mostly films traversed by an educational, instructional, or promotional agenda that, in order to enlighten viewers on an issue regarding their daily life, merge the fabled animation with an informational voice-of-God commentary.

Moreover, the investigation of nonfiction animations' paratextual materials shows that the recognition of the animated documentary as a proper filmic category became always more eradicated with the passing of decades. If in the 1940s the employment of the wording "cartoon documentary" (and of its variants) was still sporadic, by the 1950s, it had entered current usage between critics and journalists, and by the early 1960s, the animated documentary was widely recognized as a typology of film to all intents and purposes. Unwittingly, columnist Henry McLemore further proves it in a review of the 36th Academy Awards ceremony. Indeed, on April 21, 1964, in underlining the predictability of Oscar recipients' speeches, he expresses the following wish: "Some day an Oscar winner is going to say something like this: 'Thank you, but I must admit that my winning the Oscar for the best black-and-white, *animated documentary* comes as no surprise to me. I would have won it last year if my assistants hadn't been so terrible. See you next year, same place, same time'" (McLemore 1964a, 7).[4] By mentioning precisely an animated documentary as the film for which such amusing acceptance speech should be proffered, McLemore thus unknowingly provides us with the indication of it being by then already commonly understood as an out-and-out filmic form, albeit a minor one.

The Animated Documentary according to Its Producers

The usage of the term "cartoon documentary" and its synonyms on the press is not the sole element that allows stating with certainty that the animated documentary existed as a form already before the 1980s. Indeed, while, as we have already seen, scholarly, animated documentaries started receiving proper attention only in the late 1990s, the first considerations in written form on this typology of audiovisual works came much earlier. Only, they were not authored by academics, but by two leading producers of animation whose studios have employed this medium extensively also to address reality-related topics, namely Walt Disney and John Halas.

The former, during the years of the Second World War, had his studio set aside its fiction animation production and devote, instead, its efforts mainly to creating instructional and public service animated films for various governmental bodies (see Chapter 6). Since he started to do so, he not only never stopped producing fact-centered animations but has even authored a few articles on this subject matter. In particular, among these writings, there is a 1955 piece published in the *Health Education Journal* wherein the creator of Mickey Mouse discusses precisely what he terms the "documentary film cartoon" (Disney 1955, 70). With this expression, Disney identifies all those nonfiction animations "simple as ABC," conceived as "primary lessons for handicapped adults in matters most closely affecting their daily lives and fortunes" (74), that commenced to be steadily produced from the 1940s onward in order to familiarize citizens with set issues regarding their everyday in a "nonpainful" way.

More specifically, in the article, Disney brings particular educational and public service shorts produced by his studio during the Second World War in partnership with the Coordinator of Inter-American Affairs as examples of animated documentaries. Among them are *The Winged Scourge*, *The Grain That Built a Hemisphere* (1943, dir. Bill Roberts), *Water, Friend or Enemy* (1943, dir. Norm Wright), and *Defense against Invasion*.[5] These films, which deal respectively with the role of mosquitos in the spread of malaria, the history of corn, the perils of the contamination of domestic water supplies, and the importance of vaccination, are driven by a didactic impulse and, as Bill Nichols (see 1991, 34–8) would say, are "expository." That is, an argumentative logic characterizes them, and they take shape around an authoritative and seemingly objective voice-of-God commentary that addresses the viewer directly. Furthermore, while the spoken word takes up the task of moving forward the narrative, the images have mainly the function of illustrating or, more rarely, of counterpointing what is being said.

Nevertheless, such animated films are not merely informational. As Disney himself explains in the article, they have been created to inform and entertain the audience at the same time. Therefore, while the voice-of-God narration carries out the task of inducing viewers to read what they are offered to watch as referring to the social world, at the level of visuals, not only animated actors are used to dramatize what the voiceover depicts but also animation's most magical narrative devices (e.g., metamorphosis, anthropomorphism, symbolism, synecdoche, the visual metaphor, and so on) are employed. For example, *The Grain that Built a Hemisphere* visually conveys in-breeding by having two plants with human-like behavior join in marriage at the tune of Wagner's *Bridal Chorus*. Similarly, in *Water, Friend or Enemy* the idea that the water a housewife serves is contaminated is expressed graphically through having a skull materialize in a previously empty glass when the woman pours the liquid into it.

Furthermore, although in different ways, from time to time in all these shorts the voice-of-God commentary is made eccentric. For instance, in *The Grain that Built a Hemisphere*, when a gigantic plant originated from the in-breeding of two small shrubs appears on the screen, the voice-of-God all of a sudden loses its aplomb and states: "My, my, what a child!" Analogously, from the very beginning of *Water, Friend or Enemy*, it is suggested that the voiceover narrator is water itself—thus also somehow anthropomorphizing this vital liquid. In *The Winged Scourge*, instead, the animated protagonists react to the voice-of-God as if they could hear the commentary. Indeed, approximately midway through the film, the voiceover narrator tells Dopey to give the oil treatment to some mosquito larva, and the dwarf obeys.

In brief, as the films that he brings as examples of animated documentaries make clear, Disney accounted the adoption of the fabled animation to illustrate reality as one of the defining traits of this form. This is made explicit when, in the course of the article, the father of Mickey Mouse recognizes as the reference model for the creation of animated documentaries precisely *The Winged Scourge*, whose protagonists are those same imaginary characters that, in 1937, had starred in *Snow White and the Seven Dwarfs*, and, referring to this short, he writes: "It taught us a valuable lesson . . . in formulating our documentary techniques for subsequent projects. It was this: Let the informative material ride along on entertainment as much as possible; use comic anecdote and character antic freely" (Disney 1955, 74).

Disney, however, also admonishes: "But fun must never imply that the documentary cartoon is insincere" (75). In effect, he points out how in making this typology of animated works, while, on the one hand, his studio fully exploited fiction animation's graphic vocabulary and narrative devices, on the other hand, "the watchword was constant counsel and supervision by the best available authorities on any subject" (72), so as to produce films that, content-wise, were accurate accounts of the topics tackled. He states: "More than in any other field of visual communication, the documentary animator must have the required information for any subject literally at his fingertips. He conveys ideas, teaches, with his drawing pencil" (Disney 1955, 72).

Therefore, in short, what emerges from this article is, first, that for Disney animated documentary was synonym of instruction and visual education, a fact that is spelled out in the closing remarks when he describes this kind of nonfiction animations as "an invaluable supplement to textbook, lecture, and laboratory in the whole expanding sphere of education" (76). Second, it surfaces that he accounted the employment of animation's fictional mode of representation and graphic language to convey truthful and well-researched real-life facts as a typical feature of animated documentaries. Finally, he identifies works that are first and foremost public service films as animated documentaries.

On the other side of the Atlantic Ocean, in Great Britain, starting from 1940 John Halas and his wife Joy Batchelor also have produced a vast number of reality-related animations through their studio Halas & Batchelor Cartoon Films to the point that Paul Wells (2006, 159) has defined them "the foremost proponents of non-fiction animation." What is more, in order to stimulate the employment of animation at a factual end, Halas, like Disney, has authored articles on this topic. In addition, he also made use of the expression "animated documentary" way before the 1990s. In particular, in his writings, Halas uses this expression in relation to the numerous films produced by his studio "for BP, Shell, Esso, Philips, WHO, COI and many other organizations which had problems to communicate on an imaginative level" (Halas in Manvell 1980).

Among the titles he refers to with these words are, for example, the shorts from the Charley series. Each of these films sponsored by COI is expository and, combining a voice-of-God commentary with imaginative visuals, instructs the viewer on one of the social reforms that the British government introduced in the post–Second World War years. Precisely, an authoritative voiceover, which is made from time to time eccentric by having Charley dialog with it, explains how such reforms are to improve the life of the average British citizen. Meanwhile, visually, these changes are enacted and dramatized by employing in full the fabled animation. As a matter of example, in *Charley in New Town*, we can find a sequence wherein this everyman literally flies out of his office. Similarly, in *Your Very Good Health* (1947, dir. John Halas and Joy Batchelor), in order to elucidate how different an ordinary man's life can be thanks to the new personal health services introduced in Great Britain with the 1946 NHS Act, the narrative device of doubling characters is heavily used. In other words, alter egos of Charley and his family members are employed to enact what would happen if they had an accident or fell sick, marking the hypothetical nature of these doubles through color by painting their bodies in an unrealistic palette of blues.

Other examples of films that Halas regarded as animated documentaries are those that his studio has produced in the 1950s on commission of BP, among which we can recall *As Old as the Hills* (1950, dir. John Halas and Alan Crick), *The Moving Spirit* (1953, dir. Bob Privett), *Power to Fly*, and *Speed the Plough* (1956, dir. Bob Privett). These shorts, which explain respectively the origins of oil, the history of the motorcar, the developments of aviation, and the modern advancements in agriculture, are described in their advertisements as movies "made to entertain as well as to instruct."[6] In line with this claim, they are expository films that elucidate their subject matter through the fabled animation. In each of them, the factual occurrences that an authoritative, but at times eccentric, voice-of-God commentary describes are enacted and dramatized, without refraining from employing gags or animation's most magical narrative devices. For example, in *The Moving Spirit*, when an early steam locomotive nears a hill, all of a sudden, the entrance of a tunnel appears on this knoll. Analogously, the developments that have led from the converted bomber to the modern airliner are accounted for in *Power to Fly* by having the same airplane rapidly morph to acquire the shapes of the various aircraft created in-between.

In sum, like Disney, Halas also understood public service or educational-promotional films that are at the same time accurate lessons of aspects of our world and entertaining, artistic creations as animated documentaries. Not casually, on the one hand, he has written that the "value of animated documentaries lies in the fact that one could establish a close contact with the audience without boring them with dry facts" (Halas in Manvell 1980). On the other hand, he has also stated the importance of making the "research into the subject" of the film "as extensive as possible on the theory that if a hillside is exposed to enough rain there is a good chance of discovering spring" (Halas 1957, 15).[7] Therefore, not only two figures that have had a crucial role in showing how animation could (and should) have been put to use even at a nonfictional end had a shared understanding of the animated documentary but they also identified as such the same typology of works that, at the time, were referred to with this label (or its variants) in the press.

Beyond Walt Disney and John Halas

Disney and Halas were not the sole producers to recognize this same kind of films as animated documentaries, as it emerges if we look at the titles sent for consideration for the Academy Award for Best Documentary Short Subject.[8] Since 1942, when this prize was introduced, numerous animated films have been submitted for consideration in this category. Undeniably, it was Disney who opened the way once again. Indeed, on the occasion of the 15th Academy Awards ceremony—the first during which the Best Documentary Short Subject prize was given out—two of the over twenty-five titles aspiring at this recognition were in animation, *The Grain that Built a Hemisphere* and *The New Spirit* (1942, dir. Wilfred Jackson and Ben Sharpsteen), and both of them were produced by the Walt Disney Studios for a governmental body (see "All Set for the Academy's Winnahs" 1943, 2, 32). However, in the following years other producers submitted animated films that used the fabled animation to address an aspect of the real for consideration for the Best Documentary Short Subject award. In the timespan up to 1960 (i.e., the 33rd Academy Awards) we can only count thirty-one titles definable as animated documentaries and just four of them are Walt Disney Studios' productions.[9] Aside from *The Grain that Built a Hemisphere* and *The New Spirit*, the father of Mickey Mouse submitted only other two animated films in this category, namely *Man in Space* (1956, dir. Ward Kimball)[10] and *Donald in Mathmagic Land* (1959, dir. Hamilton Luske). The former, which illustrates facts, legends, and foibles regarding mankind and the conquest of outer space and has been called by reviewers a "science-factual featurette" (e.g., "Davy Takes" 1956, 26; "Ohio Outlaws" 1956, 7), was sent for the 29th Academy Awards. The latter, wherein Donald Duck visits an imaginary land of numbers, competed instead in the 32nd ones.

The majority of the titles describable as animated documentaries sent for consideration for the Best Documentary Short Subject award were submitted instead by UPA, a studio particularly active in the creation of this typology of works. More precisely, the studio submitted nine animated works in this category between 1946 and 1961: *Brotherhood of Man*, *Flat Hatting* (1946, dir. John Hubley), *Man on the Land* (1951, dir. Bill Hurtz), *Man Alive!*, *Look Who's Driving* (1954, dir. Bill Hurtz), *The Invisible Moustache of Raoul Dufy*, *Pump Trouble* (1954, dir. Gene Deitch),

Sappy Homiens (1956, dir. Leo Salkin), and *Inside Magoo* (1960, dir. Abe Levitow and John F. Becker). The first two were both sent on the occasion of the 19th Academy Awards.[11] The third one, which is an animated ballad produced for the American Petroleum Institute to illustrate the positive impact that petroleum would have had on the development of agriculture, was the title in which UPA placed its hope to gain this Oscar at the 24th Academy Awards. *Man Alive!*, *Look Who's Driving*, *Pump Trouble*, and *The Invisible Moustache of Raoul Dufy* were instead submitted respectively for the 25th, 26th, 27th, and 28th Academy Awards. Finally, *Sappy Homiens* and *Inside Magoo*, both of which are public service films made for the American Cancer Society and aimed at familiarizing the average American man with the seven dangers of cancer, were sent for consideration respectively for the 29th and the 33rd Academy Awards.

Overall, the films submitted for consideration by UPA are animated works sponsored either by a private body or, more rarely, by a public one, as in the case of the training film *Flat Hatting*, which was made for the US Navy as part of a "Flight Safety" series. Also, they tend to instruct viewers on aspects of their everyday by telling the made-up, exemplary story of an everyman. For example, to discourage pilots from flat hatting, *Flat Hatting* narrates the vicissitudes of Murphy, an imaginary aviator accustomed to engaging in this dangerous practice when alone, who ends up losing his job for this. Similarly, to prevent viewers from acting childishly behind the wheel, *Look Who's Driving*, which was created for the Ætna Casualty and Surety Company, narrates the made-up vicissitudes of everyman Charlie Younghead, an average family guy who has a car accident because he loses his temper. Likewise, *Pump Trouble*, a public service film made for the American Heart Association, illustrates facts on heart disease and encourages viewers to not diagnose themselves by recounting of another everyman, Mr. Pump, who goes to see a doctor thinking he is about to die of a heart attack but, after some checkups, discovers he has just a slight elevation of blood pressure. As in these titles, the everyman around which the story pivots tends to be a character expressly created for the film. However, in *Inside Magoo*, this role is even played by one of the studio's animated stars, the famed Mr. Magoo.

After UPA, it is John Sutherland Productions, with five titles, that sent the highest number of animated documentaries for consideration for the Oscar in the Best Documentary Short Subject category between 1942 and 1961. The titles in question, which are either public service or educational-promotional films, are *Fresh Laid Plans* (1951, dir. George Gordon), *A Is for Atom* (1953, dir. Carl Urbano), *Horizons of Hope* (1954), *The Living Circle* (1956), and *Rhapsody of Steel*, and they have been submitted respectively for the 24th, 26th, 27th, 29th, and 32nd Academy Awards. Therefore, once again, a US studio has placed its hope of winning this statuette in sponsored, entirely or partly animated audiovisual works employing in full the fabled animation to illustrate an aspect of the social world. Indeed, for instance, the largely animated *Horizons of Hope*, which deals with the progress in cancer cure and was made on commission of the Alfred P. Sloan Foundation, uses two anthropomorphic cells, a normal and a cancerous one, to dramatize the techniques for controlling cancer. Even further imbued with fictionality is the controversial *Fresh Laid Plans*, which was interpreted by many as an attack of the Brannan Farm Aid Plan (see Jack 2015, 513).[12] This short is fifth in a series of films created for the Alfred P. Sloan Foundation, but via the Harding College, to provide viewers with an economic education; it stars a talking owl, Dr. Owsley Hoot, that illustrates how wage and prices control work to the inhabitants of Eggville, an imaginary village populated by roosters and hens.

To compete for an Oscar in the Documentary Short Subject category have been also John and Faith Hubley with their *Harlem Wednesday* (1958) and *Children of the Sun* (respectively submitted for the 30th and 33rd Academy Awards). Likewise, the Warner Brothers animation department has sent for consideration in this category two works directed by Chuck Jones: *So Much for So Little* (1949) on the importance of healthcare for the 22nd Academy Awards and, for the 29th ones, *90 Day Wondering?* (1956), wherein the advantages of re-enlisting are imaginatively dramatized.

Moreover, next to leading US animation studios, smaller ones have sent their animated documentaries for consideration in this category as well. For instance, one of the titles submitted for the 25th Academy Awards is the highly imaginative and allegorical *Good Wrinkles. The Story of a Remarkable Fruit* (1952), a short produced by All-Scope Pictures for Sunsweet Growers Inc. to encourage the consumption of the Californian Sunsweet prunes. This animation stars an anthropomorphic plum named Sunny Sweet that works in Hollywood as an actor, through which is retraced the life and processing of a tenderized Sunsweet prune. Likewise, among the titles sent for the 30th Academy Awards we can find *The Hope That Jack Built* (1957, dir. Gene Deitch), a public service animation made by the Garantray-Lawrence Animation studio for the National Association of Investment Companies that explains how savings can be increased through correct investments by narrating the story of Jack and Penny Saver, an exemplary, imaginary couple who, having some extra money, seeks a way to make it grow enough for affording their dreamboat. On the occasion of the 33rd Academy Awards, within the works aspiring for the Oscar for Best Documentary Short Subject, we can instead find both *All About Polymorphics* (1959, dir. Bill Orr), a stop-motion animation on new ideas in mainstream computing produced within Thompson Ramo Wooldridge Inc., and *George Grosz' Interregnum* (1960, dir. Altina and Charles Carey), a film made by Educational Communications Corp. that uses drawings by artist George Grosz to portray Nazi brutality.

Lastly, a few non-US studios also have sent for consideration in this category works definable animated documentaries. More precisely, the British unit Larkins Studio has sent for consideration for the 23rd Academy Awards *Local Government. A History in Pictures* (1949, dir. Peter Sachs and Phil Windebank), a black-and-white short made on commission of the COI that retraces the evolution of local governance. Another British studio, Signal Films, has submitted for the 24th Academy Awards *The Story of Time* (1951, dir. Michael Stainer-Hutchins), a film sponsored by Rolex wherein stop-motion animation is used to illustrate the numerous ways in which man has measured the passage of time throughout the decades. On the occasion of the 28th and 30th Academy Awards, Joop Geesink's Dollywood has sent for consideration respectively *The Story of Light* and the coproduction with Transfilm *The Earth Is Born* (1957, dir. Zachary Schwartz), a thirty-minute partly animated film commissioned by *Life Magazine* that depicts the origins of our planet.[13] Norman McLaren's anti-war film, *Neighbours* (1952), and Roman Kroitor and Colin Low's *Universe* (1960), which uses a realistic animation to recreate the universe as it would appear to a space voyager, are instead the titles submitted by the National Film Board of Canada respectively for the 25th and 33rd Academy Awards. Finally, the Halas & Batchelor Cartoon Films studio has sent, on the occasion of the 29th Academy Awards ceremony, *To Your Health* (1956, dir. Philip Stapp), a public service film made for WHO wherein, as Malvin Wald has written on *Film in Review*, animation is employed "imaginatively to point out the boundaries of social drinking, across which drinking becomes harmful to society and the individual" (Wald 1957, 169).

It thus emerges how Disney and Halas were far from being the only animation producers to envision as animated documentaries the educational, instructional, and promotional films, abundantly produced starting from 1940, that in tackling an aspect of the real employed the fabled animation. They have simply been the ones who have put into written form what was a transnational common understanding of a typology of works which already back then was fully recognized within the film industry.

And the Oscar for Best Documentary Short Goes To . . .

In November 2015 on the pages of *The Hollywood Reporter*, Scott Feinberg has blamed the Academy of Motion Pictures Arts and Sciences for having long been following an unwritten rule that foresees not truly considering for the Oscar in the documentary feature category the nonfiction films heavily employing animation (see Feinberg 2015). In stating this, he has therefore implicitly suggested that the Academy has been resisting the idea itself of animated documentary. Certainly, it is true that in the last decade, among the titles submitted for Best Documentary Feature there have been several animated documentaries, such as *Approved for Adoption* (*Couleur de peau: Miel*, 2012, dir. Laurent Boileau and Jung Henin), *Is the Man Who Is Tall*

Happy? An Animated Conversation with Noam Chomsky (2013, dir. Michel Gondry), *Last Hijack* (2014, dir. Femke Wolting and Tommy Pallotta), and *Tower*, and none of them has even received a nomination. Nevertheless, Feinberg's implicit claim that the Academy would have been against the idea itself of animated documentary is unfair. Indeed, if, as we have seen, only in the first eighteen years of life of the prize for Best Documentary Short Subject a critical mass of animated films was submitted for consideration for this award, it has not been just because the producers envisioned these works as animated documentaries but also because the Academy received them as such, as is made evident for instance by the category change requested for the NFB-produced *Comet* (1985, dir. Sydney Goldsmith). Indeed, in 1985, this animated documentary, which illustrates the general phenomena of comets and the transformations they undergo as they approach the sun, was submitted for consideration in the Best Animated Short Subject category. After viewing the film, the members of the awards committee, however, established that the most appropriate category for it to run in was that of Best Documentary Short Subject. And they were so convinced about it that, since for that year *Comet* could not be transferred to the latter category, because the documentary screenings for the Academy members had already taken place, Goldsmith and the NFB were given the exceptional opportunity of resubmitting the film the subsequent year.[14] It is thus apparent that within the Academy also there has long been recognition and acceptance of the animated documentary as a possible approach for cinematically illustrating the real.

In fact, contrary to what Feinberg has stated, I believe we could venture into asserting that the Academy has played a role in the emergence of the animated documentary as a full-blown form. Only, it has done so mostly through its submission guidelines and its award for Best Documentary Short Subject, rather than through the one for Best Documentary Feature. Indeed, first of all, in the voting rules pamphlets that were prepared each year to provide the submission guidelines for the various statuettes awarded, sentences that show a recognition on the Academy's part of animation as a medium apt also at tackling the real have long been present. More precisely, as far back as 1942, when the Academy still considered the prizes for documentary films as "special awards" whose guidelines and procedures were to be "established by a special committee appointed for this purpose,"[15] the document providing the rules for nominations in these two categories, among others, read: "Documentary shorts are defined as those outside the general entertainment Short Subjects Award Classifications, and specifically including but not limited to shorts and *cartoons* produced by or for a Government."[16]

This sentence was retained in the Academy Awards' voting rules pamphlets also when the two statuettes destined to documentaries went from being special prizes to becoming ordinary ones. It was taken out only when, on the occasion of the 40th Academy Awards, the contents of the voting rules booklet underwent some significant revisions. Though, at this time something even more interesting occurred: the mention of animation was integrated into the general indication of what the Academy considered to be a documentary. Indeed, from 1967 to 1992 we could read the following in the paragraph devoted to documentary of the voting rules pamphlets: "Documentary films are defined as those dealing with cultural, artistic, historical, social, scientific, economic or other significant subjects, photographed in actual occurrence, re-enacted or *produced in animation, stop-motion or any other technique* and where the emphasis is on factual content. The purely technical instructional film will not be considered."[17]

Moreover, several animated films have been nominated for or even won an Oscar in the Best Documentary Short Subject category. Undeniably, if we skim through the titles nominated for this statuette in the last twenty-five years or so, we can notice the presence also of films in animation. For instance, at the 88th Academy Awards, one of the runner-ups for this Oscar was *Last Day of Freedom* (2015, dir. Nomi Talisman and Dee Hibbert-Jones), an entirely animated film wherein, using 30,000 drawings, the aural testimony of African American Bill Babbitt regarding the death sentence of his younger brother, Manny, is visualized and dramatized. Similarly, both among this category's 1998 and 1992 nominees, we can find a short that has been created integrating archival materials, still photographs, and animation: respectively Shui-Bo Wang's autobiographical account of his life in China from 1960 to 1989, *Sunrise over Tiananmen Square* (1998), and Joyce Borenstein's *The Colours of My Father: A Portrait of Sam Borenstein* (1992), which retraces the life and career of this famous painter through the testimonies of friends and family.

Most importantly, even more significant has been the number of shorts entirely or partially in animation that have received a nomination in the documentary category between 1942 and 1968. Indeed, at the 15th Academy Awards, among the shorts running "for the best achievement in Documentary Film production,"[18] there were *The Grain that Built a Hemisphere* and *The New Spirit*. The 22nd Academy Awards, instead, saw *So Much for So Little* as one of the nominees for the Best Documentary Short Subject statuette. Both *Man Alive!* and *Neighbours* were up for this Oscar four years later. Walt Disney Studios' *Man in Space* and *Donald in Mathmagic Land* were nominated for this award respectively in 1956 and 1959. At the 33rd Academy Awards, one of the candidates for such Oscar was National Film Board of Canada's *Universe*, while at the 41st Academy Awards, one of the contenders for this prize was Saul Bass' short on the nature of creativity, *Why Man Creates* (1968, dir. Saul Bass). In sum, in the twenty-seven years in question, nine have been the animated films to receive a nomination for the Best Documentary Short Subject Academy Award, and three of them—namely *So Much for So Little*, *Neighbours*, and *Why Man Creates*—have even gone on to win this Oscar.

Through the indications offered in its submission guidelines as well as by nominating for, and in some cases also awarding with, the statuette for Best

Documentary Short Subject set nonfiction cartoons, the Academy has thus, first, shown to have long recognized and accepted the existence of animated documentaries, initially identifying too as such educational, scientific, and public service films that illustrate an aspect of the real by pairing fabled animation with an informational voice-of-God commentary. Second, through the aforesaid wording used in its voting rules as well as through the nominations and awards mentioned earlier, it has inevitably contributed to boosting and "standardizing" the production of this typology of audiovisual works. In other words, in so doing, whether more or less consciously, the Academy has both encouraged the making of these animations and appointed models to look up to in creating them, therefore contributing to determining this form's characteristics.

One could argue that the fact that these films received a nomination or an Oscar for Best Documentary Short Subject beating other live-action works that are out-and-out documentaries disproves the idea of animated documentaries being animation's docudramas, consubstantiating instead the diffuse conception of them being equitable in full to live-action documentaries. However, we must not forget that the Academy has never had a docufiction category and that among the films submitted and even prized with a Best Documentary statuette, we can find even live-action works that would best be described as docufictions rather than documentaries. A case in point is Peter Watkins' sci-fi mockumentary *The War Game* (1965), which, despite attesting a never occurred nuclear attack, was prized at the 39th Academy Awards ceremony with the Oscar for Best Documentary Feature. Therefore, the presence of animated documentaries among the nominees and awardees for Best Documentary Short Subject does not necessarily disprove the idea of this form being animation's counterpart to the live-action docudrama. What it certainly further proves is instead that it was starting from the early 1940s, and not the late 1980s, that film and media professionals commenced conceiving a precise typology of audiovisual works as animated documentaries.

The Three Eras of the Animated Documentary

Based on all the above-illustrated data, if adopting Honess Roe's same criteria, we can conclude that advertisement, scientific, educational, and public service animations can be animated documentaries.[19] This is, however, not to say that a reality-related film in animation falling within one of these categories is inevitably an animated documentary. If it employs exclusively or predominantly the sober animation, as can be the case especially for scientific and educational titles, it is not an animated documentary. However, even when it is created using solely or largely animation's fictional mode of representation, it may not necessarily be an animated documentary. Indeed, if in it the reference to the real at the content level is minimal and the advertising, instructional, or propagandistic agenda is not combined to the illustration of or reflection on an aspect of our world, it cannot be ascribed to this class of films. To better understand this second case, let us compare *The New Spirit* and *Leon Schlesinger Presents "Bugs Bunny"* (1942, dir. Robert Clampett), better known as *Any Bonds Today?*. Completed a week apart, these two films are both government-commissioned and aim at leading the viewing public to adopt a behavior that would help the United States in the war effort: respectively paying income taxes and buying war bonds. Moreover, both have an animated star as their protagonist. In *The New Spirit*, it is Donald Duck, while in *Leon Schlesinger Presents "Bugs Bunny,"* it is the famous gray-and-white rabbit with a brash personality mentioned in the title (supported by Porky Pig and Elmer Fudd, who make a cameo appearance as backup singers). Despite these similarities, however, only *The New Spirit* can be considered an animated documentary. Indeed, in this title an anthropomorphic radio set that acts as the voice-of-authority, first, explains to Donald, who plays the role of "Mr. Average Taxpayer" (McGowan 2019, 96), how to fill in the tax forms and, subsequently, illustrates toward what the money of US taxpayers will be used. While having a strong propagandistic message, this film thus clearly uses imaginary figures and a fictional mode of representation to address the social world, enriching viewers' knowledge on set aspects of reality.

Leon Schlesinger Presents "Bugs Bunny," instead, amounts just to a musical number wherein the rabbit, first alone and then aided by Porky Pig and Elmer Fudd, sings a tune that encourages citizens to buy US savings bonds and stamps from the "tall man with the high hat and a whiskeys on his chin" that will soon be knocking at their door. No information on how bonds work or in what sense who invests in them acquires "a share of freedom," as the lyrics of the song say, is provided. This film is thus a blunt patriotic plea, a mere advertisement for war bonds that does not provide the viewer with any information about the social world. Therefore, it cannot be considered an animated documentary, even if it employs animation's fictional mode of representation to a promotional and propagandistic end as many other coeval animated documentaries.

Most importantly, always according to Honess Roe's criteria, we can also conclude that the animated documentary existed as a full-fledged form way before the mid-1980s. Certainly, one could contend that it is anyhow correct to consider it a strictly contemporary form, because, as Andy Glynne (2013, 73) suggests, the kind of audiovisual works that nowadays we refer to as animated documentaries "feel a little bit more 'documentary' in their consistency" than the films that were labeled as such in the past, since contemporary ones "deal with real people, real testimony and first-person thoughts and feelings." Such an argument is, however, controverted, first and foremost, by the history itself of the live-action documentary. In his

Introduction to Documentary, Nichols ([2001] 2017, 22) underlines that still today the vast majority of people associate the "expository mode ... with documentary in general." If this is the case, it is because such mode, which relies "heavily on an informing logic carried by the spoken word," has long been dominant (Nichols [2001] 2017, 122). Indeed, the "shift away from information and advocacy for a specific position on an issue to the subjective and experiential" that has brought first-person testimonies to be perceived as veridictive marks has occurred only in more recent times (Nichols 2016, xvi). As Alisa Lebow (2012, 5) has illustrated, up to the 1980s, "the emergence of the subjective voice in documentary" was "hampered by the burden of disinterested objectivity." To put it another way, in the same years in which animated documentaries like *The Winged Scourge* or *Man Alive!* were produced, live-action documentaries also tended to be predominantly expository, didactic, and propagandistic and to showcase an informational voice-of-God commentary. Thus, the elements that Glynne identifies as the hearer of a documentary consistency would not have been considered such at the time, while the presence of an authoritative voiceover narration and an expository mode of representation would have. Consequently, asserting that the many reality-related animated films produced from the 1940s onward by the Walt Disney Studios, UPA, or the Halas & Batchelor Cartoon Films studio could not be considered animated documentaries, because they do not showcase features that paradoxically at the time in which they were made would have been more easily associated with fiction than with nonfiction, would simply mean not taking into account that throughout the decades, the documentary itself has undergone an evolution and with it our very idea of what represents a veridictive mark.

That said, undeniably, as Rick Altman (1999) shows, producers, critics, and viewers are all essential players in the genrification process of films. Hence, the fact that starting from the 1940s the label "animated documentary" and its synonyms have been used by these categories of people to identify a precise typology of movies is undoubtedly an indicator that already back then it was a full-blown form. At the same time, however, Altman highlights that most of the titles which today we recognize as early masterpieces of a genre—as is *The Broadway Melody* (1929, dir. Harry Beaumont) for the musical or *The Great Train Robbery* (1903, dir. Edwin S. Porter) for the Western—were not conceived or received as part of that class of films at the time of their release because back then the genre of which they became an early flagship still did not exist as a recognized category. Therefore, these works came to be envisioned as part of a set genre only retroactively (see Altman 1999, 30–48). Consequently, why couldn't the same have been the case for the animated documentary as well?

This form did not suddenly appear out of nothing in 1940. On the contrary, starting from 1909, in the decades preceding its recognition as a class of films within the film industry, now and then, animations that already showcased the characteristics bound to become defining traits of this form were created. It is, for instance, the case of the previously mentioned *To Demonstrate How Spiders Fly* and *The Sinking of the Lusitania*. Back when they were made, these films were not referred to as animated documentaries by their makers. For example, at the time of its release the expression used to identify *The Sinking of the Lusitania* was "pen picture," a label McCay himself coined that paradoxically draws the attention more on the film's artificial genesis than on its factual content. Indeed, this expression highlights that a tool of re-creation—as the pen is—rather than of recording—as the camera is—was used to make the film. This, however, does not make such title any less an early masterpiece of the animated documentary. As a consequence, we can ascribe it—and the various titles similar to it—to this form retroactively, setting the origins of the animated documentary even further back in time than the 1940s.

More precisely, in light of all the aforesaid, I propose to reconceptualize the history of the animated documentary as formed by three macro eras:

1. a period of the origins (1909–39), characterized by the unsystematic creation of animated films which exhibited elements that have subsequently become the defining traits of this form, but that still did not display them in a shared way. Also, what distinguishes this period's films is that at the time of their creation, they were not referred to or conceived of expressly as animated documentaries;

2. a classical period (1940–85), marked by the systematic production of expository, animated lessons on aspects of the real tied to the everyday, which were not only recognized as animated documentaries but also displayed all of the form's defining traits following a unitary model;

3. a contemporary period (1986–current), during which the animated documentary has become mainly a synonym of works imbued with subjectivity that offer mostly (first-person) accounts of real-life experiences of specific, existing individuals. In particular, this period's production tends to revolve around personal traumas and states of mind. Indeed, the main characteristic of nowadays animated documentaries is that they linger more on the feelings and emotions experienced by one or more real-life people rather than on illustrating mere facts concerning them.

The entry of animated documentary in its classical period in the 1940s is unsurprising if looked at against what was occurring in the same years in the out-and-out documentary realm. Indeed, as Derek Paget has underlined, with the start of the Second World War an ample employment of the so-called judicious fiction (i.e., "sincere and justifiable reconstruction") was made within documentaries, creating in this way works that often ended up being "documentary-dramas" and setting the ground for the initiation, in the immediate postwar years, of what can be identified as the first phase of docudrama's history (Paget [1998] 2011, 174–80). Still, I believe that what has most determined animated documentary's entrance in its classical phase precisely in these years has been that planning for creating consistently such typology of animated works finally made inroads. Indeed, when the Second World War broke out, governmental bodies found themselves in need of conveying certain aspects of reality to the population in an engaging way, and, thus, they started commissioning the creation of nonfiction animated films capable to talk about topics felt as relevant in simple and entertaining terms. Consequently, animated documentaries started systematically being produced. Even if on a less regular basis, something similar had already occurred during the First World War. What changed this time around, however, was that some of the studios that were "drafted" by governmental bodies did not just think of their work on such films as an activity merely functional to help win the war that was to be dismissed as soon as peace was restored. On the contrary, they started planning to keep producing this typology of movies also once the conflict was over. A case in point is offered by the foreword of *Dispatch from Disney's*, a newsletter that the creator of Mickey Mouse wrote in 1943 to update his employees serving in military units around the world on the activities that the studio was undertaking while they were far away. Here, Disney wrote:

> Working, as we never worked before, on films for the Army and Navy, we are thinking of the time when you are coming back. Animation is proving that it can help with major problems. The lessons learned, you will apply constructively in solving the problems of peace. . . . Science, Economics, and Industry must be given a voice which all can understand. With these and a thousand other problems, the motion picture can be more helpful than any other force.
>
> That is the work to which you will return with the ending of the war. . . . Using the ways and means, which the art of animation is acquiring through films of war, you will make constructive educational films for peace. (Disney in Lesjak 2014, 19)

As these words make evident, Disney was thus already thinking of steadily carrying on making animated documentaries beyond the contingencies of the conflict. Precisely this look to the future of the form, I believe, has been crucial for the animated documentary to start being recognized within the industry as a class of films and consequently for the form to exit the "tentative" stage of its earlier days and enter its phase of maturity.

The contemporary evolution of the animated documentary in the mid-1980s was, instead, most likely influenced by the shift toward the subjective and the experiential that occurred in the documentary domain. Indeed, when it became clear that the "Direct Cinema austerities," which apparently represented the most neutral approach possible to the telling of the real, did not allow to "deliver indisputable 'objective' evidence on the screen," documentary filmmakers not only started blurring "the stark divide between documentary and fiction" (Winston 2013, 13) but also have increasingly put the subjective at the center of their films (see Nichols 2016, xvi). Since the animated documentary, as any docufiction form, tends to be affected by the changes that occur in the documentary realm itself, it has ended up mirroring this shift. In fact, documentary filmmaker Brett Morgen has declared: "Animation inherently calls into question the objective nature of documentaries. . . . It's one of the most honest approaches we can take" (Morgen in Miller 2018). Indeed, as Stuart Miller highlights, "animation changes how documentaries are perceived, undermining the conventional but misleading perspective that they are authoritative and objective. The artifice of animation keeps it real, reminding viewers that they are seeing a subjective narration" (Miller 2018). With documentary taking a subjective turn precisely because of an acquired awareness of the impossibility for a live-action camera to return the real objectively and animation proving the perfect means for honestly presenting the subjective, the animated documentary also was, thus, bound to veer toward subjectivity.

A part in the animated documentary's contemporary transformation may have, however, been played also by what has occurred in the nonfiction comics domain. If comics have influenced and nurtured animation since its early days (see Wells 1998, 17), the animated documentary also has long held with the nonfiction comic a longstanding, multifaceted relationship that has progressively strengthened over time. During this form's early age, their ties amounted mostly to some authors of animated documentaries having a background as newspaper cartoonists and perhaps at times creating works that bear close proximity to news illustrations, as is the case for McCay's *The Sinking of the Lusitania*. When the animated documentary entered its classical era, its relationship with nonfiction comics strengthened. On the one hand, at times this period's works exhibited aesthetics proper of comics. For instance, throughout the first part of *Look Who's Driving*, what everyman Charlie thinks is made visual through some borderless thought bubbles derived from comics' mode of representation (e.g., see Figure 3.1). Similarly, in *Man Alive!*, from time to time, the worries of the protagonist, Ed Parmelee, are visualized through the use of colorful thought bubbles (e.g., see Figure 3.2).

Also, like comic books ask their readers to do (Bongco [2000] 2013, 65), at times, classical animated documentaries required spectators to "fill in gaps in information" by offering some "inanimate" shots. In

FIGURE 3.1 *In* Look Who's Driving, *Charlie's thoughts are made visible using a comic book-like approach.*

FIGURE 3.2 *In* Man Alive!, *the worries of Ed Parmelee are visualized through thought bubbles.*

other words, mostly in order to reduce production's costs and time, these audiovisual works displayed here and there static images, thus leaving the viewer "to reconstitute the phenomenal continuity of movement and time" (Atkinson 2009, 266).[20] A case in point is *So Much for So Little*. In a sequence of the film aimed at explaining that, back then, many infants died due to infections transmitted to them by flies, when the voice-of-God narrator suggests ironically that to solve the problem either these insects could be trained to wash their feet or killed, visually the spectator is offered two motionless shots: first, one portraying a fly in the act of washing its legs and, subsequently, one of a man about to hunt a fly. Thus, as is the case for comics, also here the task of conferring movement is left to the spectator.

On the other hand, in this period, the practice of adapting animated documentaries into nonfiction comics set off. *Henry's Backyard: The Races of Mankind* and *The Moving Spirit: How the Motor Car Grew Up* are two early precursors of this custom. Indeed, each of them is a picture-book version of an animated documentary short, and more precisely respectively of *Brotherhood of Man* and *The Moving Spirit*. However, in the 1950s full-fledged comic book versions of animated documentaries have also appeared, as is the case of those published by Dell Comics for Walt Disney Studios works such as *The Great Cat Family*, *Man in Man in Flight*, and *Donald in Mathmagic Land*. These adaptations, which have been made by a publisher with whom the Walt Disney Studios habitually collaborated (see Becattini 2016, 45–7), share with their filmic counterparts the same expository and didactic character. The visuals reenact and dramatize what is illustrated in the captions, which, being the comic book equivalent of the voice-of-God narration, are extensively employed. Speech balloons instead tend to be reduced to a minimum. In the 1950s, UPA's *Look Who's Driving* also was adapted into a comic strip series. Indeed, perhaps prompted precisely by the fact that this animated documentary taps into the comic book aesthetics, not too long after its release, its frames have been used to create a namesake comic strip series, which has been published starting from October 14, 1954, by the newspaper *The San Saba News and Star* in cooperation with the Ætna Casualty and Surety Company (see "Traffic Safety Comic Strip Series Starts in This Issue" 1954, 8) (e.g., see Figure 3.3).[21]

In the late 1980s, what scholar Jeff Adams (2008) refers to as the "documentary graphic novel" has reached a wide diffusion. These nonfiction comics "deal textually and visually with disruptive social or political events, and their various critical devices may be said to reveal something of the underlying social configuration" (Adams 2008, 9). Examples of these texts are Joe Sacco's *Palestine*, Marjane Satrapi's

FIGURE 3.3 *One of the strips created using frames from UPA's* Look Who's Driving *and published in the newspaper* The San Saba News and Star.

Persepolis, and Art Spiegelman's *Maus*. These nonfiction comics share with contemporary animated documentaries a number of traits, among which are the subjects chosen, an autobiographical or semi-autobiographical character, the employment of a graphic language imbued with fictionality, and, from time to time, the aesthetics.[22] Indeed, not only some contemporary animated documentaries are adaptations of documentary graphic novels and vice versa[23] but also even animated documentaries that are not the transposition of a nonfiction comic may draw their aesthetics from those proper of graphic novels, as is the case for instance of the features *The Green Wave* or *25 April* (2015, dir. Leanne Pooley). Considering the ties that nonfiction comics and the animated documentary have had in the past, the close proximity that the contemporary specimens of this audiovisual form bears with the documentary graphic novel, and the fact that, although the latter started booming only in the late 1980s, successful examples of it had already emerged in the 1970s (see Adams 2008, 54), it may be possible that the documentary graphic novel also has influenced the animated documentary's mid-1980s evolution rather than simply being the outcome of the same cultural climate.

To conclude, multiple reasons may have determined the shift undergone by the animated documentary from its phase of the origins to the classical one and that which has seen it evolve into what it is today. Whatever these reasons may be, it is, however, important to keep in mind that the three macro periods of the animated documentary's history here delineated should be envisioned not as separate entities but rather as the stages of a continuous evolutionary process. In fact, first of all, as Parts II and III will make apparent, while undeniably differing in many respects, the animated documentaries produced in each of these three periods also share several macro commonalities, some of which correspond with elements that, in their writings, Walt Disney and John Halas identified as defining traits of such form.

Second, the year identified as demarcating the end of the classical period and the beginning of the contemporary one does not mark the complete disappearance of the previous approach. As will be shown in Chapter 11, expository animated documentaries akin to those created during this form's classical period are still produced nowadays, even if they represent just a minority. Similarly, as we will see in Chapter 5, during the last fifteen years or so of the classical era, animated documentaries focusing on mind-related internal processes or created around the audio recordings of real-life declarations that anticipated and prepared this form's contemporary mutation had already sporadically surfaced. In other words, the years I have identified as delimiters of each of the three macro eras of animated documentary's history are to be intended as symbolic, since they mark the advent of a gradual, nondramatic change.

Notes

1 In the second edition of his *Introduction to Documentary*, Nichols suggests that any industrial and sponsored film, regardless of its specificities, should be conceived as a work that falls at the intersection between the category of the "documentary film" proper and that of the "nondocumentary" nonfiction film. Likewise, according to him, all scientific, informational, and "how to" films would fall in the "nondocumentary" nonfiction category (see Nichols [2001] 2010, 145–7). In the 2017 edition of the book, however, while he keeps indiscriminately classing scientific, informational, and "how to" films as nondocumentaries, he no longer suggests that an industrial or a sponsored film cannot be a documentary (see Nichols [2001] 2017), thus already in part weakening the distinction that Honess Roe offers, if we consider that for her animated documentaries are in all respects examples of documentaries.

2 With the expression "inseparable paratexts," I refer to what Jonathan Gray terms "unincorporated paratexts." That is, I mean those paratextual materials that are aimed mainly at marketing the text and at suggesting to the audience which universe it presents, without adding to the storyworld of the text. Examples in this sense are film posters, print ads, reviews, and trailers (see Gray 2010, 208–10).

3 See Advertisement, *Detroit Free Press*, April 13, 1944, 4.

4 The same article has appeared under different titles in several US newspapers (e.g., see also McLemore 1964b, 4; 1964c, 4-A).

5 In the article, when providing examples of animated documentaries, Disney briefly mentions also *Hookworm* (1945, dir. Jim Algar), *Tuberculosis* (1945, dir. Jim Algar), and *Nutrition*, which was the working title for *Planning for Good Eating* (1946, dir. Gerry Geronimi).

6 For example, see Advertisement, *Sight & Sound*, January/March 1954, i; Advertisement, *Sight & Sound*, Autumn 1956, 58.

7 The same statement can be found also in Halas and Batchelor (1948, 11–2).

8 The data on the films submitted illustrated in this paragraph have been extrapolated from the following documents: Academy of Motion Picture Arts and Sciences (1944), "17th Annual Awards. Documentary Nominations Screenings," Academy Awards Reference collection, Margaret Herrick Library; Academy of Motion Picture Arts and Sciences (1951), "23rd Annual Academy Awards. Entries Received for Documentary Short Subject Award," Academy Awards Reference collection, Margaret Herrick Library; Academy of Motion Picture Arts and Sciences (1952), "24th Annual Academy Awards. Nomination Voting for Documentary Awards," Academy Awards Reference collection, Margaret Herrick Library; Academy of Motion Picture Arts and Sciences (1953), "25th Annual Academy Awards. 35 Entries Received for Documentary Short Subject Nominations," Academy Awards Reference collection, Margaret Herrick Library; Academy of Motion Picture Arts and Sciences (1954), "26th Annual Academy Awards. 26 Entries Received for

Documentary Short Subject Nominations," Academy Awards Reference collection, Margaret Herrick Library; Academy of Motion Picture Arts and Sciences (1955), "27th Annual Academy Awards. 26 Entries Received for Documentary Short Subject Nominations," Academy Awards Reference collection, Margaret Herrick Library; Academy of Motion Picture Arts and Sciences (1956), "28th Annual Academy Awards. 35 Entries Received for Documentary Short Subject Nominations," Academy Awards Reference collection, Margaret Herrick Library; Academy of Motion Picture Arts and Sciences (1957), "Documentary. 29th Awards–Short Subject Entries Received," Academy Awards Reference collection, Margaret Herrick Library; Academy of Motion Picture Arts and Sciences (1958), "30th Annual Academy Awards. 29 Entries Received for Documentary Short Subject Nominations," Academy Awards Reference collection, Margaret Herrick Library; Academy of Motion Picture Arts and Sciences (1959), "31st Annual Academy Awards. 29 Entries Received for Documentary Short Subject Nominations," Academy Awards Reference collection, Margaret Herrick Library; Academy of Motion Picture Arts and Sciences (1960), "32nd Annual Academy Awards. 35 Entries Received for Documentary Short Subject Nominations," Academy Awards Reference collection, Margaret Herrick Library; Academy of Motion Picture Arts and Sciences (1961), "33rd Annual Academy Awards. 32 Entries Received for Documentary Short Subject Nominations," Academy Awards Reference collection, Margaret Herrick Library. For all the years of which the Margaret Herrick Library does not hold a list of the entries received, motion-picture industry magazines have instead been consulted.

9   Depending on how broadly we define animation, the titles could be thirty-one as *Toccata for Toy Trains* (1957, dir. Charles and Ray Eames), which shows antique toy trains moving and was submitted on the occasion of the 30th Academy Awards, could also be included. Moreover, this figure refers just to the films employing exclusively or mostly the fabled animation, as this is a defining trait of the animated documentary. However, a few titles wherein sober animation is instead employed can be found too. It is, for instance, the case of *Human Growth* (1947, dir. Sy Wexler) and *Introduction to Feedback* (1960, dir. Charles and Ray Eames), submitted respectively for the 23rd and 33rd Academy Awards.

10 This title was first created in 1955 in the form of a television episode. In 1956, it was then made into a featurette for distribution in cinemas, and it is this second version that was submitted for consideration.

11 More precisely, *Brotherhood of Man* was submitted as a UPA production, while *Flat Hatting* was sent as a US Navy Department production, although the latter just commissioned it.

12 The president of Harding College, George S. Benson, responded to this accusation by saying that *Fresh Laid Plans* was simply "born out of the desire to help Americans better understand the advantages enjoyed in America in comparison to other nations and to help explain the fundamentals that make America tick" (Benson 1951, 260).

13 Initially, *The Earth Is Born* was supposed to be the first of four films on the origins of Earth (see "Earth Is Born" 1957, 10-F). The other titles, however, got canceled.

14 See Academy of Motion Picture Arts and Sciences, "59th Annual Academy Awards. Official Entry Blank – Documentary Awards," Academy Awards Reference collection, Margaret Herrick Library.

15 Academy of Motion Picture Arts and Sciences, "Voting Rules: 15th Annual Academy Awards of Merit for Achievements during 1942," Academy Awards Reference collection, Margaret Herrick Library, 2.

16 Academy of Motion Picture Arts and Sciences, "15th Awards: Rules for Nominations of Short and Feature Length Documentary Films for the 1942 Academy Awards of Merit," Academy Awards Reference collection, Margaret Herrick Library.

17 Academy of Motion Picture Arts and Sciences, "40th Annual Academy Awards of Merit for Achievements during 1967: Voting Rules," Academy Awards Reference collection, Margaret Herrick Library, 10; italics added.

18 Academy of Motion Picture Arts and Sciences, "Program: Fifteenth Annual Academy Awards of Merit for Achievements during 1942," Academy Awards Reference collection, Margaret Herrick Library, 10.

19 A study of the Academy Awards' voting rules pamphlets and of the works submitted for consideration for an Oscar for Best Documentary Short Subject and prized with this award also provides us with important indications concerning the documentary proper, and especially what can be and has been categorized as such over time. In particular, it makes apparent how questionable is Nichols' choice to a priori class any scientific, instructional, and "how to" film as nondocumentary.

20 More precisely, in the animated documentaries of the classical era could be either offered some shots consisting in zoom-ins and pans of the camera on a motionless drawing or, more simply, shots completely deprived of movement comprising just of a static image.

21 This comic strip series has, however, appeared also in other newspapers, including *The Alexander City Outlook*, *The Atmore Advance*, *The Etowah News-Journal*, and *The Daily Republican*.

22 For the characteristics of the contemporary documentary comics' production, see, aside from Adams 2008, also Mickwitz (2016).

23 Examples of animated documentaries that are transpositions of documentary graphic novels are *Persepolis* (2007, dir. Marjane Satrapi and Vincent Paronnaud), *Approved for Adoption*, and *Virus Tropical* (2017, dir. Santiago Caicedo).

PART II

The Rise and Affirmation of an Audiovisual Form

4

The Age of the Origins, 1909–39

An Emerging Minority

As anticipated in Chapter 1, the first animations addressing the social world came into being already in the late 1900s. Indeed, in years during which cinema, in general, was considered "a medium destined to educate" (Gaycken 2012, 67), animation also could not but start being exploited to elucidate the real. With the First World War the quantity of reality-related animations produced increased significantly since both governmental and private bodies sponsored the creation of a good number of such works. Exploiting its "ability to reduce the optical world to its haptic essence" (Crafton 2013, 297), during the conflict, animation was employed especially for making training films for instructing the soldiers, films illustrating the phases of a battle or, more broadly, of a war-related occurrence, and public information films aimed at inducing set collective behaviors in the population (see Alonge 2000, 12).

As a result, by the end of the fight, animation's potential to show the unfilmed and the unfilmable, to convey concepts in terms so simple that even the most illiterate strata of the population could understand them and to keep alive the attention of viewers, became apparent. Therefore, even once peace was restored, animation continued to be employed in nonfiction contexts, and in 1920, in the introduction to his book *Animated Cartoons*, Edwin George Lutz even went as far as to predict that it would have soon become first and foremost a medium for instructing rather than entertaining:

> Teachers now are talking of "visual instruction." They mean by this phrase in the special sense that they have given to it the use of motion-picture films for instructional purposes. Travel pictures to be used in connection with teaching geography or micro-cinematographic films for classes in biology are good examples of such films. But not all educational subjects

can be depicted by the camera solely. For many themes the artist must be called in to prepare a series of drawings made in a certain way and then photographed and completed to form a film of moving diagrams or drawings.

As it is readily understood that any school topic presented in animated pictures will stimulate and hold the attention, and that the proprieties of things when depicted in action are more quickly grasped visually than by description or through motionless diagrams, it is likely that visual instruction by films will soon play an important part in any course of studies. Then the motion-picture projector will become the pre-eminent school apparatus and such subjects as do not lend themselves to photography will very generally need to be drawn; thereupon the preponderance of the comic cartoon will cease and the animated screen drawing of serious and worth-while themes will prevail. (Lutz 1920, x–xi)

Lutz's estimates proved too optimistic, as the day in which the nonfiction animations produced outnumber the fiction ones has yet to come. However, his words are symptomatic of how already back then animation was fully recognized among makers as a medium apt also for talking about reality. Indeed, as Kirsten Ostherr (2013, 35) points out, by the 1920s animation increasingly became "the default medium for communicating with the 'average person,'" taking on "a privileged—if problematic—status within theories of visual pedagogy."

Up to the late 1930s the mode of representation of choice in creating reality-related animated films was mainly the sober animation. This perhaps happened because, at the time, when an animation addressed the real, it was mostly to educate and instruct, and "many experts felt that amusement and instruction were antithetical objectives" (31). Indeed, it was believed that if a film became too entertaining, its educative value would be lessened. Therefore, since, as we have seen, the fabled animation brings with itself precisely that amusement regarded with suspicion by the then pedagogists, while the sober one does not, between 1909 and 1939 the latter has been the go-to mode of representation for factual animations. Nevertheless, in the period in question, we can also find several films employing the fabled animation to tackle reality-related topics. And these works can be seen as proper early animated documentaries, or in any case experiments in their direction. Indeed, the fact that the label "animated documentary" started being used only in the 1940s does not mean that titles created before this time cannot be retrospectively recognized as pertaining to this form. As already underscored in Chapter 3, it is not infrequent for a filmic category to start developing before the introduction of the label with which it will subsequently come to be identified.

In particular, in the case of the animated documentary, with hindsight, one of the very first examples of the form can be considered Smith's *To Demonstrate How Spiders Fly*. Undeniably this film constitutes just an initial step in the direction of what the animated documentary will become, since it still does not showcase a full adoption of the fabled animation. For instance, as far as the setting is concerned, the viewer is not actually encouraged to build a space, given that the background is plain black and the only scenery element is the rock on which the spider is standing at the beginning of the film. Nevertheless, first, *To Demonstrate How Spiders Fly* showcases the defining elements of the animated documentary since it elucidates an aspect of the real through animation's fictional mode of representation by having an animated actor reenact a factual occurrence, inviting as such the viewer to put in place a fabled reading. Second, it even displays some of the "minor" traits that, as we will see, will recur in classical animated documentaries and beyond. Indeed, this short is expository and character-oriented, instructs while entertaining, and resorts to the "generalizing synecdoche" (Odin 2004, 91). That is, it revolves around a single character who nevertheless stands for a broader category, which in this case is that of spiders.

Smith's film has not remained alone for long on the route toward the development of the animated documentary as a coherent form. A number of animation pioneers from around the world, in the following decades, have likewise contributed to paving the way to this form's shaping. It is the case, among others, of the French Marius Rossillon and Robert Collard—better known as O'Gallop and Lortac—, the British Lancelot Speed, the Italian Luigi Liberio Pensuti, the New Zealander Len Lye, the Japanese Zenjiro Sanae Yamamoto, and the Americans Winsor McCay and Max Fleischer.

Informing the Viewing Public

Like it will be characteristic of many classical animated documentaries in the decades to follow, most of this form's early examples are intended for broad nonspecialized audiences and are produced on commission of either a government agency or a private body. As a consequence, they tend to be informed by a propagandistic or advertising agenda. In other words, they not only address reality-related topics but are also shaped by the desire to act on the factual, to influence it. Moreover, content-wise the area in which the highest number of early animated documentaries falls is that of public information. In other words, the shape that animated documentaries most frequently take between the 1910s and the end of the 1930s is that of films illustrating set correct behaviors which the viewers should keep in their everyday. Typically, they are health-related and instruct spectators on the best practices to adopt in domains such as hygiene, sex, or alcohol consumption in order to avoid making their lives miserable.

However, in so doing, these films do not follow a same pattern, nor do they showcase the same degree of factuality. Indeed, this period's animated documentaries range from works that make only a timid use of fabled animation to others that showcase a significant degree of fictionality even at the content level. Also, some take the form of made-up exemplary stories that depict the consequences of not adopting certain righteous behaviors, while others take the form of expository works wherein animation is used to stage, in a more or less imaginative and dramatic way, what the intertitles (during the silent period) or a narrator (after sound is introduced) illustrate. Examples of the first approach are titles like *It Must Be Said* (*On doit le dire*, 1918, dir. O'Galop) and *Tombolino's Hygiene* (*L'igiene di Tombolino*, dir. Luigi Liberio Pensuti, 1935 ca.),[1] where the paradigmatic story of one or more fictional characters (each of whom by generalizing synecdoche stands for a category of people) is told. In other words, this subgroup of early, public service animated documentaries uses a fictive but plausible story to induce in viewers a reflection on the importance of embracing set virtuous conducts in their everyday. As in the case of *It Must Be Said*, the foregoing can be done by comparing two characters—one that acts correctly with one whose conduct is instead ruinous—and showing how their lives turn out very differently. Indeed, the film directed by O'Galop narrates about soldiers Mathieu and Mattéo, who contract syphilis from the same prostitute. Nevertheless, while the former has a happy life because he seeks medical care before tying the knot, the latter refuses treatments, gets married immediately, and has a miserable existence. Alternatively, as it occurs in *Tombolino's Hygiene*, the protagonist can at first be a negative figure who snubs set righteous behaviors, but, once he experiences the devastating consequences of his practices, he decides to "redeem" himself by starting to adopt a virtuous conduct. For instance, the protagonist of Pensuti's film is a child named Tombolino, who ignores the basic hygienic rules. During a visit to the zoo, he hurts his leg, and, due to his refusal to use soap, the wound gets infected. He will manage to get better thanks to the prompt intervention of Dr. Perticone, but the fear of dying that he ends up facing will induce him to start caring about his personal hygiene. All these characters tend to have first names, a fact that individualizes them and thus makes their stories personal stories. Nonetheless, they can still be seen as embodying a broader category of people. In this typology of early animated documentaries can thus be identified the roots of those classical-era animated documentaries like UPA's *Brotherhood of Man*, *Man Alive!*, and *Look Who's Driving*, wherein the exemplary vicissitudes of a character are likewise used to highlight what is depicted by a voice-of-God narrator.

At the same time, however, early public service animated documentaries can also be more readily expository, as in the case of *The Alcohol Cycle*

(*Le circuit de l'alcool*, 1919) and *The Fly* (*La mouche*, 1919).[2] These two films warn respectively against the dangers of alcohol consumption and of flies, and both have been directed by O'Galop under the scientific advice of an expert, Doctor Jean Comandon. In particular, in *The Alcohol Cycle* the intertitles explain how, when consuming alcohol, following an initial moment during which life looks rosier, one can face a series of negative effects that go from loss of balance and temporary obnubilation to mental health issues and death.[3] This is visually depicted by showing a man that, after having had some glasses of wine in a bar, wobbles while going home, does not manage to let himself into his own house because he has not enough lucidity to insert the key in the keyhole, and falls asleep on the landing. Subsequently, we see him dying in prison in the throes of delirium. Similarly, in *The Fly*—which in many respects can be viewed as an unsophisticated and primeval version of an emblematic classical animated documentary, *The Winged Scourge*—the intertitles illustrate how this insect can pass on germs of any kind and spread diseases such as typhus and tuberculosis by perching first on dirt and filth and then on our food. Visually, this is returned by having a disproportionately big fly that, for instance, first alights on a rubbish bin and subsequently perches on a gigantic sugar cube and on a cake, or drinks the spit of a sick man before landing on a baby bottle. Both these O'Galop's films are thus character-oriented and have as protagonist a figure with no first name that, by generalizing synecdoche, stands for a broader category: the drunkard of *The Alcohol Cycle* represents any man who abuses of alcohol, whereas the fly of *The Fly* is any exemplar of its species. Also, their backgrounds are fully drawn and bidimensional, therefore favoring the construction of a diegesis on the part of the viewer. However, in neither film, the fabled potentials of animation are exploited in full, because, mostly, they just stage what is explained in the intertitles rather than actually dramatizing it. For instance, the fly starring in the namesake film should be a negative character. Still, first, while the intertitles demonize it, it is drawn with big, cute eyes that do not encourage to envision it as an enemy (see Figure 4.1). Second, except for the final sequence wherein a bear throws a stone at it, it does not have an antagonist. That is, no actual attempt at eradicating it is visually depicted. To the point that, years later, when editing the film to make an Italian version of it, the Luce Institute felt the need to add a final live-action sequence showing a housewife that cleans her house, covers the trash can, and puts a protective cloth on food in order to at least ward off the fly.[4] Moreover, this insect is anthropomorphized: the intertitles refer to it as a "she," and here and there it betrays human-like behaviors such as wearing shoes or standing on two legs. Still, it is a very partial personification, since for most of the film the conduct of this fly is in line with that of its species' members.

This timid use of fabled animation, however, is not proper of all the expository, public service animated documentaries produced in this period

FIGURE 4.1 *A shot of the fly too cute for being envisioned as an enemy that stars in* The Fly.

nor is identifiable just in works from the 1910s. Indeed, on the one hand, for example, in France, a year before the release of *The Alcohol Cycle* and *The Fly*, two titles like *The Slum Has to Be Conquered* (*Le taudis doit être vaincu*, 1918, dir. Lortac) and *To Resist Tuberculosis, Stay Strong* (*Pour résister à la tuberculouse, soyons forts*, 1918, dir. Lortac) saw light.[5] These films, while similarly being expository, showcase a fuller employment of the fabled animation and a higher degree of dramatization in illustrating best lifestyle practices to defeat tuberculosis. Sponsored by the Rockefeller Foundation and always created with the scientific advice of Comandon, *The Slum Has to Be Conquered* and *To Resist Tuberculosis, Stay Strong* are character-oriented and allegorically personify death as a skeleton that goes around spraying tuberculosis germs. Most importantly, in these two titles we can already find the first instances of what will become the canonical way of dramatizing the fight against an illness in classical animated documentaries and beyond: literally portraying it as a combat, and most frequently as a war-like battle, between figures embodying the disease (i.e., the villain[s]) and others representing health (i.e., the hero[s]). In fact, in both films, death finds on its path a character embodying good that literally engages in a fight with it and defeats it. In particular, in *The Slum Has to Be Conquered*, death is fought by a doctor with a cannon firing hygiene, while in *To Resist Tuberculosis, Stay Strong*, by a fit man with a healthy lifestyle (who by generalizing synecdoche represents any man who exercises in the open air) that punches him till he knocks him out.

On the other hand, works that do not make full employment of fabled animation can also be found after the 1910s as proven for instance by

Diseases Spread (*Byodoku no denpa*, 1926, dir. Sanae Yamamoto) or *The Road of Health* (1936, dir. Brian Salt). The former was produced by the Japanese Ministry of Education to promote public awareness about hygiene and illustrates how carelessness and laziness can determine the propagation of disease. Not dissimilarly from *The Fly*, this short is character-oriented, and its protagonist is a personification of "evil," and more precisely a blob-like figure, provided not only with arms, legs, and a face but also with the ability to speak,[6] that by generalizing synecdoche represents any illness. Furthermore, through succinct intertitles, the film points out some behaviors that, if put in place, could prevent the spread of disease within a household and beyond, such as avoiding eating half-cooked fish or using the water of the river to wash food or crockery, and wearing a mask when walking in the street. Through the animated visuals, it is mostly staged how not following these hygienic rules allows illness to thrive and, only rarely, is enacted how instead applying them can eradicate it. Therefore, analogously to what was noted for *The Fly*, the viewer is not offered an actual dramatization of the real-life aspects depicted. In fact, the film is not even structured as a unitary story with a narrative development but instead as a series of vignettes each of which has a different setting and stars different animated actors in the role of the Japanese citizen acting recklessly. To collate what otherwise is just a series of disconnected scenes is only the fact that they all illustrate a hygiene-related behavior and, at some point, showcase the personification of disease, which remains the same throughout the film. Finally, while up to the last sequence, in line with what is typical of the fabled animation, the characters are immersed in bidimensional backgrounds, as far as the setting is concerned the coda of *Diseases Spread* adopts a sober approach reminiscent of the map-film. Indeed, the protagonist of the film acts in front of a one-dimensional map of Japan (see Figure 4.2).

The Road of Health, instead, is a partly animated and partly live-action short sponsored by the British Social Hygiene Council that melds public information and fund-raising. Indeed, on the one hand, it stigmatizes prostitution, delinquency, and alcohol abuse as behaviors that lead to venereal diseases. On the other hand, it lingers on the vital role that the British Social Hygiene Council itself plays in the eradication of these illnesses, encouraging in the end money donations from viewers in support of this body's work. *The Road of Health* opens with a live-action portion wherein a lecturer talks about syphilis and gonorrhea, also showing the bacteria responsible for these diseases. He then turns to a drawing board and starts sketching a road that, immediately after, comes to life. It begins as such the animated portion of the short, which is by Reginald Jeffryes and consists mainly in an allegorical visualization of the Council's role in helping people affected by a venereal disease to get back on the road of health. More precisely, the viewer is shown a neat crowd walking on a sunny road that traverses a landscape with lush greenery. From this street

FIGURE 4.2 *In* Diseases Spread's *coda, the personification of disease acts in front of a map of Japan.*

(that represents the road of health) depart three paths (i.e., the path of prostitution, of delinquency, and of drink broken homes), all of which bring to the venereal disease land, a somber territory with dead vegetation. Some of the people walking on the main road detach from the rest of the crowd to take one of the three paths that bring to this land. However, thanks to the work of the British Social Hygiene Council, these people are no longer trapped in such inhospitable territory. They can get back to the road of health through a bridge whose bricks bear inscriptions such as "doctors," "nurses," "treatment centers," and so on. Therefore, unlike in the cases of *The Alcohol Cycle*, *The Fly*, and *Diseases Spread*, *The Road of Health* is not character-oriented but uses an allegorical visual language throughout and clearly distinguishes between good and evil by exploiting, for instance, the full scale of grays and black. Nonetheless, also in this case, rather than with a dramatization of what the lecturer illustrates, we are presented just with an imaginative visual transposition. Furthermore, the portions employing the fabled animation are somehow flagged as "fictional" by having just a musical score accompany them. The voice of the lecturer accompanies the animation almost exclusively in the few instances in which sober animation is made use of to illustrate data concerning attendances at treatment centers.

It thus emerges how between the 1910s and the late 1930s not only diverse approaches in developing public service animated documentaries have coexisted but also different routes have been pursued within the subgroups of works deriving from the adoption of the different approaches. Therefore, rather than by a progressive development toward what will be this form's mature shape, this period has been characterized by a range of experiments in its direction.

Beyond the Main Tendency

Not all the titles that can be considered early animated documentaries are necessarily public information films. For example, they can also come under the shape of animated records of (relatively) current events. Indeed, during the First World War years, the employment of animation in the illustration of real-life, war-related occurrences, and facts that Cohl kickstarted in 1909 with *The Battle of Austerlitz* thrived. A good number of animated films providing an account of relatively recent battles or presenting other data concerning the ongoing conflict were produced. The majority was structured as map-films and, therefore, falls out of the animated documentary domain due to an exclusive, or in any case predominant, use of sober animation. In some instances, however, the fabled animation was instead favored, giving as such life to a small number of shorts that reenact and dramatize then relatively recent war-related facts with a more or less explicit propagandistic intent which can be considered out-and-out early animated documentaries. Examples of these films—which have paved the way for a strand of works illustrating past occurrences or retracing the history of something that will flourish during this form's classical era and beyond—are, for instance, *The Sinking of the Lusitania* or *Britain's Effort* (1917, dir. Lancelot Speed), a short commissioned by the Ministry of Information that employs cut-out animation to illustrate the main challenges Britain had to face at a demographic and economic level between 1914 and 1917 due to the war.

A propagandistic agenda informs both titles. More precisely, *Britain's Effort* aims at convincing the internal front to accept the sacrifices required by the conflict in anticipation of the joys of peace times to come. Similarly, *The Sinking of the Lusitania* aspires at demonizing the Germans, to the point that, even if it purports to be an objective account of the events narrated, it selectively hides some information from the viewer in order to more readily present this nation as evil. For instance, the film avoids saying that the *Lusitania* was equipped for combat and was listed on the Admiralty Fleet Registry as an "armed auxiliary cruiser" (Canemaker 1987, 150), or that it was also carrying guns destined to the British soldiers, which might have been the cause for the fatal explosion (see Alonge 2000, 84). Moreover, both films make use of fabled animation to attest data regarding the conflict. Nonetheless, as seen for the early public information animated documentaries, *Britain's Effort* and *The Sinking of the Lusitania* do so at different levels and following different patterns. Indeed, Speed's film is based for the most part on a series of statistics. However, the data is visualized in an imaginative way that enables the viewer to build a space and put in place the operation of narrativization. More precisely, the statistical figures are staged and integrated into a narrative, albeit a highly fragmented one. Indeed, after a live-action prologue residual of the lightning sketch tradition, the events that have brought Britain to enter the war are dramatized using the fabled animation.

In particular, the 1914 German invasion of Belgium is reenacted by showing a winged Wilhelm (who allegorically represents Germany) that grabs a young woman sitting on a hillside (who incarnates Belgium) and puts a chain on her arm. At this point, Britannia wakes up a sleeping John Bull (who embodies the British population). Upon opening his eyes, he immediately realizes what is happening, gets up from the grass where he is laying, and walks out of frame with a combative attitude. It is then cut to Britannia sounding the bugle, an image symbolically indicating that the British population is called to arms. The call is answered by a gentleman, a farmer, a clerk, a fisherman, a miner, and a railway porter, who are all shown in the act of leaving their workplaces and activities and lining up next to each other. When all six of them are aligned, their clothes morph into a military uniform. Only at this point, once the viewer has thus been informed of the reasons for the war, the actual statistics concerning Britain's efforts during the conflict start being visualized. Nevertheless, once this occurs, the operations of construction of a diegesis and narrativization that up to that moment the viewer has been encouraged to put in place are not blocked. Indeed, the data is immersed in a detailed, bidimensional background and is staged in an imaginative way by employing an allegorical visual language. To make an example, the growth of the British army thanks to the inclusion of soldiers from overseas territories is not illustrated through a moving diagram as it would have conventionally occurred. On the contrary, a single soldier for each of the lands that at the time were under the British dominion (who by generalizing synecdoche stands for all the militaries drafted from that territory) is portrayed next to the animal more readily associable with the set geographic area from where he comes. We see a Canadian soldier riding through a forest on a moose, an Australian one riding on a kangaroo, a South African one standing next to a springbok, a New Zealander one with an emu, and an Indian one on an elephant. All these militaries reach the same beach where a British soldier (who by generalizing synecdoche represents the British army) is standing and magically fuse with him, determining his disproportionate growth. Precisely due to this use of the fabled animation and the then still-rooted idea that such a mode of visual representation was synonym to insincerity, the overall scientific validity of *Britain's Effort* has been questioned by many (see Alonge 2000, 49). However, paradoxically, here and there throughout the film the shots become aerial and animated maps are used to illustrate the facts narrated. These shots are not entirely sober since often the map acts just as a background to actions animated using this medium's fictional mode of representation. Nevertheless, their presence alone betrays how *Britain's Effort* is still not entirely emancipated from the then more prominent map-film approach, while at the same time not having found an equilibrium in the employment of fabled animation.

Conversely, *The Sinking of the Lusitania*, on the one hand, favors a "realistic" graphic style and mode of representation (Crafton 1982, 116; Wells 1997, 42) and opts for a more literal visual language. Yet, on the other hand, it is fully liberated from the map-film model, has a much more linear narration, and showcases a higher degree of dramatization. Indeed, McCay's film does not merely re-present a relatively current event but fully dramatizes it, for example, by focusing the attention on the death of a baby and his mother. Indeed, first, the viewer is shown an intertitle that says: "The babe that clung to his mother's breast cried out the world—*to avenge* the most violent cruelty that was ever perpetrated upon an unsuspecting and innocent people" (original emphasis). The film then closes with a heartrending scene in which we see a woman drowning with her baby, which not casually is the only character that is shown from close-up and in its integrity. Furthermore, unlike in *Britain's Effort* but similarly to what often occurs in the contemporary animated documentary production, some markers of veridiction aimed at encouraging the viewer to read the film's content as factual are present in *The Sinking of the Lusitania*. It is the case of its initial caption stating that the viewer is about to look "at the first *record* of the sinking of the Lusitania" or its live-action prologue. Indeed, as *Britain's Effort*, McCay's film also opens with a sort of *ante litteram* making of sequence reminiscent of the lightning sketch tradition. However, the one in Speed's short points to the film being a creative recreation of the facts narrated by showing the animator in the act of drawing Kaiser Wilhelm and then having the character take life. The one in *The Sinking of the Lusitania*, instead, although not returning a factual account of the film's productive circumstances,[7] invites the spectator to regard this short as the result of a rigorous reconstruction, faithful to facts and based on attentive preliminary research (see Alonge 2000, 82). Finally, always in line with what tends to occur nowadays, the paratextual materials of *The Sinking of the Lusitania* stress the fact that the film is being based on real-life occurrences. More precisely, they are inclined to present it as an account "authentic to the last detail" ("Doug Fairbanks" 1918, 5),[8] and to underline that reliable documents of the event have been used as the basis for the film. To make an example, in the *Medford Mail Tribune* it is told: "Winsor McCay obtained his first idea of the actual sinking from the noted war correspondent, August F. Beach, who was the first newspaperman to obtain the detailed stories of the survivors who reached land" ("Doug Fairbanks" 1918, 5).

In sum, it emerges how even early animated documentaries illustrating (relatively) current events, while bearing some similarities, do not anticipate the traits destined to become characteristic of this form in the same way nor are structured according to a shared pattern.

After the end of the First World War, the employment of animation to create animated records of current events dropped. Yet, as anticipated, it soon instead peaked its use to make animated lessons, and, although until the late 1930s, the sober animation was preferred in creating films aimed at explaining in layman terms an aspect of the real, this does not mean that the fabled one was never employed at such end during this period. In particular, among the animators who have contributed an early animated documentary falling in the educational domain is the other animation pioneer that, together with McCay, happens to be mentioned in the discourses on nonfiction animation, namely Max Fleischer (e.g., DelGaudio 1997, 190; Honess Roe 2013, 9). Still, the film in question is not one of the two partly animated titles illustrating Albert Einstein's theory of relativity and Charles Darwin's theory of evolution—namely, respectively *The Einstein Theory of Relativity* (1923) and *Evolution* (1925)—for which he is normally seen as an anticipator of this form. Like any other film employing animation to tackle an aspect of the social world, these two works have certainly contributed to setting the ground for the subsequent development of the animated documentary as an out-and-out form. Nevertheless, they cannot be considered actual early examples of it, since they both are compilation films created by drawing mainly on a single preexisting live-action feature—respectively *The Basics of Einstein's Theory of Relativity* (*Die Grundlagen der Einsteinschen Relativitäts-Theorie*, 1922, dir. Hanns Walter Kornblum) and *Evolution* (1923, dir. Raymond Ditmars)[9]—and their use of animation is minimal. Also, if *Evolution* at least employs the fabled animation,[10] *Theory of Relativity* utilizes the sober one. The educational early animated documentary that Fleischer has contributed is *Finding His Voice* (1929, dir. Francis Lyle Goldman and Max Fleischer), a short produced by the Western Electric Company to illustrate how sound-on-film technology works. More precisely, it does so within the frame story of how talking filmstrip Talkie helps silent filmstrip Mutie to get back in business by taking him to Dr. Western, a film surgeon specialized in voice lifting who is capable of giving a voice to the motion pictures who lack it. This film is thus character-oriented and makes use of animation's magical devices such as anthropomorphism (both Talkie and Mutie have anthropomorphic attributes and behaviors) or personification (Dr. Western is the incarnation of Western Electric). However, on the one hand, the moments wherein the frame story is told—that is, the long initial sequences revolving around Mutie's problem and Talkie coming up with the solution of going to Dr. Western's office, and the ending one with Talkie and Mutie exhibiting themselves in a musical number—are entirely imaginary and thus off-balance the film in the direction of fiction even at content level. On the other hand, in its central part, wherein the actual explanation of sound-on-film's working principles is offered, *Finding His Voice* loses most of its fictional character also at form level. More precisely, even though here fabled animation is used—for instance, Mutie and Dr. Western jump inside many of the machinery that the latter illustrates to the former—this section of the film is impacted by the then still dominant idea of sober animation, which is the most appropriate visual language for elucidating the real in animated form. Indeed, in this section, diagrammatic animations crafted exploiting the graphic vocabulary of technical drawing abound and the overall tone is more didactic with Dr. Western adopting "the pedagogical mode of address common to announcements of electrical acoustics" (Wurtzler 2007, 99).

In sum, as all the other titles addressed, also *Finding His Voice* anticipates in its way traits that will be proper of the subsequent animated documentary production, although not integrating them in a cohesive and balanced way. In particular, in this film we can identify the roots of a strand of industrial animated documentaries mixing an educational and a promotional agenda that will develop during this form's classical era and in which, as we will see, fall, for instance, works as *Pay Attention to the Label* (*Occhio all'etichetta*, 1966, dir. Giovanni Cecchinato) and other titles sponsored by Montecatini or the various shorts created by Halas & Batchelor Cartoon Films for British Petroleum, Shell, Esso, and Philips. Indeed, behind the appearance of a mild educational film, *Finding His Voice* hides also a promotional intent. In fact, it was aimed not only at presenting "sound-film technologies to theater owners, nontheatrical producers, corporate film units, and educational institutions" (Solbrig 2012, 195)[11] but also at favoring the affirmation of Western Electric's patent as the sole valid by attempting "to define film sound as a telephonic rather than a filmic technology" (193).

Another example of an early industrial animated documentary is *Down the Gasoline Trail* (1935, dir. Rockwell Barnes), a short produced for the Chevrolet Division of General Motors Corporation by a studio specialized in using animation to visualize the invisible, the Jam Handy Organization (see Oakes 2010, 101). This film, which depicts how a car's fuel system works, combines "entertainment and instruction" as well as live-action and animation, like the other nonfiction titles in the "Direct Mass Selling" series, of which it is part (Prelinger 2009, 217). However, whereas most of the latter employ (mainly) sober animation (and thus do not qualify as animated documentaries), *Down the Gasoline Trail* uses exclusively the fabled one. Indeed, meanwhile a voice-of-God narrator illustrates the voyage of fuel through the gas line of a car, brief live-action shots of the exterior of the engine's parts mentioned in the commentary are alternated to longer scenes in animation that dramatize what occurs to gasoline inside those same components.[12] In particular, we follow the journey from the tank to the exhaust line of an anthropomorphic drop of gasoline (see Figure 4.3), who by generalizing synecdoche represents this fuel as a whole. And, this drop, after jumping inside the gas tank, is the protagonist of both humorous interludes and dramatic vicissitudes (including its death toward the end of the film when it gets in the cylinder).

Therefore, similar to *Finding His Voice*, *Down the Gasoline Trail* also is character-oriented and explains in pleasurable terms the working principles of a machine that pertains to our world. In this title, entertainment and information are better blended than in Fleischer's animated documentary. Yet, a tendency to separate the amusing moments from the educational ones can still be recognized, since the humorous interludes that see the gasoline drop protagonist are often offered during pauses between the voice-of-God narrator's explanations, rather than as an illustration of its statements. Moreover, always analogously to what is seen in *Finding His Voice*, in

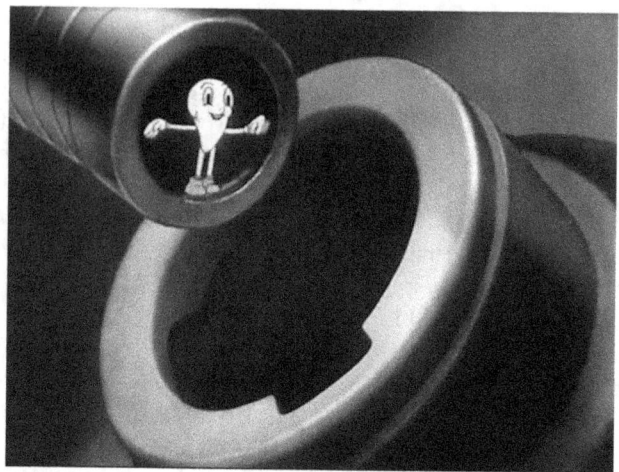

FIGURE 4.3 *The personified gasoline drop protagonist of* Down the Gasoline Trail.

Down the Gasoline Trail the promotional agenda is kept under trace. That is, there is "no explicit advertisement, in order to render" the film's message "more palatable in theatres and schools" (Prelinger 2009, 217). The Chevrolet brand is, however, subtly promoted through brand placement, and in particular by offering, both at the beginning and the end of the film, a few live-action shots of the car in whose engine the gasoline drop enters wherein the Chevrolet logo is well visible (e.g., see Figure 4.4).

If in the cases of *Finding His Voice* and *Down the Gasoline Trail*, the advertising intent is under trace, among the early examples of animated documentaries, it is possible to find also a work like *Trade Tatoo* (1937, dir. Len Lye), whose main agenda is precisely promotion. Despite being produced by the GPO Film Unit expressly to encourage the posting of mail before 2 p.m., this film is, however, more than an animated advertisement. Through adding animated words and patterns to documentary live-action footage, with this film Lye sought to "express 'a romanticism about the world of the everyday'" (Lye in Harris 2006, 72). The result is an avant-garde work that bears close proximity "to films such as Walter Ruttmann's *Berlin: Symphony of a Great City* (a 1927 documentary that Lye admired)" (Horrocks 2001, 151). In fact, precisely as Bill Nichols ([2001] 2017, 116) argues to be the case for the live-action titles adopting a "poetic mode" of documentary representation, Lye's short "explores associations and patterns that involve temporal rhythms and spatial juxtapositions." In particular, *Trade Tatoo*'s rhythm is informed both by the Cuban dance music to which it is animated and by "the movement of textual and imagistic passages" (Harris 2006, 64). Moreover, as Nichols ([2001] 2017, 117) notes to be the case for poetic documentaries, Lye's film also "draws on the historical world

FIGURE 4.4 *A frame from* Down the Gasoline Trail *in which Chevrolet's logo is well visible.*

for its raw material but transforms this material in distinctive ways." Indeed, it is composed of outtakes from live-action documentaries produced by the GPO which have been subsequently treated to optical printing manipulation and overlaid with abstract shapes from stencils (see O'Pray 2003, 45). Therefore, as Paul Ward (2005, 83) suggests, this "kinetic paean to the hustle and bustle of trade" too can be considered an animated documentary. More precisely, we can view it as an early example of an animated documentary adopting a "poetic mode" of documentary representation, and a precursor to contemporary works like Samantha Moore's *An Eyeful of Sound* (2010) and Ruth Lingford's *Little Deaths* (2010).

In synthesis, between 1909 and 1939 around the world a small number of films that exhibit traits destined to become defining characteristics of the animated documentary saw the light within various domains, anticipating some of the faces this form will have in its classical era and beyond. At the time, these works were not labeled as animated documentaries and were not made following a unitary approach. Indeed, as we have seen, during these thirty years, even when the titles deploying traits proper of the animated documentary pertain to a same domain, they employ them differently and with a dissimilar concentration. Consequently, while it is possible to recognize these films as animated documentaries retrospectively, they should be envisioned as preliminary outcomes of an ongoing experimentation aimed at finding the perfect balance between a set of ingredients, and in particular between fact and fiction both at form and content level. For this reason, I suggest considering these first thirty years of the animated documentary's history as its age of origins.

Notes

1. Zanotto and Zangrando (1973) date *Tombolino's Hygiene* between 1932 and 1934. Still, in virtue of the strong relationship it entertains with another title at which Pensuti has collaborated, *The Tavern of Tuberculosis* (*La taverna del tibbici*, 1935, dir. Lamberto Ristori), it is more likely for *Tombolino's Hygiene* to be from 1935. Indeed, these two titles even share two animated actors. Furthermore, in 1936, on the pages of an Italian newspaper *La Stampa*, *Tombolino's Hygiene* and *The Tavern of Tuberculosis* are presented as recent productions of Pensuti's studio, SICED (see m.g. 1936, 3).

2. In the 1930s, *The Fly* was renamed *War on Flies* (*Guerre aux mooches!*) (see Lefebvre 2009, 182).

3. O'Galop directed another title similarly addressing the negative consequences of alcohol consumption through an expository approach: *Great Oaks from Small Acorns Grow* (*Petites causes, grands effets!*, 1919) (see Lefebvre 2009; Neupert 2011).

4. The Italian version of *The Fly* is entitled *The Domestic Fly* (*La mosca domestica*) and is preserved in the Luce Institute Archive.

5. The attribution of these two films is debated as there are scholars who suggest that they were created by O'Galop (e.g., see Neupert 2011). However, as Lefevbre (2009, 175–6) shows, they were most likely made precisely by Lortac.

6. Speech balloons are used to return the declarations of the character.

7. Unlike shown, McCay availed himself just of two and not of five collaborators, none of whom is among the people portrayed in this live-action sequence.

8. See also "Crystal Theatre" 1918, 3. Analogously the *Twin Falls Weekly News* writes that *The Sinking of the Lusitania* is "in every way . . . as authentic as possible" ("The Orpheum Theatre" 1918, 5).

9. On magazine *The Bioscope*, *The Einstein Theory of Relativity* is presented as a film "arranged by . . . Max Fleischer" ("The Einstein Theory of Relativity" 1924, 56). Similarly, the poster of *Evolution* preserved at the British Film Institute introduces this work as a film "edited by Max Fleischer." Finally, it must be noted that Ditmars' *Evolution* is itself mostly a compilation film created by assembling preexisting materials taken from Charles Urban's film library (see Gaycken 2014b, 110), and it also showcases some rudimental animation (see McKernan 2013, 192).

10. Like the live-action sequences, this animation also is mostly recycled from preexisting works. For instance, when Fleischer explains that there has been a time wherein Earth was inhabited by dinosaurs, shots from *The Ghost of Slumber Mountain* (1918, dir. Willis O'Brien) are used.

11. *Finding His Voice* had, however, also a wide theatrical distribution. To attest it is Arthur Edwin Krows in an article on the genesis of this film written

for *Educational Screen* over ten years after its release: "When completed, it became one of the most popular short subjects of the time, and was screened in virtually every important theatre in the country" (Krows 1944, 70).

12 More precisely, some of the animated shots are completely in animation, while in others the animation is layered on still photographs of the engine parts.

5

The Classical Age, 1940–85

Soon after the Second World War broke out, the animated documentary entered its classical age, a period destined to last up to 1985, during which, across the world, a consistent number of titles characterized by a well-defined set of traits ascribable to this form were systematically produced. More precisely, during the forty-five years in question, a large portion of the global animated documentary production of the period was created by three countries: the United States, Great Britain, and Canada. In particular, the United States was the top animated documentary-producing nation during this era of the form, a fact that does not surprise considering that, in the time frame under consideration, this nation's animation industry was the strongest and its production in general dominated worldwide (see Furniss 2017, 164). In second place we find Great Britain, wherein, during this period, the creation of such works was so pervasive that John Southall (1999, 85) wrote that "the British cartoon production through to the 1980s" has been characterized by a style "based . . . upon the short factual film." John Halas and Joy Batchelor involuntarily provide us with an explanation for Great Britain's large animated documentary production when in a 1948 article they underline: "In England . . . we . . . have sponsored films, probably to a greater extent than in any other country and it is this factor which determined the form of the English cartoon and which specifies the content and approach of the script" (Halas and Batchelor 1948). Indeed, classical animated documentaries are mainly sponsored films—that is, films "financed and/or produced by companies, associations or institutions, often for purpose of advertising or education" (Masson 2012, 127). Consequently, the presence of a vast client network for animation in general, and this typology of titles in particular, favored the thriving of the form in the country. Canada, instead, ranked third, a placement that, as we will see in Chapter 8, was largely due to the presence in the country of a body as the NFB and to the extremely advantageous conditions in which the animators that gravitated around it could work.

The fact that we can identify in these three nations the main animated documentary producers does not mean, however, that they are the only countries in which this type of works saw the light during the form's classical era. On the contrary, from Australia to India to European nations such as France, Italy, Germany, Holland, or Czechoslovakia, most nations throughout the globe have to their credit at least a few animated documentaries in these forty-five years. Also, interestingly, the breadth of the corpora of animated documentaries that came to light in all these countries is not necessarily directly proportional to how developed and established their animation industry was. We will see it in Chapter 9 in relationship to Italy, where many such works were produced throughout the time frame in question, even if an embryonic national animation industry started taking shape only in the late 1950s. Another example is offered by India. Here, a continuous animation film production commenced only in the 1940s. What is more, for long, basically, the sole animated works that saw the light were those created within a governmental organization, namely the Films Division of India (see Bendazzi 2016b, 387–8; Furniss 2017, 416). Nevertheless, a good percentage of the titles produced in the country between the 1940s and 1985 were animated documentaries. Indeed, *The War that Never Ends* (1949, dir. Myna Johnson), *Metric System (Weights and Measures)* (1958, dir. G. H. Saraiya), *A Great Problem* (1960, dir. Govind Saraiya and G. H. Saraiya), *Healthy and Happy (Swasthya Aur Sananda*, 1962, dir. Pramod Pati), *A Fable Retold* (1965, dir. Pramod Pati), and *The Thinker?* (1981, dir. A. R. Sen)—which elucidate respectively methods of fighting disease, working principles and advantages of the metric system, family planning, rural sanitation, the benefits of the Cumulative Time Deposit Scheme, and environmental pollution—are only a few examples of the Indian animated documentary production during the classical age.

If, as the cases of Italy and India make apparent, rich corpora of animated documentaries saw the light even in nations with un- or underdeveloped animation industries, it is most likely because, as anticipated, the animated documentaries produced between 1940 and 1985 were created mainly on commission and, therefore, the amount of titles falling in this form that were made in each nation depended more on the presence of a clientele network (be it public, private, or mixed) and on its width than on how strong the animation industry of that set country was.

The Main Characteristics of the Era

Whatever the nation that produced them, the animated documentaries that were created during the forty-five years in question were, predominantly, sponsored expository films "for adult education" (Disney 1955, 72) that strived to offer accurate but entertaining depictions of an aspect of the real. In other words, classical animated documentaries were for the most part works produced on commission of a public or private body. Ministries, bureaus, councils, corporations, associations, and foundations are only some of the typologies of bodies that, in the course of the forty-five years in question, requested the creation of this kind of animated films and subsidized their making. As a consequence, in the animated documentaries from this period, a propagandist or a promotional agenda frequently interlocks with the ever-present informational (or informational-instructional) one. Therefore, while we can find some classical animated documentaries that are traversed just by informative intents, we more often find works that are either informational-propagandist or informational-promotional, depending on who has sponsored them and with what objectives. In fact, if we consider education as "the imparting of information and ideas" in a way that enables "the recipient to make up his or her own mind on any given issue," while propaganda as "the communication of ideas designed to persuade people to think and behave in a desired way"—or better in a way that benefits "those doing the persuading, either directly or indirectly"—(Taylor [1990] 2003, 6), almost all the animated documentary production of the classical era was at least in part propaganda. Even those works that, apparently, have a purely educational agenda often were developed to persuade viewers to adopt in their everyday a specific behavior or way of thinking that somehow benefited these films' sponsors. This is, however, unsurprising, if we consider that animation makes it relatively easy for a propagandist agenda to be pursued, since it allows the creators of the film total control over the world onscreen and thus, among others, it lets them leave out any visual element in contradiction with the message they wish to convey (see Jack 2015, 501).

Moreover, even if often they have been used also in schools as supplementary aids to textbooks, classical animated documentaries were works aimed mainly at an adult audience. Indeed, as Walt Disney underlines in his seminal 1955 article on the form, "the documentary film cartoon" has been specially developed for "reaching adults often beyond other channels of timely information" (Disney 1955, 70). However, a peculiarity of these animated works is that of presenting their subject matters in layman terms so that any viewer, regardless of his or her level of literacy and education, can easily grasp what in them illustrated.

Additionally, while a wide range of aspects of our world is addressed by classical animated documentaries, first of all, the topics tackled tend to have in common the fact of being "everyday," at least for a certain group of people. That is, frequently, classical animated documentaries addressed issues that concerned the daily life of or were of close interest to a category of people, be it citizens at large or a narrower group of persons. For example, they may deal with everyday issues of factory workers (as is the case for safety-related animated documentaries as *Three Blind Mice* [1945, dir. George Dunning], *How to Have an Accident at Work* [1959, dir. Charles

A. Nichols], or *Two Breaths to . . .* [1982, dir. George Gordon]), soldiers (as the training films *Camouflage* or the series "A Few Quick Facts" [1943–5]), or employees of a company (e.g., *Communication in the Workplace* [*La communication dans l'enterprise* 1972, dir. Jacques Rouxel]). Second, not only, as we will see, in certain moments of this era some subject matters have prevailed over others but also during the overall period, there have been domains more visited than others. In particular, the topics addressed in classical animated documentaries most frequently pertain to scientific fields like astronomy, biology, or public health. Moreover, among the films that fall into a same domain, some issues were touched upon repeatedly. Just as a matter of example, among the biology- and public health-related animated documentaries of the classical era, one can identify numerous titles dealing with sexuality—of which works like Walt Disney Studios' *The Story of Menstruation* (1946, dir. Jack Kinney) and *VD Attack Plan* (1973, dir. Les Clark) or *Baby Story* (1978, dir. Bruno Bozzetto) are examples.

Last but not least, in line with what we have seen to be proper of animated documentaries in general, this form's classical era titles also presented "solid facts in a very palatable package," as Dick Kleiner (1982, 30) puts it in writing about *Donald in Mathmagic Land*. In order to obtain films that, content-wise, are accurate in their depiction of the chosen topic, the makers of classical animated documentaries either personally conducted extensive research on the assigned subject matter or, more often, sought the advice of an expert on it. In some instances, both approaches could even be combined. A case in point is what occurred for *Horizons of Hope*. Indeed, regarding this film, we read on the pages of *Business Screen Magazine*: "Research by writers John Sutherland, Bill Scott and True Boardman, under the direction of Dr. Cornelius Rhoads and his staff of the Sloan-Kettering Institute, began almost a year before the film actually went into production" ("Sloan Foundation Tells Cancer" 1955, 122).

Generally speaking, when the advice of an expert was sought during the making of the film, his or her participation in the movie tended to be highlighted in the title sequence, so as to reinforce the "claim" that what narrated entertained "a direct relationship to the events" referenced, in a similar fashion to what docudramas do through their initial captions (Lipkin 1999, 370). More rarely, always to this end, the scientific consultant could even be made to appear onscreen, as it occurs for example in *Our Mr. Sun* or *Our Friend the Atom* (1957, dir. Hamilton Luske). Indeed, the experts who advised during the making of these two televisual animated documentaries—respectively Dr. Frank C. Baxter and Dr. Heinz Haber— also acted as these audiovisual works' voices-of-authority.

Always in line with what happens in docudramas, at the end of authenticating the film "as part-documentary" (Paget [1998] 2011, 105), selected classical animated documentaries contain also some documentary material. An example is the Czech short *How Man Learned to Fly* (*Jak se člověk naučil létat*, 1958, dir. Jiří Brdečka), an animated history of aviation in which some live-action archival materials, including shots of the Wright Brothers' first flight, are integrated. Another example is the military animated documentary on the development of airpower in the United States across the decades, *Air Power American* (1951), in whose animated visuals from time to time are incorporated (portions of) still photographs, reintroducing as such a partial indexical link with the historical facts illustrated. More generally speaking, as far as the sole visual component of classical animated documentaries is concerned, the most employed veridictive mark is, however, the medium's nonfiction language: the sober animation. This is probably because it plays a double role, since, at the same time, it helps also to clarify complex concepts (see Chapter 1).

If we take into account also sound, instead, the main marker of veridiction of classical animated documentaries is, without doubt, the ever-present voice-of-God or voice-of-authority commentary.[1] In fact, as mentioned, these works are expository. Therefore, similarly to what Bill Nichols shows to be the case for live-action expository documentaries, in these animated films the spoken word enjoys a position of dominance over the images. In other words, the latter "serve a supporting role. They illustrate, illuminate, evoke or act in counterpoint with what is said" (Nichols [2001] 2017, 122). More precisely, in the majority of cases, a voice-of-God commentary is employed. That is, it is opted for that kind of voiceover narration that is "presumed to come from someplace that remains unspecified but is associated with objectivity or omniscience," "seems literally above the fray," and supposedly "has the capacity to judge actions in the historical world without being caught up in them" (Nichols [2001] 2017, 123).

Alternatively, like it can be the case for live-action expository documentaries, a voice-of-authority commentary may be employed in place of the voice-of-God. In these cases, the narrator is, thus, no longer a disembodied voice. It is an animated character "we see as well as hear, who speaks on behalf of the film" (Nichols [2001] 2017, 42). Frequently, this character is a figure that spectators can associate straightaway to the idea of knowledge in general or on the subject addressed by the film, more specifically. For instance, in *Men of Merit (A Lantern Lecture)* (1948, dir. Peter Sachs), *Fresh Laid Plans*, or *Toot, Whistle, Plunk and Boom*, the voice-of-authority is a figure we tend to identify as the holder of knowledge par excellence, namely a professor. In *The New Spirit* and *Cold Comfort* (1944, dir. Joy Batchelor), this role is assigned to a radio, a medium that at the time was seen as a synonym of information, since it was often people's main source for news. In the German film *Great Synthesis* (1964, dir. Horst G. Koch), which was produced by Atelier H. Koch K. G. on commission of BP, an artificial intelligence, namely a computer-lecturer, acted as voice-of-authority. Similarly, in the Walt Disney Studios series *I'm No Fool...*, *The Nature of Things* (1956), and *You and Your...*, the voice-of-authority is an animated star as Jiminy Cricket, whom viewers have been accustomed to equating to wisdom since his popular role in the fiction feature *Pinocchio* (1940, dir. Hamilton Luske and Ben Sharpsteen). If these are all cases of films wherein a figure that evokes knowledge generically is employed as voice-of-authority, an example of a title wherein in this role we find a character that incarnates more specifically an expertise on the subject of the film is, instead, John Halas and Joy Batchelor's *Compost Heaps* (1943). Indeed, in this animated documentary on how to properly feed vegetables, the voice-of-authority is "a cartoon incarnation" of the then "popular gardening expert C. H. Middleton" (Price 2019, 150).

It is, however, quite common also for the voice-of-authority to be an entity whose supposed knowledge on the film's subject is derived not as much from study and research but from having a "direct" experience of that set aspect of the real. Indeed, the voice-of-authority may be, for instance, a chameleon in an animated documentary on camouflage (as it occurs in Frank Thomas' *Camouflage*), a waste bin in one on how to correctly recycle domestic waste (as in *Model Sorter* [1943, dir. John Halas and Joy Batchelor]), a scarecrow in one on agricultural matters (as in *Pay Attention to the Label* or *Speed the Plough*), and so on.

That said, in classical animated documentaries, the employment of the voice-of-authority is much less commonplace than that of the voice-of-God. Most likely, as suggested by Martin F. Norden (2011, 117) with regard to Walt Disney Studios' titles, this has been determined by a desire to contain production costs and times. Indeed, as he writes, "keeping the narrator off-screen" meant having "one less character that needed to be animated" (Norden 2011, 117).

Dramatizing Facts in the Classical Era: The Visual and Narrative Strategies

Toward the beginning of one of the most-renowned classical animated documentaries, Frank Capra's *Our Mr. Sun*, an anthropomorphic Sun affirms: "My story should be colorful, romantic, not just facts." This statement well synthesizes the general approach adopted in the construction of classical animated documentaries: offering, visually, imaginative dramatizations of the solid facts illustrated by the voice-of-God or voice-of-authority narrator. And even in so doing, similar patterns tend to be followed. Indeed, these films' settings are usually (more or less creative) animated reconstructions of real-life sites and spaces. Still, it can also happen for them to take place in completely imaginary locations, as it occurs in *Fresh Laid Plans* or *In a Nutshell* (1971, dir. Les Drew and Michael Mills), wherein the made-up village of Eggville and the fictitious country Bongolia provide the backdrop for showing, respectively, how the production and price system works and how CIDA helps developing countries.

Color, in line with what Maureen Furniss shows to occur in some animated films, is not necessarily employed in a realistic way. It is often used to create mood and atmosphere or even to convey a feeling (see Furniss [1998] 2007, 73–4). Additionally, it may be employed to undoubtedly connote a character as evil or good. As a matter of example let us take into consideration *The Traitor Within* (1946, dir. George Gordon). In this animated documentary on cancer, the fact that a cell is turning cancerous is rendered visually by having its skin become pitch black, so as to stress its acquired malignancy. Finally, color may be employed to enable the viewer to more readily distinguish the film's animated characters from one another, as it is for instance the case for the two industrial animated documentaries *Gasoline's Amazing Molecules* (1948a) and *Lubricating Oil's Amazing Molecules* (1949). In both these shorts, which discuss respectively gasoline's and lubricating oil's composition, production, and uses, the different anthropomorphic animated characters that represent the diverse molecules forming the two substances in question have each not only their own personality but also an individual color scheme—as explained on the pages of *The Hammond Times* in relationship to *Lubricating Oil's Amazing Molecules*, whose production, for this reason, ended up requiring fifty separate colors (see "Standard Oil Movie" 1949, 12).

As far as the actors starring in these films are concerned, titles wherein one or more animated stars appear onscreen may be identified. Nevertheless, this occurred only seldom and predominantly just in US productions (see Chapter 6). In the vast majority of cases the cast of a classical animated documentary was, instead, composed of novice performers, that is, animated actors expressly created for the film. This is probably because more often than not, the characters brought on screen by such performers were animated embodiments of a category of beings rather than of a specific real-life person or entity. Indeed, as John Hubley and Zachary Schwartz (1946, 361, original emphasis) point out, when in animation, a "single image can represent the *general* idea. The part can be interpreted as a symbol of the *whole*." Indeed, in order to have the viewer activate a fabled reading, it is necessary to transform the diegetic space in a discursive space (see Chapter 1). Given this fact, the capability of the medium to generalize is highly exploited in classical animated documentaries, especially through abundant use of what Roger Odin (2004, 91) refers to as the "generalizing synecdoche." This narrative device, which involves a "process of categorization" (Odin 2004, 91), consists in offering onscreen a figure that is to be interpreted as a representative of the larger category to which it is attributable. Within classical animated documentaries, this representational strategy is widely employed also when it comes to characters. Indeed, in the vast majority of cases, the characters that appear in these films act as stand-ins for a more or less large class of people, animals, or objects to which they can be traced back. In other words, they are not animated alter egos of specific beings or entities from our world that have effectively experienced first-hand the occurrences outlined. On the contrary, they are exemplary figures that embody an entire category of beings that have experienced or might experience events similar to the ones narrated in their everyday.

The generalizing synecdoche is not the sole narrative device widely employed to dramatize the real in classical animated documentaries. Among the most commonplace ones are also metamorphosis, anthropomorphism, condensation, symbolism, and the visual metaphor. Visual and situational gags are quite used too. Just to make an example, *Family Planning* (1967, dir. Les Clark) stars Donald Duck. However, this animated actor is not the protagonist of the film. He just plays the part of an onscreen assistant of the voice-of-God narrator—all that this famed character does is paint a few pictures illustrative of what the latter explains. In fact, in this film, Donald's only real role is clearly that of introducing what Disney himself has referred to as the "fun factor" (Disney 1955, 74). Put otherwise, here, his function is solely that of offering some brief moments of comedy with his clumsiness.

In classical animated documentaries more generally, the bearer of the fun factor is not necessarily a single character as in *Family Planning*, nor there is always a narrative framework dedicated to providing comic relief. In most titles, the gags are integrated into the main narrative and more than one of the film's characters ends up being the protagonist of these comedic moments. Examples are *The Romance of Transportation in Canada* and *History of the Cinema* (1956, dir. John Halas). In both films a visual or situational gag can be found almost in each of the periods in the historical evolution respectively of transportation and cinema presented.

All these representational strategies may be employed singularly or may be combined. Most importantly, within films addressing a same or related subject matter, we may even witness a standardization in the way they are used. In other words, at times, in dramatizing an identical or alike aspect of the real, the same devices may be adopted, combining them in a similar way. In fact, the chosen devices may even be declined in the same manner (e.g., a variant of the same symbol or visual metaphor may be employed to represent a set aspect of the real, a same non-human entity may be anthropomorphized in an analogous way, and so on). Emblematic is the case of medical-biological animated documentaries. In them, first of all, in line with what we have seen to occur during the early era of the animated documentary, "military-combat metaphors" are utilized in representing diseases (Ostherr 2013, 92). That is, the action of our body to contrast an illness is dramatized as a fight between two opposing formations: an evil one constituted of the microorganisms of the disease in question and a good one composed of our body's elements in charge of defeating that set illness. Second, the inside of our body tends to be depicted as a series of interrelated factories. More precisely, our brain is usually portrayed as the headquarters of several plants with different functions (i.e., all the other different internal organs) connected among them and to their headquarters through some streets (i.e., our arteries, veins, and vessels). The smaller elements present in our body, such as cells, muscles, enzymes, and so on, are instead usually pictured as workers (e.g., see *Defense against Invasion, The Traitor Within, Hemo the Magnificent,* or Elio Gagliardo's *Magic Lab* [*Laboratorio magico*, 1962] and *Anatomy of Motion* [*Anatomia del moto*, 1962]). The specialization of such workers may differ depending on the role that the components or substances they represent fulfill in our body (e.g., see Figures 5.1 and 5.2). Nonetheless, such specialisms are usually attributed following the same aim of making visually clear in an imaginative way the function absolved within our body by the substances or components that these figures symbolize. In sum, in medical-biological animated documentaries, not only a same metaphorical visual language tends to be used to portray such elements but also the latter are similarly anthropomorphized.

Furthermore, generally speaking, if we look at the animated documentary production from the classical era, we can isolate also some dominant approaches in illustrating the real that have a keystone in one of the form's abovementioned commonplace fictional narrative devices. In particular, it is possible to identify two recurrent ways of structuring these films which we can refer to as the everyman's exemplar story and the animated history. At the core of the former—which recoups, exacerbates, and rethinks a practice that, as Bill Nichols ([2001] 2017, 44) shows, was not uncommon in early live-action documentaries and consists in "using individuals as examples or illustrations. . . . using shots of specific persons as instances of larger

FIGURE 5.1 *In* The Traitor Within, *the cells forming our body are represented as assembly line workers in coveralls.*

FIGURE 5.2 *In* Magic Lab, *pepsin is portrayed as a worker involved in maneuvering a crane.*

concerns"—we can find the generalizing synecdoche. In fact, classical animated documentaries, in general, tend to be character-oriented, and often their protagonist is a human being that, by generalizing synecdoche, stands in for a (more or less) large group of people. The manifesto of this approach can be identified in a scene of *Family Planning*. Toward the beginning of the film, we see Donald Duck paint six men with distinguished racial features, while the narrator explains: "Throughout the world of course there are all sorts of men. They look different in different places and have different ways of life but basically all men are the same." Then, the voiceover states: "So, to make things easier let's put them together into one and let this one stand for all. He is a common man just like you and me." At these words, the different gentlemen painted by Donald magically merge into a single male character,[2] who, from that moment onward, acts as the embodiment of the family man category. In this way, the generalizing discursive process key to inducing the spectator to put in place a fabled reading is implemented, while at the same time offering to the film's main target audience (i.e., adult married men) a figure with which they can fully identify and whose emblematic vicissitudes can induce them to embrace a precise behavior in their everyday life, namely control the number of children they have and space their births. Indeed, generally speaking, the exemplar story approach foresees illustrating an aspect of our world by showing how a certain behavior, law, facility, or utility affects (or may affect) the life of an everyman (or more rarely an everywoman) who, by generalizing synecdoche, represents a (more or less consistent) group of people on whose ordinary life that behavior, law, facility, or utility has an impact. More precisely, these films entirely revolve around the figure of this everyman or everywoman to whom the voice-of-God or voice-of-authority narrator imparts a lecture on a precise fragment of the real, often by entering directly into dialog with him or her. As Adam Abraham (2012, 64) notes concerning the protagonist of UPA's *Brotherhood of Man*, this everyman character acts "as a stand-in for the audience and a receptacle for the lesson at hand." In other words, this figure, who is generally a male and may or may not have a forename, incarnates the attitudes of the film's target audience so that, through convincing the character of the validity of the voice-of-God or voice-of-authority's thesis, the film's intended spectators are also supposedly persuaded. For this to occur, however, full identification of the target audience with this character needs to be favored. Consequently, his racial features, clothing, and profession (when one is indicated) are developed so as to reflect those of the film's intended viewership. For example, *Brotherhood of Man* is targeted at the average Caucasian US citizen and its protagonist is a white male in pants and shirt. In *A Great Problem*, which was made for an Indian audience, the everyman around whom the film revolves is an ordinary, shirtless Indian man with white dhoti trousers and a turban on his head (see Figure 5.3).

Like the generalizing synecdoche is at the core of the everyman's-exemplar-story structure, condensation is central in the many animated documentaries that, adopting a historical perspective on the subject matter illustrated, are structured as an animated history of the object, art, field of study, or aspect of the real addressed. In fact, as in any animated documentary, these films employ "condensation in its most basic sense of distilling a large body of knowledge into a simplified, easily apprehended form," of rendering large amounts of intellectual material "in a visual language developed for maximum communicative efficiency" (Bashara 2019, 132). However, next to "an economy of representational ideas compressed within one image"

FIGURE 5.3 *The everyman protagonist of* A Great Problem.

(Wells 1998, 50), to characterize animated histories is also a condensation of time, since the intellectual material distilled is a series of events that occurred over a (more or less) ample length of time. More precisely, these animated documentaries, which retrace past events often with a progressive perspective (i.e., with the precise scope of celebrating the present and its advancements that have improved the quality of human life), tend to structure themselves as one long "episodic sequence" (Metz 1974, 130). In other words, similarly to what Christian Metz argues to be the case for this type of sequence, these animated histories tend to "string together a number of very brief scenes, which are usually separated from each other by optical devices" (Metz 1974, 130), and work as symbolic summaries of a continuous temporal course or evolution of events (see Metz 1974, 131). Each subsequent scene is marked by a leap-in-time of months, years, decades, or even centuries and dramatizes key occurrences in the historical development of the object, art, field of study, or element of the real addressed. Among the processes most heavily employed to visually condense time are the elliptical cut, "the fade out and fade in, the dissolve from one image to another, and the wipe, where one image appears to cover and replace another" (Wells 1998, 73). At times, even page-turning or metamorphosis can be employed always at the same end.

It is, however, important to note that the dominant presence of a narrative device does not exclude the use also of other ones. For example, condensation may be present in the everyman's-exemplar-story animated documentaries and the generalizing synecdoche in the animated-history ones. Moreover, one must also note that the everyman's exemplar story and the animated history are the most commonly employed approaches in structuring the narrative of a classical animated documentary but not the only ones. A less common but still fairly recurrent approach is, for instance, what we can refer to as the alternative scenario structure. In this case, two possible scenarios are presented one after the other: a negative or even catastrophic one that could be faced in case what the law, practice, behavior, element, or object on which the film focuses was not reality (or was not put in practice), and a positive or even idyllic one which corresponds (or will correspond) to our reality (once what illustrated by the voice-of-God or voice-of-authority narrator is implemented). This narrative structure is used mainly to consubstantiate clearly the importance for a certain behavior to be carried out or to show how fundamental a set practice, law, or element of the real has become in our everyday. An example of a classical animated documentary structured as such is *Dollar Dance* (1943, dir. Norman McLaren), in which, first, the hellish economic situation the population would have to go through in case of inflation is shown and, then, the comparably heavenly one faced when price control is applied.[3] Another example is *River of Steel* (1951, dir. Peter Sachs), which discloses how much more miserable our life would be without steel and, subsequently, how the presence of this metal makes our ordinary life better.

Sounding Eccentrically Factual

If it is mainly through the visuals of an animated documentary that the facts in it recounted are made "colorful" and "romantic" as desired by the Sun of *Our Mr. Sun*, sound is not exempt from some "fictionalization," or better, from a taming of its veridictive charge. As anticipated in Chapter 2, the voices-of-God and voices-of-authority of classical animated documentaries distinguish themselves from those of live-action expository documentaries in their displaying (at least from time to time) some eccentricity. This result is achieved by having such voices fall short of one or more of their defining traits. Therefore, it can be obtained in a variety of different ways. In particular, as far as the voice-of-God is concerned, the most common method consists in having the narrator address a character, instead of bypassing it and talking directly to the spectator, as Doane (see 1980, 42) shows to be characteristic of a nonfiction film's voiceover commentary. Concretely, in this case, the moments of eccentricity can be imparted to the voice-of-God via having it say something to a protagonist of the film and having the latter react to what is being said as if he or she could hear the narrator. An example can be located approximately midway through *The Winged Scourge* when the voice-of-God prompts Dopey to give the oil treatment to some mosquito larva and the dwarf obeys. In many titles, however, there may even be moments wherein the voiceover narrator and an onscreen character dialog with each other. Clear examples of this way of bestowing eccentricity to the voice-of-God commentary are offered by two shorts on planned parenthood: the Indian *A Great Problem*, which was produced by the Films Division, and the US *Family Planning*, which the Walt Disney Studios made for The Population Council. The former opens with a scene in which we see several floating faces from which a male one is singled out. Meanwhile, we hear the voiceover state: "There are four hundred million people in India, but we want to talk to you." This character—who by generalizing synecdoche represents any Indian family man—makes a gesture as if to ask the voiceover if he is referring to him and the latter replies: "Yes, to you!" At this point, a long segment of the film during which, from time to time, the voice-of-God asks a series of questions to this family man that the character answers always through body language begins. However, at the narrator's query, "Don't you care for your family?," the character outraged replies verbally by saying: "You keep out of this. My family is my business." Similarly, in the second half of *Family Planning*, there is a long section during which the family man protagonist of the film not only comments on the statements of the voice-of-God but also asks him questions (also on behalf of his wife) in what thus acquires the contours of a full-fledged conversation between the narrator and characters.

A further variant of this approach for making eccentric the voiceover commentary consists in having the latter dialog with a figure that pertains to the diegesis but is present in the film only as a voice-off. An example is the British short *We've Come a Long Way* (1952, dir. Allan Crick and Bob Privett). Here, there is a voice that, like the voice-of-God, is never embodied in an onscreen character: the voice of a captain of oil tankers. We are just suggested that, unlike that of the narrator, this voice comes from the diegesis through a series of shots showing the interiors of the captain's house and belongings. However, throughout the short, similarly to what was noted for the family men of *A Great Problem* and *Family Planning*, also this voice-off of the captain repeatedly dialogs with the film's voice-of-God, asking questions and making suggestions.

If in all its variants this method of rendering the voiceover narration eccentric entails working against the idea of it being positioned "outside the spatial and temporal boundaries of the social world the film depicts" (Wolfe 1997, 149) as a documentary's voice-of-God should instead be, the second most common approach foresees acting contrary to another defining trait of this typology of commentary: its disembodiment (see Wolfe 1997, 149). Indeed, if the voice-of-God by definition is a voice "construed as fundamentally unrepresentable in human form," in order to confer it some eccentricity in many classical animated documentaries it may instead be loosely associated with the body of an onscreen character. This may be done in one of the following two ways:

1 via suggesting (even if just briefly) that to speak is a figure from within the diegesis; or
2 via having the voice-of-God narrator report sentences possibly pronounced, or even just thought, by an onscreen character.

In order to understand concretely what the former method consists in, let us consider *So Much for So Little*. In this short, there is a scene during which the voiceover, after illustrating all the diseases an infant can catch following his first year of life, addresses the protagonist of the film and says: "But don't worry, John. That's where your health officer—*that's me*—comes into the picture." While this last sentence is being pronounced, the character of the health officer appears onscreen. As such, the voice-of-God is clearly linked to this figure but without ever properly embodying it in him (e.g., the character never even moves his lips), and thus without making it become a voice-of-authority.

In the case of *So Much for So Little*, we can find only a couple of brief moments in which the voice-of-God narration is tied to the character of the local health officer. However, there are also titles wherein the commentary is left in this limbo between being a voiceover and a diegetic voice for a more consistent portion of the film's duration. It is the case of *T for Teacher* (1947, dir. Peter Sachs) or *Water, Friend or Enemy*. Throughout the second half of Sachs' short, which illustrates how to correctly prepare and serve tea, we see onscreen an animated professor. It is never explicitly said that the commentary is from this character and we never see him move his lips. However, from how it is combined to visuals representing the professor, the voice-of-God commentary is repeatedly led back to this character, leaving the viewer with the doubt that it may rather be a voice-of-authority. Similarly, in Wright's short, via having the narrator talk in the first person and associating at the outset of the film his words to shots of water, from the very beginning it is given the impression that to speak is the spirit of water—thus also somehow anthropomorphizing this vital liquid, even if just through the juxtaposition of sound and image. Indeed, for instance, the film opens with the image of a waterfall followed by a tracking shot through which the journey of its water is shown. Sound-wise, these images are accompanied by the following statements: "I am friend to every living creature. I am power, roaring, thundering, filling life, and mighty oceans. I am cloud and mist and river. I am dew that sparkles flowers." In so doing, the voiceover is thus yoked to water while at the same time remaining extradiegetic.

Examples of titles wherein the voice-of-God is, instead, made eccentric via having it return alleged declarations of an onscreen character are offered, among others, by the Indian short *Metric System* produced by the Films Division and the British *Down a Long Way. The Story of an Oil-Well* (1954, dir. Bob Privett), which has been made by Halas & Batchelor Cartoon Films on commission of BP. In the former film, we can find a sequence showing how the current measuring system in India is confusing. Here, as part of his commentary, the narrator reports a possible dialog between the owner of a shop and a customer. Indeed, for instance, sound-wise, the following words of the narrator accompany the shots of a suck that enters a green shop, asks for some rice, contests how it is measured, and then buys it:

> Like the people of the South for his everyday food, a suck wants rice. So, he goes to the green shop. The man at the shop sells rice by measure.
> "Oh no," says the shuck, "in Bengal we buy it by weight."
> "Take it or leave it," says the man at the shop. "This is the way we do it in the South."

As such the voice-of-God temporarily comes to be linked to the bodies of the characters, while remaining a voiceover.

Similarly, in *Down a Long Way*, after a first portion of the film where the voice-of-God narration is through and through a voiceover, there is a long scene during which the commentary is yoked to an onscreen character. More precisely, after stating that a geologist must deduce the existence of a reservoir of oil by what he sees on the surface, all of a sudden, the voice-of-God starts voicing the alleged thoughts of the character that onscreen represents this category of scientists. The narrator's statements shift from being in the third person to becoming in the first person, suggesting as such that they are the thoughts of the character that we see intent in assessing where the reservoir of oil may be. In this film, the voice-of-God commentary is further made eccentric by introducing in the second half of the film another voiceover narrator, whose voice is similarly linked to that of a character, and namely to the figure of the driller. As in the other cases analyzed, also the two voices of *Down a Long Way*, however, are connected to an onscreen body but never embodied in it, thus remaining midway between an actual voice-of-God and a diegetic voice.

Quite commonplace in making the voice-of-God eccentric are also other two approaches that entail playing with the relationship image-sound:

1. literally translate into visuals the metaphors that the narrator uses, as it occurs for example in *Defense against Invasion*, where, when the narrator compares the human body to a city with factories, it is exactly as such that the inside of our organism is visually represented; or
2. reduce significantly the presence of the commentary in favor of long moments wherein the animated visuals, accompanied just by extradiegetic music, are left to speak for themselves (e.g., see *As Old as the Hills, Animal, Vegetable and Mineral* [1957, dir. Louis Dahl], *The Energy Picture* [1959, dir. John Halas and Gerald Potterton], and *Of Stars and Men* [1964, dir. John Hubley]).

Further ways in which eccentricity may be conferred to the voiceover narrator entail, instead, depriving the tone of the commentator of its characteristic neutrality. Practically, this can be achieved via having the narrator:

1. speak in rhyming couplets (as it occurs in many British titles [see Chapter 7]);
2. adopt a lyrical tone (like it happens in various Italian titles [see Chapter 9]);
3. adopt a comedic or satirical tone (as, for example, in *The Romance of Transportation in Canada*, whose commentary "wryly delivered" by Guy Glover [Wright 2019, 47] is pervaded with "earnest drollery"[4]);
4. temporarily quiet down to let a song take up its role (as is the case of *Man on the Land*, wherein an original folksy ballad by Terry Gilkyson keeps replacing the voice-of-God in illustrating the evolution of agricultural practices, or in *Understanding Stress and Strains* [1968, dir. Hamilton S. Luske], *Steps Towards Maturity and Health* [1968, dir. Les Clark], *The Social Side of Health* [1969, dir. Les Clark] and *Physical Fitness and Good Health* [1969, dir. Less Clark], wherein there are one or more moments during which information on the

aspect of the real tackled is provided through songs specially created by Mel Leven);[5] or

5 momentarily lose its composure (as it happens, for instance, in *The Grain That Built a Hemisphere* when, at the appraisal on screen of a gigantic plant originated from the in-breading of two small shrubs, the voiceover narrator drops briefly his neutrality and states: "My, my, what a child!").

Finally, in a same classical animated documentary, often more than one of the strategies here described may be employed. Just as a matter of example, let us consider *T for Teacher* and *Energetically Yours* (1957, dir. David Hilberman). In the former not only, as seen, the commentary is left in a limbo between being extradiegetic and diegetic but also is in rhyming couplets, and there is a scene in the first part of the film wherein the narrator reports a sentence possibly pronounced by the onscreen character of the sloppy maid and, a little later, one allegedly proffered by the figure of the customer. Similarly, in the latter, which was commissioned by the Standard Oil Company and illustrates how man has harnessed energy sources across the decades, the voice-of-God is repeatedly characterized by a witty tone and visual literalization of the narrator's metaphorical words abound. For instance, when the voiceover says that man is the sole creature on earth that "moves mountains and rivers," we see the onscreen character representing mankind push away a mountain with a finger. Or, when the narrator says that, thanks to the many kinds of fuels at his disposal, man now has hundreds of invisible servants at his commands, such as phantom housemaids, icemen, cooks, dishwashers, laundresses, and electronic babysitters, onscreen we see all these ghosts in the act of helping a member of the family protagonist of the short. Moreover, there is also a case in which, as part of his commentary, he reports sentences allegedly pronounced by the onscreen characters. Indeed, when the discovery of fire is illustrated, at a certain moment, referring to the character representing mankind, the voiceover states: "What he is probably trying to say is: 'Guess what I did today, dear? I found something that will keep us warm, cook our food and allow us to see in the dark'."

Like voices-of-God, voices-of-authority also are made eccentric in classical animated documentaries. In order to obtain such result, some of the same approaches seen for the voice-of-God, such as having them talk in rhyming couplets (e.g., see *Men of Merit*) or start singing all of a sudden (as it occurs in the final sequence of *Pay Attention to the Label*), may be employed. However, the way in which they are most frequently conferred eccentricity is through the figure cast for this role. Even when it is opted for a figure that in the eyes of the viewer is undoubtedly synonymous with knowledge and expertise, such as a professor, this character is rarely an animated human being. It is more often a clearly fictional entity with at least some fantastic traits. Indeed, the voices-of-authority of classical animated documentaries are often talking, anthropomorphic animals or objects. Moreover, especially in Great Britain (see Chapter 7), in some classical animated documentaries, a figure that appears out of part may even be cast as voice-of-authority. In other words, a character that is unclear on what basis it should be speaking on behalf of the film about that set aspect of the real may be chosen—a case in point, the voice-of-authority of *The Case of the Metal Sheathed Elements* (1973, dir. Sid Mould) is Sherlock Holmes, but what makes this fictional figure an expert on the construction and use of metal sheathed elements? In a few cases, the characters employed may even more or less explicitly disclose that they are not actual experts on the film's topic (e.g., the men acting as voices-of-authority in *I'm Glad You Asked That Question* [1970, dir. Nancy Hanna, Keith Learner, and Vera Linnecar] and *Refining* [1983, dir. Denis Gilpin]).[6]

A Tripartite Era

As shown, it is possible to identify a series of traits that recur in the animated documentaries produced during the forty-five years of the form's classical era. However, during this period some changes also occurred, especially in terms of the aspects of the real more addressed and the aims with which this kind of animated works were created. In fact, the form's classical era can further be divided into three subphases:

1. an affirmation phase (1940–5);
2. a consolidation phase (1946–67); and
3. a phase of gradual transition toward the contemporary animated documentary approach (1968–85).

More precisely, during the affirmation phase, which has been short and coincided more or less with the years of the Second World War, precisely the ongoing global conflict determined the content, agenda, and target audience of classical animated documentaries, along the lines of what in the same period occurred for animated works in general. Indeed, retaining the lesson learned on the occasion of the Great War, during the Second World War, the medium of animation became "part of the arsenal that governments" drew upon in fighting the conflict, since it was recognized as "an effective means of imparting information and developing support for the war effort, as one element in a larger agenda of propaganda aimed at uniting citizens in their respective countries" (Furniss 2017, 160). In particular, as John Hubley and Zachary Schwartz (1946, 360) put it, "[b]ecause of wartime necessity, pigs and bunnies" collided "with nuts and bolts"—which is how educational shorts used to be called within the film industry—and many animated documentaries saw the light worldwide. In effect, the number of such works produced between 1940 and 1945 was so consistent that it determined the affirmation of the animated documentary as a recognized and recognizable audiovisual category, as proven by the fact that it was in these years that an expression for labeling them started circulating among film critics and industry members (see Chapter 3).

Entering into detail, during this affirmation phase, animated documentaries were mostly produced either by or on commission of a governmental body—be it a ministry, a state agency, or any other kind of governmental organization[7]—had mainly an informational-propagandist or, more often, an instructional-propagandist character, and tended to deal with war-related topics, or better, with issues whose understanding by the population a set government considered paramount for winning the war. In the vast majority of cases, this period's animated documentaries were targeted at the ordinary citizen and either tackled happenings that the population was facing due to the outbreak of the global conflict—such as, for instance, rationing (e.g., *Point Rationing of Foods* [1943, dir. Chuck Jones], *Providing Goods for You* [1944, dir. Philip Ragan] or *Cold Comfort*) or price control and inflation (e.g., *Dollar Dance* or *A Few Quick Facts: Inflation* [1944, dir. Osmond Evans])—or behaviors people were encouraged to embrace in their everyday life to support the war effort—like, for example, salvage (as in *Model Sorter*) or payment of taxes (as in *The New Spirit*). Therefore, usually, these animated documentaries provided citizens at least with some instructions on how to correctly implement a set conduct in their daily life or face a certain event. At the same time, however, this period's animated documentaries were often also traversed by instances of social propaganda, exploiting the fact that "animation can carry important messages in an accessible form which meets little resistance or suspicion in audiences" (Wells 1995, 62–3). Therefore, an instructional (or informational) and a propagandist agenda tend to cohabit in the titles of these five years.

During this first subphase, various public health-related animated documentaries, which instruct on proper hygienic practices and conducts to embrace for preventing the spread of a set disease (e.g., see *The Winged Scourge, One Pair of Nostrils* [1944, dir. Carl Giles], or *Insects as Carriers of Disease* [1945, dir. Bill Roberts] and the other "Health for the Americas" shorts) also were created. Indeed, as Kirsten Ostherr has pointed out, during and after the Second World War, "the medium of film attained a uniquely privileged status in promoting world health" (Ostherr 2018, 285). It was, thus, inevitable for health-concerned animated documentaries to also start being created sooner rather than later, given such form's vocation to instruct and educate the viewing public. Unlike the other animated documentaries produced in this period, the focus of this strand of titles was obviously not an aspect of the real directly connected with the coeval global conflict.

Nevertheless, in many cases, the concept of war is present, even if just at a representational level through the employment of military imagery and of the habitual war-related metaphors and similitudes which foresee comparing the eradication of a disease to a battle.

Once the Second World War ended, the animated documentary form was not abandoned or set aside, as it had instead happened after the First World War. It was simply reconverted to peacetime use. Indeed, in line with what Walt Disney hoped for and encouraged to do in his 1945 article for *The Public Opinion Quarterly*, after the global conflict came to a close, "[t]he generation that used the motion picture to help train its fighters and its workers" made of animation a "tool in the labor of enlightenment, civilization and peace" (Disney 1945, 125). And, for the classical animated documentary started a new subphase during which this form did not simply outlive the end of the Second World War. It thrived, coming even to reach an unprecedented boom between the late 1950s and early 1960s. Since, between 1946 and 1967, the number of titles definable as animated documentaries that was created worldwide either remained stable or faced a growth,[8] we can refer to this subperiod as the consolidation phase of the classical animated documentary.

Considering that, as we have seen, this form has long been largely dependent on sponsorship, its flourishing during this subphase of the classical era was probably determined, among others, by a broadening of the entities that commissioned such works. Indeed, similarly to what can be observed for the documentary film (see McLane [2005] 2012, 167, 176), in the decades in question, next to governmental bodies, who kept ordering animated documentaries, also private foundations, associations, and the industry became increasingly active in commissioning (or even internally producing) titles ascribable to this form. In fact, during this subphase, the industry in particular progressively became the principal sponsor of these animated works in many nations, coming to represent at the same time a vital force and a resource for the development of the form. Consequently, while instructional-propagandist animated documentaries continued seeing the light, the majority of the titles created were either informational-promotional or, at least apparently, just informational—since the companies who commissioned them often did so with a (hidden) advertising purpose. Titles that have been made with the latter aim are, for instance, the US *Good Wrinkles*, the British *Pan-tele-tron* (1957, dir. Digby Turpin), or the Italian *Fertilizers* (*I concimi*, 1960), as we will see more in detail respectively in Chapters 6, 7, and 9.

As far as the nature of these animations is concerned, another shift in trends also occurred during the twenty-one years of the classical era's consolidation subphase: it became more frequent for the animated documentaries produced to inform and enlighten viewers on aspects of the real which impacted more or less closely on their everyday than to impart them how-to instructions concerning a daily life issue, as it was instead predominantly the case for wartime classical animated documentaries. To put it as McLane, similarly to the documentary production that has seen the light between 1945 and 1952, the animated documentary of the consolidation subphase intends "to serve the community rather than to persuade or indoctrinate and to meet the need of audience for information about and understanding of certain subjects" (McLane [2005] 2012, 163)—or better it apparently intends to do so since, like anticipated, some underlying propaganda can often be identified even in this period's titles. In particular, now, works that trace the evolution of an aspect of the real across the decades (as is, among others, the case of the Dutch *The Story of Light* and *Light and Mankind*, the Czech *How Man Learned to Fly*, the British *Speed the Plough* and *History of the Cinema*, or the Canadian *Family Tree* [1950, dir. George Dunning and Evelyn Lambart] and *The Romance of Transportation in Canada*) abound. This is, however, not to say that animated documentaries offering how-to instructions disappear completely. They keep being made, but in a lesser number. In fact, the presence of practical indications is still quite commonplace, especially in the titles dealing with hygiene, health, or safety issues. For instance, the British short *Modern Guide to Health* (1946, dir. John Halas and Joy Batchelor) instructs viewers on a series of health-related topics, ranging from how to correctly sunbathe to the right posture to keep when at work. Similarly, the US films *How to Have an Accident in the Home* (1956, dir. Charles Nichols) and *How to Have an Accident at Work* indicate to their spectators what precautions to adopt in order to avert home-related and workplace-related accidents respectively. The Indian short *Healthy and Happy* gives, instead, to its target audience (i.e., the inhabitants of India's rural areas) some rules of hygiene and sanitation to observe for eradicating sickness and disease.

During the consolidation period of animated documentary's classical era, many of the titles created were conceived with a general audience in mind, as in the previous subphase. Nevertheless, numerous works aimed primarily at more specific groups of people were also produced. For instance, one can find titles targeted to the employees of a set company (as the British films *Enterprise* [1951, dir. Peter Sachs] and *Balance 1950* [1951, dir. Peter Sachs], whose primary intended audience was ICI employees, or *Sales Promotion. The Key to Efficiency* [1953, dir. Bob Privett and Digby Turpin], which has been created mainly for showing to BP's staff, and in particular to its salesmen), a category of potential consumers (e.g., the Italian titles *Pay Attention to the Label* or *The Soil Is Hungry* [*La terra ha fame*, 1961, dir. Giovanni Cecchinato], which are mainly targeted at farmers), or of workers (as *Three Blind Mice*, which is intended principally for factory workers).

As far as the subject matters tackled are concerned, during these twenty-one years, science-related topics tend to prevail. This is unsurprising considering that animation proves a medium particularly apt for illustrating scientific concepts as it allows to visualize metaphors and analogies, which "are universal tools for explanation" that enable to attach "concrete, everyday meanings to theoretical ideas or scientific assumptions" (van Dijck 2006, 8). More precisely, from paleontology to mathematics, from geology and geography to physics, the range of scientific fields touched upon by this period's animated documentaries is quite ample. However, there are three areas in which the greatest number of this subperiod's scientific animated documentaries falls: astronomy, biology, and public health. After hard science, the other domains to which the titles from this subperiod of the classical era pertain more often are economics, safety, and technology and progress. More specifically, as far as the latter category of works is concerned, technological advancements in a variety of fields that range from agriculture to transportation are illustrated, usually retracing the historical evolutions that have brought to the current technology. Therefore, while, generally speaking, during the consolidation subphase, the recurrent subject matters differed from those of the affirmation subphase, like the ones of the latter period, the topics tackled remained strongly connected with the current social and political events. Indeed, first, numerous titles that directly addressed issues specific to the postwar times—such as new social reforms and practices or economic matters relevant to the period in question—saw the light. Just as a matter of example, between the late 1940s and early 1950s animated documentaries on concepts key to the Marshall Plan like Jacques Asséo's *Story of a Rescue* (*Histoire d'un sauvetage*, 1949) and *Productivity* (*Productivité*, 1951), which explain respectively how this plan works and what the principles of productivity are, or Peter Sachs' *Without Fear* (1951), which illustrates the importance of breaking down borders within Europe, were made. Second, even the many other films that tackle apparently "timeless" topics—such as mathematics, agriculture, astronomy, and so on—are pervaded by and return that general optimism in science and technology characteristic of the years of the economic boom and the space race during which they were created.

In 1968, the classical animated documentary entered its third and final subphase, which can be envisioned as a transitional period toward the form's post-1985 personal and experiential turn. Indeed, during this third subphase, expository works in keeping with those proper of the two previous subperiods of the classical era remained dominant. In particular, be they created for the big or the small screen, the animated documentaries that most frequently saw the light in these last seventeen years of the form's classical era were scientific informational and safety-related instructional titles. Examples of the former are the various astronomy-related films that Sidney Goldsmith created at the NFB (e.g., *Satellites of the Sun* [1974], *Starlife* [1983], or *Comet*), or *Homo Technologicus* (1981) and the other series of shorts that Bruno Bozzetto made for the Italian television RAI. To this genre of the animated documentary pertain, for instance, also Jacques Rouxel's *Atoms and Electricity* (*Des atomes et l'électricité*, 1975), *Journey through Electricity* (*Voyage en électricité*, 1981–3), and *Blood* (*C'était le sang*, 1982). The first two are series created on commission of the EDF company that, in each episode, explain respectively an aspect of nuclear power and a different notion of electricity physics, using animated actors

FIGURE 5.4 *A red blood cell as personified in* Blood.

that visually dramatize what a voice-of-God narrator illustrates. The third one instead is a short made for ECPA, wherein, not dissimilarly from Disney's *Defense against Invasion*, futuristic personified figures embody the various components of blood of which the voice-of-God narrator explains the functions (e.g., see Figure 5.4).

Safety-related instructional animated documentaries from this period are, instead, for instance, Pierre L'Amare's *11 Steps to Survival* (1973) on the measures to take in case of a nuclear attack, Gordon's *Two Breaths to . . .* on how to prevent from falling victim of a fatal accident on the workplace due to oxygen deficiency, or David Eady's *Play Safe* (1978) and *Safe as Houses* (1983), which instruct children on how to avoid electricity-related accidents when playing outside and when in the house respectively.

Furthermore, in these last seventeen years of the classical era, titles pertaining to the genre resulting from the crossover of the scientific and the safety-related animated documentary that can be referred to as the health animated documentary were still produced. It is, for instance, the case of the so-called *Upjohn's Triangle of Health* series. The latter is formed by four shorts made at the Walt Disney Studios between 1968 and 1969 on commission of the Upjohn Pharmacy Company: *Understanding Stress and Strains* on the consequences that prolonged stress can have on our body; *Steps Towards Maturity and Health* on how a man should pay attention to cultivate at the same time his physical, mental, and social health because they are all equally important for his well-being; *The Social Side of Health* on how a man needs to socialize in order to conduct a fully healthy life but has to pay attention with whom he does so; *Physical Fitness and Good Health* on the importance of staying active and exercising our bodies. In 1979, *Understanding Alcohol. Use and Abuse* (1979, dir. John Ewing and Sam Harvey), an add-on to this series on the perils of alcohol abuse, was also produced.

Moreover, the animated histories also keep being quite common during this third subphase of the classical era. For example, from this period is Albert Barillé's successful TV series *Once Upon a Time . . . Man* (*Il était une fois . . . l'Homme*, 1978) that retraces the history of mankind from the early Stone Age up to the present day—offering even some speculations on the future in its final episode, "Once Upon a Time . . . the Earth and Tomorrow?". This French series, which counts twenty-six episodes of about twenty-six minutes each and offers a rigorous but entertaining treatise of the historical periods tackled, has the peculiarity of focusing on the everyday of history, on what characterized the life of the ordinary people in each period addressed. To this end, its protagonists are a number of stereotypical characters that in each episode interpret a same role but adapted to the historical moment the action is set in. As Barillé himself has explained, Maestro, Peter, Jumbo, Pierrette, The Pest, The Dwarf, and the other protagonist of *Once Upon a Time . . . Man* "do not have a precise nationality and can be white, yellow, red, or black according to where the action takes place. They are of all time. They are symbols" (Barillé in Elausti et al. 2016, 30).

Next to all these works fully aligned with the canons of the classical animated documentary, between 1968 and 1985, titles that, either in their entirety or just under some respects, anticipated the form's contemporary production also started, however, to gradually see the light. Indeed, we can identify precisely in 1968 the beginning of this third subphase of the animated documentary because in this year came into fruition *Why Man Creates*, a first successful example of these anticipatory titles. This Oscar-winning short is still a sponsored film. More precisely, it is an industrial animated documentary, since Kaiser Aluminum and Chemical Corporation produced it.[9] Nevertheless, in many respects, *Why Man Creates* is closer to nowadays subjective and experiential animated documentaries than to those of its own time. It anticipates contemporary titles, first of all, in that it focuses on an inner process and tries to make it understandable to everybody. Secondly, it offers a depiction of the sensations behind the creative process rather than illustrating its working principles. Referring to *Why Man Creates*, Bass has declared: "My intent was not to attempt to explain the creative process in physiological or psychological terms, but rather to express to the audience how it feels and what it looks like to work creatively and in committed way. It's an emotional film, not an explaining type of film" (Bass in Rosser 1977, 239). Indeed, this short is not an expository work that imparts a lesson to the viewer. On the contrary, as Jan-Christopher Horak (2014, 2) puts it, it is a "free-form essay, a hodgepodge of film notes that asks many more questions than it answers." Always Horak notes:

> *Why Man Creates* eschews the "voice of God" narration of many other documentary films of the period, which presuppose a passive audience; instead, Bass attempts to engage viewers in an active process of questioning

and exploration. Significantly, *Why Man Creates* never directly answers the central question of its title, freeing each audience member to take away his or her own thoughts after seeing the film. (Horak 2014, 334)

Even the film's first segment, which adopts a historical approach to the subject matter, is far from being an illustration of how creativity has evolved across time. It is purely functional to conveying that "[o]ne idea builds upon all the ideas before it, but adds something new of its own" (Bass in Coynik 1972, 208). In fact, as Horak (2014, 336) points out, in this segment, "[r]ather than strictly chronologically, Bass groups events by the nature of the endeavor."

Saul Bass' film did not remain for long an isolated case. Perhaps on the push of its Oscar win in the Best Documentary Short Subject category, in the following years, in many nations, titles that foreshadowed the form's post-1985 turn by showcasing characteristics that were to become dominant traits of the contemporary animated documentary production started seeing the light. Still, not only the making of such films remained unsystematic but they also did not necessarily exhibit all the elements that became characteristic of the animated documentary after 1985 nor displayed them in a shared way. On the one hand, in these years titles that foreshadowed only timidly the post-1985 animated documentary appeared. In other words, films that overall maintained an expository character and anticipated just a few of the form's future dominant traits were made. Examples are the Australian short *Art* (1974, dir. Bruce Petty) or the US cinematic transposition of Erik Erikson's monograph *Childhood and Society*, *Everybody Rides the Carousel* (1975, dir. John and Faith Hubley). Both these films showcase an eccentric voice-of-God narration and visually offer an imaginative dramatization of what the narrator explains. However, *Art*, which depicts how art movements are connected to historical and social change, offers the point of view of its author on its subject matter. *Everybody Rides the Carousel* avoids adopting the purely didactic-informational approach to its subject matter that usually characterizes classical animated documentaries. Also, it makes visible a series of states of mind. More precisely, this animated feature pictures the different "psychosocial crises" an individual undergoes in each of the eight stages in which a man's life can be divided. In so doing, it returns at the same time "outer and inner realities" by having "inner images" react and counteract "with the 'real' events" of the characters' lives (Hubley 1975, 220). Indeed, as John Hubley himself explains, among others, *Everybody Rides the Carousel* was also born out of an urgency to find "less simplistic ways of showing an emotional conflict or nervous response" through animation than those offered, for instance, in some of "Disney's early Pluto the dog shorts" (Hubley 1975, 219). In other words, with this feature, the Hubleys meant also to unearth how animation can be employed "to describe with greater sensitivity the complexities of the inner self" (Hubley 1975, 220). As such, while not divesting the expository approach, they concurred in laying the foundations for the development of contemporary animated documentaries' use of animation for representing inner states.

On the other hand, it is possible to find films that completely abandoned the expository approach proper of the classical animated documentary, anticipating in full what would have gone on to become the form's dominant production after 1985. It is, for instance, the case of the Canadian *Interview* (1979, dir. Caroline Leaf and Veronica Soul) or the Australian *Ned Wethered* (1983, dir. Lee Withmore). As many post-1985 animated documentaries (see Chapter 10), both shorts are by female animators and are explicitly autobiographical, first-person narrations imbued with subjectivity. More precisely, mixing animation and live-action, in *Interview* Leaf and Soul reveal their dreams, fantasies, and frustrations. Referring to this film, Soul has declared: "We were trying to do a new form of documentary in which the technique would indicate the personality. Everything we did, any kind of altered motion, the colors of the person, whatever we showed on the screen would tell something about the person you'd never know if you followed them with a live-action camera" (Soul in Pilling 1992, 46). *Ned Wethered* is, instead, an animated memoir centered on the director's recollections of her childhood, and more precisely of an old family friend, Ned Wethered, who used to visit frequently her house when she was young. Also, this film is mostly in animation but ends with a live-action sequence wherein we see Withmore, first, holding a photograph of Wethered and, then, drawing him as if to stress that what the viewer has been recounted up to that moment was not invented but rather was an animated dramatization of real-life occurrences.

Titles from this transitional subphase of the classical era that can be considered in full forerunners of the transformations the animated documentary has undergone from 1986 onward are, however, for instance also the Japanese *Pikadon* (1978, dir. Renzō and Sayoko Kinoshita) or the Swedish *Holiday Home* (*Semesterhemmet*, 1981, dir. Birgitta Jansson) and the British TV series *Animated Conversations* (1978–81) and *Conversation Pieces* (1982–3). *Pikadon*—which, as it will become the case for many contemporary animated documentaries (see Chapter 10), was independently produced (see Pilling 1992, 33)—reenacts what the inhabitants of Hiroshima experienced on the morning the atomic bomb hit their city. In making this film, the directors conducted extensive research into the accounts of Hiroshima survivors so as to convey the events of the attack as accurately as possible (see Kornhaber 2020, 232). In particular, Renzō and Sayoko Kinoshita have used drawings and notes from the survivors as the basis for their film. *Holiday Home*, which in its opening credits is explicitly presented as an animated documentary,[10] offers a portrayal of the daily life in a summer camp for old, disabled people in Jutland using documentary sound recorded at the holiday house in question.[11] Similarly, in each installment of the BBC-produced *Animated Conversations*, a real-life dialog recorded in an ordinary day-to-day situation is animated. Indeed, among the films forming this series are, for instance, Peter Lord and David Sproxton's *Confessions of a Foyer Girl* (1978) and *Down and Out* (1979) and Bill Mather's *Hangovers* (1978), wherein eavesdropped conversations of two usherettes in a cinema foyer, a homeless pensioner with the staff of a Salvation Army shelter, and the patrons of a bar with a hungover female bartender, respectively, were animated. The same occurs also in the *Conversation Pieces* series commissioned to Aardman Animation by Channel 4 precisely after the success obtained by the two shorts this studio made for BBC's *Animated Conversations*. As Sibley (1998, 52) would put it, in the *Conversation Pieces* animations also "realistic human figures" act out "small, intimate dramas based on true-life situations." Unlike *Interview* and *Ned Wethered*, none of these films is thus autobiographical. However, they also abandon in full the expository approach proper of the classical era. As Charles DaCosta and Fatemeh Hosseini-Shakib (2006, 32–3) note specifically for Aardman Animations' shorts, these works all "avoid commentaries, offer no solutions, and make no suggestions." In addition, as far as *Pikadon* is concerned, the same use of testimonies from people who have experienced the events dramatized traceable in many post-1985 animated documentaries can be identified. Indeed, this short is based on testimonies from the survivors of the bombing. Only, instead of aural recollections of the event (as it has become commonplace after 1986), written ones were used. Similarly, *Holiday Home*, *Animated Conversations*, and *Conversation Pieces* exude subjectivity since, in offering a "look in on life as it is lived"—as Bill Nichols ([2001] 2017, 133) would say—they stem from conversations of specific individuals which inevitably return their very personal viewpoint on that aspect of the real. Indeed, like it is commonplace for present-day animated documentaries (see Chapter 10), these films are based on audio recordings of real-life conversations that are made eccentric by embodying them in animated characters.[12] The only difference between these shorts and the post-1985 animated documentaries is that, while the latter tend to use as their basis interviews, these earlier works employ recordings of (eavesdropped) real-life dialogs. Consequently, whereas nowadays interview-driven animated documentaries can be considered the result of a contamination of the form with instances of cinema vérité and its participatory mode of representation, works such as *Holiday Home*, *Animated Conversations*, and *Conversation Pieces* are closer to Direct Cinema and its observatory approach. Not casually, referring to *Conversation Pieces*, Brian Sibley (1998, 52) underlines: "With their overlapping dialogue, false starts and unfinished sentences, these films have all the hallmarks of fly-on-the-wall TV reportage."

In short, during this third subphase of the classical era, even when fully abandoning the expository approach, the animated documentaries that anticipate the subjective and experiential turn of the form do not do so following a unitary approach. The seventeen years spanning from 1968 and 1985 can, therefore, be seen as preparatory for the affirmation of the animated documentary as we know it today but nothing more than that since not only in this period the expository approach remained dominant but also a clear shared alternative mode of representation had not yet emerged.

To conclude, in general, the animated documentaries of the classical era were characterized by a common mode of production and representation with the result that, overall, the works created during these forty-five years form a unitary and distinguishable corpus of films. Still, like it is commonplace even for the most codified film genres (see Altman 1999), during the over four decades in question, the form did not remain static and unchanged. It kept evolving in response to the changes in clientele and the shifts in the social and political context that took place, with the result that, as seen, it is possible to further divide this era of the form into three subperiods.

Notes

1. In particular, the presence of a voiceover narration is an element that classical animated documentaries share not only with live-action documentaries but also with docudramas (see Paget [1998] 2011, 104).
2. This newly formed character has Indian traits, most likely because the film had the Indian public as its primary target audience. Indeed, in India, family planning was a much-felt issue at the time.
3. My use of the terms "hellish" and "heavenly" here is not casual as in dramatizing these two moments McLaren recurs to elements immediately associable to hell in the first case (e.g., red flames or the dollar sign that morphs into a devil) and to heaven in the second one (e.g., the dollar sign with a halo or the use of light-blue backgrounds).
4. Press-sheet of *The Romance of Transportation*, 1952, Pressbooks Collection, BFI Ruben Library.
5. The songs employed pertain to popular music genres that, at the time, were considered unsuitable for use in a nonfiction film. Indeed, as John Corner (see 2002, 362) points out, in the period in question, the conviction that, whenever non-diegetic music was employed in a live-action documentary, it had to be a piece of classical music was established.
6. For a discussion of the voices-of-authority of these two films, see Chapter 7.
7. If, as seen in Chapter 3, in defining which titles could be entered for an Academy Award in the Best Documentary Short Subject category at first, it was specified that "*cartoons produced by or for a Government*" (Academy of Motion Picture Arts and Sciences, "15th Awards: Rules for Nominations of Short and Feature Length Documentary Films for the 1942 Academy Awards of Merit," Academy Awards Reference collection, Margaret Herrick Library, my emphasis) could also compete, it is likely precisely because the vast majority of the animated documentaries initially produced during the form's classical age fitted such definition.

8. The peak growth reached by the animated documentary between the late 1950s and early 1960s is mirrored in the number of films pertaining to this form submitted for consideration for the Academy Award for Best Documentary Short Subject (see Chapter 3).
9. On the genesis of *Why Man Creates*, see Horak (2014, 328–30).
10. More precisely, in the title sequence of the film the viewer can read: "En animerad dokumentärfilm av Brigitta Jansson" (trans. "An animated documentary by Brigitta Jansson").
11. For a treatise of this film, see Ajanovich-Ajan (2019, 107).
12. Unlike what is commonplace for contemporary animated documentaries, in the case of *Holiday Home*, a close resemblance with the people to whom the voices we hear pertain was even sought, a fact that is stressed in the last sequence of the film itself. Here, it is switched from animation to live-action and we see, first, the hand of Jansson that picks up from the set one of the statuettes used in the film, and then, the disabled persons that these figurines impersonate look closely at their plasticine counterparts and comment upon them.

6

The United States

The US Animated Documentary Goes to War

In the United States, the classical era of the animated documentary started later than in other nations. Here, the first instances of the affirmation subphase can be identified in Paul Fannell's *Broken Treaties* and *How War Came*, two one-reel current events shorts in Dunningcolor produced by Cartoon Films Ltd. and released by Columbia respectively on August 1 and November 11, 1941 (see "Dunningcolor Puts Out New Picture" 1941, 14). These animated documentaries—which were supposed to be the first two installments of a six-part series entitled "This Changing World" but end up remaining the only titles in it—are full expressions of the first subperiod of the classical era in their being expository works that present the events leading up to the outbreak of the Second World War and the subsequent Nazi conquest of Poland. Also, both films open with brief live-action shots of their voice-of-authority, news commentator Raymond Gram Swing—who a year before had authored a book made up of his talks from March 1939 to the outbreak of war (see "Book Reviews. *How War Came*" 1940, 16)[1]—seated at a desk introducing the subject matter. Then, and for the rest of the shorts' duration, live-action is abandoned in favor of animation, and Swing is reduced to a voiceover narrator. And, in this, *Broken Treaties* and *How War Came* even anticipate what will become a recurrent approach in US classical animated documentaries, and in particular in televisual ones: the employment of live-action for showing the real-life expert chosen as voice-of-authority and of fabled animation to dramatize the occurrences he illustrates.

However, in Fannell's shorts—and especially in *How War Came*—there is still a consistent presence of sober animation in the form of animated maps which makes these films overall more transitional titles between the form's period of the origins and its classical era than full-fledged examples of the latter. Even better, *Broken Treaties* and *How War Came* can be seen as a "false start" of the affirmation subphase in the nation, as the first instances of a phase that never was, a fact that could explain also why these two films remained the sole installments of the "This Changing World" series. Indeed, these titles were developed in a moment in which both the US animation and documentary productions were still very much in continuity with those of the 1930s, because the country was yet to get involved in the Second World War and thus the widening global conflict had yet to impact profoundly on its filmic production as it was instead occurring in the nations that were already fighting (see respectively Mollet 2017, 61–106; McLane [2005] 2012, 137).

A change in the US film industry, in general, and the actual opening of the animated documentary's classical era, in particular, took place only after the nation entered into the global conflict—which is unsurprising considering that, like seen in Chapter 5, worldwide the affirmation subphase of the classical era has been strongly linked to the war contingencies. Following the Pearl Harbor attack, animation was quickly "mobilized for war" to "capitalize on the effectiveness of the medium ... as a channel for persuasion and for emphasizing the importance of patriotism and sacrifice in the wartime climate" (Mollet 2017, 107–8). Governmental agencies put under contract the main animation studios to produce films in support of the war effort and an animation unit was even created as part of the Army Air Force's own studio, FMPU. In no time, a consistent number of animated titles wherein warfare finds representation or that anyways tackle aspects of the ongoing conflict saw the light (see Shull and Wilt 2004). A good portion of these films are fictional works—be they designed purely for entertainment or to deliver a propaganda message—but many were also the nonfictional titles made. Of the latter, the vast majority employs predominantly or exclusively the sober animation for illustrating the chosen aspect of our world—like for instance Walt Disney Studios' training films *Four Methods of Flush Riveting*, *Fundamental Fixed Gunnery Approaches* (1943), or *Fog* (1943) and the other "aerology" titles (see Baxter 2014, 27)—and thus falls outside the animated documentary category. However, between 1942 and 1945, next to these sober animations, took shape also a small corpus of nonfiction titles wherein fabled animation was prevalently employed that can instead be considered animated documentaries.

The forebear of such works can be identified in a film that the Walt Disney Studios created for the US Treasury Department immediately after the nation entered the global conflict: *The New Spirit*. This short, which utilizes the everyman's-exemplar-story structure, made evident the effectiveness of the animated documentary form in informing and prompting viewers to implement set behaviors in their everyday. As reported on the pages of magazine *Look*, from a poll conducted among US citizens on whether or not the "picture had any effect on their willingness to pay" taxes, "37 percent replied that it had" ("Walt Disney, Teacher of Tomorrow" 1945, 23). This success of *The New Spirit* inevitably incentivized national governmental agencies to commission other such works (see Klein 1993, 186), thus determining a flourishing of the classical animated documentary.

More precisely, during wartime, in the United States, the Army and Navy, the Office of War Information, and the OCIAA were among the main sponsors of this type of animations. Also, animated documentaries were produced for two different audience groups: civilians and soldiers. The vast majority of those targeted at the former category of viewers were created at the Walt Disney Studios—which is not astonishing if we consider that "[b]y the end of 1942" this company is "the primary Hollywood contributor towards government training and film propaganda" (Mollet 2017, 107)—, are works of social propaganda, and, in particular, have either an informational-propagandist or an instructional-propagandist character.[2] Also, they tend to employ more often a voice-of-God narration than a voice-of-authority one. And, when the latter is used, the "This Changing World" series' approach is often favored over the one of *The New Spirit*, wherein an animated character (i.e., an animated radio) covers instead this role. Examples are *Defense against Invasion* and *Victory through Air Power*. In both titles, the voice-of-authority is a male figure (respectively a doctor and Major Alexander P. Seversky, the author of the nonfiction book of which the film is an adaptation) and live-action shots of him are alternated to animations wherein what he illustrates is imaginatively reenacted.

Moreover, from issues purely linked to warfare as the employment of aviation in combating the enemy (addressed in the partly animated feature *Victory through Air Power*) to others that concern more the home front life as the payment of taxes (*The New Spirit*) or the control conflict between reason and emotion (*Reason and Emotion* [1943, dir. Bill Roberts]), these civilian-targeted titles cover an ample range of subject matters. Nevertheless, it is also possible to identify two subject areas that have recurrently been touched upon. The first one is food and nutrition. Examples of titles tackling this topic are *The Grain that Built a Hemisphere*, Jones' *Point Rationing of Foods*, which illustrates the working principles of the point rationing system and the reasons behind the rationing of canned and processed foods, or the two US Department of Agriculture-sponsored shorts *Food Will Win the War* (1942, dir. Hamilton Luske) and *Something You Didn't Eat*. Indeed, Luske's film offers an account of the amount of food produced in US farmlands in 1942, while Algar's one explains (especially to housewives) how to use the basic seven groups of food essentials in order to have a well-rounded diet.

The second subject area repeatedly addressed in wartime, civilians-destined classical animated documentaries has been health and hygiene. For instance, during these years, the Walt Disney Studios produced for the OCIAA the already mentioned *The Winged Scourge*, *Defense Against Invasion*, and *Water, Friend or Enemy* as well as the "Health for the Americas" series. The latter is made up of several shorts especially conceived for Latin American audiences that deal with health-care issues such as tuberculosis (in *Tuberculosis* [1945, dir. Jim Algar]), personal cleanliness (in *Cleanliness Brings Health* [1945, dir. Jim Algar]), prenatal and infant care (in *Infant Care* [1945, dir. Jim Algar]), the hookworm (in *Hookworm* [1945, dir. Jim Algar]), and environmental sanitation (in *Environmental Sanitation* [1946, dir. Graham Heid, Earl Bench, and Ben Sharpsteen]). Health and hygiene have been the focus also of three animated documentaries produced as part of "Reading for the Americas," another series that the Walt Disney Studios created during the war years on commission of the OCIAA expressly for circulation in Latin America. This series was conceived for teaching reading to unschooled audiences through a combination of "*motivation* films, which would inspire illiterate adults with a desire to learn," and "*teaching* films, which would accomplish the actual work of teaching students" (Kaufman 2009, 156). Nevertheless, it ended up being a "combined health/literacy series" with its motivation titles, *The Human Body* (1945, dir. Bill Roberts), *The Unseen Enemy* (1945, dir. Bill Roberts), and *How Disease Travels* (1945, dir. Bill Roberts), being so similar to the "Health for the Americas" films that, as J. B. Kaufman suggests, they can be envisioned simply as "additional entries in that series" (Kaufman 2009, 162–4). Just as a matter of example, *The Unseen Enemy*, which focuses on disease and microbes, even stars Careless Charlie (Ramon in the Spanish version), the everyman figure who incarnates any humble man that is often protagonist of the "Health for the Americas" shorts (see Shale 1982, 56).

Whatever the topic in them addressed, another characteristic of the wartime, US classical animated documentaries conceived for civilians is a heavy usage of fabled animation. In fact, they may at times contain some sober animation. However, in most cases, they are characterized not only by that prevalent use of fabled animation necessary to qualify as animated documentaries but also by diffuse employment of the medium's devices more immediately associable to fiction. This is, however, unsurprising considering that the majority of these titles are from the Walt Disney Studios and, as we will see more in detail in the paragraph devoted to this company's classical animated documentary output, Walt Disney saw in entertainment a defining trait of the form. In particular, the generalizing synecdoche is abundantly present in these civilians-targeted wartime animated documentaries, a tendency that once again is aligned with these films being mainly from the Walt Disney Studios, whose Second World War propaganda output, in general, tends to have "a higher symbolic content," as Richard J. Leskosky (2011, 45) notes.

Finally, as far as narrative strategies are concerned, instead, there is not a dominant approach. The everyman's-exemplar-story structure adopted in *The New Spirit* can be found in various other civilians-destined titles but often only in embryonic form. For example, the first half of *The Winged Scourge* illustrates the negative effect that getting malaria would have on the life of a man that represents any American. However, this figure remains basically just an extra, never becoming the protagonist of the film. The main character of the film's first half is the malaria mosquito. In the short's second half, we have instead several everymen as protagonists. As Disney (in Lesjak 2014, 179) himself has pointed out, in order to show "how simple it is" to "get rid of mosquitoes" some fabled "ordinary citizens," namely the Dwarfs, are brought in. Yet, it is seven of them and not one that by generalizing synecdoche represents an entire category as we have seen to be peculiar of the everyman's-exemplar-story structure. Not dissimilarly, *Reason and Emotion* initially dramatizes the control conflict that occurs inside our brains between the two title processes by focusing on what occurs in the head of Junior, an every child who grows to become an everyman. More precisely, the film shows how inside his brain a personifications of emotion and one of reason battle for who has to take control. Nevertheless, not only soon the attention shifts to what occurs inside the head of an everywoman and, subsequently, of an every-German, but also the real protagonists of this first portion of the short are the two personifications of reason and emotion and not Junior. And, in the remainder of the film, the baton passes over to the characters representing the reason and the emotion of the average woman and the average German citizen.

The US classical animated documentaries of the affirmation phase made for soldiers, instead, are works that for the most part have been shown exclusively to troops—who represented a much larger audience than one may think if we consider that by 1945 the military "counted for 20 percent of the country's male *total* labor force" (Smoodin 1993, 77, original emphasis). Such films focused on teaching "important lessons" to soldiers, many of whom at the time had little to no literacy skills (Furniss 2017, 154).[3] Undeniably, these animations often were still conceived to induce their viewership to embrace a certain behavior or sentiment and a few even contained overt propagandistic references. For example, *Weapon of War* (1944) is traversed by explicit anti-German propaganda. Indeed, this short talks about racial and religious hatred comparing it to a bottle of poison that Germany has used to infect, first, its own citizens and, then, other populations from all over the globe. The short ends showing how Germany would have tried to spread such poison also in the United States with no success. In particular, the last sequence shows a vendor trying to fool a group of US citizens (including a few soldiers) into buying the toxic potion that metaphorically represents racial and religious hatred, but these figures resist the temptation of getting a bottle of it and blow a powerful raspberry that causes the salesperson to literally fly away.

A further example is *A Few Quick Facts: Japan* (1945). This short, which was screened as part of the *Army-Navy Screen Magazine*, is composed of three segments, each of which tackles a different topic concerning Japan. However, the issues related to this country are chosen in the service of anti-Japanese propaganda. For instance, the second segment of the short entitled "Sato-san" focuses on how at the time Japanese citizens were highly regimented and even thinking "unapproved thoughts" was considered a crime prosecuted by a special police enforcement, the Thought Police. In doing so, Japan is presented as a repressive and unliberal nation. Similarly, in the third segment, "Earthquake," it is narrated that, when on September 1, 1923, an earthquake devastated Japan, the United States promptly helped the nation by donating food, medicines, and clothes, therefore not even too subtly portraying the nation as an ungrateful backstabber.

In most US military classical animated documentaries created between 1942 and 1945, however, the propagandistic elements tend to be almost covert. As a consequence, such films give the impression of being shaped by a purely didactic or informational agenda. More precisely, some of these animated documentaries instruct on military techniques—often adopting the traditional teaching methodology of offering both negative and positive examples (or "good and bad exemplars") (Leskosky 2011, 59). It is the case of *Camouflage, Position Firing* (1944, dir. John Hubley and Chuck Jones), or *Elementary and Pylon Eights* (1944, dir. Gus Arriola), wherein basic techniques of camouflage, the right approach to position firing, and the correct procedures for executing some flight maneuvers like S-turns, elementary figure eights, and pylon figure eights are explained, respectively. In this group falls also the flight safety short *Dive Bombing Crashes* (1945), which illustrates how to avoid accidents when dive-bombing.

Other titles deter behaviors seen as unconstructive. Examples are *A Few Quick Facts: Inflation* and *The Enemy Bacteria* (1945). The former discourages overseas soldiers from purchasing too many goods in the stores of the foreign cities and villages they are stationed in so as to avoid generating an inflation that would reduce the spending power of the local population. The latter, which was created at Walter Lantz Productions, deters surgeons from not scrubbing thoroughly before operating by showing how staphylococcus and streptococcus bacteria can easily penetrate and proliferate in the body of a patient, causing an infection.

Still other titles simply inform troops on aspects of the real linked to their job or, more generally, to the ongoing conflict. It is, for instance, the case of *Voting for Servicemen Overseas* (1944), which explains to overseas soldiers how they can cast their vote in US elections and why it is important to do so, or *Another Chance* (1944), wherein how the then recently funded United Nations work is clarified. In this third subgroup also falls *A Few Quick Facts: About Fear* (1945, dir. Zack Schwartz), which illustrates what fear is and how it acts on the human body.

Finally, it is also possible to find a few titles which do more than one of the foregoing. This happens in particular in some of the shorts that form the "A Few Quick Facts" series. Indeed, while a number of the titles in the series, such as the already mentioned *A Few Quick Facts: Inflation* and *A Few Quick Facts: About Fear*, deal with a single subject, others have instead a fragmentary structure and are formed by three or four segments, in each of which is briefly tackled a different topic, pursuing at times a different objective. Let us consider, for instance, the second title in the series, which was included in the *Army-Navy Screen Magazine* n. 22. In this short some statistics concerning Air Transport Command planes and ships of the US Navy are sequentially presented, and basic information on Chinese soldiers is illustrated. The film then closes by explaining how 17 percent of fires that start in US posts are caused by soldiers smoking in bed, a practice that the short discourages. More precisely, similarly to what usually occurs in the Private Snafu series, this last segment teaches "by negative example" (Arnold 2017, 115), and specifically through showing a soldier smoking in bed that ends up starting a fire. Therefore, we have a more informative portion followed by one aimed at deterring a behavior considered unconstructive.

Next to an apparent dominance of the educational and informational side over the propaganda one, another element that distinguishes these military animated documentaries from those aimed at civilians is their being created by a more diverse group of studios. In fact, in this corpus of films, we can still find some titles that come out of the Walt Disney Studios such as *Camouflage*, *Another Chance*, and *Voting for Servicemen Overseas*. Yet, they constitute a minority.[4] Most of the animated documentaries intended for soldiers exclusively are by other animation studios. Just to make a few examples, *Elementary and Pylon Eights* and *Position Firing* are from FMPU's animation unit. *Weapon of War* was storyboarded at FMPU but produced at the MGM animation studio, while *Dive Bombing Crashes* was made at Warner Brothers. *A Few Quick Facts: Inflation* and *A Few Quick Facts: About Fear* are instead from the future UPA, Industrial Film and Poster Service. Precisely the "A Few Quick Facts" series represents the example par excellence of this involvement of a plurality of studios in the making of soldiers-aimed animated documentaries, since even the titles of which it is composed come from different production companies.

This involvement of a greater number of studios in the making of military animated documentaries has caused such corpus of films to be less unitary than the one destined to civilians in terms of animation style and approach to the subject matter. They can go from being highly fabled as *Camouflage* (wherein not only no sober animation is used but also the fun factor is insisted upon, for instance through the long initial sequence that sees the voice-of-God narrator prompt the chameleon who will subsequently become the film's voice-of-authority to camouflage to a series of different backgrounds, or the recurrent gag of a soldier rushing to the latrine in a straight line, undoing his colleagues' trace concealment work) to mildly fabled as *Elementary and Pylon Eights* (wherein not only there is a significant presence of sober animation but also the entertainment element is limited to a few gags involving Wilbur Wrong and a cow). In addition, in military animated documentaries we can find deployed as diverse narrative strategies as the variant of the alternative scenario used in *Elementary and Pylon Eights* (wherein each maneuver is shown performed first wrongfully by an inept aviator, Wilbur Wrong, and then correctly by the good Wilbur Wright), the hypothetical conflictual situations involving the two imaginary nations of Highland and Lowland utilized in *Another Chance* to illustrate how the United Nations work, or a military variation of the everyman's-exemplar-story structure as in *Position Firing*. Indeed, here, how to correctly position fire is taught by focusing on the difficulties of every-soldier Trigger Joe in transitioning from firing against enemy planes by instinct to doing it "scientifically." Moreover, the narration may be mildly fragmentary as in these latter two films, highly fragmentary as in the first titles in the "A Few Quick Facts" series, or unitary as in *Camouflage* or *A Few Quick Facts: Inflation*.

That said, a few recurrent traits can be identified. First of all, military animated documentaries tend to have among their protagonists one or more soldiers, or better every-soldiers, so as to provide their audience members with characters that represent them and in which they can identify. In particular, there are even titles as *A Few Quick Facts: Inflation*, *A Few Quick Facts: About Fear*, and (albeit just briefly) *Voting for Servicemen Overseas* that star the then famed Private Snafu. Indeed, this everyman, or better every-soldier, character created at Warner Brothers by Theodor Geisel, P. D. Eastman, and Chuck Jones was the protagonist of a namesake non-animated documentary series (and precisely, of twenty-six "modern military fables . . . leaving a practical moral as a denouement," as Christopher Dow [2003] puts it) that had brought him to get identified as the average soldier par excellence. Thus, occasionally, in the same years, he has been employed also in animated documentaries made by other studios (see Arnold 2017, 115).[5]

Second, with a few (partial) exceptions as *Elementary and Pylon Eights*, *Camouflage*, or *The Enemy Bacteria*, the voice-of-God narration tends to be favored over the voice-of-authority one. And when, as in *Elementary and Pylon Eights*, *Camouflage*, *Dive Bombing Crashes*, or *The Enemy Bacteria*, there is a voice-of-authority, either the latter is only sparsely shown leaving its declarations mostly disembodied, or a voice-of-God narrator is also present. For example, the narration we hear in *The Enemy Bacteria* can be considered a voice-of-authority as it is feigned that to narrate the consequences of not properly scrubbing is a bacterium. Yet, this voice is never clearly embodied into one of the many animated bacteria that we see. Therefore, it remains midway between a voice-of-God and a voice-of-authority. *Camouflage*, instead, starts with a voice-of-God narration which, however, after having introduced the topic and an expert of camouflage as the chameleon is, gives way to the latter. Therefore, the film shifts from having a voice-of-God narration to having a voice-of-authority one. Something similar happens in *Dive Bombing Crashes*. In the film's first part, a voice-of-God narrator guides the viewer through the animated reenactment of an actual 1944 fatal accident that occurred to a pilot as a result of forgetting to look at his altimeter during a steep dive.[6] In the second part, instead, to instruct on how to avoid such casualties from happening is a voice-of-authority, and namely an animated version of the character created in 1943 by cartoonist Robert Osborn and Commander Seth Warner for a column in the *Bureau of Aeronautics Newsletter*, old aviator Grampaw Pettibone.

Finally, although, as seen, these soldiers-destined animated documentaries can be characterized by different degrees of fabledness, they tend to steer clear from an unconscionable use of fabled animation and often recur to good chunks of sober animation or live-action. This has likely been mostly due to the fact that there was a need for such titles to be completed quickly. However, a part in this generous use of live-action or sober animation may have been played also by the existing debate on whether or not an amusing film educates less its viewer (see McGowan 2019, 105). Balancing the employment of the entertaining fabled animation with some more "serious" sober animation or live-action may have been perceived as a good compromise for avoiding any risk of endangering the soldiers' learning process while still informing them in a pleasurable way.

In Times of Peace: Elements of Continuity

The restoration of global peace did not determine an abrupt shift in the US classical animated documentary production. If this has been the case, it is, on the one hand, because in this nation the transition from a wartime to a peacetime animated documentary production started when the Second World War was still ongoing, with some of the late-wartime titles having been made already with a view to the future. That is, if the subject matter allowed it, references to the specificities of the wartime context were avoided, favoring instead a more timeless approach to the topic tackled in order to enable the resulting film to find equal application in postwar America. This eye-to-the-future attitude is, for example, what, according to Richard Shale (1982, 60), guided Walt Disney Studios' choice to end *Something You Didn't Eat* with the average family protagonist, the Jones, enjoying a dinner served on silver that is far from the frugal meals US citizens could have during wartime years with rationing in place. Indeed, since it was not linked to the specific social context of the war, *Something You Didn't Eat* could keep being used to educate the US population on proper nutrition also after the end of the conflict.

On the other hand, governmental agencies did not stop ordering animated documentaries once the war ended. Obviously, the subject matters tackled changed to reflect the new historical circumstances. Yet, both civilians-destined and soldiers-aimed titles kept being sponsored. Examples of the former are *Expanding World Relationships* (1946, dir. David Hilberman), the Oscar-winner *So Much for So Little*, *The Adventures of Junior Raindrop* (1948, dir. Carl S. Clancy), *Multiple Screening* (1950, dir. David Hilberman and William Tytla), and *You Can Be Safe from X-Rays* (1952). The animated history *Expanding World Relationships* was created by UPA for the US State Department and illustrates how, since 1789, thanks to the progress of science and technology, communications and transportation have become easier and faster and, consequently, relationships between people across the globe have expanded. The US Department of Agriculture's Forest Service commissioned the partly animated and partly live-action *The Adventures of Junior Raindrop*, which, following the journey of an anthropomorphic raindrop through a watershed, explains to what negative consequences poor watershed management can lead. *So Much for So Little* was made at Warner Brothers for the US Public Health Service "to stimulate interest . . . in local health services and to raise the question in the mind of the public: Do we have a good local health service?.."[7] The safety animated documentary aimed at personnel of photo fluorographic units *You Can Be Safe from X-Rays* was also created under the auspices of the US Public Health Service. To produce this film that, focusing on the exemplar figure of the animated X-ray technician Ike Isodope, illustrates how to properly handle X-ray equipment was, however, no longer Warner Brother but the Communicable Disease Center. Finally, *Multiple Screening*, which depicts the key role mass screenings have in detecting illnesses in their early stages, was created by the Communication Materials Center of the Columbia University Press in collaboration with Tempo Productions and its sponsor was a local governmental institution, namely the Pennsylvania Department of Health.

Among the government-sponsored civilians-targeted classical animated documentaries from the postwar years, *Story of a Rescue*, *Productivity*, and *Without Fear* deserve a mention. These titles sponsored by the short-lived, independent governmental agency US Economic Cooperation Administration distinguish themselves for having been ordered to European studios and not to American ones, despite the United States certainly not being in lack of animators qualified for the job. More precisely, the French studio Les Gémeaux produced both *Story of a Rescue* and *Productivity*, while *Without Fear* was created at Larkins Studio. This curious decision may have been taken, at least in part, because, since these films were expressly made for circulation in Europe, having European studios make them would have avoided incurring in the kind of culturally inappropriate representational choices that, for instance, the Walt Disney Studios made when creating animated documentaries for a Latin American audience during the war years.[8]

If thus the range of US governmental agencies that commissioned animated documentaries in the postwar years remained ample, the most active ones in this sponsorship activity were the defense departments. Indeed, while the end of the Second World War marked the termination of most military animated wartime stars' careers such as those of Snafu, Trigger Joe, and Mr. Hook Military (see Mc Gowan 2019, 106), it did not determine a halt in the creation of training and safety animated documentaries aimed at soldiers. In fact, the various US military departments kept commissioning such works. For instance, between 1946 and 1949 the Department of the Navy sponsored numerous flight safety shorts, the vast majority of which were animated documentaries. We can recall, among others, the already mentioned *Flat Hatting* and *Disorientation Crashes* (1946), which explain respectively the importance of going on instruments in situations of low visibility; *Landing Accidents* (1946), on why a pilot should never daydream when landing an aircraft; *Join-Up Collisions* (1946), on how to avoid join-up collisions; *Emergency Landing on Land* (1947), which illustrates the do's and don'ts of an emergency landing; or *Bailing Out* (1949), on the procedures to follow when bailing out from an airplane. These animated documentaries tend to be characterized by an attention to the psychological aspects of the situations addressed (e.g., the fear connected to parachuting oneself from a plain in *Bailing Out* or the psychological origins of flat hatting in *Flat Hatting*) and by nonlinear narratives wherein flashbacks, flashforwards, and mental sequences can often be found. Most importantly, with a few exceptions like *Flat Hatting*, which only dramatizes and condemns a negative behavior, these films tend to employ the traditional good-and-bad-examples teaching methodology, with the first part consisting normally in the staging of one or more avoidable accidents caused by a pilot's reproachable behavior in a set circumstance and the second amounting to the illustration of how an aviator should instead act in that situation. Although there are a few titles—like, for instance, *Join-Up Collisions*—in which the accidents presented involve each a different aviator, generally the story of a single pilot (e.g., Murphy in *Flat Hatting*, Morton in *Disorientation Crashes*, Fred Diddle in *Landing Accidents*, or Lt. McGarkle in *Bailing Out*) that represents any pilot is told, thus adopting (at least in the first part) the everyman's-exemplar-story approach. The explanation of how to correctly behave in the circumstances tackled by the film may also be presented through the every-pilot protagonist, as it happens in *Landing Accidents*, *Disorientation Crashes*, or *Bailing Out*. Indeed, in the first two titles, Fred Diddle and Morton become "voices-of-authority" and describe respectively to the guests of a dinner party how to properly land a plane and to fellow pilots how to act in situations of low visibility. Not dissimilarly, in *Bailing Out*, the explanations on how to correctly parachute oneself from a plane are provided by the voice-of-God narrator but are visually enacted by Lt. McGarkle. Alternatively, a different onscreen figure who acts as the film's voice-of-authority may instruct on the correct behaviors to keep in the situation tackled by the short. When the latter is the case, Grampaw Pettibone is usually employed to this end, therefore drawing some continuity between these postwar safety animated documentaries and wartime ones.

And, the US Army, Air Force, and Navy-sponsored military animated documentaries saw the light also beyond the 1940s. For instance, the Raphael G. Wolff Studios in 1951, Warner Brothers in 1955, and the D4 Film Studios

Inc. in 1964 made for the US Department of the Air Force respectively the propaganda-riddled animated history *Air Power American*, which in its second part explicitly promotes the US Air Force and its personnel (likely with a recruiting aim), the promotional *A Hitch in Time*, a Chuck Jones' short encouraging re-enlistment that employs a gremlin as voice-of-authority, and the training film *Refrigeration: Principles of Mechanical Refrigeration*, which, making use also of some sober animation, explains how mechanical refrigeration works. Similarly, in 1956 and 1957 at Warner Brothers, Chuck Jones directed for the US Army respectively *90 Day Wondering?* and *Drafty, Isn't It*, both of which are promotional animated documentaries aimed at recruiting soldiers. More precisely, following in the wake of what was already done with *A Hitch in Time*, these shorts, which star the animated everyman Ralph Phillips, incite respectively at reenlisting and at joining the army by exposing the advantages of so doing and dismounting existing false myths regarding military life through anthropomorphic conscience-like figures with telling names (i.e., Re-Pete in *90 Day Wondering?* and Wille N. List in *Drafty, Isn't It*).

On top of all the foregoing, even if now to sponsor such titles are predominantly foundations and the like and only seldom governmental bodies, the strand of health-related animated documentaries emerged in the war years persisted also during the form's consolidation phase and beyond. In fact, in the United States, animated documentaries "on matters of general public health" not only did not disappear after the end of the Second World War but also, similarly to what McLane notes with regards to live-action documentaries, became "more plentiful . . . than before" (McLane [2005] 2012, 175). From the menstrual cycle (*The Story of Menstruation*) to the advantages of publicly financed health centers (*So Much for So Little*) to mass screening approaches (*Multiple Screening*) the range of issues addressed is wide. However, be it cancer, tuberculosis, venereal infections, heart problems, stress-related disorders, or just the common cold, the majority of such films focuses on a specific disease or group of diseases. Most importantly, whatever their specific subject matter, like wartime ones, peacetime health-related animated documentaries were mostly aimed at non-medical audiences—even if titles conceived instead specifically for health-care workers were not completely absent, as proven for instance by a film like *You Can Be Safe from X-Rays*.

Moreover, like many of their wartime equivalents, most post-1945 classical health-related animated documentaries taught by bad and good example and adopted the everyman's-exemplar-story structure. Their lead characters, who voice the fears and concerns that the viewing public may have around the specific disease or health-related matter addressed, tend to be almost exclusively male figures. Just to make a few examples, the protagonist of *How to Catch a Cold* (1951, dir. Hamilton Luske), Walt Disney Studios' short on the common cold and how it can spread within a community, is an average family man that meaningfully goes by the name of Common Man. Similarly, in *One of Sixteen Million* (1968, dir. R. Drew) the audience learns about arthritis through the vicissitudes of middle-aged man George Brown, in *Rodney* (1950, dir. Lu Guarnier) about tuberculosis through the story of an average young man named Rodney, and in *Pump Trouble* about heart issues through Cordell Pump, a hypochondriac man in his forties. Female figures appear generally only in secondary roles, and mainly in those of wife or girlfriend of the protagonist or of nurse. An everywoman is chosen as protagonist only when a strictly feminine issue is presented, as it occurs for instance in Walt Disney Studios' *The Story of Menstruation*.

Finally, always like their wartime predecessors, peacetime health-related animated documentaries incite viewers to adopt set good practices in their daily lives. Only, now, the most encouraged custom is that of having regular physical checkups and seeking medical advice immediately when not feeling well. Indeed, as Cantor (2020, 183) notes in relation to the three cancer-focused shorts *Man Alive!*, *Sappy Homiens*, and *Inside Magoo*, such titles are often prevention-oriented and tend "to persuade men to seek early detection and treatment," be it for specific diseases or in general (e.g., see *Multiple Screening* or *So Much for So Little*'s second-last sequence). At the same time, however, such films tend to also dismantle common misconceptions and myths existing around their subject matters. For instance, *Inside Magoo*'s concluding sequence, which illustrates what a checkup for cancer consists of, aims at preventing misconceptions around such practice. Similarly, in *One of Sixteen Million* and *The Traitor Within*, there are scenes wherein myths concerning respectively gout and cancer are first presented and then undone.

To put it briefly, some continuity between the wartime US animated documentary production and a part of the post-1945 one can be detected and not just in the years that immediately follow the end of the global conflict.

The Newness of Peacetime Animated Documentary

The existence of elements of continuity between the pre- and post-1945 classical animated documentary production does not mean that, on the whole, no significant change occurs. In fact, transformations can be found at various levels, and first and foremost at those of the studios involved in producing such films, the type of organizations sponsoring them, their distribution, and the aspects of the real addressed. Indeed, first of all, while the Walt Disney Studios will continue to be an important protagonist of the animated documentary scene also long after the end of the Second World War, most of the other studios active in the creation of wartime animated documentaries ceased making such works, or even business operations altogether, as soon as peace was restored. Over the years of the classical era's consolidation subperiod, new companies, however, started producing animated documentaries, including UPA, John Sutherland Productions, Tempo Productions, Warner Brothers, Lee Blair and Bernie Rubin's Film Graphics Inc., and Faith and John Hubley's Storyboard Productions. In fact, in the course of the form's consolidation subphase, the first two companies even ended up jeopardizing Walt Disney Studios' position as the US leading animated documentary producer. Despite being best known for fictional works as the Gerald McBoing Boing series, UPA has devoted much energy to the making of nonfiction animations and has contributed a rich number of qualitative animated documentaries, which tend to be characterized by the adoption of the exemplar story approach and to revolve around a willful everyman "who must learn a lesson that could save his life" (Abraham 2012, 99). In fact, it seems that UPA's approach in making this type of film has been more that of applying a precise artistic vision to the different subject matters they have been requested to tackle rather than bending to the wills of each client and letting the different sponsors dictate the characteristics of their animated documentary production. The case of *Man on the Land* with UPA intentionally using music "to undermine the potency of the rhetoric" of the sponsor's message makes it apparent (Ostherr 2018, 283).

Similarly, as animator Bill Scott puts it, John Sutherland Productions specialized in the making of "didactic films: films to impress, films to persuade" (Scott in Scott 2001). And, among the titles it produced, which have often been made on commission of industrial giants (see Segrave 2004, 101), many are animated documentaries. Not dissimilarly from UPA's ones, a good number of such films revolve around an everyman (e.g., Freddie in *Going Places* or Mr. Finchley in *Working Dollars* [1957, dir. Carl Urbano]). A number of these films, however, have instead as protagonists personified objects or substances (e.g., the atom in *A Is for Atom*, the cancer cells in *The Traitor Within* and *Horizons of Hope*, or the missile in *A Missile Named Mac* [1962, dir. Carl Urbano], whose personification is accomplished through sound) or anthropomorphic animals (e.g., *Fresh Laid Plans*). In fact, even though many of the films that form it are directed by the same person, Carl Urbano, John Sutherland Productions' corpus of animated documentaries tends to be more heterogenous than that of UPA, and not just as far as the approach to the subject matter is concerned. The level of fabledness also tends to vary from title to title, ranging between mild (as in titles like *A Missile Named Mac* or *The Traitor Within*) and high (as in *The Story of Creative Capital* [1957, dir. Carl Urbano], which is even punctuated with brief musical numbers starring an elf/voice-of-authority with magic powers). Paradoxically, in this diversity we could, however, identify a unitary approach consisting of letting the subject matter and the requests of the animated documentary's sponsor dictate the shape of the final film.

This, however, does not mean it is not possible to detect some trends in creating such works also for this studio. For instance, John Sutherland

Productions' animated documentaries relied more on drama than on comedy, since Sutherland believed that "an excess of humor might so confuse members of the audience that they could miss the educational point altogether" (Jack 2015, 493).⁹ Also, often this studio's animated documentaries were characterized by a nonlinear temporality. Emblematic in this sense is *Fresh Laid Plans*, which starts with the owl/voice-of-authority jumping on a train to escape an angry crowd, and its core portion, wherein the Brannan Farm Aid Plan is referenced, is framed as a long flashback that explains why the character ended up being chased.

During the classical era's consolidation phase, in the United States, we witness changes in respect to the form's affirmation subperiod also as far as to where animated documentaries find distribution. Filmic titles may have their showings either in cinemas or within the nontheatrical circuit, and thus in such places as schools, clubs, or industrial plants. By the mid-1950s, however, an increasing number of made-for-television animated documentaries also started to be created, mainly in the form of series (or episodes of a series), as it frequently is the case for the nonfiction works created for this medium (see McLane [2005] 2012, 199). The richest production of classical televisual animated documentaries was undoubtedly the Walt Disney Studios' one, which includes such titles as *I'm No Fool…, The Nature of Things, This Is You, The Great Cat Family, Our Friend the Atom*, and *Man in Space*. Nonetheless, among the animated documentaries made for television in the United States, Frank Capra's *Our Mr. Sun, Hemo the Magnificent, The Strange Case of the Cosmic Rays* (1957), and *The Unchained Goddess* (1958) also deserve a mention. Indeed, Eric Smoodin (2004, 221) goes as far as to define such titles their "decade's most inventive educational films, along with those produced by Walt Disney." These four one-hour televisual works had teenagers as their main target audience. More precisely, they were created with the goal "to attract America's young minds into scientific careers" (Capra in "Bell Shows Hemo the Magnificent" 1957, 12) and have been the first four specials in "The Bell System Science Series," an animated documentary series sponsored by Bell System that comprised also other five titles, four of which were produced by Warner Brothers Pictures (i.e., *Gateways to the Mind* [1958, dir. Owen Crump], *Alphabet Conspiracy* [1959, dir. Robert B. Sinclair], *Thread of Life* [1960, dir. Owen Crump], and *About Time* [1962, dir. Owen Crump]) and one by the Walt Disney Studios (i.e., *The Restless Sea* [1964, dir. Les Clark]).¹⁰

A further respect under which the post-1945 animated documentary production differs from the pre-1945 one is the subject matters tackled in them. Since, as anticipated in Chapter 5, the classical animated documentary production, in general, tends to be a son of its times, after the end of the Second World War also in the United States, overall, we witnessed a shift in the aspects of the real addressed in such works to reflect the historical changes faced by the nation. Just as a matter of example, in the immediate postwar years titles like *Brotherhood of Man* or Philip Stapp's *Boundary Lines* (1946) and *Picture in Your Mind* (1948) that dealt with race relations— a topic that, as McLane ([2005] 2012, 163) notes, was quite tackled in nonfiction cinema in general in this period—were produced. Also, there was no shortage of works illustrating the practices and guiding principles of American industrial capitalism, like for instance *Make Mine Freedom* or *Meet King Joe*, which fall in that "genre of sponsored educational films" on business economy-related topics, whose emergence was spurred in the immediate postwar years by tensions between industrial management and organized labor (Jack 2015, 494). And animated documentaries referable to the "economic education" efforts that began "just as the Truman administration's developing orientation toward containment of Soviet expansionism . . . foreshadowed the Cold War to come" continued to see the light also in the following decade (Jack 2015, 494–5). In fact, overall, during the consolidation phase of the classical era, a rich number of economy-related animated documentaries were created. Among them, "Fun and Facts about American Business," a series of nine pro-capitalism titles on the working principles of the US economic system and the benefits of free enterprise, stands out.[11] We can, however, recall also Robert Lawrence Productions' *The Hope That Jack Built*, which the National Association of Investment Companies sponsored to explain the role of investment companies to prospective investors (see "Platable Facts for Investors" 1957, 41), or the two John Sutherland Productions directed by Carl Urbano *What Makes Us Tick* (1952) and *Working Dollars*. Both these films, which explain respectively what stocks are and how an average man can put his money to work, have been commissioned by the New York Stock Exchange. Indeed, the latter organization was driven by the belief that it was important for people to understand the workings of a capitalistic society and saw in films a good vehicle for achieving this objective (see "The Woman's Viewpoint on Investments" 1963, 39–40). John Sutherland Productions, however, have created also other two important titles in cooperation with E.I. du Pont de Nemours & Company. The films in question, which were made for the Chamber of Commerce of the United States—in whose program of work audiovisual materials in the 1950s were progressively given always greater importance (see "Speaking to America" 1957, 39)—are *It's Everybody's Business* (1954), on the United States' free-enterprise ideology, and *The Story of Creative Capital*, which, as *Business Screen Magazine* puts it, "tells the origin of invested funds in popular terms" (38).[12]

Analogously, in the 1950s, with the mounting of Cold War tensions and the resulting development by the federal government of "an aggressive campaign to promote educational projects that enhanced scientific, technological and mathematical learning around all levels of American society" (Norden 2011, 115), the production of hard science-related animated documentaries boomed.

Actually, from the 1950s and up to the end of the classical era, the majority of the animated documentaries produced in the United States dealt with issues falling in a branch of science—be it astronomy, physics, mathematics, biology, or medicine—and popularized such topics. These works were filled with optimism in the capabilities of man and science to the point that even in a film as *Hemo the Magnificent* which is so imbued with Catholic religion that it opens with a biblical quote, we can hear a character (i.e., Mr. Writer) state that "the man of science will solve" all the unanswered questions of life. In other words, such faith in science was so pervasive that, in his works, the profoundly Catholic Frank Capra "tries to create a common ground between science and religion—both are ways for the optimistic and the curious to think about our world and our place in it" (Gunter 2012, 198).

Still, this flourishing of science-related animated documentaries cannot be ascribed only to a desire of reflecting the then-current historical moment. If a booming of this kind of works could happen it was undeniably also, to a certain extent, because the animated documentary form is particularly apt for conveying factual science-related discourses that would otherwise prove difficult and tedious to a general audience. As Frank Capra has declared, "[c]artoons can bring clarity, impression, humor and alacrity to otherwise pedantic discourses. With this device, you can eliminate extraneous material easily—as well as holding the audience's attention" (Capra in "Bell Shows *Hemo the Magnificent*" 1957, 12).

To another extent the kind of entities sponsoring animated documentaries in the United States in these years played a role in this blooming of scientific titles. In fact, generally speaking, as we will see, post-1945 classical animated documentary's last major shift away from the wartime production happened at the level of the typology of bodies sponsoring such works. After 1945, the titles commissioned by governmental agencies soon came to represent only a small portion of the animated documentaries produced. The array of entities that commissioned the making of such works enlarged significantly to include organizations as diverse as the Museum of Modern Art (sponsor of *The Invisible Moustache of Raoul Dufy*), the United Auto Workers (sponsor of *Brotherhood of Man*), the non-profit film foundation Julien Bryan's International Film Foundation (sponsor of Philip Stapp's *Boundary Lines* and *Picture in Your Mind*), or corporations like Kimberly-Clark and General Electric, just to name a few. In particular, the main typologies of sponsors were now, on the one hand, associations, foundations, and the like and, on the other hand, the industry. To be exact, both these macro-categories of entities were by this time not new to supporting the creation of nonfiction animated films. For instance, as Victoria Cain (2012, 230) points out, the conviction of "the film's educational potential" had long since taken root among the officers at the United States' most powerful philanthropic foundations, bringing many such institutions to sponsor research and experimentation in the educational film genre already prior to the outbreak of the Second World War. And some of these "early" titles commissioned were (partly) in animation, albeit they tended to use the medium's sober language. Similarly, before 1945, on multiple occasions there had been cases of industries supporting the making of animated films addressing the real and, as seen in Chapter 4, in a few instances the resulting titles were even full-fledged examples of early animated documentaries. So, what actually changes now is that the industry and associations, foundations, and the like start regularly subsidizing the making of out-and-out animated documentaries to the point that the first one quickly grew to become the leading sponsor of such works, followed by the others. And, as we will see, within both categories many were the bodies that either operated within the realm of science at large or had scientific progress at the heart of their agendas.

As far as the associations, foundations, and societies that sponsored classical animated documentaries after 1945 are concerned, a good chunk of them had public health-related scopes. Indeed, among the sponsoring organizations that fall in this group, we can find entities as the National Tuberculosis Association (sponsor of *Rodney*), The Arthritis Foundation (sponsor of *One of Sixteen Million*), the American Heart Association (sponsor of UPA's *Pump Trouble*), and especially the American Cancer Society, which repeatedly subsidized the making of animated documentaries during the consolidation phase of the form's classical era. At this last organization, following a change in leadership in 1944, films in general came to be seen "as an indispensable part of an integrated range of mutually supportive methods of public education and cancer control" (Cantor [2007] 2008, 42). Consequently, the American Cancer Society started "making movies central to their efforts" (Cantor [2007] 2008, 56) and a growing number of films was produced, broadening also the range of media employed in making them to include animation. In the 1950s, with a director of Public Education as Chester Williams, who was convinced that "the audio-visual medium reaches more people more effectively than any other technique of mass education" (Williams in Ross 1959, 28), the organization availed itself even further of films to "dissipate the many fears that stand between many people and the possibility of being cured of cancer" (Ross 1959, 28). More precisely, the American Cancer Society increasingly exploited movies "to get men and women to their doctors for health checkups, to acquaint the entire population with the seven danger signals which mean cancer, to get across the idea that many cancers can be and are being cured and to translate the charitable impulses of the public into making donations to fight cancer" (Ross 1959, 28). And among the titles sponsored by this organization between 1946 and 1960, five were animated documentaries. More specifically, in the 1940s, both *The Traitor Within* and *To Save These Lives* (1949, dir. David Hilberman), which was made by Tempo Productions and illustrated how a community can be reached with information about the early treatment of cancer, with a view to inducing people to enlist as volunteer workers for the local public education programs of the American Cancer Society, were commissioned. Subsequently, this organization subsidized the making of the three UPA shorts targeted at male viewers: *Man Alive!*, which has been the first cancer education film to use humor throughout (see Cantor 2020, 184), *Sappy Homiens*, and *Inside Magoo*.[13]

That said, obviously not all the foundations, associations, and societies that sponsored animated documentaries in these years had public health-related scopes. For instance, a foundation that subsidized a great number of such films during the classical era's consolidation phase was the Alfred P. Sloan Foundation, which, as Caroline Jack points out, was originally instituted "with a focus on increasing public understanding of economics" (Jack 2015, 497). And the majority of the titles it commissioned dealt precisely with economics. Indeed, albeit "hid" behind Harding College so as to ensure the films to be more effective,[14] between the second half of the 1940s and the early 1950s the Alfred P. Sloan Foundation ordered to John Sutherland Productions the "Fun and Facts about American Business" series, in whose titles, on the sponsor's request, the fun factor has progressively been more present so as to increase their likelihood of finding theatrical distribution (see Jack 2015, 492–3). Subsequently, the Foundation also commissioned at Warner Brothers the making of three highly fabled "lessons on economics and capitalism" that feature Sylvester the Cat (Sachleben and Yenerall 2004, 33): *By Word of Mouse* (1954), on the free-market capitalist system; *Heir-Conditioned* (1955), on the benefits of good investments; *Yankee Dood It* (1956), on methods of capitalism. These three films were all directed by Friz Freleng, who was by then not new to working on an animated documentary as he had written the Oscar-winner *So Much for So Little* together with Jones. In making these economy-focused shorts, however, he went a bit overboard with the fun factor to the point that they substantially amount to fictional cartoons featuring Sylvester the Cat "that break in the middle for a brief lesson" (Schneider 1988, 98). In short, in line with its scope, the Alfred P. Sloan Foundation commissioned mostly economy-related titles. Nevertheless, interestingly, among the animated documentaries that it sponsored, we can find also a public health-concerned short as *Horizons of Hope*.

As far as US industrial animated documentaries are concerned, the range of companies that commission such works after the end of the Second World War is also vast. We find firms as diverse as the food industry Sunsweet, the insurance company Ætna Casualty & Surety, or the radiocommunications corporation CBS, just to name a few. However, first of all, there are business sectors that tend to commission animated documentaries more actively than others. It is the case of the automotive one with its related industries. The short on how to properly handle tools *The ABC of Hand Tools* (1946), the four ones on internal combustion engine *The ABC of Internal Combustion Engines* (1948), *The ABC of Internal Combustion Engines. The Automobile Engine* (1948, dir. Gordon Sheehan), *The ABC of the Diesel Engine* (1950), *The ABC of Jet Propulsion* (1954), the film illustrating how Chevrolet's then-innovative transmission system works *Turboglide* (1958), The Calvin Company's partly animated and partly live-action short on deep-tillage *Dividend in Depth* (1954), Portafilms' *A Spark in Time on the Firing Line* (1962) on the automobile ignition system and spark timing, and Transfilm Incorporated's *Energetically Yours* are only some of the many titles whose making has been prompted by a company falling in this business sector.[15] Second, among the companies sponsoring animated documentaries in this period, the number of those in whose activity science and its advancements are key is high. It is the case of many businesses falling in the mentioned automotive sector but also, for instance, of a corporation as AT&T/Bell System, whose president Cleo T. Craig, as Frank Capra underlines, insisted precisely that "since science is what his company is selling, science is what the Bell System should sponsor" (Capra in Niderost 2014).[16] In fact, many classical industrial animated documentaries can be considered outcomes of what Eric Smoodin (2004, 220) identifies as a tendency of "science corporations during the Cold War" to interact "with the education and entertainment industries to consolidate their influence in the national economy and on governmental science policy."

The Commonalities behind the Apparent Diversity

Behind an apparent heterogeneity determined by the ample spectrum of bodies that sponsored them, studios that created them, and subjects in them tackled, post-1945 US animated documentaries tend to showcase some shared traits. First of all, as anticipated, regardless of the topic addressed, they often praise scientific discoveries and suggest that Americans have to thank scientists if their standard of living is better than that of previous generations. This is particularly evident if we consider this period's animated histories, which echo the creed, then diffused in the United States, that the nation's mission "was to lead the world in the unfolding of an ever finer tomorrow, that the direction of history, in America at least, was onward and upward" (Chambers 1958, 197). Indeed, in such animated documentaries, the review of the developments that have brought to the introduction of the set material, object, or practice around which the film revolves is reduced to a tool for making apparent precisely how the current well-being of US citizens is indebted to a series of past discoveries, and thus for suggesting that it is mainly thanks to science if an always greater life will be possible for mankind.

This faith in science and progress can be found throughout this period's animated documentaries but it usually finds its fullest expression in concluding scenes that foreshadow an always better future. Just to make a few examples, *So Much for So Little* ends with the voice-of-God narrator stating that thanks to well-staffed health departments, the then mortality rate of babies in the country is likely to decrease in the future. In *Rhapsody of Steel*'s last sequence it is suggested that, in the future, steel will make possible the departure of the first spaceship. Similarly, in the final scene of *It's Everybody's Business* it is stated that, if the United States will manage to keep the foundation of its business system strong, its citizens will "be able to maintain and improve" their way of living and "continue to build a better life for themselves and their fellow men in the world of tomorrow."

Second, during the classical era's consolidation subperiod, the exemplar story approach became always more diffused in the US animated documentary production to the point of making a timid appearance even in some of those titles that chose not to actually adopt it. The two John Sutherland Productions' shorts *It Never Rains Oil* (1953, dir. Arnold Gillespie) and *It's Everybody's Business* are examples in this respect. The former opens with a long sequence illustrating how omnipresent oil is in the daily life of everyman Stanley McGrokel (and for extension in that of the viewer), giving thus the impression that the entire film will revolve around this character. However, from the second sequence onward the short abandons the exemplar story approach. It goes on to explain how oil is discovered and extracted. Subsequently, it focuses on what the percentage depletion plan that was developed in 1926 entails and how it has encouraged the discovery of new oil deposits, all without McGrokel ever even being mentioned. This everyman appears again only in the brief concluding scene of the film. He remains thus confined to the narrative's framework. Similarly, *It's Everybody's Business* as a whole cannot be said to showcase an exemplar story structure, but some of its sections do. For instance, the principles informing the US business system are introduced by illustrating the exemplar story of the hatmaker Johnathan, who stands for all workers.

A third recursive trait in this period's US animated documentaries is the presence of scenes that explicitly demolish false myths and misconceptions concerning the set aspect of the real addressed by the film. In fact, this practice was not just a peculiarity of health-related animated documentaries. It can be found also in titles that tackle other subject matters. Take, for instance, the industrial animated documentary *It Never Rains Oil* or UPA's *Brotherhood of Man*. In the former, we can find, for example, brief scenes wherein existing beliefs and myths around where oil can be found and how an oil well works are, first, visually dramatized. Then, the voice-of-God narrator explicitly states that they are wrongful conceptions, and, finally, where oil is effectively located and how an oil well truly operates is illustrated both aurally and visually. Likewise, *Brotherhood of Man* is entirely built around the deprogramming of rooted misconceptions concerning races by showing how, unlike often erroneously believed, no substantial biological diversities set apart men of different ethnicities. Only skin color and a few other similar "frills" distinguish them.

It becomes progressively more commonplace for the animated characters protagonist of these films to have some lines, gradually bringing as such these works even closer to docudramas. Undeniably, the voice-of-God narration is still quite employed. For instance, we keep finding shorts like Portafilms' *A Spark in Time on the Firing Line*, wherein all the talking is done by a voice-of-God narrator, while the leading character, a personified mouse on roller skates, is reduced to a mute, "visual" assistant. That is, this animated actor does not go much beyond obeying orders imparted to it by the voiceover narrator that are aimed at clarifying visually what the latter states. Yet, as it occurs for instance in *Brotherhood of Man* or *The Hope that Jack Built*, starting with the beginning of the consolidation subphase in US animated documentaries it becomes always more frequent for the voice-of-God narration to retreat here and there to let the characters talk among them or dialog with the voice-of-God itself. Indeed, instead of just reacting to what is stated by the voiceover narrator through actions and facial expressions, characters may now verbally interact with it: they may ask questions, verbalize their understanding of what he says, or object to his statements. It may even happen that the voice-of-God narration is alternated with a voice-of-authority one, as it occurs for instance in *Rodney*. This short on tuberculosis starts and ends with a traditional voice-of-God narration but, in its central part, it is an onscreen doctor who illustrates how tuberculosis is spread, how its germs behave in a human organism, and what the treatments for this disease are. A further example is offered by *Gasoline's Amazing Molecules*. In it, a voice-of-God narration is employed but there also are a couple of scenes wherein a talking, animated carbon atom voiced by Ken Carpenter acts as a voice-of-authority.

In fact, with the consolidation subphase, we witness also an increase in employment of the voice-of-authority narration within classical US animated documentaries, even if at times it is just either in alternation with a voice-of-God narrator or a hybrid between a voiceover and an actual voice-in. Indeed, there are also cases of films in which the lines are never lip-synched by the onscreen character to which they can be led back. Take for instance *A Missile Named Mac*. Through the use of first-person pronouns, it is suggested to viewers that the voice they hear pertains to the onscreen missile protagonist of the film and can thus be classified as an eccentric voice-of-authority rather than as a voice-of-God. Yet, this animated character does not have a mouth and, therefore, the lines pronounced are not lip-synched by it, remaining suspended between a full-fledged voice-in and a voiceover. Another example is offered by *Turboglide*. Here, the transmission is personified into Mr. T, and, by way of the words spoken by the character as well as by way of how sound is treated, it is made clear that it is this animated figure that illustrates to the viewer how Chevrolet's Turboglide transmission works. However, the words we hear are never shown to come out of Mr. T's mouth, with the consequence that the narration stays a voice-in for the most part.

That said, be it full-fledged or hybrid and its employment partial or exclusive, the voice-of-authority is increasingly present in US animated documentaries and this role may be performed either by an animated character or by a real-life figure, as it occurs for example in *Our Friend the Atom* or *Dividend in Depth*, wherein physicist Heinz Haber and the film's alleged animator himself respectively take it over. Also, the voice-of-authority may equally be an expert by knowledge or by practice. That is, it may be a scientist (e.g., Dr. Frank Baxter in *Our Mr. Sun*, *The Unchained Goddess*, and the other animated documentaries in "The Bell System Science Series"), a professor (e.g., the owl professors in *Fresh Laid Plans* and *Toot, Whistle, Plunk and Boom*), a doctor (e.g., the animated physician in *Rodney*), or even the personification of common sense, as it occurs in *How to Catch a Cold*. Nevertheless, it may as frequently be an animated figure or element that, on the topic addressed by the film, has expertise by direct experience, for example, because it is an object or substance directly involved in the process or phenomenon explained. Indeed, we may find a personification of the transmission that acts as voice-of-authority in a film about the working principles of Chevrolet's Turboglide transmission (as it occurs in *Turboglide*), a personification of gasoline in the form of a "modern genie" in a short about the discovery and development of this refined petroleum (as in Carl Urbano's *Fill 'Er Up!* [1959]), or a missile in a film about the targeting system of missiles (as in *A Missile Named Mac*).

As a matter of fact, a further characteristic of this period's US animated documentaries is the tendency for abstract concepts and inanimate objects or substances key to the film to be personified. Indeed, while we have seen this to occur frequently within the titles by John Sutherland Productions, it has not been exclusive to this studio's production. For instance, the two shorts produced by Jerry Fairbanks Inc. for Standard Oil Company Indiana, *Gasoline's Amazing Molecules* and *Lubricating Oil's Amazing Molecules*, have as protagonists personified molecules and atoms, each with its own personality and individual color scheme as well as with a distinctive shape devised from the structural pattern with which scientists normally draw it (e.g., see Figures 6.1 and 6.2) (see respectively "Progress through Science" 1948, 35; "Standard Oil Movie" 1949, 12). Moreover, in both films, from time to time we hear them talking and, at the end of *Lubricating Oil's Amazing Molecules*, even singing in unison (Figure 6.3).

Similarly, Capra's *Our Mr. Sun* stars an animated sun with human-like facial traits and the ability to speak. In Walt Disney Studios' already mentioned *How to Catch a Cold*, common sense is anthropomorphized in a tiny man. The protagonist of John Sutherland Productions' *A Is for Atom* is Dr. Atom, a personification of this infinitely small particle (see Figure 6.4). In *The ABC of Internal Combustion Engines*, *The ABC of Internal Combustion Engines. The Automobile Engine*, *The ABC of the Diesel Engine*, and *The ABC of Jet Propulsion*, air, fuel, and ignition are portrayed as goofy cartoon characters with anthropomorphic qualities and precise

FIGURE 6.1 *An advertisement of John Sutherland Productions that well synthetizes the studio's tendency to adapt its "style" to the needs of the client.*

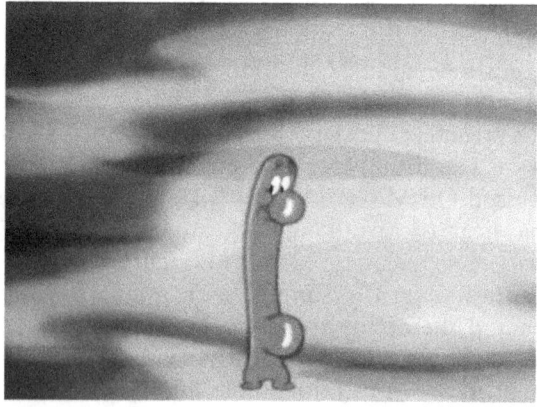

FIGURE 6.2 *The personification of a fuel oil molecule in* Gasoline's Amazing Molecules.

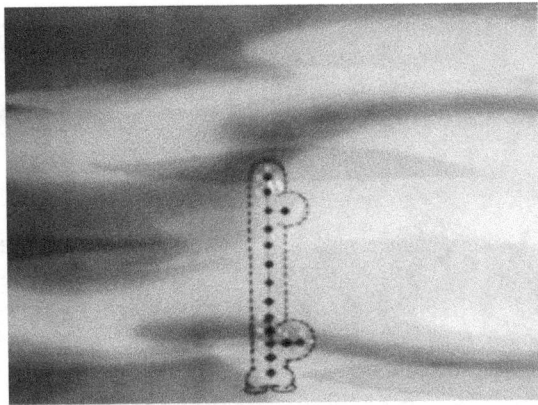

FIGURE 6.3 *A shot revealing how the shape of* Gasoline's Amazing Molecules' *personified fuel oil molecule is devised from its habitual scientific graphic visualization.*

FIGURE 6.4 *The personification of the atom in* A Is for Atom.

personalities—that undergo little changes from one title to the other despite the films being produced by different studios (see Figure 6.5).[17] And this list of examples could go on forever because this practice of personifying the inanimate was quite rooted among the US producers of post-1945 classical animated documentaries.

Furthermore, it was also commonplace for post-1945 US animated documentaries to be part of a two-media project that, alongside film, involved print. More precisely, in various cases, this period's animated documentaries had a tie-in booklet or comic book. As seen in Chapter 3, in the years in question at times such titles were supplemented by picture books (e.g., *Brotherhood of Man*) or comics (in the form either of a comic

FIGURE 6.5 *Air, fuel, and ignition as portrayed in* The ABC of Internal Combustion Engines *and its "sequels."*

strip series as for *Look Who's Driving* or of a comic book as for *The Great Cat Family, Man in Man in Flight,* and *Donald in Mathmagic Land*) created using artwork from the film. There were also cases of animated documentaries that had word-driven companion print publications, as was for instance for *The Story of Menstruation, Gasoline's Amazing Molecules, Lubricating Oil's Amazing Molecules,* and *Dividend in Depth.* Indeed, for *The Story of Menstruation* the tie-in booklet *Very Personally Yours,* which, differently from the film, contains plenty of references to Kottex's products for feminine hygiene, was created. In this publication, some artwork from the Disney short is present but acts just as an illustration of the written text. Similarly, *Gasoline's Amazing Molecules* had a tie-in booklet entitled *Gasoline's Amazing Molecules. The Inside Story of Modern Gasoline,* in which "the story of modern gasoline manufacture" is told through a combination of written text and artwork from the film (*Gasoline's Amazing Molecules* 1948b, 13). For its sequel, *Lubricating Oil's Amazing Molecules,* "a booklet in color showing scenes from the film and describing the refining operations" also was created, as pointed out in *The Hammond Times* ("Standard Oil Movie" 1949, 12). *Dividend in Depth,* instead, as we learn from an advertisement published in the magazine *The National Future Farmer,* had even both a companion book, *Farming the 3 Dimensions,* and a tie-in "cartoon booklet" entitled *Power Farming* ("Catching on Like Wildfire!" 1955, 6).

During the classical era's consolidation phase, the relationship that an animated documentary entertained with the print medium could, however, also be one of derivation. That is, some films were instead based on a booklet, pamphlet, or book. For instance, Herb Lamb Productions' shorts illustrating the working principles of an internal combustion engine, *The ABC of Internal Combustion Engines* and *The ABC of Internal Combustion Engines. The Automobile Engine*, were adaptations of General Motors' 1944 booklet *A Power Primer* as are Film Graphics Inc.'s *The ABC of the Diesel Engine* and Sound Masters Inc.'s *The ABC of Jet Propulsion*. John Sutherland Productions' animated history of capital and industry in the United States, *The Story of Creative Capital*, was based on the 1955 booklet *This Is du Pont: The Story of Creative Capital*, while John and Faith Hubley's feature *Of Stars and Men* was a cinematic version of the namesake 1959 book by astronomer Harlow Shapley. Analogously, the airing of Walt Disney Studios' animated documentary television episode *Our Friend the Atom* was preceded by the publication of *The Walt Disney Story of Our Friend the Atom*, a tome authored by scientist Heinz Haber (who in the animated documentary acts as a voice-of-authority), illustrated by the studio's artists, and prefaced by the father of Mickey Mouse himself. Among the examples of films that are an adaptation of a print publication, there is also *Brotherhood of Man*. Indeed, in addition to having a tie-in picture book, this film was also based on the Public Affairs pamphlet *Races of Mankind* by Ruth Benedict and Gene Weltfish. In fact, as *Brotherhood of Man*'s case demonstrates not necessarily the relationship that a postwar classical animated documentary entertained with the print medium had to be either one of origin or derivation. Both could also be in place for the same title.

Finally, we can identify also a commonality that concerns specifically the industrial animated documentary production. Such films were not all created with the same audience in mind. They were made either for internal use or, more frequently, for circulation among the general public, in which case they thus fell in the public relations film category.[18] In some cases, multiple versions of the same title were even produced, one for each intended audience group. Take for instance the two pairs of animated documentaries created by Jerry Fairbanks Inc. for Standard Oil Company (Indiana): *Gasoline's Amazing Molecules*/*The Inside Story of Modern Gasoline*, and *Lubricating Oil's Amazing Molecules* (distributed by the United States Bureau of Mines under the title of *The Story of Lubricating Oil*)/*The Inside Story of Lubricating Oil* (1949). The first two films are twin productions on how gasoline is obtained targeted at different audiences. That is, they are nearly identical; only the former was created for public showing, while the latter was created "for Standard employees and for dealer merchandising clinics" and, therefore, the way in which the voice-of-God narrator presents the subject matter is adjusted to meet the needs of the different typology of spectators ("Progress through Science" 1948, 36). Likewise, *The Inside Story of Lubricating Oil* is nothing other than a "special version for dealer and company employee showings" of *Lubricating Oil's Amazing Molecules*, which was instead aimed at a general audience. And its differences from the latter short amount to the presence of "some detail on the Standard Oil product, Permalube Motor Oil," which is instead not present in the film for public distribution ("Standard Oil Movie" 1949, 12).

Regardless of their intended audience or sponsoring company, classical industrial animated documentaries shared the fact of being in all and for all industrial films, a term used to denote all works "commissioned and used as a communication tool by corporations and business associations (*excluding advertising spots*)" (Zimmermann 2009, 104, my emphasis). Consequently, while not being advertisements in the true sense, they tended to have a promotional agenda, which, however, was frequently concealed behind the appearance of a purely informational film. Certainly, it is possible to find also works such as *Good Wrinkles*, *A Missile Named Mac*, and *More Than Meets the Eye*, whose promotional agenda is explicit. Indeed, the first one showcases not only a heavy brand and product placement within the animated visuals (e.g., see Figure 6.6) but also a substantive live-action sequence wherein, in illustrating how Sunsweet tenderized prunes can be cooked in different, succulent ways, a packet of this product repeatedly appears within the frame.

In *A Missile Named Mac* the brand image is carried out through the commentary from the very beginning when the animated missile that here acts as a voice-of-authority states: "The telephone company asked me to tell you what the people at the Bell Laboratories and Western Electric are doing." Similarly, if, as a reviewer of the *Business Screen Magazine* nicely puts it, in its first part *More Than Meets the Eye* deals "with the impact of sound on listener's imagination" ("CBS Network Presents" 1952, 31), its second half is substantially an advert for the medium of radio in general and CBS in particular. In fact, toward the end of the short, a long sequence is devoted to presenting stats and data regarding CBS specifically and to pitching it as the radio where companies should advertise their products.

FIGURE 6.6 *An example of brand placement in the animated visuals of* Good Wrinkles.

In other words, the film closes with a full-fledged advert of the same radio network that commissioned it, making its promotional aim blatant.

However, explicitly promotional industrial animated documentaries like *Good Wrinkles*, *A Missile Named Mac*, and *More Than Meets the Eye* were a minority. In most cases, to be pursued in making such works was rather the path encouraged by Walter Lantz, who, as Malcolm Cook and Kirsten Moana Thompson (2019, 20) point out, "urged that sponsored film should be indirect in its approach and that 'placing the sponsor's films should be subtle and not impose itself on the audience's attention at all', but rather '[offer] a really instructive—and/or amusing—view of the product or industry'." Indeed, in most industrial animated documentaries, the name and brand of the sponsoring company were subtly integrated within the animated visuals and devoted very little screen time or even relegated just to the film's paratexts, and more precisely to its opening or ending credits. As Thomas Heinrich and Bob Batchelor point out specifically regarding Walt Disney Studios' *The Story of Menstruation*, classical industrial animated documentaries, in general, have been part of "a rapidly growing marketing trend when corporations commissioned 'informational' productions to paddle their wares" (Heinrich and Batchelor 2004, 121) and, in many cases, were made for distribution in schools. In order to prevent criticism of commercializing the classroom, such films had a dominantly educational character. Also, product and brand placement had to be minimal and, possibly, subtle. Take for instance *Rhapsody of Steel*. Referring to this Technicolor, high-budget short the reviewer of the *Motion Picture Exhibitor* writes: "This is a 'no charge' subject. The only ad plug is at the very end" ("The Short Parade" 1960, 4711). Nonetheless, *Rhapsody of Steel* was made "as part of US Steel's campaign against competing steel imports and alternative materials like aluminum" (Prelinger 2006, 79), with the additional goal of promoting careers in the steel industry (see Boschen 2018). However, all these aims have been pursued by telling a history of steel that exposes how important this metal has been for mankind and how present it now was in the daily life of a US citizen. For instance, we can find a long sequence starring an every-family wherein, accompanied only by the music originally scored by Dimitri Tiomkin and performed by the Pittsburg Symphony Orchestra,[19] various objects made using steel that punctuate the everyday of ordinary Americans are shown. The sequence, however, is preceded and followed by expository scenes, with the result that overall, the audience's impression is that of viewing an informational rather than a promotional work.

Other examples are the stop-motion short *Live and Let Live* (1947) and *Look Who's Driving*, sponsored by Ætna Casualty & Surety Company, or *Dividend in Depth*. In *Live and Let Live*, some space is devoted to the sponsoring insurance company in the opening credits which not only list it as the film's sponsor but also celebrate it as a firm "which believes that the indispensable function of an insurance company is not only to make financial reimbursement in case of loss, but also to do its utmost to prevent that loss from occurring." Likewise, in *Look Who's Driving*, Ætna Casualty & Surety Company is briefly mentioned complete with its logo as the film's sponsor in the opening and end credits. For the rest, however, both films are safety animated documentaries devoid of any promotional character. In particular, *Live and Let Live* presents a series of possible car accidents and illustrates how each of them could have been prevented. Teaching by negative example within an everyman's-exemplar-story structure, *Look Who's Driving* instead tackles the problem of "improper mental attitudes that cause motorists to drive at excessive speed, fail to stop at a through way, or try to gain a few seconds by passing on a hill" ("Safety Film" 1954, 15). Not dissimilarly, overall, *Dividend in Depth* showcases an informational character. First, it explains why hardpan forms and why it endangers the fertility of the land. Subsequently, it illustrates why tridimensional farming is "the solution" to this problem. Undeniably, toward the end, *Dividend in Depth* contains some product placement in the form of footage of Caterpillar tractors at work, but these images are fully integrated into the informational narrative, leaving the advertising intent concealed.

The Animated Documentary according to Walt Disney

Although during the consolidation phase, UPA and John Sutherland Productions threatened their leadership position, the Walt Disney Studios have unquestionably been the United States' greatest producers of animated documentaries during the classical era. If this has been the case, it is mostly because Disney devoted much energy throughout his career to producing educational works in general and animated documentaries in particular. After the United States entered the Second World War, he feels that "Mickey and Donald Duck should not be used for profit while the war is on" but decides to have them star instead "in educational pictures" ("Mickey Mouse and Donald Duck" 1944, 6). And, in 1942, his company's output went from being for the most part fictional films purely aimed at entertaining the audience to becoming for the four-fifths informational-propagandist works (e.g., see "Disney's War Effort" 1942, 8), a fact that spured the national press to state that he had "turned teacher" ("Teacher Disney" 1942). Although not all, many such works are animated documentaries, and, through leading his studio in the creation of a rich corpus of these government-sponsored titles, Disney brought it "to develop a 'voice of scientific authority'" (Norden 2011, 117), on which he continued building in the postwar years and beyond. Indeed, despite the passing of decades, Disney kept considering "the documentary film cartoon . . . a widely applicable medium for instructional purposes," a form with almost limitless "possibilities in the broad areas of education" (Disney 1955, 70). In fact, interestingly, during the consolidation phase, he even exceeded in committing to the animated documentary form by producing a number of such works without being prompted to do so by a sponsor. Indeed, although, among the studio's post-1945 animated documentary production, we find various titles (e.g., *The Story of Menstruation*, *How to Catch a Cold*, *The ABC of Hand Tools*, and *The Story of Oil*) that were created "on invitation"—as Disney itself puts it (Disney 1955, 70)—, he also produced many that were not the result of a sponsorship, including *Donald in Mathmagic Land*, *The Great Cat Family*, and the Oscar-winner short *Toot, Whistle, Plunk and Boom*. And in this Disney represented such an anomaly that it does not surprise that in the obituary published at his death, Newman Rosenthal (1966, 4) writes about him: "I believe, that above all other of his accomplishments, Walt Disney will be accepted, even by the profession, as a great teacher."

From hand tools (i.e., *The ABC of Hand Tools*) to the formation of planet Earth (i.e., *A World Is Born* [1955]) to family planning (i.e., *Family Planning*) to the basic principles one must follow to be safe on the workplace (i.e., *How to Have an Accident at Work*), the studio's animated documentaries throughout the decades have addressed the most disparate topics. However, the approach adopted in developing them has remained basically unchanged and is well synthesized in this golden rule that, as underlined by David R. Smith, Disney required his artists to abide by when they were working on the three space-related titles *Man in Space*, *Man and the Moon* (1955, dir. Ward Kimball), and *Mars and Beyond* (1957, dir. Ward Kimball): "First get the material straight, then find the way you can tell it in an entertaining fashion" (Disney in Smith 2016, 498). Indeed, the first step taken at Walt Disney Studios when producing an animated documentary was to acquire all the needed information on the chosen subject. There were two ways in which the animators would do so: through conducting research on it directly or consulting an expert on the topic. The former has been, for example, the approach adopted for the industrial short *Story of Oil*, concerning which we read on *Business Screen Magazine*: "The Disney people put months of library research into historic and geophysical study. One portion of the crew even went through a concentrated two-week course in geology to pick up background for depicting underground formations" ("Story of Oil" 1955, 5A). The latter is instead the case, for instance, of *Our Friend the Atom* or *The Story of Menstruation* (for which was hired as a consultant the gynecologist Mason Hohl)—and, when this approach was adopted, the presence of the expert was underlined either just through the film's credits or even by having him act as the film's voice-of-authority.

Once the needed information was obtained, the task of the animator was to translate it "in the world's oldest language—pictographs"—employing "symbols the most backward and illiterate of people could comprehend and profit by" (Disney 1955, 72–4). Indeed, Disney not only identified in its visual component the key part of an animated documentary but also believed that the target to keep in mind when creating this typology of films should have been "untutored people" (Disney 1955, 74). Therefore, he required such animated works to be at the same time of "unquestionable accuracy" and elementary in their portrayal of facts (Disney 1955, 74). In other words, extending what scholar Giaime Alonge notes in relationship to the wartime titles, this studio's animated documentary production has been informed by a "manifestly populist and anti-intellectualistic educational model, comparable to the *Reader's Digest*'s editorial line" (Alonge 2000, 179, my translation).

The second principle followed at Walt Disney Studios in making animated documentaries was to inform in an entertaining way, since, "although it has been said by pundits of psychology that painful experience is the most effective spur of memory," the father of Mickey Mouse believed "the fun factor" to be "even more potent," "a sure way into the minds and hearts of people" (Disney 1955, 74). This approach concretely translated, first of all, in the inclusion of some humor in the film. Disney considered "a linear sight joke" to be "a quick way to a beholder's mind—to acceptance of a statement or a premise" (Disney 1955, 74). He adds also: "It works as well with adults as with children; is as agreeable to the sophisticated as to the ignoramus, by that strange spell the moving cartoon can exert" (Disney 1955, 74). However, as Bob Cruz notes with regard to the *I'm No Fool...* series, the humor of Walt Disney Studios' animated documentaries tended, in general, to be "deliberately low-key," most likely "so that it would not distract from the main message" (Cruz 2011, 137).

In these films, instead, those "magic" representation devices peculiar to the medium of animation such as metaphor, synecdoche, and personification are abundantly employed. Emblematic in this regard is the case of *Food Will Win the War*, which, as John Baxter (2014, 57) points out, basically, "is made up almost entirely of mind-numbing statistics." Yet, such data is visualized by translating into animated images the imaginative comparisons that the voice-of-God narrator utilizes to give viewers a better idea of the amount of food to which the numbers provided correspond. As a result, the film ends up being populated by such fabled images as a moon made out of cheese, a dam from which fruit juices gush out, or a planet Earth with anthropomorphic features whose face is hit by a gigantic pie (e.g., see Figure 6.7).

Certainly, at times, we can encounter titles characterized by a timid employment of fabled animation like *The Story of Menstruation*. However, upon investigating such works, we may discover that, if they are less fabled, it is for reasons that go beyond Disney's will. For instance, as Heinrich and Batchelor (2004, 123) explain, for *The Story of Menstruation* the depiction

FIGURE 6.7 *Planet Earth as represented in* Food Will Win the War.

of a smiling embryo was originally considered but had to be discarded because "the image violated school policies that prohibited the showing of nude figures in classrooms." The employment of a renowned Disney character as protagonist was also evaluated, and the idea was abandoned only because it risked preventing the intended viewership from identifying with it (see Heinrich and Batchelor 2004, 123).

While it ended up not occurring in *The Story of Menstruation*, there are, however, also various animated documentaries produced by the Walt Disney Studios wherein one of the company's popular actors is cast. For example, in *The New Spirit*, *Donald in Mathmagic Land*, and the safety shorts *How to Have an Accident in the Home* and *How to Have an Accident at Work*, the leading role was given to Donald Duck, which we can also find in *Family Planning* in a minor part. Analogously, *You and Your...*, *I'm No Fool . . .* and the series "meant to reveal to children the underling logic of natural adaptation, *The Nature of Things*" (Sammond 2005, 348), all feature Jiminy Cricket as voice-of-authority.

The employment of such animated stars is obviously functional to raising these films' entertainment value but not only to that. If some of Walt Disney Studios' most popular animated actors have repeatedly appeared in the company's animated documentaries, it is mainly because, as he specifies in relationship to the use of Happy, Doc, Bashful, Grumpy, Sleepy, Sneezy, and Dopey in *The Winged Scourge*, Disney believed that his studio's animated stars "exercised more authority with their amusing antics" on the viewer than any real-life expert (Disney 1955, 74). And, when employed in this context, stability in their star image was sought attentively not only at the level of their appearance—by having them look and dress like they did in the fictional animated films that brought them to fame—but also at that of personality, through the insertion of moments wherein the defining traits of their star persona surface.[20] Let us consider for instance *The Winged Scourge*. Here, for example, we can find a scene wherein, in line with its characterization offered in *Snow White and the Seven Dwarfs*, Sneezy produces a sneeze of such a gale force capacity that it makes the rowing boat he is steering go as fast as a motor one, whereas Sleepy is briefly shown in the act of yawning while working (see Figure 6.8).

Moreover, within animated documentaries, often these animated stars—like it can be the case for real-life ones (see Dyer and McDonald 1998)—become a tool for propagating set good practices and social values that are felt to be "in danger." For example, in *The Winged Scourge*, the dwarfs' image of hard-working figures not particularly attentive to cleanliness is exploited to convey the message that malaria is such a dangerous disease that even the less keen on hygiene, like Doc, Grumpy, and the other dwarfs, understand the importance of adopting the measures necessary to keep away mosquitos from their homes. Analogously, in *The New Spirit*, the disproportionate enthusiasm and the clumsiness that characterize Donald Duck are used respectively to convey to the spectators the message that paying their income taxes is less painful than it can seem and that, if a bungle like the famous duck can effortlessly do so, they cannot but find it extremely easy.

In fact, more generally speaking, most Walt Disney Studios' animated documentaries share the objective of impacting on the real by having set good habits and values take root among their viewers. Indeed, such works usually contain at least a segment wherein how-to advice concerning the topic tackled is provided. In particular, the teaching method employed was that of offering

FIGURE 6.8 *Sleepy yawning while working in* The Winged Scourge.

first negative and then good behavioral examples in one or more specific situations connected to the topic of the film. Let us consider for instance *The ABC of Hand Tools* and *How to Catch a Cold*. In the former, first, the everyman and everywoman protagonists, Primitive Pete and Mrs. Primitive Pete, are shown in the act of misusing hammers, screwdrivers, and other utensils. Immediately afterward, the viewer is presented, instead, with the proper employment of such tools. Likewise, in the latter, first Common Sense shows how Common Man has passed on his cold by behaving irresponsibly in order to then highlight what one should do when ill to avoid "spreading" his "germs to a lot of innocent people." Similarly, in the second portion of each episode of the *I'm No Fool...* series—wherein safety matters are more properly tackled—, wrong and correct behaviors are dramatized through two characters, respectively a small boy named You, who stands for any careful kid, and a teenage called Fool, who represent all careless youngsters.

A final recurrent trait of Walt Disney Studios' animated documentaries is the inclusion of scenes functional at conferring "an air of seriousness" to the film that are set in a classroom (as in *Toot, Whistle, Plunk and Boom*) or wherein anyways the voice-of-authority—be it a real-life expert or an animated character as Common Sense in *How to Catch a Cold* or Jiminy Cricket in the *I'm No Fool...* series—stands beside a blackboard or among stacks of books when explaining something (Van Riper 2011, 91).[21]

Disney's Greater Role

The Walt Disney Studios and their founder have had a greater role in the development and expansion of the classical animated documentary than simply producing one of the richest corpora of such works following well-defined principles. First of all, it was always from this studio that many of the animators responsible for the non-Disney US classical animated documentary production came. UPA was established by three artists, Schwartz, Hilberman, and Bosustow, who left the Walt Disney Studios during its 1941 strike (see Abraham 2012). Tempo Productions was in turn an offshoot of UPA whose founders were Schwartz and Hilberman (see Maltin [1980] 1987, 327). John Hubley, who has created animated documentaries both with UPA and, later, with his own studio, was also a Walt Disney Studios' employee and left the company after the 1941 strike. Prior to co-funding with Bernie Rubin Film Graphics Inc. in New York, Lee Blair had worked at the Walt Disney Studios as a color director on important projects, including *Saludos Amigos* (1942, dir. Norman Ferguson). Herb Lamb Productions, which made *The ABC of Internal Combustion Engines*, was established by former Disney production manager Herb Lamb together with a former Disney animator, Tom Codrick. Finally, before establishing John Sutherland Productions in 1945, Sutherland had worked at the Walt Disney Studios for approximately three years "in the capacity of a Story and Gag Man, as well as Writer," as we learn from a letter of reference that the father of Mickey Mouse himself wrote for him on December 19, 1940.[22] And he remained in good standings with Disney as proven by the fact that, years later, when the president of Harding College, George S. Benson, was seeking a studio with which to collaborate for creating the "Fun and Facts about American Business" series, the father of Mickey Mouse recommended John Sutherland Productions for the job (see Jack 2015, 499). Moreover, the art director of one of John Sutherland Productions' most-renowned titles, *Rhapsody of Steel*, is Eyvind Earle, who not only had prior collaborated for Walt Disney Studios but, during her time at the studio, had even worked on an animated documentary, namely *Toot, Whistle, Plunk and Boom*. In short, we could thus very well say that the leading non-Disney US producers and directors of classical animated documentaries were (at least partly) trained at the Walt Disney Studios and it would be naïve to think that the work experience at this company did not have a somewhat influence on their subsequent work.

Even more importantly, Disney has been pivotal in showing the potential of the animated documentary not just in times of warfare but also in those of peace, leading the way both in the employment of the form in response to the Second World War needs and in its reconversion to peacetime uses toward the end of the global conflict. Indeed, the war was still not even over when the US press announced that he was foreseeing "a 'world of tomorrow' in which films" would have played "an important part in the education of adults and children" ("Mickey Mouse and Donald Duck" 1944, 6). And he did not restrict himself to tracing this path. He also encouraged others to follow in his footsteps in using animation for teaching the real by way of writing articles on the subject (e.g., Disney 1945 and 1955) as well as offering to entities that were looking into creating instructional or informational nonfiction audiovisual works his studio's production as a possible reference model. Emblematic of how he has sustained the peacetime development of the form is a fact occurred in 1946. Upon learning that the Catholic Cinematographic Center was looking into creating films that illustrated the main Catholic teachings, Disney donated to this organization a copy of the three titles that in his 1955 article "Animated Cartoon" he identifies as examples par excellence of his animated documentary production: *The Winged Scourge*, *Defense against Invasion*, and *Water—Friend or Enemy*. In February of that year, *The Roman Observer* announced:

> ARI informs that the great creator of cartoons, Walt Disney, has offered to the Catholic Cinematographic Center his three most recent didactic shorts as a sign of sympathy and ideal collaboration to C.C.C.'s catechism films project. The three cartoons by Walt Disney are in colors and ... address three hygiene-related issues: do not drink contaminated water, get vaccinated, be afraid of malaria. They are three lessons ...

that youngsters find fascinating thanks to the beautiful and whimsical gimmicks . . . the C.C.C. technicians admire these three shorts and are considering following Walt Disney's narrative methodology in creating their catechism films. ("La collaborazione di Walt Disney" 1946, 3, my translation)

From this episode it emerges well the kind of commitment and dedication Disney has put in having the animated documentary become the go-to audiovisual form for instructing viewers in the United States and beyond, and thus how key he has been to its development and flourishing.

Notes

1 The book written by Swing in 1940 is entitled *How War Came*, exactly as one of the two animated documentary shorts into which it has shortly after been adapted.

2 They often contain moments of explicit anti-German or, more rarely, anti-Japanese propaganda.

3 A few of these animated documentaries have also been made available to civilians but only in a second moment. It is, for instance, the case of *Weapon of War* which was first offered as part of the *Army-Navy Screen Magazine* but was later released also in theaters.

4 This is not due to the Walt Disney Studios having created little nonfiction animations for a soldiers-formed audience. On the contrary, the production of the studio in this sector has been consistent. Yet, in these years, in making such films, the Walt Disney Studios tend to favor the use of sober animation and thus for the most part have given life to works that fall out of the animated documentary category. For more on this Disney production, see Baxter (2014, 23–33).

5 If, as Aylish Wood (2007, 166) highlights, *A Few Quick Facts: Inflation* and *A Few Quick Facts: About Fear* break away "from the conventional narrative structures evident in other Snafu cartoons," it is not only due, as she suggests, to their "minimal use of spatial detail" but also to the fact that the other works are fictional stories with a teaching while these two are proper informational animated documentaries. For a more detailed description of these two titles and an analysis of their style, see Abraham (2012, 57–8), Bottini (2019, 29–30). For a discussion of the Private Snafu series instead, see Smoodin (1993, 72–95), Dow (2003), Fisher (2018), McGowan (2019, 101–6).

6 The voiceover specifies that what the viewer is being presented is a "case history taken at random from official Navy files."

7 Association of State and Territorial Health Officers (1949), "Proceedings of the Forty-Eight Annual Conference of the Surgeon General, Public Health

Service and Chief, Children's Bureau of the Federal Security Agency with State and Territorial Health Officers, State mental Health Authorities, State Hospital Survey and Construction Authorities," October 19 and 22.

8   For instance, when making *Water—Friend or Enemy*, the color red has been used to symbolize contaminated waters. Yet, to the Latin American population, this color is a synonym for joy and life and thus it did not give viewers the desired impression of death and sorrow (see Kaufman 2009, 141).

9   This is, however, not to say that comedy is absent in John Sutherland Productions' animated documentaries. For example, in *A Missile Named Mac* we can find various comic moments, including one that has as protagonist a duck that recalls Duffy Duck.

10 For an analysis of the entire series, see Niderost (2014).

11 The titles in the series are *Make Mine Freedom* (1948), *Going Places* (1948), *Meet King Joe* (1949), *Why Play Leap Frog?* (1949), *Albert in Blunderland* (1950), *Fresh Laid Plans*, *Inside Crackle Corner* (1951), *Dear Uncle* (1952), and *The Devil and John Q.* (1952).

12 In particular, both shorts are the result of "a cooperative practice in which industry pays for production of a film subsequently promoted and distributed by the Chamber" ("Economic Facts for John Q. Public" 1957, 35). On this practice, see also Jack (2015, 494).

13 For an in-depth analysis of these three films, see Cantor (2020).

14 Jack (2015, 502) explains as such the Sloan Foundation's choice of keeping concealed its role as sponsor of such animated documentaries: "Sloan and Benson agreed on the correctness (and thus the factuality) of free-enterprise economic ideology, but neither man was under the illusion that the public would accept a lecture on the social benefit of free enterprise from a managerial source."

15 In particular, the first five films were all sponsored by General Motors, *Turboglide* by Chevrolet, *Dividend in Depth* by Caterpillar Tractor Co., *A Spark in Time on the Firing Line* by the producer of spark plugs Champion Spark Plug Co., and *Energetically Yours* by the oil-producing company Esso.

16 The titles making up "The Bell System Science Series" are not the sole animated documentaries that came to life thanks to this corporation. We can also recall *The Thinking Machine* (1968, dir. Henry R. Feinberg), a short animated by John Snyder which stars a talking animated robot-computer and was produced by a film unit internal to the company referred to as Bell Telephone Laboratories.

17 In *The ABC of Internal Combustion Engines*, there is a long sequence wherein the voice-of-God narrator introduces the three characters and their personalities are outlined. For instance, Air is depicted as "a big, happy looking fellow" that "is usually lazy and languid, an easygoing sort of character," while Fuel is portrayed as "an explosive little rascal," "a tough little character."

18 At times, titles originally conceived for internal showing have been received so well by the employees of the sponsoring industry that they have ended up being used also as public relation films, as it occurred for example for a John Sutherland production on "the liquid of modern man's progress," oil: *It Never Rains Oil* (see McGrain 1956, 37).

19 For an analysis of the film's music, see Palmer (1990, 153–5).

20 Animated actors bring to an extreme Christine Geraghty's concept of the "star-as-professional" (see Geraghty 2000, 197–9). Indeed, since it is entirely "manufactured" and controlled by a studio, their star image can be characterized by a degree of stability and coherence that is hardly achievable when the star is a real-life human being. Second, always in virtue of their very ontology, they exist as actors only in order to be a certain character, to the point that in their case the actor becomes indistinguishable from the character and vice versa.

21 When it comes to voice-of-God and voice-of-authority, instead, there seems to not be a shared policy. We can equally find one or the other, and when the latter is the case, it may be either an animated character or a real-life person to cover this role.

22 Walt Disney (1940), "Letter of Introduction for John Sutherland," Howard W. Fleming collection, Margaret Herrick Library.

7

Great Britain

Instructing the Home Front through the Animated Documentary

When the Second World War broke out in September 1939, the British government came to find itself in need to inform and instruct the population on a high number of everyday issues. Cinema was soon identified as a suitable medium for fulfilling this task (see Wells 2006, 165–6). Especially starting from 1941, the MOI commissioned an increasing number of public information and propaganda films, a good portion of which in animation. As Daniel J. Leab (2007, 50) points out, "[t]he MOI's leadership believed that propaganda could be entertaining as well as convincing and that cartoons could usefully put across the agency's message." As a consequence, during the war years, through its commissions, the MOI became "a steady and reliable source of funding" for the national units working with this medium. It enabled as such the birth and development of various new studios—among which were, for instance, Halas & Batchelor Cartoon Films or Analysis Films (see Burrows 1986, 277, 280)—as well as a general "growth of British animation" (Southall 1999, 76–7).

It is in this context that the British classical animated documentary started developing. Indeed, among the many public information and propaganda animations sponsored in these years by the MOI, we can find this nation's first classical animated documentaries. This, however, is not to say that all the animations commissioned by the MOI in the first half of the 1940s can be considered examples of animated documentaries. Among the titles made employing such medium under the sponsorship of this ministry, we can also find films that deliver their message via telling a fictional story and that, therefore, while being examples of animated propaganda, cannot be considered animated documentaries. For instance, it is the case of John

Halas and Joy Batchelor's *Dustbin Parade* (1942) and *Cinderagella or Rags to Stitches* (1944). Both prompt British citizens to salvaging their waste but to do so by recounting highly imaginary vicissitudes. The former tells the story of four anthropomorphic pieces of scrap (i.e., a bone, an empty tin, a toy, and a plastic tube) joining up and being transformed into a shell. The latter, instead, narrates a wartime version of the *Cinderella* tale whose protagonist is a sad, anthropomorphic old rag. This piece of scrap, with the help of a fairy godmother, is recouped, transformed in a brand-new nurse uniform, and can thus attend the imaginary "War Service Ragtime Ball" at the castle, where it meets the prince, who is "a remade rag himself." Yet, undeniably, fictional titles like *Dustbin Parade* and *Cinderagella* constitute only a small portion of the animated production that have seen the light under MOI's auspices. Most of the animated films created on commission of this ministry during the war years employ, instead, the fabled animation to illustrate (even if often just very briefly) an aspect of the real, and thus classify as full-fledged animated documentaries. Therefore, interestingly, the classical animated documentary in Great Britain took shape as part of that same wartime cinema of which "[t]he drama-documentary" soon came "to be recognized as 'the key representational form'" (Chapman 2007, 16).

One of the very first titles referable to as a classical British animated documentary is *Filling the Gap* (1942), a short wherein, combining fabled animation and a voice-of-God commentary, it is explained why all citizens should start growing vegetables in their gardens. This film is directed by Halas and Batchelor, whose unit, Halas & Batchelor Cartoon Films, was among the most active studios in the making of animated documentaries during the Second World War in the UK.[1] Yet, it was not the only one. Among the other units that produced a number of these works in the period in question were, for instance, also Dufay-Chromex and Film Traders. In particular, after Halas and Batchelor, the figure that, in the war years, was most active in the creation of animated documentaries in Great Britain was Henry J. Elwis, who not only directed several such films for Dufay-Chromex but, in 1944, also personally produced a few titles through its own short-lived unit, Elwis Films.

Regardless of who made them, British wartime animated documentaries tended to share some traits. First of all, they were generally part of a larger public campaign and had ordinary citizens as their primary target. Second, they often took the form of the then so-called trailers: that is, informational and instructional films of about eighty seconds that were designed for attaching to the newsreel and contain "messages of immediate public importance" (Chapman 2015, 91). Content-wise, instead, this period's animated documentaries tackled mainly war-related issues connected with the everyday of the British public, such as salvaging, rationing, economizing, and so on. For instance, we can find titles on the recycling of domestic waste (*Salvage Saves Shipping* [1943, dir. G. M. Hollering], *Model Sorter*, or *Bones, Bones, Bones* [1944, dir. John Halas and Joy Batchelor]), on the rationing of fuel or electricity consumption (respectively *Cold Comfort* and *Peak Load* [1944, dir. G. M. Hollering]), on the cultivation of one's food (Halas and Batchelor's *Filling the Gap*, *Compost Heaps*, or *Blitz on Bugs* [1944]), on the proper handling of set everyday objects so to make them last longer and, consequently, avoid facing unnecessary expenses (*Bristles and Brushes* [1944] or *Leather Must Last* [1945, dir. Henry J. Elwis]), and so on. In sum, in line with what was commonplace for British nonfiction films in general during the Second World War, animated documentaries also tended to be "related in one way or another" to what was judged "needed in the national interest" (McLane [2005] 2012, 149). In particular, their main aim was to encourage viewers to adopt in their daily life set behaviors considered key for enabling the nation to win the conflict. Perhaps in order to more clearly convey the idea that adopting the suggested conducts was a way for British citizens to contribute to fighting the enemy from their homes, these animated documentaries often evoked the conflict also through the visual choices made in dramatizing their subject matter. An example is the decision to portray pests moving into a plant in *Blitz on Bugs* as an army attacking by air, land, and underground.

Next to the many titles focusing on behaviors that it was felt viewers needed to implement to enable the nation to defeat the enemies, we can, however, find also a small number of animated documentaries on topics that, while still concerning British citizens' everyday life, are not specifically linked to wartime contingencies. For instance, we can find health-related animated documentaries such as *One Pair of Nostrils* and *More Hanky Panky* (1945, dir. Henry J. Elwis) that illustrate the importance of the use of handkerchiefs in preventing the spread of the common cold. Or we can encounter safety ones as Elwis Films unit's *It Makes You Think* (1944) and Dufay-Chromex unit's *Tombstone Canyon* (1945, dir. Henry J. Elwis), which focus respectively on how easily a fire can start and on the importance of taking care when crossing the road. Still, also in these shorts, the conflict tends to be somehow recalled. Let us consider, for example, *One Pair of Nostrils* and *More Hanky Panky*. In the former, germs are represented as paratroopers. At the beginning of the latter, instead, the voice-of-God narrator describes the employees of the every-factory (which, by generalizing synecdoche, represents any factory) in which the film is set as people that "work to knock out Germany."

Whether they addressed a wartime issue or not, the animated documentaries created in the UK during the first half of the 1940s tended to blend information and instruction. Indeed, as scholar Giaime Alonge points out to be more generally the case of all British animated propaganda from these years, such films also provided mainly practical advice on the topic tackled, "without ever attempting at organizing a more complex discourse on war and its objectives" (Alonge 2000, 131, my translation). Titles such as *Bristles and Brushes* and *Model Sorter* well exemplify this characteristic of such period's British animated documentaries. In the former, a voice-of-God narrator informs viewers that the life of brushes and bristles can be prolonged by taking care of them and teaches how to do so. At the same time, visually, we see a hospital wherein an anthropomorphic exemplar for each type of brush and bristle mentioned (which by generalizing synecdoche represents its entire "species") is treated as one should for ensuring it a long life. Similarly, in *Model Sorter*, after a woman dumbs her trash in bulk, a voice-of-authority, first, points out that the proper recycling of scraps can help defeat the enemies. Subsequently, it instructs spectators on how to correctly sort their waste, aided in this by the various pieces of trash themselves, which magically group in the right way. In brief, the instructional dimension not only tends to always be present in Second World War British animated documentaries but also, as these examples make clear, often predominates.

Another trait common to most of these works is a marked eccentricity of their voice-of-God or voice-of-authority narration. For instance, we can find titles such as *Salvage Saves Shipping*, *One Pair of Nostrils*, and *Leather Must Last*, wherein the voice-of-God narrator talks in rhyming couplets. We also encounter films such as *Bones, Bones, Bones*, whose commentary is structured as a conversation between two men: one that keeps asking questions and a more informed one that answers them, enlightening his curious interlocutor (and consequently the viewer) on how bones can become "weapons of war," since fertilizers, glue, and explosives can be made from them. Similarly, there are various works wherein an anthropomorphic diegetic object plays the voice-of-authority role. Examples are *Model Sorter* or *Cold Comfort*, wherein this role is undertaken by a waste bin and a radio, respectively.

Moreover, we can even find a title such as *Peak Load*, whose voiceover commentary not only is in rhyming couplets but also purports to come from a load meter displaying electricity consumption, and thus to be a voice-of-authority. Indeed, even if, unlike in *Model Sorter* or *Cold Comfort*, the meter has no human features and is not shown in the act of talking, in the second scene of the film, while visually an animated representation of it is offered, we hear the narrator state: "I am a load meter, and I display electric power as it burns away." Therefore, although just orally, the meter is anthropomorphized, and it is suggested that it is this object to speak.

This overt eccentricity of the soundtrack was part of a more general trend to make these works highly entertaining, most likely due to a need to captivate and maintain the attention of the viewing public to ensure that they were reached by the message conveyed. Referring more generally to the trailers sponsored by the MOI, the *Documentary News Letter* states: "Who wants to listen to a housewife when you can hear a talking hen? . . . The trick stuff packs more punch, gets a clearer message across and is more entertaining" ("New Documentary Films" 1943, 182). In fact, we can notice in this period's British animated documentaries heavy use of fabled animation, in the sense that they abundantly employ all those devices more immediately associable to the medium's fictional production. For instance, often these animated documentaries heavily star (talking) anthropomorphic objects (as it occurs, among others, in *Bristles and Brushes*, *Model Sorter*, *Cold Comfort*, *Blitz on Bugs*, and *Bones, Bones, Bones*), but they can even visualize idioms, as it happens in *Peak Load*. Indeed, in this title produced by the Film Traders unit, in conveying the idea that excessive domestic consumption of electricity during morning hours (a time during which "war factories need it most") can determine a power overload, the saying "the straw that breaks the camel's back" is repeatedly referenced and literally transposed into animated visuals, even going as far as to represent the electricity course around a load meter in the shape of a camel.

In sum, what distinguishes the British animated documentary production of the classical era's affirmation subphase is a good degree of experimentalism. In other words, it tends to "play" with what in Chapter 5 we have seen to be the conventions of the form during its classical period in order to create works capable of complying with the then pressing imperative of capturing the attention of the viewing public.

The British Animated Documentary in Peacetimes

Even if the development of the classical animated documentary in Great Britain was initially triggered by specific communication needs contingent to the Second World War, the end of the conflict, and thus the consequent disappearance of the necessity that had sparked the emergence of this typology of films, did not determine a stagnation or a decline of the form. Undoubtedly, with the exclusion of Halas & Batchelor Cartoon Films—which long remained the main producer of animated documentaries in the country—, the units active in creating animated documentaries during the Second World War ceased to make such films once peace was restored. However, between 1946 and 1985, there were companies other than Halas & Batchelor Cartoon Films that engaged in making one or more animated documentaries. It is the case, among others, of the Pearl & Dean studio, Nicholas Cartoon Films Ltd., Biographic Films, Leeds Animation Workshop, Antony Barrier Productions, the documentary unit World Wide Pictures, or Larkins Studio, which even came near "to challenging Halas & Batchelor's supremacy" in the field (Burrows 1986, 280). In fact, overall, a significant number of animated documentaries were produced in the decades following the conclusion of the war.

These works also continued to be mainly sponsored films. It was no longer the MOI alone—which in the immediate postwar was dismantled—that commissioned them but a range of public and private bodies did so. Indeed, in line with what, in the late 1950s, John Huntley (1956–7, 4) pointed out to be the case for the national animation production in general, the vast majority of the classical animated documentaries produced in Great Britain after 1945 were made on commission of one of two typologies of entities:

1 "official bodies, government departments or international authorities";
2 industries.

More precisely, as far as the first kind of sponsors is concerned, the body that had commissioned the highest number of animated documentaries had undoubtedly been the COI, namely the "technical service department for the ministries to use for the production of campaign materials, with a committee of ministers and one of officials supervising liaison" that from early 1946 took up the MOI's heritage (Boon 2008, 153). As Timothy Boon explains, "[t]here has been sensitivity that, if information were continued to be run as a ministry, there would undoubtedly be accusation of party political use" (Boon 2008, 153). Therefore, the MOI was replaced with what Jane Chapman (2015, 129) describes as a "public-sector advertising agency" charged with the task of facilitating "the publicity needs of other [government] departments." And, like the MOI, the COI—which immediately embarked "upon an extensive programme of public information films" that will end up exceeding "even the height of wartime production in its quantity" (Chapman 2015, 124)— tends to favor animation over live-action for the making of such works (see Wells 2019, 111). As a consequence, in the course of its life, this department ended up also sponsoring the making of numerous animated documentaries which, unlike MOI's ones, often were more than just trailers. Indeed, even if eighty-second animated documentaries were seeing the light (especially in the immediate postwar years), the majority of post-1945, COI-commissioned works falling in this form were longer and more articulated than the wartime titles. In terms of the aspects of the real tackled, instead, a wide range of issues was covered over the years, with economic matters and social reforms being, however, two of the most addressed topics. The former is, for instance, at the core of the trailer *Export or Die* (1946, dir. John Halas), which explains to British citizens why they should sacrifice their luxuries for export,[2] or of Halas and Batchelor's *Farmer Charley* (1947), *Charley's Black Magic* (1947), and *Robinson Charley* (1948), which deal with the implementations needed within the farming industry to meet the national demand, postwar coal prices, and international trade respectively. Examples of COI-sponsored animated documentaries on social reforms instead are: *Charley in New Town*, on urban planning; *Charley's March of Time* (1947), on the National Insurance Act 1946; *Your Very Good Health*, on the benefits of the NHS Act 1946; *Charley Junior's Schooldays* (1948), on the Education Act 1944; the more recent *The Colombo Plan* (1962), on the namesake plan for Cooperative Economic Development in South and Southeast Asia; and *Referee* (1976), on the Race Relations Act 1976.

However, the COI is not the sole institution falling in Huntley's first category one can find behind the classical animated documentaries produced in Great Britain between 1946 and 1985. On the one hand, during the time frame in question, other national bodies commissioned one or more such works first-hand. Just to make some examples, in the immediate postwar, the British Council sponsored *Magna Carta. The Story of Man's Fight for Liberty* (1946), a colored short that, interspersing animated reenactments with prints and live-action dramatizations, traces the development of personal freedom and civil rights in Britain across the centuries. The Royal Navy directly commissioned to the documentary unit World Wide Pictures the eight-part series *Flight Safety and You* (1976–7), which, integrating animation and live-action, instructs on set safety procedures, such as pilot's pre-flight checks or the proper use of ground support equipment. The Sheffield City Court and the Welsh Association of Community Health Councils sponsored respectively the short *Council Matters* (1984, dir. Leeds Animation Workshop), on the services provided by local authorities, and *You and Your Health* (1979, dir. Harley Jones), on the aids offered in Wales by CHCs (i.e., the official consumer advisory bodies that help individuals with any problem concerning the NHS other than clinical matters). On the other hand, one can also find a small number of classical British animated documentaries commissioned by foreign governments and geared toward international audiences. It is, for instance, the case of Halas & Batchelor Cartoon Films' *Dam the Delta* (1958, dir. Joy Batchelor), which was commissioned by the Netherlands Government Information Service to promote the so-called Delta Plan, a project aimed at protecting the land around the Rhine-Meuse-Scheldt delta from sea flooding. Another example is Larkins Studio's controversial *Without Fear*, which discontented its sponsor, the US Economic Cooperation Administration, for its framing of European integration "in terms of defense against communist aggression" rather than in those of economic cooperation as it had been previously done, for instance, in French studio Les Gémeaux's *Story of a Rescue* (Fritsche 2018, 90).[3]

As far as industry-sponsored animated documentaries were concerned, instead, they started to increasingly emerge in the early 1950s, and thus when "the use of film as a medium of public and works relations and publicity generally" became more prominent "in the mind of industrialists" (Hoare 1952, 175). In other words, in Great Britain, industrial animated documentaries commenced to appear as soon as "the film in industry" started to become "more and more the recognized and established method of informing and influencing public opinion" (Hoare 1952, 178). Like Chapman (2015, 160) notices to have been the case for industrial live-action documentaries, animated ones were also commissioned by private corporations and nationalized industries. Indeed, the British industrial animated documentary production of the classical era can be divided into two macro groups, as far as their sponsorship is concerned. On the one hand, we have titles made under the auspices of bodies such as the British Iron and Steel Federation (*River of Steel* and *Earth Is a Battlefield* [1957, dir. Richard Taylor and Roger MacDougall]), the Gas Council (*Piping Hot* [1959, dir. John Halas] and *I'm Glad You Asked That Question*) and its replacement, the British Gas Corporation (*Super Natural Gas* [1975, dir. Nick Spargo]), and the Electricity Council (*The Case of the Metal Sheathed Elements* or *Play Safe* and *Safe as Houses*).

On the other hand, there are various animated documentaries sponsored by leading private corporations, like, for instance, BP (e.g., *The Moving Spirit*, *Power to Fly*, *Speed the Plough*, *We've Come a Long Way*, and the various other titles created at Halas & Batchelor Cartoon Films, or Larkins Studio's *Refining* and World Wide Pictures' *Gas Naturally* [1984, dir. Clive Mitchell]), ICI (Peter Sachs' *Enterprise* and *Balance 1950*), Rolex (Signal Films' *The Story of Time*), Philips (*Pan-tele-tron* or *For Better, For Worse* [1961, dir. John Halas and Peter Sachs]), and Barclays Bank (*The Curious History of Money* [1969, dir. Anne Jolliffe and Beryl Stevens]). This second typology of works was often traversed by a promotional agenda, which, however, in line with these animations being industrial films and not advertisements, remained undercurrent. Indeed, these works tended to illustrate an aspect of the real linked to the domain in which the corporation sponsoring them operated, often adopting a historical perspective. And, not dissimilarly from what was noted for most US industrial animated documentaries (see Chapter 6), when the firm or one of its products was referenced, it was done "subtly," so as not to undermine these films' overall educational character. Examples are the cases of *The Curious History of Money* and *Pan-tele-tron*. The former, which was produced by Larkins Studio in association with the Film Producers' Guild, illustrates the evolution of payment methods in England across the decades. Starting from barter and ending with the then recently introduced credit card, via cash, banknotes, checks, bills of exchange, and credit transfers, it explains how each of such forms of payment works. Reference to Barclays is made only on two occasions in the form of product placement. More precisely, a shot portraying a drawn Bank Giro Credit paper slip by Barclays and one representing the Barclaycard are briefly offered when respectively what a credit transfer and a credit card are is described (e.g., see Figure 7.1).

Similarly, *Pan-tele-tron*, which was instead made by the Pearl & Dean studio, is an animated history of telecommunications wherein Philips is referred to by integrating some objects (among which a rotary phone, some cameras, and a building) bearing either its logo or its name (e.g., see Figure 7.2). Unlike in *The Curious History of Money*, here, Philips is also mentioned in the commentary, but only at the very end of the film to suggest that the company is synonymous with telecommunications. Therefore, once again, it draws attention to the corporation sponsoring the animated documentary without undermining the film's overall informational character.

FIGURE 7.1 *A shot of a Bank Giro Credit paper slip by Barclays from* The Curious History of Money.

FIGURE 7.2 *A frame from* Pan-tele-tron *wherein there are some cameras with the Philips logo.*

Especially from the 1960s onward, however, next to governmental bodies and corporations, also some classical animated documentaries made under the auspices of a third typology of sponsors saw the light in Britain: national and international foundations and non-profit organizations. Examples are Joy Batchelor's *The Commonwealth* (1962), which illustrates the Commonwealth of nations looking at its benefits, people, ideology, and institutions, and Doron Abrahami's *Spare a Thought* (1978), wherein how Great Britain has exploited its colonial territories at commercial level is explained. Indeed, the former film was sponsored by the Nuffield Foundation and Commonwealth Institute. The latter was made on the commission of Christian Aid and Oxfam.

Whatever body sponsored them, from 1946 onward, British classical animated documentaries have tended to lose that instructional dimension dominant in the wartime works to become more purely informative. That is, these animated documentaries abandoned the wartime inclination at imparting practical advice on the aspect of the real addressed and focused instead on illustrating and describing that set part of our world. In particular, a good number of these animated documentaries are characterized by a historical approach to their chosen topic. In other words, they take the shape of animated histories. As we have seen, this was often the case for the industrial classical animated documentaries sponsored by private corporations. However, it was not exclusive of such works. It is possible to find numerous animated documentaries tracing the historical development of an aspect of the real also outside the realm of the corporation-sponsored titles. It is, for instance, the case of *Dam the Delta*, wherein the Delta Plan is presented as the latest in a long series of actions undertaken by the inhabitants of the Netherlands since 2000 BC to contrast the encroachment of the sea along their coasts. Other examples are the already mentioned *Magna Carta* or COI-sponsored works like *Men of Merit*, *First Line of Defence* (1949, dir. John Halas and Joy Batchelor), and *Local Government*. In *Men of Merit*, which combines stop-motion and hand-drawn animation, a "puppet lecturer" illustrates the development of electricity (Lloyd 2019, 203-4). In *First Line of Defence*, using just fabled animation and some brief captions, the evolution of flight is traced. In *Local Government*, mainly through a montage of still drawings, the history of local governance from its first inception in Saxon times to the current days is presented.

The fact that most post-1945 British classical animated documentaries had an informative rather than an instructional character, however, does not mean that they no longer aimed at inducing the adoption of a certain behavior in the spectator nor that all the titles falling in this form made after the end of the Second World War were informational. On the contrary, first of all, we can find British classical animated documentaries produced after 1946 that, despite having a predominantly informative character, aimed at prompting viewers to adopt a set way of conduct. Just to make an example, the primary goal behind *Men of Merit* was not to enrich the knowledge of British citizens around the history of electricity but to encourage them to avoid using electrical equipment in peak hours (an issue that is introduced by having a power cut interrupt the talk and force the lecturer to carry on by candlelight) (see Lloyd 2019, 203-4). Second, instructional titles that, in continuity with the wartime production, offered practical advice on a specific aspect of the real were still identifiable within the post-1945 British animated documentary production. The topics on which they imparted dos and don'ts were the most varied. They range from the golden rules to follow for serving a good cup of tea, which are laid down and showed by the animated professor protagonist of *T for Teacher*, to the health-related good practices to adopt in day-to-day life, illustrated in John Halas and Joy Batchelor's *Modern Guide to Health*.[4] Safety is, however, the aspect most touched upon, with the series *Flight Safety and You* or the shorts *A Mortal Shock* (1950),[5] *Play Safe*, and *Safe as Houses* being some examples. That said, these instructional works represent only a small portion of the overall British animated documentary production of the decades in question.

If the post-1945 production differed from the wartime one with regard to the ratio of information and instruction, there were other respects under which the titles of these two periods showcased instead a good deal of continuity. The first one concerns their target audience. Indeed, undeniably, after 1945, it became more commonplace also to find animated documentaries intended for a specific category of people. It is, for instance, the case of *Enterprise* and *Balance 1950*, both of which are examples of industrial animated documentaries targeted at the employees of their sponsoring company. As explained on the pages of the magazine *Film User*, in the early 1950s, "ICI believes in explaining its trading and financial operations to its workers. . . . ICI feels that workers and staff should understand the financing of the company, if only to see how great a provision is made for the future, and how much is paid out in wages and salaries" ("Films for the Workers" 1952, 335). Therefore, the corporation commissioned to Larkins Studio these two animated documentaries intended for internal circulation, which respectively explain the structure of ICI and dramatize the company's balance sheet of 1950, detailing how the corporation had spent its money that year.[6] Other examples of titles created with a specific target in mind are *T for Teacher*, *Flight Safety and You*, and *Referee*. Created by Larkins Studio on commission of the Tea Bureau, *T for Teacher* is a black-and-white animated documentary on how tea should be stored, prepared, and served that, as Lloyd (2019, 202) points out, was conceived with "trainee catering and domestic science students" in mind. Analogously, as its subject itself makes evident, the series *Flight Safety and You* had its target audience in naval aviation personnel. *Referee*, which explains how the then recently established Race Relations Board was there to aid all citizens receive the same, fair treatment regardless of their race, was instead clearly aimed at a British South Asian audience. This is made apparent through the choice of having a British citizen of Indian origins as its everyman protagonist.

In sum, under the perspective of the target audience, some changes occurred between the pre- and post-1945 British classical animated documentaries. Nevertheless, like their wartime counterparts, the majority of the titles produced from 1946 onward that fall in this form were targeted at a general audience. In particular, they were mostly aimed at British citizens at large, a fact that tended to be emphasized by having characters with whom anybody could easily identify as their protagonists. Emblematic is the work done around the clothing of Charley, the middle-aged man drawn by Joy Batchelor and serving as "the figure representing the attitudes and opinions of an audience" in Halas & Batchelor Cartoon Films' "Charley" series (Southall 1999, 79). Precisely to favor anybody's identification in this character regardless of their social milieu a long musing was done around how to dress him. Halas and Batchelor themselves recount: "Charley's clothes gave a great deal of trouble. If he didn't wear a tie the working mane might take umbrage, if he did, he was dangerously near the white-collar-worker. In the end, a very plain tie was balanced by a boiler suit" (Halas and Batchelor in Southall 1999, 80).

The second element that unites pre- and post-1945 classical animated documentaries is the tendency to play with the conventions of the form, experiment around its canons, and reinvent them. In particular, precisely like their wartime counterparts, post-1945 British animated documentaries were characterized by a marked eccentricity of the voice-of-God or voice-of-authority narration. For instance, when a voice-of-God commentary was opted for, it might have been in rhymes, as Manvell points out to occur frequently in the titles produced at Larkins Studio (see Manvell 1955, 82). Alternatively, the unseen and omniscient narrator could have repeated aural interactions with the character(s) protagonist of the film. This happens, for instance, in Halas & Batchelor's *Your Very Good Health* and *Charley's March of Time*. The protagonist of these two shorts, Charley, not only is addressed directly by the voice-of-God narrator more than once but also repeatedly looks into the camera and comments or questions the assertions of the unseen narrator as if the latter was a figure located behind the camera with whom he was having an actual conversation. Another example in this sense is *Flight Safety and You*. Here, the voice-of-God constantly dialogs with Lionel, the animated bluebird erected as Royal Navy's flight safety symbol that stars in all the episodes of the series. Even more interesting is the case of *Super Natural Gas*. This film's main character is Willo the Wisp, a floating personification of methane with the facial features of the actor who voices it, Kenneth Williams. This entity does not just aurally interact with the omniscient voiceover narrator, commenting on what he states. At times, it also substitutes him in the telling of the history of natural gas, therefore partially becoming an eccentric voice-of-authority.

Analogously, in the animated documentaries that, in place of a voice-of-God, employed a voice-of-authority—which in Great Britain have been unusually numerous throughout the classical era—for this role were often chosen engaging rather than authoritative animated characters. In other words, instead of undertaking the conventional route of casting in this role a figure that the viewer immediately associated to credibility and knowledge (such as a professor or a scientist) was opted for characters capable of "sugaring the pill of information" (*Charley Junior's School Days* 1950, 13), as noted on the pages of the *Monthly Film Bulletin* in relationship to the celestial nurse used as a voice-of-authority in *Charley Junior's Schooldays*. More precisely, these eccentric voices-of-authority could be highly fabled figures as, for instance, a talking object (e.g., the scarecrow of *Speed the Plough*) or animal (e.g., the wise, old owl of *Play Safe* or the cat of *Safe as Houses*, which are voiced respectively by Brian Wilde and Judi Dench), a popular fictional character (e.g., Sherlock Holmes in *The Case of the Metal Sheathed Elements*), or a supernatural entity (e.g., the spirit of coal reminiscent of the ghosts of Christmas Past, Christmas Present, and Christmas Yet to Come of Charles Dickens' novella *A Christmas Carol* used in *Charley's Black Magic*). Alternatively, they might have been ordinary men or women who (more or less explicit) counterposed themselves to the traditional figure of the expert. Examples of this second case are the voices-of-authority of *I'm Glad You Asked That Question* or *Refining*. Indeed, in *I'm Glad You Asked That Question*, this part is played by a clumsy man in a light-blue suit who from the outset betrays little familiarity with the role to the point of starting his speech giving his shoulders to the camera. Moreover, he also keeps looking at his notes and is completely lost when his flashcards accidentally fall on the floor and get mixed up. Similarly, the voice-of-authority of *Refining* is an ordinary man who escaped from the guided tour of a BP refinery that he has already taken more than once. This character repeatedly counterposes himself to the tour guide in a lab coat that embodies the actual expert on the topic. Indeed, he presents himself as a figure capable of explaining the information exposed by the tour guide in simpler and more understandable terms. Finally, it is also possible to find voices-of-authority that showcase a mixture of ordinariness and highly fabled traits since they are apparently average human figures, who, however, have fantastic attributes. For instance, in *Council Matters* "a char who uses her vacuum cleaner as a flying broomstick" explains how a local authority functions (Lant [1993] 2006, 165). Similarly, in *Charley Junior's Schooldays* a nurse who tends to children still to be born illustrates the benefits of the Education Act 1944.

In addition, more generally, when an eccentric voice-of-authority was employed, it was not infrequent for it to expose the information on the topic in question as part of a dialog with another fabled diegetic character unfamiliar with that subject matter who can be seen as a filmic alter ego of the viewer and with whom the latter can identify. For instance, the nurse of *Charley Junior's Schooldays* explains the advantages of the Education Act 1944 to a still to be born Charley Jr. The owl of *Play Safe* and the cat of *Safe as Houses* expose the dos and don'ts around electricity as part of a conversation with a young robin and a dog respectively. In *The Case of the Metal Sheathed Elements*, Holmes illustrates how metal sheathed elements are constructed and used while dialoguing with his assistant Dr. Watson.

Even at the level of visuals, like their wartime predecessors, post-1945 British classical animated documentaries were not afraid of exploiting in full animation's most fictional devices nor refrained from including scenes finalized only at entertaining the viewer to the point that the commentary could be temporarily absented during them. Examples in this sense can be the many comic antics involving the Greek god Zeus and his messenger Hermes, of which is interspersed *Pan-tele-tron*, or those having as protagonist the eccentric voice-of-authority and star of *I'm Glad You Asked That Question*. The British post-1945 animated documentaries that overall showcased the most extreme deployment of fabled animation were, however, the ones from Larkins Studio. In the immediate postwar years and up to the mid-1950s, this company was home to Peter Sachs, who "understood the power of animation to capture the audience's attention through a contemporary visual vocabulary that imaginatively conveyed information in a condensed and often unexpected manner" (Lloyd 2019, 200). Sachs personally directed a number of the company's first animated documentaries, shaping what will remain the studio's approach to the form also after his departure. And, next to constant reinvention of classical animated documentary's canons and the employment of a modernist style characterized by "angular figures, clear-cut lines and sharply-defined backgrounds, in which detail is reduced to a minimum" (Huntley 1956–7, 6), a characteristic of his work was precisely an overt employment of fabled animation without, nevertheless, ever sidelining the factuality of what was illustrated. This characteristic of Sachs' works has lived on also after he departed from the studio as it becomes clear from some declarations of female animator Beryl Stevens dating to 1972. Stevens, who joined Larkins Studio in 1956 and later moved up the ranks internally to become the company's managing director, worked on numerous of the unit's animated documentaries—including *Refining* (of which she has been the scriptwriter) and *The Curious History of Money* (which she co-directed). And in a 1972 interview with *The Leader-Post*, she stated: "A good cartoon can do a valuable job in short circuiting complicated facts and figures which would otherwise take a long time to read and absorb" (Stevens in Pulling 1972, 13). However, in talking about her conception of sponsored animated documentaries, she also added that "[a]musing sponsored films are all very well but they must have a strong backbone of facts," which is why in scriptwriting them she opted for the following approach: "I write the script twice. The first time 'straight' with all the facts, the second time 'crooked' when I introduce the fun" (Stevens in Pulling 1972, 13). From these words, it emerges how Stevens had a vision of the animated documentary very close to that of Sachs.

If, when it comes to Larkins Studio's shorts, the same abundant use of fiction animation's devices proper of the titles from the Second World War years can be identified, in many of the other post-1945 works falling in this form the excessively fabled character proper of most wartime animated documentaries was instead tempered a bit either through limited use of sober animation or combining fabled animation with live-action. This second approach is noticeable also in titles from the immediate postwar years (e.g., see *Magna Carta*), but became highly employed especially between the early 1970s and the end of the classical animated documentary era. And, it can be read as an attempt to integrate in these works some of that indexicality between the film and our world that Honess Roe (see 2013, 29–30) shows to be a prerequisite for an audiovisual work to be accepted as a documentary. Also, this incorporation of live-action in British classical animated documentaries has taken two alternative forms:

1. the alternation of animated and live-action scenes, as it happens for example in *Magna Carta, You and Your Health*, or *Gas Naturally*; and
2. the insertion of animated characters in live-action backgrounds, as is the case, for instance, for *Flight Safety and You, Play Safe, Safe as Houses*, or *Refining* (e.g., see Figure 7.3).

Furthermore, with the 1970s, titles in which this indexical link with reality was instead introduced through sound also saw the light. This, however, occurred only in a limited number of works forerunning the contemporary animated documentary production, such as the observational shorts forming the *Animated Conversations* and *Conversation Pieces* series, which, in returning a portrayal of a fragment of the everyday, used audio-recordings of eavesdropped, real-life conversations as their basis. In sum, at the level of mode of representation, there is mostly continuity between the pre- and post-1945 British animated documentary production, but some variances can also be detected.

FIGURE 7.3 *A shot from* Refining *wherein the animated voice-of-authority is inserted in a live-action background.*

The Classical Animated Documentary according to Halas and Batchelor

As already anticipated, the leading British studio in the production of classical animated documentaries has unquestionably been Halas & Batchelor Cartoon Films. Out of it a high number of qualitative titles attributable to the form were produced—some of which went on to receive awards even outside of the national borders.[7] Also, its two founders, John Halas and Joy Batchelor, repeatedly advocated the use of animation to tackle the real, inevitably playing an important role in the development of the abundant classical British animated documentary production. Indeed, like Disney in the United States, Halas and Batchelor swiftly understood that animation has a "value both as a means of presentation and teaching" (Halas 1957, 15), and, when "well used, can help to explain what is going on outside our personal sphere ... more clearly than is possible through the live-action film, which suffers from the same limitations as the human eye and ear" (Halas and Manvell [1959] 1976, 133). Halas (in Manvell 1980) has written: "John Grierson ... proclaimed the documentary film the creative interpretation of actuality. The animated film is admirably suited to this same definition with the additional fact that it is also able to penetrate beyond the surface of actuality and show a reality beyond that which the live action lens can detect." In other words, he and his wife quickly realized that animation in certain circumstances can prove superior to live-action for telling the real because it has abilities that the latter lacks. Indeed, "where live action particularizes, animation generalizes, and in the process makes what it seeks to explain universal" (Manvell 1980, 134). Moreover, animation has abilities that live-action has not, such as the power:

1 [t]o visualise the invisible. . . .
2 [t]o solidify the intangible. . . .
3 [t]o characterise and symbolise. . . .
4 [t]o re-create the extinct, inaccessible to normal filming. (Halas 1957, 15)

Besides, Halas and Batchelor quickly became aware also that "cartoons can make entertainment out of the presentation of facts, figures, systems and ideas" (Halas and Manvell [1959] 1976, 116), and therefore can "inform and entertain at the same time" (Halas 1956, 6)—or, as it is put in the adverts of the animated documentaries created by the studio for BP, "entertain as well as ... instruct"[8]—a fact that positively affects the reception of the data conveyed through them. Thus, the two British animators rapidly comprehended that this medium allows getting information across more readily by enabling to make a point "painlessly—either deriving a dramatic impact from the subject or winning the sympathy and good humor of the public because of what was in effect the aesthetic impact of the film, the graphic charm or force of its presentation" (Halas 1956, 133).

It is important to note that the two spouses effectively partook this understanding of the medium's applicability in a nonfiction context and equally contributed to shaping the studio's animated documentary production. At first glance, it could seem that the mastermind behind the unit's animated documentaries was the sole Halas, while Batchelor had a more purely executional role, since, as seen in Chapter 3, next to having (co-)directed a good number of such works, the former alone has signed almost all the writings wherein is expressed the vision of the studio on the form.[9] Nevertheless, first, as Paul Wells (2014, 76) points out, Batchelor also "believed that animation could be readily used in the service of social good." Second, besides co-directing and, in several instances, even solo directing some of the studio's animated documentaries—as it has been the case, for example, for *Dam the Delta*, *The Commonwealth*, or *The Colombo Plan*—, she has solely scripted most of them. So, even if Halas "was the face that people saw" and "the primary figure associate with the company" (Stewart 2014, 16), he cannot be considered the only mastermind behind this production.

Furthermore, the animated documentary for them appeared to be more than an opportunity for raising the money needed to self-finance their more renowned fictional works. It was a form in which they were fully invested. To prove it is the fact that, while most of the works produced by Halas & Batchelor Cartoon Films that fall in this category were created on commission of a government agency or a private corporation in line with what back then was generally the case for this typology of titles in Great Britain, on a few occasions from the studio came out also "independent 'free'" animated documentaries: that is, titles "made for themselves rather than commissioned by sponsors" (Stewart 2014, 18). It is the case of *History of the Cinema*, an account of the development of moving pictures since their early days,[10] or *History of Inventions* (*La storia delle invenzioni*, 1959), a short directed by Bruno Bozzetto that Halas co-produced.

That premised, Halas & Batchelor Cartoon Films' animated documentary production is diverse in terms of topics addressed and modes of presenting them. Certainly, there are some aspects of the real that have been addressed more than once. It is, for instance, the case of aviation and its history, which has first been illustrated in *First Line of Defence* and, years apart, in *Power to Fly*—although making different choices in terms of mode of narration and graphic style. However, all in all, this unit has produced animated documentaries on a large spectrum of topics, as Halas (1956, 6) himself points out when he writes: "The subject of practically every film we make differs from the last. Our subject today may be the history of agriculture and our audience a specialized technical group, and tomorrow we may be required to outline in comprehensible terms for the general public the theory of alcoholism and its effect on human society."

Similarly, we may find a same image or animated actor in more than one of the studio's animated documentaries. For instance, the latter is the case of the shorts forming the so-called Charley series or of the wartime shorts *Filling the Gap* and *Compost Heaps*, where the same anthropomorphic cauliflower can be found. Examples of films that share an image are instead *The Moving Spirit* and *The Colombo Plan*. In both shorts one can see rail tracks and galleries that progressively take shape at the advancing of a train. In *The Moving Spirit*, it happens when, in tracing the history of the motor car, the introduction of "steam engines on wheels" that moved on "its own level track" is illustrated. In *The Colombo Plan*, instead, it occurs when it is explained that, thanks to the Colombo Plan, new railroads would have been built. Still, overall, Halas & Batchelor Cartoon Films' animated documentaries were not marked by a unitary approach to the subject matters addressed or a shared mode of presentation. This is due to Halas and Batchelor having always seen the form and style of the narration as an aspect that should be subordinated to the topic tackled as well as to the film's objective and intended audience. In a 1948 article, the two animators declared that they tend to base the structure of a script and a film first and foremost on "what has to be said and to whom" as well as on "what kind of effect the film is intended to produce" (Halas and Batchelor 1948, 11). The consequence of letting these three parameters dictate the form of the film is that, for instance, among Halas & Batchelor Cartoon Films' corpus of animated documentaries one can find titles interspersed with gags wherein the entertaining moments abound and, at times, the facts illustrated may even be satirized (e.g., see *Piping Hot*, *History of the Cinema*, or *For Better, For Worse*) as well as a film like *The Colombo Plan* that is characterized by serious tones throughout. Indeed, the adoption of this approach meant that the number of entertaining elements showcased, the mode of narration and the fictional devices used, the graphic style employed, and the quantity of sober animation present (if any) could all vary significantly from one of the studio's short to another, even within the same series. Let us consider, for example, the Charley series. These seven shorts have in common a character (i.e., Charley), the design, and the relationship between entertainment and information, since they all have a same target audience in which they aim to produce an identical effect. However, these are pretty much the only elements that they share. Indeed, depending on what economic matter or social reform they illustrate, they are structured differently. In some of them, a voice-of-God narrator was used, while in others, a voice-of-authority was preferred. From one film to the other, the weight of Charley in the narrative changes. He can go from having a mere walk-on part, as in *Charley Junior's Schooldays*, to having the leading role, as it occurs in *Charley's March of Time* or *Farmer Charley*. Finally, the fictional device that each film heavily exploits changes: in *Your Very Good Health*, it is doubling characters; in *Charley's March of Time*, time travel; in *Charley's Black Magic*, a Dickensian spirit; and so on.

Yet, more generally speaking, the choice of letting the subject matter, the target audience, and the desired effect dictate the structure and form of the film may not be the sole reason behind the diversity of Halas & Batchelor Cartoon Film's animated documentaries. The latter can, in part, be accounted also to a drive toward experimentalism that, despite not having been as pronounced as at Larkins Studio, characterized this unit as well. Discussing animation in general, Halas recognizes: "From the very beginning of the cinema this medium was a platform for new ideas and new approaches in cinematography" (Halas 1957, 15). At the same time, he also identifies in sponsored documentaries a terrain for experimentation when he writes:

> The kind of film service developed by the documentary movement in Britain during the nineteenth-thirties might not at first seem to offer any substantial place for the cartoon. But in *Night Mail* the documentary film-maker was already using the soundtrack with the same kind of calculation as the animator in his work, and *the spirit of experiment that inspired the best sponsored documentaries in Britain at that time gradually extended until it drew in the cartoon itself*—initially during the War years, when animated propaganda films were produced. (Halas and Manvell [1959] 1976, 116, my emphasis)

For instance, a film as *First Line of Defence*, wherein, instead of the then commonplace voice-of-God commentary and voice-of-authority, a limited number of brief captions is used to convey the facts concerning the history of aviation—thus leaving mainly to the animated visuals the task of communicating its evolution across the decades—, may, therefore, be seen as the result of a desire to experiment a different approach rather than of the belief of this being the most apt way for narrating that aspect of the real.

Nevertheless, one could argue that, at a macro level, it is possible to identify two alternative approaches that have been recurrently adopted throughout the decades at Halas & Batchelor Cartoon Films in making animated documentaries. On the one hand, as Halas (in Manvell 1980) himself has pointed out, part of his studio's titles falling in this form are "in the format of argument between two opposing views." More precisely, "an advisory voiceover"—that the characters can hear—or a voice-of-authority explains to the protagonist of the film an issue concerning his or her everyday life, gradually persuading the character of the validity of what is stated (Wells 2014, 67). In particular, as Paul Wells notes to be the case for *Modern Guide to Health*,[11] in these argumentative animated documentaries the voice-of-God or voice-of-authority, who exercises "a playful tension between the ignorance of the subject (the audience) and the role of the expert," tends to convince the character by "offering a demonstrably positive outcome as a consequence of undertaking the suggested actions" (Wells 2014, 67). Also, the addressed character is usually an everyman "representing the attitudes and opinions of an audience" (Southall 1999, 79). Moreover, he is conceived so that the whole sector of the viewing public to which the film is targeted can easily identify with him. The studio's finest examples of these everymen are the already mentioned Charley or George, the protagonist of *Think of the Future* (1956, dir. John Halas), an animated documentary explaining why the more a worker produces, the better future is ensured to everyone. The very first instance of this everyman figure within a Halas & Batchelor Cartoon Films' animated documentary can, however, already be identified in *Filling the Gap*, whose nameless protagonist represents all British citizens. Therefore, his design not casually recalls the universal pictorial symbol for man used in the Neuraths' Isotype graphic language.

On the other hand, in line with what we have noted to be quite commonplace for the classical British animated documentary in general, an even more significant number of the studio's titles adopt a historical perspective on their subject matter. Exploiting the possibility "to compress a time period of several hundred years into a few minutes" that animation gives (Halas in Manvell 1980), they summarize the evolutions that have brought a set element of the real (e.g., agriculture [*Speed the Plough*], aviation [*First Line of Defence*, and *Power to Fly*], the motor car [*The Moving Spirit*], the tankship [*We've Come a Long Way*], the film industry [*History of the Cinema*], and so on) to acquire its present traits. More precisely, in many cases, the focus is posed on showing how across the decades a problem has progressively been solved so as to foreground why the latest advancements in that set sector represent an essential step forward for the everyday life of mankind in general, the inhabitants of specific territories, or a set category of people. Emblematic are two of the titles created by the studio for BP with the aim of bringing "vitality and color to their public relations, clarifying complex technical and scientific processes with distinctive artistry" (Manvell 1980): *We've Come a Long Way* and *Animal, Vegetable, Mineral*. The former does not simply illustrate the history of the tankship. It depicts how, from the 1860s onward, its design has been progressively changed to overcome the difficulties that hauling oil poses. Similarly, *Animal, Vegetable, Mineral* is not as much about the evolution of lubricants across the centuries as on how the introduction of multi-grade oils represents the culmination of a long journey undertaken to solve the problem of friction, which started as far back as the Ancient Egypt era.

More generally speaking, in these animated histories, condensation processes as the elliptical cut, the dissolve, the wipe, and the fade out and fade in are obviously heavily employed. It is not infrequent, however, also the adoption of "metamorphosis as narrative transition" to "elide . . . time and space" (Wells 1998, 66). For example, in *Piping Hot*, the idea expressed by the voice-of-God that, due to people never taking baths, for centuries, dirt and disease have been common causes of death even among rich people is synthetically represented by the image of an aristocrat's carriage that morphs in a coffin. In *Power to Fly*, the evolutions from the converted bomber to the large passenger aircraft are concisely illustrated through having a single plane of the former kind that, while flying in the sky, rapidly morphs into different models before acquiring the shape of the latter airplane type. Analogously, in *The Moving Spirit*, the reconversion of the motor car industry after the end of the Second World War is symbolically summarized through showing a series of military motor vehicles that, in moving away from a landscape devastated by the conflict and entering one where peace reigns, mutate into automobiles for civilian use (see Figures 7.4 and 7.5).

Finally, in these animated histories, a same animated actor whose clothing changes according to the fashion of the different decades or centuries touched upon may be used, as it occurs, for instance, in *Speed the Plough*. However, it is more commonplace for a different character to be employed for each period, perhaps to stress the change of decade or century further.

It is, thus, undeniable that, in terms of approach and development of their subject matter, Halas & Batchelor Cartoon Films' animated documentaries showcase some recurrent patterns after all. Yet, in line with the principle of subordinating the form of the film to both its subject and target audience, first, these two formats are not the only ones to be employed. Second, they are never rigidly applied and can even be mixed in the same title. We can find, for instance, animated documentaries as

FIGURE 7.4 *A military motor vehicle moving away from a landscape devastated by the conflict in* The Moving Spirit.

FIGURE 7.5 *The military motor vehicle transformed into an automobile for civilian use after entering a landscape wherein peace has been restored in* The Moving Spirit.

Think of the Future and *Charley's March of Time* that, while being mainly argumentative, also offer historical insights on their subject matters. In both cases, however, the past is illustrated to prove to the character the validity of what the voice-of-God narrator has stated. In particular, in *Charley's March of Time*, the character is brought back in time to experience how, in the past, people had much less social securities, so to prove to him that the National Insurance Act 1946 is an important step forward for British citizens, even if it will require a greater economic effort on their part. Likewise, in *Think for the Future*, George is made to experience the working and living conditions of the past to demonstrate to him that they were much worse than those of the present days. In both the films, the adoption of a historical perspective is, thus, not an end in itself. Rather, it is functional to the argument.

In a nutshell, Halas & Batchelor Cartoon Films' approach to the animated documentary form has been varied but consistent enough for some patterns to be identifiable. Each time Halas, Batchelor, and their team have proven capable of finding original but coherent ways to illustrate and explain the assigned topic. And, even if a distinctive Halas & Batchelor animated documentary style may not have been developed, especially between the early 1940s and the late 1950s, through their works and writings, the two founders of this unit have exercised an important influence on the definition and evolution of the national approach to the form. From their studio have come out works that simultaneously are perfect exemplifications of what the British animated documentary has been during its classical era and high points of this period's production that other national companies have looked up to in creating their own films. In other words, this unit has been capable of making titles that have been at the same time classics and reference models of the classical British animated documentary production.

Notes

1. For a more in-depth treatise of the work Halas & Batchelor Cartoon Films did for the MOI, see Price (2019), Wells (1995).

2. Other examples of trailers dealing with postwar economic matters are John Halas and Joy Batchelor's *The Keys of Heaven* (1946) and *More Exports* (1947). In this category, *Watch the Fuel Watcher* (1946), which focuses on saving power at the workplace, can also be included.

3. In *Story of a Rescue*, European integration is framed specifically as the sharing of surplus goods among European nations. A man dressed in clothes habitually associated to a certain nation (whom for generalizing synecdoche stands for the population of that set country) is shown in the act of throwing a good that the country in question produces in excess to a man of another nation, who does not have it and who in turn throws to the citizen of a different country a good his nation has in abundance, and so forth (e.g., a Frenchman receives from a Scot a jacket and throws a bottle of wine to a Swiss).

4. In particular, *Modern Guide to Health* explains, among others, the posture to keep when working, how to correctly sunbathe, how children should be dressed to favor their correct growth, and what to do before going to bed to ensure oneself a restful sleep.

5. More precisely, *A Mortal Shock* warns viewers of the dangers of electric shock in the bathroom.

6. *Balance 1950* is not the sole title illustrating a balance sheet that was animated at Larkins Studio. For instance, this unit is also responsible for the animated segments of the partly animated short *Money and Steel* (1959, dir. Robin Cantelon). However, this title sponsored by the British Iron and Steel Federation cannot be considered an animated documentary. Indeed, in this case, sober animation is mainly employed for illustrating the balance sheet of a typical plant.

7. For example, *Modern Guide to Health* obtained the first prize at the Brussels World Film Festival in 1947. *As Old as the Hills* and *Power to Fly* received the first prize at the Venice Film Festival in the documentary category in 1950 and 1954, respectively.

8. See, for instance, the advert for *The Moving Spirit* that has appeared on *Sight and Sound*, 23 (3), 1954: i, or the one for *Speed the Plough* published on *Sight and Sound*, 26 (2), 1956: 58.

9. For instance, see Halas in Manvell (1980), Halas (1956), Halas (1957).

10. *History of the Cinema* was, however, later bought by Philips of Eindhoven to promote the sale of film projectors (see "The John Halas Story" 1964, 42).

11. Although, due to its fragmented and sketchy structure, it is not fully an expression of Halas & Batchelor Cartoon Films' argumentative animated documentaries, *Modern Guide to Health* shares various elements with them.

8

Canada

The birth of the Canadian animation industry is conventionally traced back to John Grierson's 1941 decision of entrusting Norman McLaren with the task of setting up an animation department at the NFB (see Beaudet 1978, 71; Handling and Jean [1999] 2000, 838; Bendazzi 2016a, 129). Indeed, up to this moment, the nationally created animations amount to a handful of titles resulting from sporadic and unconnected experimentations with the medium. With the establishment of the NFB studio, instead, Canada started finally boasting a systematic and continuous production of animated works.

Interestingly, behind the creation of the NFB animation department, and consequently the exiting of Canadian animation from its long age of origins, there is a Disney nonfiction animated film. Indeed, after its establishment in May 1939, with the mandate "of helping 'Canadians in all parts of Canada to understand the ways of living and the problems of Canadians to other parts the world's'" (McLane [2005] 2012, 131–2), the NFB at first focused its efforts on the creation of live-action documentaries. Animations, instead, seem to have been considered a typology of works that could have been commissioned externally, if needed. In fact, at the beginning of 1941, Grierson was already trying to find a way to have McLaren—who now lived in New York—collaborate with the NFB. Still, as it emerges from some letters that the Scottish animator exchanged with his family, when first getting in touch with McLaren in January 1941, Grierson was just looking into the possibility of having the NFB commission him "one or two . . . films" (McLaren in Dobson 2018, 67). Then, on April 3rd of the same year, Grierson was invited to attend a presentation at the Walt Disney Studios, during which were screened some of the company's works, in order to make apparent the training and educational potential of animation. Among the films shown was *Four Methods of Flush Riveting*, which struck a chord in Grierson, making him realize that animation has "a capacity for simplifying the presentation of pedagogical problems as documentary films have not" (Grierson in Shale 1982, 16). This realization brought the Scottish documentarist to commission the Walt Disney Studios' four promotional shorts encouraging viewers to buy the Canadian war bonds—namely *The Thrifty Pig* (1941, dir. Ford Beebe), *7 Wise Dwarfs* (1941, dir. Richard Layford), *Donald's Decision* (1942, dir. Ford Beebe), and *All Together* (1942, dir. Jack King)—as well as *Stop That Tank!* (1942, dir. Ub Iwerks), a training film aimed at teaching soldiers how to use the Boys antitank rifle properly (see Baxter 2014, 12–16).[1] At the same time, however, the viewing of *Four Methods of Flush Riveting* likely made Grierson understand the importance of having an animation department at the NFB. He probably realized that, in this way, the institution would have been able to make this typology of works internally. Indeed, when he reached out to McLaren again in July 1941, it was no longer only to have him make a couple of films. It was to offer him "a permanent position" at the NFB. Also, significantly, as the Scottish animator underlines in a letter to his parents, Grierson wanted him there precisely for creating "films for publicizing things like War Savings and so on" (McLaren in Baxter 2014, 68).

Although at the roots of its birth there is a nonfiction film, the NFB studio has produced many fictional animations. Nevertheless, since its inception, it has devoted at least part of its energies to making films about our world. Moreover, not all the reality-centered animations that over the years have come out of this studio are animated documentaries. A case in point is Jodoin's 1960 series "Antenna Fundamentals." Created for the Royal Canadian Air Force, the titles forming this series are training films that clarify the principles of radio wave transmission making use only of sober animation.[2] Therefore, despite tackling an aspect of our world, they cannot be considered animated documentaries. Many of the reality-related animations created over time by the NFB animators, however, do qualify as animated documentaries. In fact, the establishment of NFB's animation department did not mark just the birth of the Canadian animation industry but also the beginning of the animated documentary's classical era in this nation. Indeed, this is the studio wherein, during the war years, the titles that inaugurated this age of animated documentary's history in Canada were produced.

Furthermore, the NFB studio will remain the primary Canadian producer of animated documentaries throughout this form's classical age. Between 1941 and 1985 another studio also frequently used animation in nonfictional contexts: Crawley Films. From 1939—when Frank Radford Crawley and his wife Judith established it—to 1982—when it went out of business—this studio produced many (partly) animated sponsored films addressing our world. In most cases, however, sober animation was used. Only a few titles of Crawley Films' extensive production can be considered animated documentaries. It is, for instance, the case of *Child Behavior Equals You* (1972), a short created with the counsel of child specialists for the Vanier Institute of the Family. This film employs fabled animation to explain what motivates both good and bad behavior in children from infancy to adolescence and how the conduct of adults has a significant influence on the development of a youngster.

Additionally, some of the animators that in the decades worked for the NFB studio eventually left it to set up their own companies. A case in point is Gerald Potterton. This animator, who, as we will see, during his permanence at the NFB, worked on various animated documentaries, in 1968 left the studio to establish his own company: Potterton Productions. With it, he produced mostly fictional films both in animation and live-action. Still, he also made, for Place Bonaventure, *The Trade Machine* (1968, dir. Gerald Potterton), an animated documentary that illustrates the history of trade.[3]

Finally, more toward the end of the classical period, there have been also some televisual animated documentaries created by studios other than the NFB. Exemplar is the case of *Eureka!* (1980–1), a series targeted to kids that in each of its thirty episodes illustrates a different concept in physics combining a voice-of-God narration and fabled animation. This series, which stars a clumsy animated ordinary man, was made by studio Grafilm Productions Inc. for TVOntario.

In brief, some animated documentaries have also been produced outside of the NFB studio during this form's classical era. Still, they amount to a handful of titles. The NFB, instead, gave life to a rich and varied corpus of such films, rapidly coming to achieve also international recognition for its work in this field. Indeed, while, unlike suggested by Strøm (2003, 55, my emphasis), in the period in question the NFB was not "*the* leading producer of animated documentaries in the world"—a title that belonged to the Walt Disney Studios—, it certainly quickly rose to be one of the world leader producers of such films.

The War Years

During the years of the Second World War, the NFB produced about seventy animated films (Alonge 2000, 149). Not all of them were, however, actually made by its personnel. Although, upon arriving in Ottawa, McLaren personally recruited several young local talents—among which were Evelyn Lambart, George Dunning, Jim MacKay, and René Jodoin—, it took some time for the NFB studio to become fully operational.[4] As a consequence, in order to satisfy the need for animations for the National War Financial Committee's campaigns, many titles were commissioned to external animators. Indeed, the five shorts ordered to the Walt Disney Studios in 1941 were not the only ones to be outsourced. For instance, US animator Philip Ragan made at his studio thirty-one of the about seventy animated films produced by the NFB during the Second World War (see Alonge 2000, 162–4).

Moreover, despite a good number of the NFB animations from these years, like most coeval animated documentaries, were propaganda films aimed at inducing Canadian citizens to adopt certain behaviors in their everyday, only a reduced number of them were actual examples of the form. Most titles were just fictional animations or experimental works with a message. Exemplar is the case of *Stitch and Save* (1943, dir. Jim MacKay), a black-and-white short starring two worn-out outfits, a female and a male one, that get magically remodeled into "new" garments to the sound of a jazz tune. This film is not a dramatization of factual data; nor does it enrich the viewer's knowledge on the topic of remodeling clothes, even just minimally. It merely urges Canadians to alter their old garments rather than buying new ones through three captions that say: "Use it up! Wear it out! Make it do! Mend and make do save buying new! Mobilize your old clothes!" It, therefore, is a propaganda film but not an animated documentary.

In brief, overall, during the Second World War, the NFB produced a consistent number of animations, many of which share some traits with animated documentaries. Though, only a few of them are full-fledged examples of the form made by McLaren and his team. It is, for instance, the case of *Dollar Dance*, a drawn-on-film "lesson of monetary politics" addressing in particular wartime inflation and price control; *More Pigs* (1944, dir. Laurence Hyde), which illustrates how to properly care and breed pigs; or the safety film *Three Blind Mice*, wherein, using cut-out animation, the importance for factory workers to respect some basic security rules is highlighted.

These films already showcased two characteristics that, although at different levels, will end up marking the entire NFB animated documentary production: diversity and innovation. More precisely, these first works were diverse from each other as well as from the dominant animated documentary model. Indeed, as it was peculiar of all NFB animations of the time (see Cote 1956–7, 16), such films differ among them for the topics addressed and techniques employed. Simultaneously, however, they also are proof that, when Grierson chose to entrust the task of establishing the NFB animation department to an artist with a marked experimental approach like McLaren based on the conviction that, under his guidance, the studio would produce animations capable of setting themselves apart from Hollywood ones (Strøm 2003, 55–6; Bastiancich 1998, 47–9), he made the right call. Indeed, these works bestow an originality that makes them stand out from the coeval animated documentary production. This does not mean that they entirely rethink each and every aspect of what, in Chapter 5, we have seen to be the standard structure of the classical animated documentary. Every title reimagines just a few elements of it—one of which tends to be the voiceover narration—but does so in a marked way. Consider, for instance, *Dollar Dance* and *Three Blind Mice*. Like we have seen to be commonplace for classical animated documentaries, both films are character-oriented and fully exploit animation's anarchic potential at the graphic and narrational level. Indeed, the protagonist of *Dollar Dance* is a dollar sign with anthropomorphic traits (i.e., it is provided with legs and feet that enable it to walk) that stands for the average income of a Canadian citizen. Also, at times, it morphs into other objects or figures (e.g., into goods or services that one can buy with it). Analogously, *Three Blind Mice* revolves around three anthropomorphic mice in overalls that represent careless factory workers who injure themselves because they do not respect basic safety rules (e.g., checking if a machine has its guards securely fastened before using it or not walking under a loaded crane). Moreover, as it usually occurs in this period's animated documentaries, the visuals of both films are a dramatization of the factual notions illustrated in their soundtracks. In short, overall *Dollar Dance* and *Three Blind Mice* follow the then-dominant animated documentary structure.

However, they also reinvent some of its elements. More precisely, in *Dollar Dance*, first of all, the dramatization of what is described in the soundtrack is more abstract than usual, with the dollar sign moving and morphing over backgrounds that are either plane-colored or extremely essential. Second, a first-person ballad-like song on inflation, conceived to give the impression that to sing is the dollar sign itself, replaces classical animated documentaries' typical omniscient voice-of-God commentary. In so doing, not only the dollar sign is further anthropomorphized but also the tendency to make eccentric the voiceover narration of animated documentaries is brought to the extreme, letting entertainment override veridiction. Although the film, thus, showcases only a few deviances from the dominant animated documentary structure, they are sufficient to endow it with an overall significant allure of originality.

Likewise, in *Three Blind Mice*, the voice-of-God narration is replaced with an adapted version of the famed namesake nursery rhyme. Moreover, while the three protagonists of the film stand for an entire category—as is commonplace in animated documentaries—, they do not represent each a different group of people by generalizing synecdoche. On the contrary, as anticipated, they all stand for the same one, namely factory workers. Therefore, once again just a few "oddities" with regard to the dominant animated documentary model are present. However, since they are quite evident, they are enough to make the film stand out from the coeval production.

In Times of Peace

Grierson always "considered the war as a temporary diversion" from what represented the actual work of the NFB, namely "express . . . the multiplicity of views that constituted the country's reality" (Evans 1991, 4). Nevertheless, once the Second World War ended, many politicians no longer saw the necessity for a government-owned film agency, and, even if the NFB managed to survive and adjust to peacetime needs, its size was cut (see Evans 1991, 6–15). This reduction did not affect the animation department, which, instead, started growing, with more artists being invited to join it. In particular, between 1945 and the mid-1950s several figures who contributed to the development of the Canadian animated documentary started working at the studio: Colin Low, Wolf Koenig, Sidney Goldsmith, Gerald Potterton, and Robert Verrall.

In the immediate postwar years another fact also occurred that paved the way for the flourishing of NFB's animated documentary production. When, in 1948, the NFB was reorganized into four production units—namely Unit A, B, C, and D—, McLaren and the other animators joined Unit B, whose main areas of activity were scientific, cultural, and animated films. This unit, which from 1951 had its director in Tom Daly, came as such to be formed by a mixture of documentary and animation filmmakers, a perfect premise for growth in the production of animated documentaries. The proximity between these two typologies of filmmakers brought them to not consider documentary and animation as separate categories of filmmaking. As Strøm (2003, 57) explains, "[w]hen they had an idea for a film, they chose its form based on what was most suitable for it; animation was one of many possible ways of expressing a particular idea."

That said, for the actual growth of the NFB-produced animated documentaries to start occurring, it took a couple of years from when Unit B was established. Consequently, between the end of the war and the beginning of the new decade, the number of animated documentaries created was still limited compared to that of all the animations made. Examples of titles from these years are *Time and Terrain* (1948, dir. Colin Low), *A Story about Breadmaking in the Year 1255 A.D.* (1948, dir. Robert Verrall), and the two shorts created for the Department of National Health and Welfare using colored paper cut-outs, *Stanley Takes a Trip* (1947, dir. Jim MacKay and Grant Murno) and *Teeth Are to Keep* (1949, dir. Jim MacKay). Made with the aid of the Geological Survey of Canada, Low's film retells the geological history of this nation. It, thus, represented the first example of a scientific NFB animated documentary, a typology of works that, in the decades to come, was gonna bring to the studio much international acclaim, including an Oscar nomination. *Time and Terrain* showcased characteristics that were to become recurrent traits of this NFB corpus of films, such as the adoption of a realistic graphic style and the absence of characters. Indeed, the visuals of this film consist solely in a succession of realistic animated landscapes that are illustrative of what the voice-of-God commentary explains to have occurred to the Canadian terrain across the centuries. This choice of looking precisely at the geological development of Canada, instead of more generally at that of planet Earth, also anticipates a future tendency of the NFB animated documentary production. Indeed, in the decades to come, many will be the films with a national focus. Similarly, Verrall's short, which depicts the various passages that in medieval times were necessary to obtain bread, anticipates a strand of history-focused animated documentaries that developed starting from 1950. There is, however, a significant difference between *A Story about Breadmaking in the Year 1255 A.D.* and NFB's post-1950 animated histories. While the latter films mostly tackle aspects of Canadian history, *A Story about Breadmaking in the Year 1255 A.D.* looks at Britain.

Both *Stanley Takes a Trip* and *Teeth Are to Keep* are, instead, public service films and represent the natural peacetime continuation to NFB's wartime animated documentary production. More precisely, the former explains the importance of a balanced diet by telling the story of Stanley, a lethargic boy to whom some animals illustrate what food he should eat. The latter, instead, which will rise to become one of NFB's most popular titles (Strøm 2003, 63), describes, first, the functions of the various teeth and, then, the actions one needs to undertake in order to keep them healthy. Like *Stanley Takes a Trip*, it does so within the framework of the daily activities of little Roger and his family, who by generalizing synecdoche represents all families. Both films were targeted to kids and, overall, conformed to the then-dominant animated documentary structure. Elements of inventiveness are, however, present at a stylistic level. For instance, in *Teeth Are to Keep*, the same two frames showing respectively a piece of cutlery (which symbolizes the action of eating) and a toothbrush (which indicates the action of brushing one's teeth) next to the heads of Roger and his family members are repeated for three consecutive times, in order to stress also visually the message that teeth need to be brushed immediately after eating (see Figures 8.1 and 8.2).

In the 1950s the production of animated documentaries at the NFB flourished. As Guy L. Cote notes, to be typical in general of the studio's

FIGURE 8.1 *A frame from* Teeth Are to Keep *showing a piece of cutlery next to the heads of Roger and his family members.*

FIGURE 8.2 *A frame from* Teeth Are to Keep *showing a toothbrush next to the heads of Roger and his family members.*

animation production, "diversity . . ., both in the multitude of purposes" from which the films were executed "as well as in the variety of animation techniques" adopted (Cote 1956-7, 16), is one of its characteristics. And, paradoxically, it remained the chief shared trait of the NFB animated documentary production for all the form's classical era. Indeed, the animated documentaries produced between 1950 and 1985 ranged from public service and instructional films to works aimed at familiarizing the viewer with specific organizations, from animated histories to scientific films. And the works falling within each of these subgroups address the most varied topics. For instance, among the titles produced in this period, there are public service films such as Potterton's *Fish Spoilage Control* (1956) on the proper methods for handling fish from boat to dinner table, Pierre Hébert's *Population Explosion* (1968) on the ways for counteracting the demographic problems of the world, and Pierre L'Amare's *11 Steps to Survival*.[5] There are also instructional films targeted at a specific group of viewers, as is the case of *Huff and Puff. A Story of Hyperventilation* (1955, dir. Grant Crabtree), which was created for the Royal Canadian Airforce to inform aircrews on the dangers of hyperventilation at high altitudes. At the same time, however, we can also find works detailing the role and functioning of an organization, like *In a Nutshell*, which was sponsored by the Ministry of International Cooperation and illustrates how CIDA helps developing countries. Moreover, the animated histories created in this period were numerous. Among them are *Family Tree, The Romance of Transportation in Canada, A Tale of Mail* (1966, dir. Donald Stearn and William Canning), and *Tax: The Outcome of Income* (1975, dir. Veronika Soul), which offer a historical survey respectively of the settlement of Canada, transportation in Canada, the Canadian Post Office, and the national taxation system. Furthermore, as anticipated, many are the scientific animated documentaries created in these years, with the period from 1970 to 1985 seeing a peak in their making. This sub-corpus of films also showcases an internal diversity in terms of fields of science addressed. In particular, among the scientific domains within which titles ascribable to it fall, there are geology, mathematics, and physics. Indeed, this sub-corpus of animated documentaries comprises titles such as Low's *Riches of the Earth* (1954) and *A Thousand Million Years* (1954).[6] Produced with the support of the Geological Survey of Canada and animated by Sidney Goldsmith, these two films illustrate Canada's geological resources, explaining how they have taken shape through the ages. Yet, NFB's sub-corpus of scientific animated documentaries also encompasses films such as *Ten: The Magic Number* (1973, dir. Barrie Nelson), which was produced for the Metric Commission and offers an introduction to the metric system, or works such as *Energy and Matter* (1966, dir. Robert Verrall), which depicts what energy is, and *Harness the Wind* (1978, dir. Sidney Goldsmith), which surveys the attempts at controlling and using wind energy that have been made throughout the decades. However, the two fields of science to which the most significant number of these animated documentaries pertain are astronomy and paleontology. In the former domain falls the famed *Universe*, a film originally conceived for classroom use that returns an image of the cosmos as it may appear to a space voyager (see Evans 1991, 76).[7] Between the early 1970s and the end of animated documentary's classical era, Goldsmith also directed several astronomy-related titles, among which are *Satellites of the Sun*, *Starlife*, and *Comet*. These films focus respectively on the solar system, the evolution of a star, and the phenomenon of comets. Examples of NFB animated documentaries ascribable to the field of paleontology are, instead, *Origin of Life on Earth* (1972, dir. Kenneth Horn), the installment of the series "Canada Vignettes" *Woolly Mammoth* (1979, dir. Bill Maylone), *64,000,000 Years Ago* (1981, dir. Bill Maylone), *Five Billion Years* (1981, dir. Joyce Borenstein), and *Journey through Time: The Human Story* (1983, dir. George Geertsen).

Finally, there are titles such as *Neighbours* and *Interview*, which are so diverse from the rest of NFB's classical animated documentaries that are standalone. More precisely, McLaren's film is an anti-war parable traversed by a "social message about the covetous of man, about the irrationality of using violence to solve solutions" (McLaren in Dobson 2018, 103). In other words, it is a work that defies classification to the point that the appropriateness of awarding it with an Oscar in the Best Documentary Short Subject category has even been called into question (see Dobson 2018, 102). *Interview*, instead, is simply a work ahead of its time. Indeed, if looked at in respect to what the animated documentary has become today, there is no doubt of it being an example of an autobiographical animated documentary. Still, at the time in which Leaf and Soul made it, it was a film "outside the box."

As anticipated, diversity can also be found within this period's NFB animated documentaries at the level of the techniques used. They range from the cel animation of *The Romance of Transportation in Canada* to the pixilation of *Neighbours*, from the stop-motion used by Maylone in his shorts *Woolly Mammoth* and *64,000,000 Years Ago* to the animated paintings adopted by Goldsmith in *Satellites of the Sun* or *Comet* or the cut-out animation employed in *Population Explosion*. Not to mention that there are works, such as *Tax: The Outcome of Income* or *Interview*, which result from a combination of techniques and materials. Moreover, it is possible to find throughout the decades in question several shorts formed of a succession of still drawings to which a sense of movement is imparted using camera pans or zooms and ambient sound. It is the case of *The Structure of Unions* (1955, dir. Morten Parker), *A Is for Architecture* (1960, dir. Gerald Budner and Robert Verrall), *Samuel de Champlain* (1964, dir. Denys Arcand), *Extinction of the Dinosaurs* (1976, dir. Paul Bochner), and the installment of the "Canada Vignettes" series *Wop May* (1979, dir. Blake James), which illustrate how a union works, the history of architecture, the life of explorer Samuel de Champlain in New France from his settlement to his death in 1635, the theory for which a sudden temperature change would have brought to the extinction of dinosaurs, and the deeds of Wop May, Canada's leading bush pilot in the 1920s, respectively. For instance, referring to *A Is for Architecture*, producer Daly declared that the static drawings are lively thanks to "Verrall's inventiveness in adapting the limits of the animation camera and apparatus of the time to more sophisticated needs of the human eye's curiosity" (Daly in Jones 1996, 99). However, depending on how one defines animation, these titles are so original technique-wise that they may or may not be considered animated works and thus animated documentaries.[8]

Precisely since diversity is the main common trait of the NFB animated documentary production, there are no other characteristics shared by all these films. However, one can identify some tendencies that unite part of the titles. More precisely, we can find characteristics that are communal to the majority of the titles falling within a specific subgroup of NFB's animated documentaries. For instance, many of the studio's scientific animated documentaries, regardless of the technique employed, strive for graphic realism. Nevertheless, we can refer to this as a tendency but not as a shared trait since, among these films, one can also find works that go in the opposite direction, as is the case of *Energy and Matter*. Indeed, director Robert Verrall, who considered "the comic aspect of laughter, satire, and parody" to be "particular assets" of the animated "medium in that they can transmit the truth less pompously and perhaps more directly" (Polonsky 1969, 3–4), but refrained from employing comic antics in this title, in line with this vision, adopted a childlike graphic style (see Figure 8.3).

Moreover, it is likewise possible to spot several traits that are shared by many NFB animated documentaries, regardless of the subcategory to which they

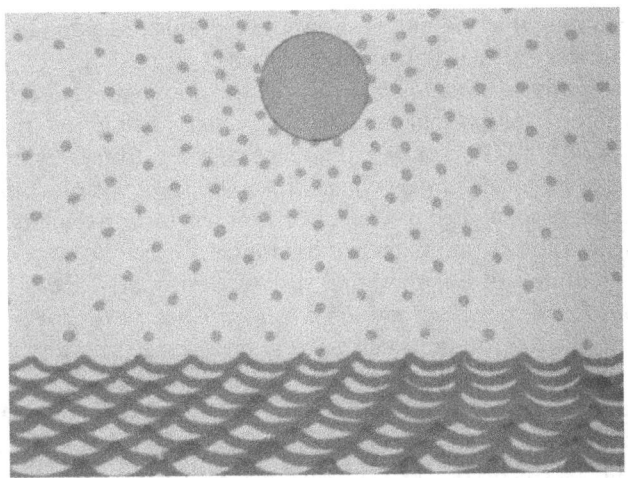

FIGURE 8.3 *A sun shining over the sea as represented in* Energy and Matter *employing a childlike graphic style.*

pertain or who has authored them. Once again, however, the characteristics in question are not identifiable in all the films, nor are necessarily all present in a same title and therefore can be considered just tendencies. The first one entails maintaining a Canadian focus on the subject matter addressed. As it may already have been evident from the brief synopsis provided, this Canadian perspective tended to be especially adopted when the animated documentary produced retraces the history of something or somebody. If this was the case, it was because NFB's main aim has always been that of helping Canadians better understand their country and one of the approaches used in order to meet this goal has been to produce films retracing the nation's socio-cultural history (see Page 1991). Just as a matter of example, it is not by chance if a film such as *The Romance of Transportation in Canada* was produced, since the development of the transportation system has been an essential aspect of the Canadian economic history (see Page 1979, 27). Yet, this focus on Canada can be found, for instance, also in some of the scientific animated documentaries. It is the case of Low's *Riches of the Earth* and *A Thousand Million Years*, which focus on the Canadian geological resources, or Maylone's *64,000,000 Years Ago* and *Woolly Mammoth*. Indeed in *64,000,000 Years Ago*, instead of broadly talking about the dinosaurs and prehistoric animals that used to inhabit Earth as it normally occurs in this typology of animated documentaries, just those that lived in the central plains of North America are presented. Similarly, *Woolly Mammoth* opens with the voice-of-God narrator informing viewers that "the last Woolly Mammoths *in Canada* died nearly 10,000 years" earlier, highlighting from the very beginning that the film is about these prehistoric animals' life on the Canadian territory rather than about the species in general.

A second recurrent trait was a refusal of the dominant character-oriented approach, which, always in line with diversity being the main shared characteristic of NFB's animated documentaries, translates in different practices. In some cases, it was chosen to make films with no characters at all, as it occurs for instance in *Origin of Life on Earth*, which is comprised just of a succession of animated landscapes. In other instances, animated actors were employed, but they had just walk-on parts. Examples in this sense are *Satellites of the Sun* and *Five Billion Years*. In the former, the only characters are two astronauts, who get very little screen time and whose faces viewers never even get to see, because either they are just tiny figures within an extreme long shot or are wearing a hard-shell space suit. In fact, in two instances a close-up shot of one of these astronauts is offered. Yet, on both occasions, his face is hidden behind a helmet with a visor that either reflects his surroundings or becomes a sort of screen on which Earth places he is missing are projected. In *Five Billion Years*, instead, when the development of life on planet Earth is illustrated, an animal for every species mentioned is shown. However, each appears in a couple of shots at most. Also, it does not do much more than walking across the frame. In yet other cases, measures to block that individualization of the characters, which, as seen in Chapter 5, is instead searched for in most animated documentaries, can be found. For instance, in *Fish Spoilage Control*, instead of having a single fish or spoilage bacteria as representatives of their respective categories, we tend to be shown a school of fishes and an army of spoilage bacteria (see Figures 8.4 and 8.5). Therefore, viewers are encouraged to see them as a category rather than as individuals representing a category.

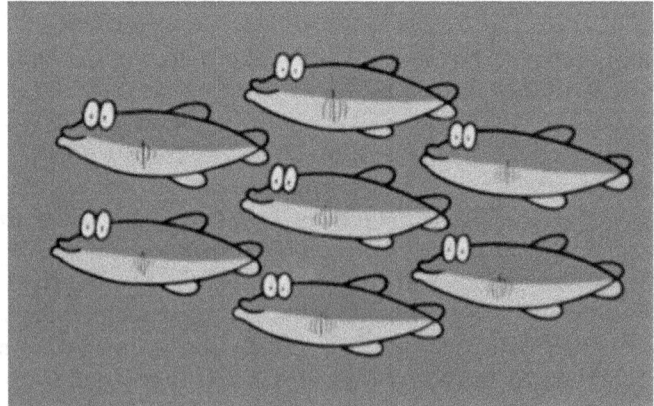

FIGURE 8.4 *The school of fishes that stands for its category in* Fish Spoilage Control.

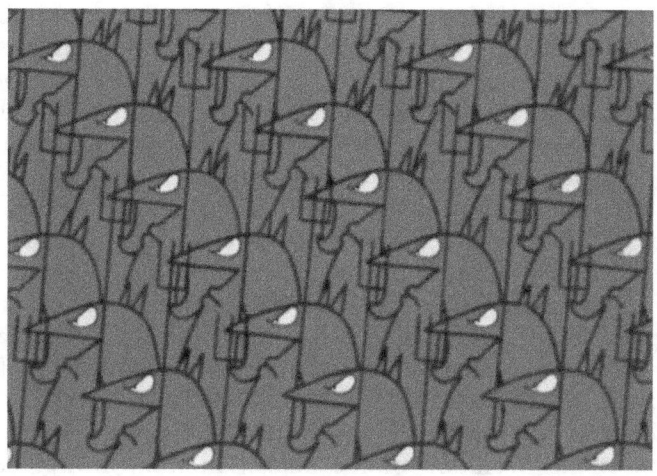

FIGURE 8.5 *The army of spoilage bacteria from* Fish Spoilage Control.

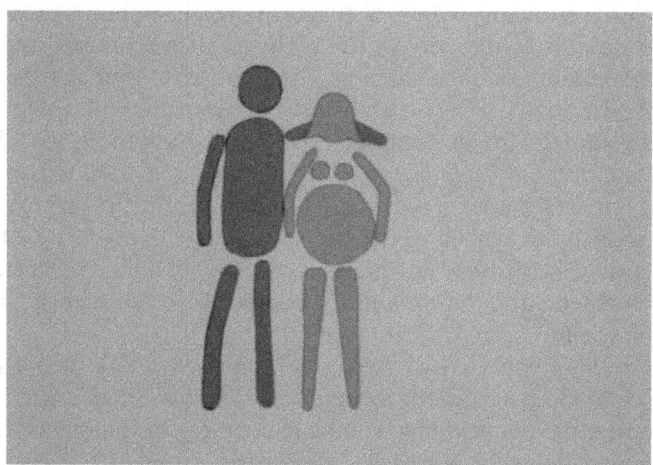

FIGURE 8.6 *The faceless and nameless animated human protagonist characters of* Population Expansion.

Likewise, always in order to prevent individualization, in *11 Steps to Survival* and *Population Expansion*, the animated human characters' protagonist are nameless and are represented as faceless gendered pictograms (e.g., see Figure 8.6).

Finally, we can also find cases in which more than one of these approaches was combined, as it occurs in *Family Tree*. Indeed, in this film, when animated actors are used, they have walk-on parts, even if the figure they are interpreting has had an essential role in the settlement of Canada. Exemplar is the case of Samuel de Champlain. He established the first settlement in Quebec City and yet appears only in a brief shot. On many occasions, however, although the voice-of-God commentary evokes the action of human figures, no characters are used to represent them visually. As a matter of example, consider the relatively long sequence of the settlement of the United Empire Loyalists in what today are the provinces of Nova Scotia, New Brunswick, Quebec, and Ontario. While the voice-of-God narrator explains that the colonists adventured in these areas and "opened up new sections of the land," visually we are, first, shown an oxcart that travels through a woodland landscape. Then, exploiting the "magical abilities" of animation, we are presented with trees that disappear, leaving empty land, where some log houses take shape. In this way, the use of characters was thus avoided.

Another tendency identifiable within the NFB animated documentary production is the liberation of the animation from always being just a dramatization of what is illustrated by the voice-of-God narrator to reducing its presence. Exemplar is the case of *64,000,000 Years Ago*. Here, the interventions of the voice-of-God are very brief and interspersed with relatively long moments wherein the soundtrack amounts just to Peter Bjerring's music or to the cries of the prehistoric creatures we see fighting, mating, or tending at their babies. More or less long scenes with no voiceover commentary, wherein only music accompanies the animation, can, however, be found also throughout *Population Explosion*, *The Romance of Transportation in Canada*, and *Satellites of the Sun*, among others. Particularly interesting is also the case of *Huff and Puff*, wherein there are relatively long moments in which the soundtrack is made up of just the sound of a man breathing. Furthermore, in *Neighbours*, the voice-of-God narration is absent, and the soundtrack consists solely of a musical score by McLaren himself.

Always in this perspective of freeing the animated visuals from the "yoke" of the voice-of-God narration, in many of the studio's classical animated documentaries, the commentary is introduced only in the second sequence. In fact, the first sequence is reduced almost to a paratext of the film. More precisely, in a similar way to what Elena Dagrada ([1996] 2005) suggests being the case for the opening of Woody Allen's *Manhattan* (1979), the first sequences of many classical animated documentaries by the NFB studio are an overture to the actual film. Indeed, the Italian scholar highlights how, not dissimilarly from the overture of an opera, in the first sequence of Allen's movie elements key to the film are introduced—as the city of New York or the music of George Gershwin—but the action proper does not start. It begins only with the second sequence (see Dagrada [1996] 2005, 63–8). Likewise, the first sequence of many NFB animated documentaries sets a framework for the narration and offers visual hints to what aspect of the real will be addressed. The subject of the film, instead, commences being tackled only when, in the second sequence, the voice-of-God narration starts. For instance, *Fish Spoilage Control* opens with a man entering a restaurant and ordering a fish to the sound of Eldon Rathburn's music. *The Romance of Transportation* begins with an aviator parachuting himself in the middle of a congested street and landing literally on a traffic warden always on the notes of a Rathburn tune. *11 Steps to Survival* starts with the animation of an atomic bomb being launched and exploded accompanied just by the noises that this action produces. From these initial sequences, we thus more or less explicitly apprehend that the films will deal respectively with fish, transportation, and nuclear explosions. Yet, the actual topics of these shorts—respectively fish spoilage, the evolution of transportation in Canada, and how to protect oneself in case of a nuclear attack—commence being illustrated only once, at the beginning of the second sequence, the voiceover chimes in. Another interesting example of an overture-like first sequence can be found in *Energy and Matter*. This film begins with a sequence wherein, first, we see the sun reach with its rays a portion of the ground and an apple tree grow in that spot. Subsequently, we see a cow eat one of the tree's apples and a child drink a glass of milk and start pedaling on its bicycle. All these actions occur solely to the sound of Robert Fleming's music, leaving the viewer to guess where the link between these images rests. It is only when, in the second sequence, the voice-of-God narration chimes in that viewers are explained why this succession of shots was shown. Indeed, while we see the same images again, the voiceover narration clarifies that their common thread is energy.

The first two sequences of *Energy and Matter* are illustrative also of a further tendency trackable within NFB's animated documentaries: a de-linearization of the film's narrative through the animated visuals. Indeed, in the second sequence of Verrall's short, when the voiceover starts informing viewers on the role of energy—thus moving forward the account—, most of the frames from the first sequence are repeated. In so doing, the animated visuals neutralize the linearity of the voice-of-God commentary, determining the narrative to become disjointed. Another film wherein this de-linearization of the narrative through the animation occurs is, for instance, *Fish Spoilage Control*. In this animated documentary, the same shots of a fish being hooked and thrown on a pile of other fishes that open the section of the film explaining how spoilage bacteria can multiply are repeated in the short's second half. In particular, they are shown for the second time as soon as the narrator commences to illustrate how one can prevent the bacteria from spreading. Although aurally the narration progresses, the reiteration of the shots folds the narrative into itself, since viewers are given the impression of being presented not with two consecutive moments but with alternative scenarios.

However, this de-linearization of the narrative wasn't necessarily obtained through the repetition of shots. Exemplar is the case of *The Romance of Transportation in Canada*. In this short, what sound-wise is a linear narrative becomes circular through the animation. Still, this circularity is not determined by a repetition of images. It is determined by the fact that, at the level of visuals, the last section of the film provides a conclusion to the occurrences shown in the already mentioned first sequence of the short.

Moreover, it is possible to find also animated documentaries whose narrative was de-linearized through both repeating shots and offering a visual conclusion to earlier occurrences. Consider, for instance, *Huff and Puff*. This short, which was scripted and animated by Grant Murno and Gerald Potterton, opens with a sequence wherein, while the voice-of-God narrator explains how hyperventilation can endanger a pilot's life, a pilot getting nervous, passing out due to overbreathing, and losing control of his aircraft is shown. This initial sequence ends with a shot of the aircraft going down at high speed that fades to black. The voiceover then explains that, although being essentially a "flying problem," hyperventilation "can occur anywhere," and we are shown an average man who, at a fair, gets overexcited while watching an erotic film in a kinetoscope, starts to hyperventilate, and faints. A detailed explanation of what biologically caused him to overbreathe—illustrated through the employment of the so-called X-ray animation—concludes this central portion of the film and, up to this point, the pilot's and the average man's collapse due to hyperventilation seem to occur at subsequent times and, therefore, the film's overall narrative appears to be fragmented but linear. Immediately after, however, the same shot of the aircraft going down which closed *Huff and Puff*'s first sequence is repurposed, followed by new shots of the airplane being about to crash on that same fair where the average man has passed out. We then see the pilot recover his senses just in time, thus avoiding causing a major accident. Through this repetition of a shot followed by fresh ones providing a conclusion to what was shown in the film's first sequence, the idea conveyed, in retrospect, is that the happenings presented visually in the initial sequence of the short and those shown in its central portion are simultaneous rather than subsequent, as it could instead have seemed at first. In other words, through these animated visuals *Huff and Puff*'s overall narrative is de-linearized, since such shots end up suggesting that we are in the presence of a case of temporal overlap.

In sum, while the only actual common trait of NFB's animated documentaries was diversity, numerous were the characteristics shared by just a portion of the titles created. These recurrent elements can, however, be viewed only as tendencies, since there are also plenty of animated documentaries by the studio that are character-oriented, have an omnipresent voice-of-God commentary, do not have a focus on Canada, or have a linear narrative. Most of these tendencies have an element in common: they foresee the (partial) abandonment of a trait proper of the dominant classical animated documentary structure. In other words, through them originality was injected in these films.

In effect, if, aside from diversity, a second shared trait can be identified within the NFB animated documentary production, it is innovation. The latter can be of different types and degrees. It can take the shape of a (partial) rethinking of the typical structure of the classical animated documentary or of a technical innovation, as it is, for instance, the case for *Universe*. In creating this film, the ambition was to return a "sense of the organic wholeness of the universe and the remarkable fact that any human being, bound to this planet for a lifetime, could nevertheless extend his or her perception in an unbroken thread of awareness all the way out from our solar system to the limits of visibility" (Daly in Jones 1996, 78). In order to achieve this result, the film had to be tridimensional and thus a new technique, which Low (in Glassman and Wise 1999, 29) has defined "animation with motorized movement," had to be developed. More precisely, as Evans (1991, 75) illustrates, co-director Kroitor, with the help of mathematical wizard Brian Salt, created the so-called "'Kroitorer,' a machine that enabled one to shoot the photographs as if a hand-held camera had been there at the time." In other words, a device that "achieved what the computer-assisted animation camera would do when it was invented a dozen years later" was developed (Evans 1991, 75).

Moreover, whether technical or formal, or both, the innovation present in NFB classical animated documentaries could be more or less marked. We can find titles that are highly innovative such as *Neighbours*, which is so experimental that it outruns its existing categorizations, or *Interview*, which is so ahead of its time that it anticipates the subjective turn that the animated documentary will undergo in the mid-1980s. Nonetheless, many are also the films that, in line with what up to its dismantlement in February 1964 has been a dominant approach within Unit B, showcase a "balance between structure and innovation" (Jones 1996, 68). An excellent example in this sense is *Fish Spoilage Control*. Directed and animated by Potterton, who had joined the NFB only two years earlier after having worked as an assistant at the Halas & Batchelor Cartoon Films studio, this short, on the one hand, as we have seen, presents formal innovations in respect to the classical animated documentary structure, such as an overture first sequence, a disjointed narrative, and a refusal of the character-oriented approach. On the other hand, the fight against spoilage bacteria's spread is traditionally represented as a conflict between good and evil. Indeed, the voice-of-God narrator presents it as the "battle to keep fish fresh" in which ice, water, and proper storage are the "weapons" necessary to man in order to win the combat. Also, spoilage bacteria are pictured as red devils holding a pitchfork, so as to clarify that they are the villains to be defeated (see Figure 8.5). In brief, in this short, there is an amalgamation of innovation and tradition that translates into the overall film being mildly original.

If both innovation and diversity could become the common denominators of Canada's classical animated documentary, it has been thanks to the idyllic conditions in which NFB animators operated. Indeed, NFB being a state-financed institution with the mission of educating viewers already made it the perfect environment for the animated documentary to thrive. However, the fact that, thanks to Grierson's foresight, the funding system in place impeded interference of the government at the creative and content level left animators free to experiment. It allowed them to undertake new paths and develop works that, while fulfilling their aim of informing viewers, retained artistic quality.

Notes

1 For an in-depth treatise of the titles made by the Walt Disney Studios for the NFB, see Honess Roe (2011).

2 The series comprises *Propagation* (1960), *Bandwidth* (1960), and *Directivity* (1960), which illustrate respectively how antennas propagate radio waves, how their bandwidth can be increased, and how they can become more directive. Other examples of films using sober animation to address a factual topic, and that thus are not animated documentaries, are: *Rythmetic* (1956, dir. Norman McLaren and Evelyn Lambart), which can be seen as an experimental math lesson; *The Origins of Weather* (1963, dir. Joseph Koenig), wherein the factors that produce the various climates on Earth are illustrated; and *Continental Drift* (1968, dir. Co Hoedeman), which explains the theory of continental drift.

3 Originally Place Bonaventure, whose construction was completed in 1967, was conceived, among others, as a trade center. The film's ultimate aim was thus to draw attention to this destination of the building by presenting it as the ultimate evolution in the history of trade.

4 Although the first animation produced at the NFB dates 1941, the animation unit effectively came into existence only in 1942 (see Evans, Véronneau and Todd 1991, xxxiii).

5 *Fish Spoilage Control* and *11 Steps to Survival* were sponsored by the Department of Fisheries and Emergency Planning Canada, respectively.

6 A revised version of *Riches of the Earth* was also made in 1966.

7 Despite having been conceived for classroom use, *Universe* ended up proving of general interest. Indeed, when it was completed, the space race between the United States and Soviet Union was well underway, with the successful launch of Sputnik 1 having occurred three years earlier. There was, thus, a general desire for films on astronomy (see Jones 1996, 79).

8 For a summary of the main definitions of animation and a treatise of how difficult it is to identify a shared definition of it, see Husbands and Ruddell (2019). Since the appropriateness of defining these films as animations may be questioned, I have chosen to not use them to exemplify the various tendencies that, as the chapter shows, are identifiable within the NFB animated documentary production. However, the characteristics illustrated can be found in these works as well.

9

Italy

The Rise of the Italian Classical Animated Documentary

In the early 1940s Italy still lacked a proper animation industry. The national production consisted of just a handful of artisanal shorts mostly born out of experimentations with the medium by individuals (Rondolino 2003, 191). A few attempts were underway to making animated features, but with the Second World War ravaging the nation, they had to be halted and it was necessary to wait till 1949 for the first Italian feature-length animations to be released in cinemas.[1] Still, the idea of animation being a medium for addressing also factual topics was already widespread in the mid-1930s, to the point that when, in 1936, Nicola Dessy wrote a short handbook on the animated cartoon, he ended it with these words:

> But the animated cartoon, born to laugh and make laugh, born to exalt the caricature and "animate" flowers, to give the word to anthropomorphized animals finds also great application in the domain of cultural and didactic cinema. The new film industries, that today are equipped for the creation of scientific and didactic films, have at their disposal rich facilities for making animated cartoons, which, in their schematic form, find great application especially for physics, mathematics, and statistics. The use of animated cartoons in didactic films raises the greatest interest among the sages, it develops their cognitions, it perfects their ability to retain. For these reasons this "animated" material strides to become an integral part of the school curricula. (Dessy 1936, 10, my translation)

As it emerges from this excerpt, in the second half of the 1930s, sober animation was still considered the default language to use for addressing factual topics through animation.

Nonetheless, not only, in these years, as we have seen in Chapter 4, experiments in the direction of the animated documentary were already being made in Italy too but also a slow transition toward the form's classical phase was underway. Indeed, between the late 1930s and early 1940s, the medium's fictional mode of representation started increasingly being employed in creating animations tackling the real, to the point that titles wherein its presence progressively equates—or even exceeds—that of the sober animation came into fruition. Exemplary of this evolution is a corpus of films created as part of what Teresa Biondi (2010, 386) refers to as INCOM's "animation project." INCOM was a film company devoted to the making of nonfiction films established in 1938, and its founder, Sandro Pallavicini, who believed in the need to "'spectacularize information' through inserting fictional segments in documentaries," had sensed the potential benefits of using animation—which he considered an "avant-garde of communication"—in nonfiction contexts (Biondi 2010, 386). Therefore, in 1939, he established an animation department at INCOM and appointed Pensuti as its director. This department's main production consisted of a series of nonfiction animations based on the reports published daily by the Ministry of War (see Biondi 2010, 386). Among the titles made were: *War Front* (*Fronte di guerra*, 1940, dir. Vittorio Gallo), on the advance of Nazi forces in Europe up to the occupation of France; *The Decline of an Empire* (*Tramonto di un impero*, 1940, dir. F.lli Amadoro), on the supposed progressive decline of the British Empire; *The Map of Europe* (*La carta d'Europa*, 1941, dir. Domenico Paolella), on the history of the old continent; and *The Beginning of the End* (*Il principio della fine*, 1942, dir. Liberio Pensuti), on England's contended attempts to block the Italian expansion in Africa.[2] All the shorts in this series are at their core map films that—in line with what Giuseppe Fidotta (2014) shows to be the case for fascist documentaries in general—meld propaganda and educational intents. Indeed, they employ a succession of animated maps to illustrate relatively current events. However, the map often ends up acting just as a background to actions animated using this medium's fictional mode of representation. Moreover, a few titles also showcase consistent portions wherein the maps are absent, and the fabled animation is used exclusively to portray what the voice-of-God commentary depicts. It is the case of the two anti-British propaganda films, *The Decline of an Empire* and *The Beginning of the End*. More precisely, in the former the presence of the maps is minimal, and many are the scenes making full employment of animation's fictional mode of representation. Just to make a few examples, the simultaneous devaluation of the sterling and alleged loss of authority of the British monarchy are represented by showing a coin wearing a crown that, first, sits on a throne located at the top of a staircase and, then, rolls down the stairs together with its tiara. Analogously, the voice-of-God's ironical statement that England would have ceded some of its colonial territories—among which were the islands of Antigua, Terranova, and Bermuda—to the United States in exchange for "superb ships" is accompanied by shots of shabby boats—some of which even have the appearance of paper boats made by a kid—that move to a musical score which stresses their slowness. In this film, the fabled animation was, thus, used more to translate into figurative images the concepts expressed by the voice-of-God narrator than to effectively reenact the occurrences he depicts, as it was instead commonplace for classical animated documentaries. However, this short represents a step in the direction of the emergence of an Italian classical animated documentary.

An even more evident example of this transition being underway also in Italy is *The Beginning of the End*. In this short, after the first part that heavily employs animated maps to illustrate Italy's colonial adventures between 1870 and 1906, the use of fabled animation becomes predominant. Indeed, in the second part of *The Beginning of the End*, visually, the alleged attempts of Britain to obstruct the Italian expansion in Africa between 1934 and 1940 are presented employing almost exclusively the fabled animation. In particular, the latter was often used to reenact and dramatize the factual occurrences illustrated by the voice-of-God narrator, such as the events concerning the 1934 assault to the Welwel garrison. Therefore, in this film also the way in which the fabled animation was employed is very close to what was characteristic of the animated documentary's classical era.

In parallel to the emergence of nonfiction films that set aside the sober animation for the fabled one, between the late 1930s and the early 1940s, the public service animations produced went progressively from being fictional stories with a message to becoming fact-based lectures on ordinary matters that were characterized by the use of animation's fictional mode of representation. We can find examples of this second kind of transformation among the shorts created for the Italian National Federation against Tuberculosis. As Miriam Posner (2012, 102) shows to have been peculiar also of the Red Cross Seal films, these works sought to make gospel of both hygiene and philanthropy. In particular, they were made with the double objective of stigmatizing the behaviors that can favor the spread of tuberculosis and prompting the population to sustain the governmental efforts in defeating this disease by buying the so-called anti-tubercular stamp. Among the most popular titles in the series, there are works, such as *The Tavern of Tuberculosis*,[3] that attain this dual aim through the telling of fictional stories. However, films such as *Public Threat n. 1. Life and Mishaps of the Koch Bacillus* (*Il pericolo pubblico n. 1. Vita e misfatti del bacillo di Koch*, 1938, dir. Liberio Pensuti and Ugo Amadoro) and *Water Hammers* (*Colpi d'ariete*, 1940, dir. Liberio Pensuti), wherein animation's fictional mode of representation was used to illustrate true-to-life facts, were also made. In particular, *Public Threat n. 1* is a hygiene film, which in many respects anticipates Walt Disney Studios' *Defense against Invasion*. It opens with a live-action scene set in a classroom, during which a teacher, who will be the voice-of-authority of the film, calls one of its young pupils at his desk and invites him to look at the *Koch bacillus* through a magical microscope. At this point, the words of the teacher become a voiceover to an animated dramatization of how tuberculosis can be transmitted and what the *Koch bacillus* does to our organism. More precisely, entirely animated scenes with others wherein the animation is incorporated in live-action shots are alternated, visually. The *Koch bacilli* are represented as evil anthropomorphic creatures that penetrate the lungs of a person and destroy them with pickaxes, jackhammers, and explosives. In other words, they are conventionally presented as the villains of the film, graphically conveying their evil nature by having them wear a white, pointed hood that immediately recalls the Ku Klux Klan's costume (see Figure 9.1). Once the action of these bacilli on human lungs has been explained, the film cuts back to the live-action classroom setting. The short then ends with a sequence wherein the behaviors to follow in order to prevent the spread of this bacterium that the professor, in voiceover, lists are visualized, using just live-action.

As it emerges from this description, in *Public Threat n. 1* the telling of a fictional story identifiable in other titles in the series is abandoned in favor of an illustration of scientific facts in simple but fabled terms. Therefore, this short can already be considered a full-fledged example of an Italian classical animated documentary.

If *Public Threat n. 1* combines animation and live-action, *Water Hammers* is almost entirely in animation and, after a first sequence wherein how man has gone from fighting against diseases with magic to combating them with science is explained, presents the results that the fascist government attained with its anti-tubercular campaigns between 1931 and 1940. Limited use of sober animation is made. However, for the most part, the fabled one

FIGURE 9.1 *The* Koch bacilli *as depicted in* Public Threat n. 1.

is employed. Indeed, the film is characterized by a graphic language rich in synecdoche, similitudes, and metaphors. The stamps and posters created each year for the anti-tubercular campaigns come to life and are presented as the good. Tuberculosis, instead, is classically depicted as a villain to combat and defeat, explicitly referring to it as man's "greatest enemy." Only, in this case, it is represented, first, as a Medusa-like creature and, subsequently, as a boulder that needs to be crumbled. A dramatic character is also conferred to the animation through the music of Raffaele Gervasio. Thus, although this film is fragmented, is not character-oriented, and uses captions instead of the voice-of-God commentary, it too can be considered an early classic animated documentary.

In brief, in Italy first examples of classical animated documentaries could already be found between the late 1930s and early 1940s. Soon, however, with the escalation of the Second World War and the subsequent fall short of a government, as the fascist one, that actively sponsored this kind of works, the Italian animated documentary faced a downturn. Indeed, up to the mid-1950s, it became rarer for this kind of animated works to see the light.

Nonetheless, in 1949, two facts that set the ground for the resumption of the Italian animated documentary occurred. On the one hand, in October 1949, in film magazine *Sequenze* an abridged translation of the 1945 article written by Disney for *The Public Opinion Quarterly* to underline how the use of animation to recount aspects of our world should have been kept up also in peacetimes appeared (see Disney 1949). To this date, the idea of animation being among the tools available to filmmakers for recounting the real was already fully rooted in Italy too. This is exemplified by the fact that a year earlier, in giving pieces of advice to amateur filmmakers in an article for film magazine *Ferrania*, Luigi Veronesi wrote that, in order to create a didactic, scientific, or industrial documentary, one "must know the technique of animation" and equip himself with "an animation stand" (Veronesi 1948, 31). However, since in these years the Disney production was an important point of reference for Italian animators and, as we have seen, Disney adopted—and preached the adoption of—the fabled animation in creating fact-based works, the publication of his article most likely concurred in legitimizing the employment of this medium's fictional mode of representation to tackle factual occurrences.

On the other hand, on December 29, 1949, the Italian parliament passed the so-called Andreotti Law, a legislation on cinema establishing, among others, that 3 percent of each show's box office revenues was to be awarded to the producers of the shorts screened before the feature films,[4] premised that they met minimum technical, artistical, and cultural standards. Also, it was specified that for shorts all "films of between 250 and 2000 meters, *even if in animation,*" were intended.[5] Moreover, the same law also established that, if a short was a documentary, it could be awarded an extra 2 percent of the box office revenues, if an appointed committee recognized it of exceptional technical or artistic quality. And, the standards to meet for being deemed of exceptional quality were very low, if we consider that already being a color film sufficed. Therefore, with this law, a short-form animated film in colors that addressed an aspect of the real could aspire to be awarded more money than a fictional animated film. As a consequence, even if in writing this legislation Andreotti intended to encourage the development of the documentary production proper, this law contributed to boosting the creation of animated documentaries as well, since it set the conditions for this kind of works to start being made also in the absence of a sponsor.

Between Promotion and Education: The Golden Age of Animated Documentary in Italy

In the first half of the 1950s, we can find some examples of animated documentaries. For instance, fortified by the existence of the Andreotti Law that ensured filmmakers interested in pursuing the creation of documentary shorts at least a recovery of costs, between 1952 and 1955 Michele Gandin carried out the project of a filmic encyclopedia, known as *Learn About* (*Conoscere*), aimed at "enabling 'millions of people of every social backgrounds' to 'go to school without even knowing it'" (Bertozzi 2008, 146). In practice, he oversaw the making of a series of documentary films each formed of three three minutes entries illustrating different topics that began with the same letter. Some of these entries are animated documentaries, as is the case of the one inserted in *Learn about n. 10* and entitled "Individual Freedom" ("Libertà individuale," 1955), wherein the fabled animation is used to depict the limits of Italian citizens' individual freedom.

However, for the flourishing of the Italian classical animated documentary to take place, it will be necessary to wait until the second half of the 1950s. Indeed, in these years, new important outsourcers of fact-based animations emerged, namely the leading Italian companies. As Pierre Sorlin (2013, 424) has underlined, "[a]fter the war the impressive takeoff of Italian industry was emphasized by a wealth of documentaries," and in the 1950s, various companies—among which we can recall Edisonvolta, Montecatini, Lepetit, and Olivetti[6]—even developed their film departments. The number of industrial documentaries produced soon came to be so consistent to justify the birth in 1957 in Monza of the first Italian festival devoted to this typology of audiovisual works. Most importantly, animation in general, and the fabled animation in particular, came to be heavily employed within these films. Even the companies that have started their film departments, however, did not produce such animations internally. They outsourced them to one of the many animation studios that, in the meantime, had come into being especially in the Milan area thanks to the advent of the advertisement TV show *Carousel* (*Carosello*, 1957–77, RAI), which determined an exponential rise in the demand for animation.[7]

Obviously, not all the then leading Italian companies chose to resort to fabled animation for their films with the same frequency. In Olivetti's films, for instance, we find more often an employment of the sober animation. Indeed, the number of actual animated documentaries that in the years have been produced by this company's film department is very limited, an example being the partly animated and partly live-action short on the history of electric energy: *The Devil in the Bottle* (*Il diavolo nella bottiglia*, 1968, dir. Sergio Spina). In contrast, in Montecatini's films, when animation is present, the fabled mode of representation is mostly employed. The Italian industrial animated documentary par excellence can, in fact, be identified in a title that came out of this company's film department: the award-winning *Pay Attention to the Label*, animated at the Gamma Film studio. Moreover, it is important to note that, within the production of a same company, just a part of the films made contained some animation, and among those that do showcase it, the quantity of it present may vary greatly. Consider, for instance, Montecatini's production. We can find shorts such as *Phosphorus. Life for the Plants* (*Fosforo. Vita per le piante*, 1956, dir. Giovanni Cecchinato) that contain just a few animated interjections, and therefore cannot be considered animated documentaries even if they employ the fabled animation. Indeed, the ones that can be defined as animated documentaries are just those that not only make use of the fabled animation but also either have consistent portions in animation, like for instance Giovanni Cecchinato's *How to Feed Plants* (*Come si nutrono le piante*, 1960), *Fertilizers*, and *Agricultural Plot* (*Il terreno agrario*, 1969), or are entirely in animation, such as Cecchinato's *The Soil Is Hungry* and *Pay Attention to the Label*.

Precisely Montecatini, whose film department had been one of the most active since its very inception (see Bertozzi 2008, 142), produced the greatest corpus of industrial animated documentaries in Italy. This does not surprise if we consider who this company's target audience was and what was the purpose with which these films were created. Indeed, as Yvonne Zimmermann (2009, 107) underlines, "[i]ndustrial films were never produced haphazardly. They were, instead, always commissioned for specific reasons on a specific occasion" and had a specific addressee. In the case of Montecatini's animated documentaries, the target audience was a social category as Italian farmers that is "extremely diversified . . . and, overall, scarcely inclined to conceptual abstractions" (Mosconi 1991, 69). In other words, a subject matter had to be illustrated to them in essential, easily understandable, and, at the same time, captivating terms, which is exactly what the fabled animation allows to do. Therefore, this had to be the go-to mode of representation. Also, as Fiorello Zangrando (1968, 30) highlights, animation allowed to overcome the technical or the temporal and seasonal limits that would have been instead faced if trying to use the sole live-action in tackling certain subjects as the soil's microbial life or the action of fertilizers on the plants.

Moreover, the reason why these films were made was to present new products, such as complex fertilizers or fungicides. Therefore, theoretically, they are "representative films" (i.e., films which demonstrate "the functioning of products to potential costumers") (Zimmermann 2009, 105). An advertising agenda can be identified, but it remains undercurrent, never transforming into proper sales pitches. Let us consider, for instance, *Fertilizers*, the Montecatini animated documentary wherein this publicity agenda surfaces the most. This short is structured as a partly animated lecture on the different typologies and functions of manures. Nevertheless, here and there, shots portraying one of the various kinds of manure sacks that Montecatini had put on the market are briefly offered. Still, such shots are well integrated with the rest of the film's visuals, and the viewer is never explicitly prompted to buy the company's products. In fact, generally speaking, these films' promotional agenda is disguised behind an educational appearance. That is, on the outside, Montecatini's animated documentaries are either instructional or educational films that address matters close to a farmer's everyday working life, such as the composition of the soil, fertilizers, or herbicides. In other words, in what is a sophisticated approach to promotion, these films do not explicitly encourage growers to purchase this corporation's new substances. They, instead, describe the chosen aspect of a farmer's day-to-day reality in such a way that availing themselves of these products in their activity cannot but appear to them the right thing to do. For instance, *The Soil Is Hungry* never prompts farmers to use Montecatini's complex fertilizers. Instead, first, it explains that, due to an increase in the global population, more people need to be fed. Subsequently, it shows how complex fertilizers increase the productivity of the soil while simultaneously saving time and money. The commercial aim is thus concealed behind a more foregrounded educational objective.

That said, one must note that Montecatini's animated documentaries do not showcase a same graphic style nor a uniform representational approach, even if they were all directed by the same person, namely Giovanni Cecchinato. Exemplar is the case of how nitrogen, phosphorus, potassium, and calcium—the four nutrients essential for a plant's healthy life—are portrayed in these films. Indeed, in *How to Feed Plants*, *Fertilizers*, and *The Soil Is Hungry* these elements are personified as anthropomorphic figures. However, the animated actors used to interpret such figures change from one film to the other (e.g., see Figures 9.2 and 9.3).

Likewise, although a good number of these titles use a voice-of-God narration, we can also find a film such as *Pay Attention to the Label* that, similarly to what occurs in Halas & Batchelor Cartoon Films' *Speed the Plough*, has its voice-of-authority in a knowledgeable anthropomorphic scarecrow who instructs inept farmer Attilio on the proper use of fungicides. Additionally, there are still other shorts wherein both the voice-of-God

FIGURE 9.2 *Nitrogen, phosphorus, potassium, and calcium as represented in* How to Feed Plants.

FIGURE 9.3 *Nitrogen, phosphorus, potassium, and calcium as represented in* Fertilizers.

narration and the voice-of-authority are used. It is the case of *The Soil Is Hungry*, where we have both a voiceover narrator and two voices-of-authority in the form of an animated professor (in the central section of the film) and an animated farmer (in the last portion of the short). In brief, Montecatini's animated documentaries are heterogeneous, and this is mainly because the company's film department did not commission its animations all to the same studio. Just to make an example, *Land Tilling* (*Lavorazione dei terreni*) and *The Soil Is Hungry* are both from 1961 and have both been directed by Cecchinato, but their animation is respectively from Pagot brothers' studio, OPEC, and the studio Elettra Film.

The Italian animated documentary production of the 1960s did not amount just to industrial films. In fact, with the late 1950s commenced what we can define as a golden age of the Italian animated documentary which saw the production of this kind of works literally explode. Indeed, the various animation studios that in these years either emerged or enlarged themselves to respond to an increasing demand for animated shorts generated by *Carousel* tended to diversify their production taking up also other projects. Just as a matter of example, next to the many advertisements created for *Carousel* and animations made on commission of leading companies, Gamma Film also produced several scientific animated documentaries, among which is *Man and Space* (*L'uomo e lo spazio*, 1965, dir. Roberto and Gino Gavioli).[8]

Most interestingly, toward the end of the 1950s, we also saw the emergence of two non-sponsored animated documentaries from a young filmmaker destined to become a leading figure in the Italian animation panorama: Bruno Bozzetto. His first animated film was *Tapum! The History of Arms* (*La storia delle armi*, 1958), a witty animated documentary that retraces the evolution of weapons and at the same time passes comment on it.[9] Prompting Bozzetto to tackle precisely this subject were his high-school studies. He has declared: "discovering the infinite variety of ways that men have come up with to slaughter themselves stimulated me to create a work that, other than being witty, could say something interesting on man itself" (Bozzetto 2017, pos. 1177–83, my translation). His main inspiration in making this short was, however, Walt Disney Studios' *Toot, Whistle, Plunk and Boom*. Bozzetto himself has explained:

> Disney, indirectly, has contributed to the idea of *Tapum!*, with a film made almost behind his back, a short which later went on to win an Oscar: the 1953 *Toot, Whistle, Plunk and Boom*. The impulse came from the fact that the film was beautiful, it had grotesque characters similar to those I created, limited animations, a very fine graphic taste, and it entertained and at the same time instructed the viewing public on something: the evolution of music. (Bozzetto in Pollone and Sclaverani 2014, 13–4, my translation)

If in creating his first animated documentary he looked up at Disney, as anticipated in Chapter 7, his second one, *History of Inventions*, was even co-produced by another leading figure in the making of this typology of films, John Halas. Indeed, *Tapum!* was selected for screening at the 11th Cannes Film Festival and here Bozzetto had the chance of meeting Halas, who offered him a short apprenticeship at his studio (Paoletti 2003, 151). During his time in London, Bozzetto made *History of Inventions*, which is a filmic adaptation of the 1956 nonfiction book *This Man, This Inventor* (*L'uomo, questo inventore*) by Dino Beretta and Roberto Costa. However, the Italian animator felt limited rather than inspired by working with Halas as he found the latter's conception of animated documentary too strict. In an interview Bozzetto recalls that Halas crossed off his comic antics when they conflicted with the accuracy in the portrayal of the subject. For example, Bozzetto remembers having storyboarded the following scene: "there was a man from the stone age that fell in the water and when he came back above water thanks to a tree stump, in practice discovered the boat. Then, like Eega Beeva, I had him extract from a pocket an outboard engine, attach it to the tree stump, and run off. Soon after he met a cop who fined him" (Bozzetto in Liberti 2007, 44). And, referring always to this scene, the Italian animator recollects: "Halas told me it was not good because at that time motors did not exist and asked me to cut it" (Liberti 2007, 44).

After *Tapum!* and *History of Inventions*, Bozzetto began working at fiction animations, but, in the course of his career, he often reverted to the form that led him to success. For instance, in 1978, he directed *Baby Story*, which explains the stages of human reproduction in elementary and entertaining terms. This film stands out from the many other sexuality-related classical animated documentaries created all over the world due to Bozzetto's original graphic choices in visually dramatizing what is explained by the voice-of-God narrator. For example, he represents the ovum as a prosperous Rapunzel-like queen trapped in an egg, who is waiting for one of the anthropomorphic spermatozoa with male features that enter the vagina to get to her (Figure 9.4).

In 1981, Bozzetto also started a long-lasting collaboration with the weekly, late-evening educational TV show *Quark* (1981–94), which enabled his studio, Bozzetto Film, to create in less than a decade about ninety animated documentaries. Under the belief that animation "allows to penetrate beyond a superficial attention" (Angela in Mosconi 2003, 79), the

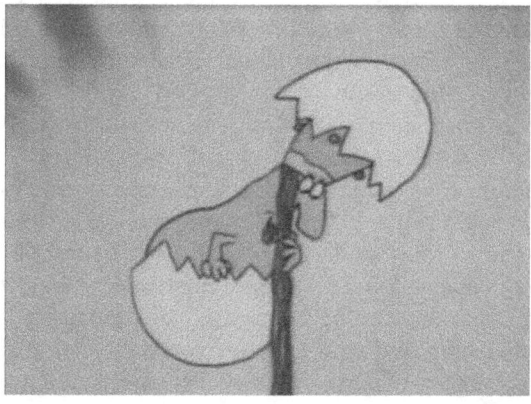

FIGURE 9.4 *In* Baby Story, *Bozzetto represents the ovum as a prosperous Rapunzel-like queen trapped in an egg.*

author and presenter of *Quark*, journalist Piero Angela, commissioned short animated documentaries to Bozzetto Film on a variety of topics ranging from the theory of relativity to overcrowding, from imagination to genetic engineering. These animated documentaries are all characterized by a voice-of-God commentary performed by Angela himself and showcase a tripartite structure consisting of an initial enunciation of the theme, a relatively in-depth treatise of the topic in question, and a conclusion, which often entails in a summary of what is previously explained. The peculiarity of these works is that—as Elena Mosconi (2003, 81–2) points out—the animation is used not just to visualize what the voice-of-God depicts but also to offer a reading of the scientific discourse presented, to pass comment on what the voiceover narrator states. In so doing, with these shorts, Bozzetto thus carries through a rethinking and personalization of the animated documentary form undertaken since *Tapum!*.

Walking through Science with Corona Cinematografica

While, as we have seen, many Italian studios were active in the creation of animated documentaries during this form's classical period, there is one that produced a particularly rich corpus of such films outside of the sponsorship system: the animation department of Corona Cinematografica. Indeed, in 1960, the film studio Corona Cinematografica, which had been founded in Rome in 1954 by brothers Ezio, Fulvio, and Elio Gagliardo, established an animation division that, as Gianni Rondolino (2003, 331) has pointed out, went on to become "a backbone of the Italian animation cinema" between the mid-1960s and early 1970s. It produced hundreds of titles, taking part even in international projects.[10] Furthermore, around it gravitated some of the leading artists of the then Italian animation panorama, such as Gibba, Pino Zac, Manfredo Manfredi, and Guido Gomas. And, since its early days, Corona's animation department devoted part of its energies to the creation of works referred to in their production documents as cartoon documentaries.[11] Indeed, one of the three founders of Corona, Ezio Gagliardo, was under the belief that "the documentary and the animated film are cinematic forms that have to be devoid of inferiority complexes with regard to cinema as conventionally understood" (Gagliardo in Carioti 1972, 185). In other words, he considered documentary and animation "with no doubt as valid and vital" as the live-action fiction cinema (Carioti 1972, 185), and, since combining these two forms gave the resulting shorts greater chances of obtaining the monetary subsidy awarded to short films by the government, dozens of animated documentaries were produced. Indeed, after the introduction of the Andreotti Law, with a series of subsequent measures that culminated in the 1965 law 1213, the committee appointed to judge the quality of the films was given always greater importance and the subsidy came to take always more the shape of a quality prize.

In terms of graphic style, Corona's animated documentaries are heterogeneous. We can find shorts employing the so-called O style, as is the case of *Heredity* (*Ereditarietà*, 1966, dir. Rodolfo Besesti and Elio Gagliardo), wherein curvilinear mice are used to dramatize Mendel's laws of heredity. Nevertheless, we can find also many titles characterized by the I style, an example being *Eye's Magic* (*Magia dell'occhio*, 1963, dir. Gibba), in which angular and bidimensional figures are used to illustrate the functioning of the human eye. Moreover, we can find films such as *The Specific Gravity* (*Il peso specifico*, 1966, dir. Rodolfo Besesti), wherein a mixture of curvilinear and angular characters is used to explain what specific gravity is and how Archimedes would have discovered it.

This stylistic diversity is most likely due to Corona's animated documentaries not being all from the same animator. Several artists were involved in their making, including a few female ones. For instance, Antonietta Campanelli was responsible, together with Demetrio Laganà, for the animations of *Adventure in the Cell* (*Avventura nella cellula*, 1962, dir. Gibba), *The Birth of Earth* (*La nascita della Terra*, 1962, dir. Gibba), *Magic Lab*, and *Anatomy of Motion*, wherein the composition and the life stages of a cell, the formation of our planet, how our digestion process works, and the complexity of human motion are illustrated respectively. Carla Ruta, in collaboration with Sandro Marinelli and Rodolfo Torti, animated *The Specific Gravity*. Rita Ciucci, who is normally remembered just for having been an employee of Corona's Ink and Paint department (e.g., see Verger 2010, 97), was, instead, the animator for *Heredity* and *Psychology of Color* (*Psicologia del colore*, 1965, dir. Rodolfo Besesti and Elio Gagliardo), a short that tackles the perception of colors. Undeniably, however, the artist who contributed the most, in various capacities, to this studio's animated documentaries has been Gibba, the animator renowned for having directed in 1948 the only neorealist animated film, *The Last Shoeshine* (*L'ultimo sciuscià*), and who has been the head of Corona's animation department from its foundation up to 1965. In particular, Gibba directed *The Plant of the Senses* (*La centrale dei sensi*, 1961) and *The Solar System* (*Il sistema solare*, 1961)—which depict respectively how the human brain works in relation to the five senses and the main satellites of the Sun—as well as the already mentioned *Adventure in the Cell*, *The Birth of Earth*, and *Eye's Magic*. There are then titles such as *Magic Lab*, *The Miracle of Blood* (*Il prodigio del sangue*, 1962, dir. Elio Gagliardo), and *Anatomy of Motion* for which he is credited as the head animator—and, for the first and the third, also as the scriptwriter—but of which he most likely was the director as well, even if they were officially presented as works by Elio Gagliardo. Indeed, in his autobiography, the animator explains how more than once Gagliardo asked him to formally hand over the paternity of his works to him (see Guido

2008, 129), and from the topics addressed to how they are dealt with, these three films showcase continuity with the ones officially directed by Gibba (see Formenti 2014, 11–12). Moreover, Gibba collaborated in the capacity of animator to animated documentaries effectively directed by others. It is the case of *The Art of Photography* (*L'arte della fotografia*, 1962, dir. Giampaolo Mercanti) and *The Painters of Prehistory* (*I pittori della preistoria*, 1962, dir. Elio Gagliardo), which are partly animated and partly live-action shorts informing the viewer respectively on photography and cave painting.

Generally speaking, Corona's animated documentaries are educational films addressing science-related topics. Even the few titles that constitute an exception to this general trend as they are animated histories are, however, riddled with science. It is, for instance, the case of *The Art of Photography* and *The Conquest of the Sky* (*La conquista del cielo*, 1968, dir. Rodolfo Besesti), which illustrate respectively the invention and evolution of photography and the development of aviation across the decades. *The Art of Photography* has a lengthy final section wherein the historical approach is abandoned in favor of an illustration of the working principles of photography. Similarly, *The Conquest of the Sky* is interspersed with relatively long scenes in which the physical laws behind flight are explained. If science is, thus, omnipresent in Corona's animated documentaries, a wide range of domains within it is covered through these films, including biology, meteorology, genetics, astronomy, paleontology, and physics.

In line with what was characteristic of classical animated documentaries, Corona also combined the use of fabled animation with a scientifically accurate treatise of the chosen topic. Indicative of how there was an attention to creating entertaining but truthful works is, for instance, the wording used in the script treatment of one of these films, *Adventure in the Cell*: "The documentary wants to be a journey through a cell. . . . The journey is imaginary but not fantastic since . . . the documentary will search for reality and expose in exact terms what science knows on the cell."[12] Always in accordance to what we have seen to be commonplace for classical animated documentaries, in creating these animated documentaries too the advice of an expert of the topic addressed—who in most cases was Rodolfo Ghione—was sought and this detail was underlined in the opening titles of the films.

Furthermore, as was customary for classical animated documentaries, the ones produced by Corona also were characterized by a scripted voiceover narration, subject to moments of eccentricity, that guides the viewer through the topic tackled without refraining from using similitudes and metaphors. More precisely, these films' voice-of-God commentaries were made eccentric partly in more "traditional" ways, such as that of having the animation literally translate into visuals similitudes and metaphors used by the narrator to explain the real. An example is the representation, in *The Plant of the Senses*, of the human eye as a stylized movie camera after the voiceover compares it to one. Still, the device most employed for making the voiceover eccentric consists in having the narrator switch, at some point, from a didactic to a lyrical tone. This shift can be found especially in the final sequences of such films, where the sentences pronounced by the narrator tend to become highly poetic, creating, as such, a contrast in respect to the plainly didactic ones proffered up to that moment. For instance, in *Adventure in the Cell*, the voiceover concludes the explanation of how the cell was discovered and what happens inside it with these words: "This occurs in the magnificent, microscopic city wherein it is guarded the secrets of life, of which the cell is the purest image." Similarly, in *The Birth of the Earth*, the final sentence pronounced by the voice-of-God narrator is: "In the warm womb of the sea the lifeless matter receives the gift of life."

Other characteristics shared by these films are as follows: the fact of being made using the hand-drawn animation technique; the presence of a musical score expressly composed by musician Franco Potenza, Alberico Vitalini, or Sandro Brugnolini, who regularly collaborated with Corona; a certain fragmentation at the level of narrative; and a limited animation in a more literal sense than that popularized by UPA. Indeed, in these films, we can frequently encounter scenes composed of static drawings to which is conferred movement by having the camera pan or zoom on them. Also, a drawing can be repeated more than once within the same title or even recycled in other films. A case in point are two shots portraying respectively a bison and a couple of hunters in cave paintings-style that we can find in the concluding sequence of *The Painters of Prehistory* as well as in the initial one of *Anatomy of Motion*. Furthermore, shots wherein to be animated are sketches rather than full drawings can be found. Exemplar is a scene from *Adventure in the Cell* where the voice-of-God states that in the eighteenth century no attention was paid to the discovery of the cell. Indeed, here, what is animated are precisely the sketches of two couples intent on dancing who are wearing eighteenth century period clothing (see Figure 9.5).

This limited animation, however, is the result not of a particular conception of the animated documentary but rather of Corona's animation department having been asked by the Gagliardo brothers to keep costs to a minimum and "impress the maximum amount of footage possible with just a few drawings" (Guido 2008, 125). Indeed, the producers saw animated documentaries merely as a cash machine. That is, they produced them in high quantity because they represented the typology of films that could have them gain more easily the governmental quality prize. However, in order to not just go even thanks to the prize but earn money out of it, the Gagliardo brothers urged their animators to make works that met the minimum requirements for obtaining the prize while keeping production costs as low as possible.[13] Since the judging committee had low standards, the repetition of a same shot or the use of a sketch rather than a full drawing did not prevent a film from being considered qualitative.

FIGURE 9.5 *Two sketched couples dressed in clothes from the eighteenth century that are shown in the act of dancing in a scene of* Adventure in the Cell.

The same reason can be identified behind an abundant presence of sober animation in many of these titles as well as for the fact that, while many of them do contain some characters, only a small number is actually character-oriented.[14] The case of *Meteorology* (*Meteorologia*, 1965, dir. Elio Gagliardo) is proof of how the reference point of Corona's animation department was the then-dominant animated documentary model and the reduction of fabled animation's presence or the detachment from the character-oriented approach seen in their works was just a result of the need to economize. Indeed, this film in its final version has no character and makes such a consistent use of sober animation that it is borderline from being an animated documentary and just a nonfiction animation. However, originally, it was to be called *The Weather, Tomorrow* (*Il tempo, domani*), its director was supposed to be Gibba, and its script treatment said: "Making use of the technique of the animated cartoon are illustrated some physical traits of water and air. Will be especially illustrated some characteristics little known to the general public. A puppet represents 'water' and another puppet will be 'air'."[15] Therefore, it was supposed not only to use fabled animation but also to have two leading characters.

In fact, Corona's animated documentaries tend to be very classical in the way in which they represent their subject matters. First of all, they are inclined to recur to what, as seen in Chapter 5, during this era of the form, had progressively become the conventional ways of making visual a certain aspect of the real in fabled terms. Just to make a few examples, in *The Miracle of Blood*, the action of white blood cells to contrast the inflammation that bacteria provoke if they manage to get in the human body through a wound is represented as a battle between good (i.e., white blood cells) and evil (i.e., bacteria) that in the end sees the former triumph on the latter.

Likewise, in *Anatomy of Motion*, the pyramidal cells responsible for our voluntary movements that are located in our brain are represented as busy receptionists, along the lines of how the brain is portrayed in Capra's *Hemo the Magnificent* (see Figures 9.6 and 9.7).

Second, the way in which set topics are illustrated and dramatized tends to be the one most commonly employed within the classical animated documentaries tackling that aspect of the real. For instance, in *The Age of Monsters*, which is the second installment of a trilogy on the development

FIGURE 9.6 *The pyramidal cells responsible for our voluntary movements as represented in* Anatomy of Motion.

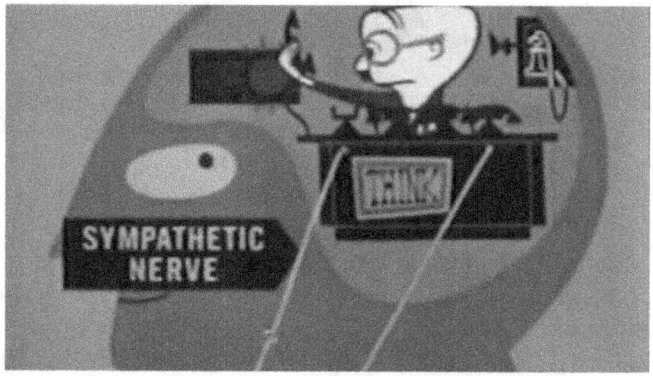

FIGURE 9.7 *The representation of the human brain in* Hemo the Magnificent.

of life on planet Earth scripted by Guido Gomas and directed by Giuseppe Maria Bruscolini, the fights between carnivorous and herbivorous dinosaurs are traditionally dramatized by showing a tyrannosaurus rex have a bloody close combat with a brontosaurus and defeat it.[16] Additionally, this fight even ends with blood from the now almost dead brontosaurus spilling on the camera lens, anticipating as such that "graphic verité" approach (Hight 2008, 17), which, as we will see in Chapter 11, will become recurrent in the strand of contemporary animated documentaries dealing with paleontology that the success of *Walking with Dinosaurs* will kickstart. Analogously, *The Conquest of Sky* is very similar to Halas & Batchelor Cartoon Films' *Power to Fly* in its being visually a parade of means for human flight, interspersed with moments wherein the science behind flight is illustrated. Simply, since Corona's film, unlike that from the Halas & Batchelor Cartoon Films studio, had to stay within the ten minutes length required for being admissible to the governmental quality prize, *The Conquest of Sky* depicts only the fundamental steps in flight's history, while *Power to Fly* addresses also lesser-known ones.

In sum, Corona's animated documentaries not only showcase a certain homogeneity among them in many respects but also were created with the classical eras' dominant animated documentary approach in mind, even if it may not always be evident at first sight as the animation department often had to scale down the original idea in order to meet the Gagliardo brothers' request to keep costs and efforts to a minimum in making these films.

Moreover, unfortunately, Corona's animated documentaries have not been seen by many Italians. Produced in order to gain the quality prize, they were screened just enough to qualify for it, which means that they have appeared only for a few days in a limited number of cinemas unevenly distributed across the country. In addition, paradoxically, these shorts were often shown before films restricted to that same young audience for which they were instead mainly intended. For example, although *Anatomy of Motion* was rated as a film viewable by a general audience, when on May 18, 1963, it was projected at cinema Delle Terrazze in Rome, it was combined with the titillating comedy *The Masseuses* (*Le massaggiatrici*, 1962, dir. Lucio Fulci). Analogously, in May 1963, *The Art of Photography* was screened at Triest's Supercinema and Udine's Cinema Astra respectively before the salacious documentary *Sexy Africa* (*Africa Sexy*, 1963, dir. Roberto Bianchi Montero) and *Diamond Head* (1962, dir. Guy Green).[17]

In the decades following their first release, a number of these titles had international distribution. For instance, in 1978, an Arabic edition was made for *Anatomy of Motion*, *The Plant of the Senses*, and *The Miracle of Blood*, among others, and Nexus Film secured their distribution rights for the Libyan noncommercial circuit.[18] Still, generally speaking, even the afterlife to their first screening has not been particularly remarkable for Corona's animated documentaries.

Nonetheless, these films, as well as the industrial ones created for Montecatini by various Milanese animation studios or Bozzetto's very personal ones, are proof of how, during the animated documentary's classical era—and in particular between the late 1950s and the end of the 1960s—also in Italy the production of works pertaining to this form thrived. Indeed, many of the nation's leading animators at some point in their career approached the animated documentary form and not all of them necessarily did so within the sponsorship system. If this has been possible, it has been mostly thanks to a series of laws that, even if not intentionally, have not only favored the production of these typologies of films but also granted the opportunity to make them in a regime of greater artistic freedom.

Notes

1 The first two Italian feature-length animations have been *The Dynamite Brothers* (*I fratelli Dinamite*, 1949, dir. Nino and Toni Pagot) and *The Singing Princess* (*La rosa di Bagdad*, 1949, dir. Anton Gino Domeneghini). For a more in-depth treatise of Italian animation up to 1949, see Zangrando (1968), Rondolino (2003), Antonini and Tognolotti (2008); Scrimitore (2013).

2 Other titles in the series are *A Prison* (*Una prigione*, 1940), *England vs Europe* (*Inghilterra vs Europa*, 1940, dir. Raoul Quattrocchi), *The True Face of England. Facts and Mishaps of the English Domain in the World* (*Il vero volto dell'Inghilterra. Fatti e misfatti del dominio inglese nel mondo*, 1940, dir. Domenico Paolella), *The Pioneers* (*I pionieri*, 1940, dir. Gianni Franciolini), *Two Populaces, a War* (*Due popoli, una guerra*, 1941, dir. Ugo Amadoro), and *Rome and Carthage* (*Roma e Cartagine*, 1941, dir. Liberio Pensuti). For a description of these works, see Scrimitore (2013, 117–48).

3 In particular, *The Tavern of Tuberculosis* narrates the imaginary story of a young balilla who, finding himself face to face with a personification of tuberculosis and its bacilli in a dirty tavern, calls to his rescue an army of anthropomorphic anti-tubercular stamps. The latter combat the disease and defeat it. The film even contains a musical number of clear Disney derivation wherein the *tuberculosis bacilli* dance and sing.

4 Since the 1930s, a law that obliged Italian cinemas to screen shorts before feature films was in place (see Aprà 2017, 13–14).

5 See "L. 29 Dicembre 1949, n. 958—Disposizioni per la cinematografia," *Gazzetta Ufficiale*, 301, 31 December 1949.

6 Edisonvolta, Montecatini, Lepetit, and Olivetti are respectively a power, a chemical, a pharmaceutical, and an information technology company. For a discussion of the film departments of the Milan-based companies, see Mosconi (1991).

7   For an in-depth treatise of the main animation studios active in Milan, see Ghirardato 1991. Aired for the first time on February 3, 1957, just before prime time, *Carousel* was a daily TV show composed of a series of advertisements each lasting two minutes and fifteen seconds. However, its peculiarity was that only in the last fifteen seconds references to the product promoted could be made, while the rest of the short had to tell a story (at least apparently) unrelated to the brand it advertised. A few animated films that apparently addressed real-life topics were made for *Carousel* too, as is the case of a series of 1959 advertisements on musical instruments made in 1959 by Gamma Film to promote Alemagna's sweets Charms. However, these shorts melded fact and fiction also at the level of content. Therefore, while they can still be considered as animated docufictions, they cannot be termed animated documentaries.

8   For a detailed treatise of Gamma Film's activity throughout the years, see Zane (1998).

9   Bozzetto is not the only one, among the future leading Italian animators, to work on fact-based animations in these years. In the early days of their careers, Giulio Gianini, Emanuele Luzzati, and Pino Zac contributed animated segments for otherwise live-action documentaries. For instance, Zac worked on the animated sequences of *The Atom in the Sea* (*L'atomo in mare*, 1961, dir. Virgilio Tosi), while Gianini was author, alone, of the animated segments in *Renaissance Today* (*Risorgimento oggi*, 1962, dir. Michele Gandin and Giambattista Cavallaro) and, with Luzzati, of those in *Operation Quality* (*Operazione qualità*, 1966, dir. Virgilio Tosi).

10 For instance, in 1974, Corona co-produced, with the Halas & Batchelor Cartoon Films studio, *European Folk Tales*, a series of thirty-three animations adapting traditional tales from different European countries.

11 More precisely, the Italian expression used was "documentario a cartoni animati." For example, see Document Prot. 01741/GF/brm—Authorization request for the employment of Elio Galiardo as the cameraman for *Adventure in the Cell*, June 7, 1962, Cineteca di Bologna, Collection Corona Cinematografica.

12 Document n. 255—Script treatment of *Adventure in the Cell*, 1962, Corona Cinematografica collection, Cineteca di Bologna.

13 Among the titles that effectively went on to obtain the quality prize, there are *The Conquest of the Sky*, *Heredity*, *Eye's Magic*, *Psychology of Color*, and *The Age of Monsters* (*L'età dei mostri*, 1966, dir. Giuseppe Maria Bruscolini).

14 Examples of Corona's character-oriented animated documentaries are *The Specific Gravity*, which has as its protagonist an animated Archimedes, or *600,000 Years on Earth* (*600.000 anni sulla Terra*, 1966, dir. Giuseppe Maria Bruscolini), which stars a prehistoric man who by generalizing synecdoche represents all those people who have lived in the early ages of planet Earth.

15 Script treatment of *The Weather, Tomorrow*, July 7, 1964, Corona Cinematografica collection, Cineteca di Bologna, Collection, folder 206.

16 The first and the third titles in this trilogy are respectively *From Space to Life* (*Dallo spazio alla vita*, 1966) and *600,000 Years on Earth*.

17 See List of documentaries' box office revenues n. 31, June 22, 1963, Corona Cinematografica collection, Cineteca di Bologna, Binder "Compenso ad agenti ed esercenti." Both *The Masseuses* and *Sexy Africa* were restricted to under eighteen years old, whereas *Diamond Head* to under fourteen years old.

18 See Concession to Nexus Film of Arabic editions' noncommercial rights, November 20, 1978, Corona Cinematografica collection, Cineteca di Bologna.

PART III

The Contemporary Production, 1986 and Beyond

10

Private Truths and Inner Realities

The Post-1985 Innovations

In describing the creation of the famed British animated documentary on autism, *A Is for Autism* (1992, dir. Tim Webb), former Channel 4's commissioning editor for animation Clare Kitson explains that, at first, "the storyboard featured comments by experts and parents, as well as the autistic people themselves. Later on, it would become clear that the comments of the autistic people were far more poignant and equally informative in their way, so they would constitute the whole soundtrack" (Kitson 2008, 125). This description of *A Is for Autism*'s genesis is emblematic of the shift that the animated documentary, in general, has undergone with the second half of the 1980s. Indeed, since 1986 this form has veered always more decisively toward the subjective. The expository and seemingly objective approach characteristic of its classical era has been undermined by a personal and experiential one consisting of tackling an aspect of the real from the particular viewpoint of one or more people that are living or have lived it. Like what can be observed for the coeval docudrama (see Paget [1998] 2011, 275–7), the direct witness testimony has thus been imported also into the animated documentary, making it, however, not simply one of the elements used to tell the real as in the docudrama but instead the core one, a cornerstone of these works. In fact, as the docudrama, the animated documentary has come to reflect the changes that the documentary itself has undergone. Indeed, the witness testimony has become such a central element in the post-Griersonian documentary that Brian Winston suggests that the best way to describe the latter is as "the narrativized recorded aspects of witnessed observation received as being a story about the world" (Winston 2013, 24).

To better understand this change that the animated documentary has gone through, let us consider, for instance, the NFB-produced short *Minoru:*

Memory of Exile (1992, dir. Michael Fukushima). This film addresses a historical fact: the 1942 internment of Japanese Canadians in concentration camps in the name of national security. Still, instead of doing it in an expository way as it would have occured in an early or classical history-concerned animated documentary, it does so by dramatizing the first-person oral testimony of the director's father, Minoru, who, as a kid, experienced first-hand those events. Together with his family, he was, initially, deported from Vancouver, where he had lived all his life, to a concentration camp in New Denver and, subsequently, obliged to move to a Japan hostile to him due to his Canadian citizenship. Therefore, as scholar Monika Kin Gagnon (2007, 280) puts it, "*Minoru* undertakes a filmic representation from within the Japanese Canadian community directly affected by the internment, rather than from a perspective outside it," demonstrating "a notable shift from the so-called objective narrators' voices" proper of earlier animated documentaries.

Another clear example of the animated documentary's post-1985 turn toward the subjective is offered by Mischa Kamp's *Naked* (*Bloot*, 2006). This series engages with a topic as puberty, which had already been at the center of several previous animated documentaries. However, while classical animated documentaries on the subject generically explain the biology of this delicate stage in an adolescent's life, *Naked* is interview-driven and presents in each of its episodes the emotions and sensations that set pubertal transformations elicited in a specific teen. For instance, unlike the classical *The Story of Menstruation*—which describes what occurs inside the body of a female during the menstrual cycle and illustrates the dos and don'ts in the days she has her period—, the episode of Kamp's series on the topic, "Ilham (13)," offers an account of the feelings that the first bleeding has arisen in a Muslim girl. More precisely, what is, here, animated and visually dramatized is the testimony of an adolescent named Ilham that focuses on the embarrassing (as the loss of her pad in the pool) and feelgood (as her mother's hug when she told her she had become a woman) moments she experienced on the occasion of her first menstrual cycle. Therefore, in sum, similarly to what was noted for *Minoru*, in *Naked* biological phenomena are addressed from the subjective and personal perspective of people who have experienced them, lingering on the sensations and emotions these facts have arisen in them.

Even just from these two examples it, thus, becomes evident how post-1985 animated documentaries tend to be (at least in part) first-person narrations, imbued with subjectivity, which pay attention to and insist on the feelings that the real-life events portrayed elicited in chosen people who have experienced those facts first-hand. Also, these audiovisual works often are interview-driven. Furthermore, returning the emotional dimension of the occurrences narrated has become so important that it can even determine from which viewpoint a factual occurrence is told, as has been the case for *25 April*. This feature film tackles New Zealand's participation in the conflict that took place in Gallipoli between February 1915 and January 1916. However, the facts are told from the subjective perspective of six New Zealanders who, with different roles, have taken part in the events by reenacting and dramatizing what they had written at the time in their diaries, memoirs, and letters to the family. The rationales that female filmmaker Leanne Pooley followed in choosing precisely those six people were explained by the director herself:

> There were specific things I was looking for, and there were certain events I wanted to cover. I wanted there to be a soldier who was there for the entire campaign. Obviously, I needed at least a couple of my characters to be at Chunuk Bair. In terms of New Zealand [culture], it was the most important battle: we actually mark 8 August [when the troops arrived at Chunuk Bair] as a really important date here, rather than the day of the landing. I wanted to find individuals who wrote in a way that expressed, not just the event, but how they felt about the event. . . . I was looking for journals with more emotional expression about how they experienced the conflict and how they felt about each other. (Pooley in Pfeiffer 2016, 92)

Recounting the feelings of the New Zealander soldiers, doctors, and nurses who were in Gallipoli was thus considered key by Pooley to the point that the presence or not of this dimension in the original testimonies became for her a criterion for selecting whose stories to tell.

Emotions are, however, only one of the many intangible internal processes of mankind that find representation in post-1985 animated documentaries. As director Shira Avni (2011, 86) has pointed out, contemporary animated documentaries tend "to illustrate . . . memory, emotion, interior states, and first-person sensory experiences difficult to re-create as effectively in other forms of cinema." Indeed, the animated documentary as a form today has come to be very much focused on making visible inner truths, a respect under which it is close to German Expressionism. Emblematic of this shift in the employment of animation to tell the real is a declaration by Femke Wolting, the co-director, together with Tommy Pallotta, of *Last Hijack*, a feature on the life of experienced Somali pirate Mohamed. In illustrating the genesis of her film, she has affirmed: "In the beginning, we thought we could use animation to visualize the moments we couldn't film in the real world. . . . The function of animation changed when we were editing. We decided to use the animation in a more expressive way to show Mohamed's fears and dreams in a subjective way" (Wolting in Murphy 2014, AR18).

The title that perhaps best exemplifies this characteristic of the form is, however, Chris Landreth's *Ryan*, which not by chance on the pages of *Cinema Scope* has been described as "a near-perfect synthesis of reportage and expressionism that sums up the deep contradictions of its subject"

("*Ryan* and *Alter Egos*" 2005, 50). By adopting an approach that he refers to as "psychorealism" (Kriger 2012, 151) in dramatizing the recording of conversations he had with fellow animator Ryan Larkin and a few other people who used to be close to the latter, Landreth visualizes also what is going on both in his and his interviewees' heads. For instance, once Larkin enrages in talking about how lack of money can be limiting, all of a sudden, red spikes come out of his head (see Figure 10.1). Similarly, when the fear of creative paralysis experienced by a young Larkin is brought up, threads of color envelop his face and immobilize his legs and arms. Moreover, as Honess Roe (2013, 130) points out, throughout the film the "characters wear the internal as physical wounds, visibly betraying their personal issues and psychological baggage."

Post-1985 animated documentary's focus on human inwardness has determined the emergence of new strands of works. For instance, a substantial group of titles focusing on those medical conditions that cause an atypical perception of the real, like mental disorders (e.g., Andy Glynne's 2003 shorts from the *Animated Minds* series *Fish on a Hook*, *The Light Bulb Thing*, *Dimensions*, and *Obsessively Compulsive*), synesthesia (*An Eyeful of Sound*), autism (*A Is for Autism* or *Snack and Drink*), Down's syndrome (Shira Avni's *Tying Your Own Shoes* [2009] and *Petra's Poem* [2012]), Asperger's (Glynne's *An Alien in the Playground* [2009] or Mike and Tim Rauch's *Q&A* [2010]), and so on, has been produced. Moreover, a considerable number of animated documentaries providing an account of memories "of a *personal past*" (Voci 2010, 62, my emphasis), and in particular of past traumatic experiences, such as abuse (*Daddy's Little Bit of Dresden China* [1988, dir. Karen Watson]), a loss (*His Mother's Voice* [1997, dir. Dennis Tupicoff]), internment in a concentration camp (*Minoru*

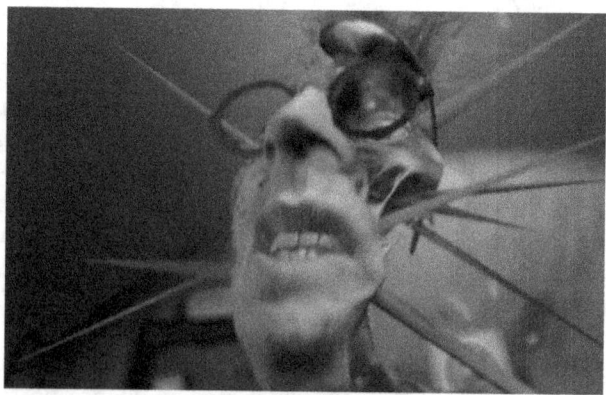

FIGURE 10.1 *In* Ryan, *red spikes come out of Larkin's head when he talks about how limiting lack of money can be.*

or *Silence*), domestic violence (*Survivors* [1997, dir. Sheila Sofian]), and so on, have also seen the light.[1] These works capture "the emotional and not only the factual dimension of one's memory" (Voci 2010, 61). Like Renov notes to be the case for the live-action autobiographical documentary, the truths offered are, thus, "often those of the interior rather than of the exterior" (Renov 2008, 41). And, this occurs even when the filmmaker and the subject of the film do not coincide. Exemplar is the case of *Another Day of Life* (2018, dir. Raúl de la Fuente and Damian Nenow). This feature film is an animated memoir on the three months spent by journalist Ryszard Kapuściński in Angola in 1975 amid a violent civil war and is an adaptation of the namesake nonfiction book written by the war correspondent himself on this experience. Clearly, Kapuściński has had no part in the making of this animated documentary since he had long been dead when it was made. Still, filmmakers la Fuente and Nenow insist also on the emotional dimension of memory in retelling the journalist's story. Indeed, similarly to what occurs in a film as *Waltz with Bashir*, which is instead fully autobiographical, in *Another Day of Life*, next to sequences wherein the facts of those three months are reenacted, one can find also scenes with a dream-like quality that dramatize the sensations and states of mind of the protagonist.

More generally, always as Renov points out to occur for the contemporary live-action documentary, in the last three decades or so, the animated documentary also has increasingly become an audiovisual form "of 'personal voices'" and the presence of "a substantive autobiographical dimension" has come to be a recurrent trait of these films (Renov 2008, 48). More precisely, on the one hand, we can find several explicitly autobiographical contemporary animated documentaries. It is the case, for instance, of *Daddy's Little Bit of Dresden China*, in which Watson tells the story of how she was repeatedly molested by her father while growing up. Other examples are *My Universe Inside Out* (1996, dir. Faith Hubley)—which, as Renov (2008, 42) puts it, is "a whimsical and highly elliptical account of the artist's 72 years that is short on facts but rich in the evocation of childhood memory, sensory experience, and the quotidian pleasures of family life"—or the already mentioned *Sunrise over Tiananmen Square* and *Waltz with Bashir*. We can also find works that can be considered in full autobiographical even if the person they focus on was only the co-director of the film as in the case of the features *Persepolis* and *Approved for Adoption*. These two animated documentaries are, one, about Marjane Satrapi's struggles of growing up during the Islamic revolution and, the other, about Jung Henin's difficulties in being an international foster child. Still, Satrapi and Henin have co-directed them with another filmmaker, respectively Vincent Paronnaud and Laurent Boileau. Nevertheless, the films remain adherent to the namesake autobiographical graphic novels of which they are an adaptation, a fact that suggests Paronnaud and Boileau have been involved mainly to bring to the project the filmmaking know-how Satrapi and Henin lacked due to their being graphic novelists and not animators. Something similar can be argued for the web series *Flavours of Iraq* (*Le Parfum d'Irak*, 2018, dir. Léonard Cohen). Consisting of twenty episodes of about three minutes each, the series offers an intimate account of the relationship that French-Iraqi journalist Feurat Alani has had with his family's country of origin, Iraq. *Flavours of Iraq* was directed and animated solely by Léonard Cohen since Alani had no filmmaking or drawing skills. Still, Alani had an active part in its making: not only is the series adapted from a thread of 1,500 tweets he wrote in the summer of 2016 but he has also acted as its screenwriter and narrator.

On the other hand, there are also many partially autobiographical post-1985 animated documentaries. Indeed, often, although formally they have as their protagonists and subjects figures other than their directors, contemporary animated documentaries end up being in (minimal) part about them too, in a similar way to what Renov notices to be the case for Michael Moore's live-action documentaries (see Renov 2008, 48). In particular, filmmakers make themselves present within the film by having an onscreen character that represents them and/or through (more or less consistent) aural interventions. Let us consider, for instance, *Minoru* and *Is the Man Who Is Tall Happy?*. As already mentioned, the protagonist of the former is not its director, Michael Fukushima, but his father. The soundtrack of the short, however, contains, next to the recollections of Minoru, also some interjections by the director, during which, from time to time, he offers some information about himself. For instance, toward the end of the film, referring to his father, Michael declares: "I am a Canadian because he struggled to remain a Canadian." Similarly, a little earlier, meanwhile visually are shown a series of photographs portraying a young Michael next to his father, aurally the director, first, explains that in his family many issues were never an object of conversation and, then, comments: "Those silences are a large part of my identity, my heritage." Not dissimilarly, *Is the Man Who Is Tall Happy?* is about American linguist and philosopher Noam Chomsky. Nonetheless, the film opens with Gondry sharing with the audience information about himself, and especially, himself as a director. For example, he informs the viewer on how he discovered Chomsky and what brought him to use animation for the film, while visually is shown an animated character sitting at the drawing table and making a film that represents him. And, similar brief sequences in which the director starts talking about himself can be found also in other parts of the feature. These moments in which Fukushima and Gondry talk about themselves inject, even if just briefly, an autobiographical dimension to their films.

There can, however, be also titles wherein the director makes himself or herself even more present than it occurs in *Minoru* and *Is the Man Who Is Tall Happy?*. Examples are *Ryan* and *Irinka & Sandrinka* (*Irinka et Sandrinka*, 2007, dir. Sandrine Stoïanov). Theoretically, the former short is a portrayal of animator Ryan Larkin. Nevertheless, as Steve Fore (2011, 285) has underlined, its "subject is as much Landreth's very personalized understanding of and response to Larkin as it is a portrait of Larkin himself." Indeed, the director makes himself present within the frame as a character by dramatizing also the interview situation and not just the content of the interviews he did. Also, significantly he opens the film with a scene set in a public bathroom wherein this animated Landreth informs the viewer about his own past traumas. Only after having talked about himself for a while, he states: "But I'm getting off of subject here, I'm afraid. This story is about Ryan." Despite such declaration, through this scene, Landreth thus makes apparent from the outset that the film is as much about him as it is about Larkin, and therefore that it is in part an autobiographical work. Analogously, *Irinka & Sandrinka* is based on recordings of an aural interview of director Sandrine Stoïanov to her Russian aunt Irene and focuses mainly on the difficult childhood of the latter. Nevertheless, the director not only inserts herself as a character but also "uses animation to weave together her aunt's memories and her own childhood fantasies of being a young Russian aristocrat" (Honess Roe 2013, 152). Therefore, not dissimilarly from what Landreth does in *Ryan*, Stoïanov also exploits the device of the interview situation to carve out a space for talking about herself in the film.

Finally, there are also animated documentaries to which an autobiographic dimension is conferred operating in reverse. That is, instead of inserting moments wherein the director foregrounds himself or herself, the subjects of the film are involved in the making of the animated visuals. It is, for instance, the case of *Little Voices*, *A Is for Autism*, or *Tying Your Own Shoes*. Indeed, as scholar Juan Alberto Conde Aldana (2018, 48, 53) underlines, *Little Voices* contains some animations made using the drawings executed in colored pencil and crayon by the children protagonists of the film themselves. This fact is underlined also in the initial caption wherein we read: "In Colombia, there are about one million children displaced by violence. This film was told and drawn by some of them." Likewise, the visual track of *A Is for Autism* also contains drawings from all the persons affected by autism of which we hear the declarations in the soundtrack. Moreover, one of the interviewees, nine-year-old Daniel Sellers, has significantly contributed to the creation of the animations. Indeed, Kitson (2008, 126) explains: "The initial idea had been for the autistic collaborator to do only the repetitive drawings, the 'inbetweens'. As it turned out, after minimal tuition in the principles of animation, Daniel was able to produce key drawings, leaving Tim and animator Ron MacRae to fill in the inbetweens." Analogously, the four protagonists of *Tying Your Own Shoes*—Petra, Matthew, Katherine, and Daninah—are responsible for all the animations contained in the film, which therefore ends up returning their self-portraits. Director Avni (2011, 84) explains:

> *Tying Your Own Shoes* provides a forum for this group of artists with Down syndrome to portray themselves as they wish to be seen, through

their own voices and artwork, rather than through the usual filters—family, caregivers, teachers, or the medical community. Combining live video interviews with each artist's beautiful animated self-portrait work and personal narration, the film provides an intimate window into the world of Down syndrome, as experienced from the inside.

Anvi (2011, 87) adds: "*Tying Your Own Shoes* attempted to be as *subjective* as possible—the artists were involved in every editing decision and had full veto power to ensure that the film represented them as they wish to be seen."

This presence of an autobiographic dimension in contemporary animated documentaries is linked to a further difference existing between the pre- and post-1985 examples of the form: the production conditions in which they are made. Indeed, within the animation realm broadly speaking, the 1980s and 1990s have been characterized by "a new emphasis on the director" and the emergence of a substantive independent production, favored, among others, by the development of college programs devoted to animation and the growth of a festival circuit wherein these titles could find an audience (Furniss 2017, 315). In line with what has been occurring for animation in general, since 1986, animated documentaries have gone from being mainly films made on commission that, thus, had to reflect the needs of their sponsors (as they were during the classical era) to being mostly creator-driven works independently produced.[2] And, as Maureen Furniss (2017, 321–2) points out, when free to explore the subjects they want, artists tend to create "introspective works focusing on the artist's own life or issues of particular concern to the artist," which explains why it is often possible to find at least some autobiographical elements within contemporary animated documentaries.

The expansion of the independent production has been also one of the factors that—together with the growth of college animation programs and the funding policies of arts institutions and televisions becoming more attentive to financing also women's works (see Pilling 1992, 5–6)—has determined a rise in the number of female animators. Mirroring this general trend and, in proportion, even outdoing what has been occurring within the broader animation realm, since the second half of the 1980s, the number of females involved in the creation of animated documentaries has exponentially increased in size. Indeed, while female animators who have (co-)authored animated documentaries could already be identified during the classical era—for example, Joy Batchelor, Beryl Stevens, Nancy Hanna, and Vera Linnecar in the UK; Faith Hubley in the United States; or Evelyn Lambart in Canada—, they represented a minority. In more recent times, instead, the women (co-)responsible for the creation of one or more of such works have almost outnumbered the men. Shira Avni, Anna Bergmann, Liz Blazer, Joyce Borenstein, Sylvie Bringas, Anca Damian, Ann Marie Fleming, Jacqueline Goss, Hanna Heilborn, Dee Hibbert-Jones,

Mischa Kamp, Gillian Lacey, Ellie Land, Ruth Lingford, Samantha Moore, Ng'endo Mukii, Marjut Rimminen, Nina Sabnani, Marie-Josée Saint-Pierre, Marjane Satrapi, Sheila Sofian, Sandrine Stoïanov, Nomi Talisman, Karen Watson, Lee Withmore, Femke Wolting, and Orly Yadin are only some of the many women from around the world who in the last three decades or so have (co-)directed audiovisual works that employ the fabled animation to dramatize an aspect of our world. There have also been cases of animated documentaries authored by women's collectives, such as the UK-based Leeds Animation Workshop, which has made social issues the main topic of its animated works, or the Australia-based Southern Ladies Animation Group, which in 2003 has created *It's Like That*. In fact, even if, paradoxically, a title by a male filmmaker (i.e., *Waltz with Bashir*) is normally taken as the example par excellence of this form's contemporary production, one could very well say that the post-1985 animated documentary is mainly a female's business, considering the number of women who retain authorship of these works. Indeed, despite being largely independent productions, these works are not dismissible as a feminine subgenre of the form as Paul Wells (1998, 198) somehow suggests to be, instead, usually the case for female-independent animations when he argues that, in them, one can identify "a specific *feminine aesthetic* which resists the inherently masculine language of the live-action arena, and the most dominant codes of orthodox hyper-realist animation which also use its vocabulary." In fact, from an examination of the contemporary animated documentaries (co-)directed by women, it emerges that the latter not only tend to not auto-segregate themselves into the feminine aesthetic but have even been progressively moving away from it. Indeed, contrary to what Wells shows to be the case for the animations that are expressions of the feminine aesthetics, their works usually do not challenge the animated documentary form by breaking with its conventions nor address exclusively issues of women's interest. In fact, extending what Maria Lorenzo Hernández (2010) shows to be the case for nowadays animated autobiographies, one can very well assert that contemporary animated documentaries by female filmmakers tend to tackle universal issues and concerns. Actually, their films may not even have female figures as their protagonists (e.g., see *Curlic: The Path to Beyond* [*Crulic: Drumul spre dincolo*, 2011, dir. Anca Damian], *Chris the Swiss* [2018, dir. Anja Kofmel], and *Last Hijack*). And, if they do, the characters in question often do not act as representatives of womankind but rather of an ungendered category of people, such as adults with Down's syndrome (as in *Tying Your Own Shoes*), persons with sleep disorders (as in Ellie Land's *Sleepless* [2016]), or wrongfully convicted citizens (as in Sheila Sofian's *Truth Has Fallen* [2013]).

Finally, with animated documentaries having gone from being mostly sponsored films to becoming mainly independent and author-driven works, even the geography of the animated documentary production has faced some changes. Canada and the UK have kept and reinforced their role as world-leading producers of this typology of animations, outperforming even the United States, which, however, still is a prominent maker of such audiovisual products. If Canada and the UK have been able to maintain a leadership position in the field, it is most likely due to the presence in these nations of bodies that have financed the production of this kind of works leaving freedom of expression to their makers, as it has been the case of Channel 4 between the 1989 and 1999 for the UK and still is the case of the NFB for Canada. In Europe, after the UK, other nations with an important production of animated documentaries are Sweden and France (see Martinelli 2012, 23; Ajanovic-Ajanć 2019, 99). Although more limited than the Canadian or British one, the Australian production is also substantial, most likely thanks to this typology of works having found particular support from the Australian Film Commission (see Velin 2009, 14).[3]

The animated documentary as a form seems to be instead less visited in Asian countries. In fact, for instance, in her 2010 monograph scholar, Paola Voci (2010, 62) writes: "In China . . . docuanimation is a . . . still quite unexplored development in film/video-making." An exception is represented by Israel, where, after the international success of *Waltz with Bashir*, films that "fit comfortably within a definition of animated documentaries" have increasingly been made (Friedman 2017, 187). This, however, does not mean that we cannot find contemporary animated documentaries from Asian nations other than Israel. Examples are the Indian *Flood of Memory* (2008, dir. Anitha Balachandran), on the monsoon of 2006 and the impact it has had on the lives of the inhabitants of the Barmer district in Rajasthan, or the Japanese *Megumi* (2008, dir. Hidetoshi Ômori), on the 1977 abduction of a thirteen-year-old Japanese girl, Megumi Yokota, by North Korea. We can also recall the Chinese autobiographical works *Preserved Voices* (*Liu sheng*, 2004, dir. Zhou Tingting) and *Ketchup* (2012, dir. Chunning Guo and Baishen Yan) or the Korean *Herstory* (*So-nyeo-i-ya-gi*, 2011, dir. Jun Ki Kim), *Never Ending Story* (2014), *Tear* (2015), and *For Her* (2017, dir. Kim Junki), on those young females, known as comfort women, who were forced into sexual slavery by Japanese soldiers during the Second World War.[4]

Like in Asia, in Africa also the animated documentary form is still scarcely practiced compared to what occurs in Europe and America, and yet also here we can find contemporary examples of the form. It is, for instance, the case of the Congolese *Kinshasa, September Noir* (1992, dir. Jean Michel Kibushi), on the military coup of Kinshasa that took place on September 23, 1991; the South African *Beyond Freedom* (2005, dir. Jacquie Trowell), wherein the topic of apartheid is tackled through the testimonies of various persons who have experienced it; or the Mozambican *The Grandchildren's Mother* (*A Mãe Dos Netos*, 2008, dir. Isabel Noronha and Vivian Altman), which focuses on Elisa, an old woman who has been left to care for her fourteen grandchildren after HIV killed her son and his eight wives.[5]

Moreover, if we have witnessed a general growth in the production of animated documentaries worldwide in the last decades, there have been also nations that go against this trend. It is the case of Italy, where, with the drastic reduction of the monetary state support toward the documentary film, the national production of animated documentaries has dropped significantly in respect to what, in Chapter 9, we have seen to have occurred during the classical age. Unquestionably, examples of the form can still be found, as is, for instance, the case of the short *On Your Doorstep* (*Sottocasa*, 2010, dir. Daniele Baiardini, Giulia Sara Bellunato, Mauro Ciocia, and Clyo Parecchini), wherein the stories of three homeless people living in Turin are narrated from their perspective. Yet, they are much more limited in number than those made during the classical era. Moreover, if certainly in the last ten years or so in Italy even some feature-length works that have been deemed animated documentaries have been produced,[6] the works in question are only partially in animation and the live-action component often overrides the animated one so consistently that they end up being borderline between actual animated documentaries and documentaries with animated interjections.

Lastly, if all nations today have under their belt the production of at least a few short-form animated documentaries, since the late 2000s, the number of long-form works made also has been growing. Indeed, if feature-length animated documentaries have long started seeing the light, before this date they were exceptions rather than the norm. After the worldwide success obtained by *Persepolis* in 2007 and *Waltz with Bashir* in 2008, the long-form has instead increasingly been chosen all over the globe to narrate our world through fabled animation. Among the feature animated documentaries made in the 2010s, we can recall the US-produced *Truth Has Fallen* and *Tower*, the Colombian *Little Voices* and *Virus Tropical*, the New Zealand *25 April*, the German *The Green Wave*, the Romanian-Polish *Curlic*, the French *Is the Man Who Is Tall Happy?*, the French-Belgian *Approved for Adoption*, the Italian-French *Samouni Road* (*La strada dei Samouni*, 2018, dir. Stefano Savona), the Swiss-Croatian-German-Finnish coproduction *Chris the Swiss*, the Dutch-Irish-German-Belgian *Last Hijack*, and the Polish-Spanish-Belgian-German-Hungarian *Another Day of Life*.

To this must be added that, in line with this animated docufiction form's long lasting tendency to take in the transformations that occur within the documentary realm, animated documentary projects that can be described as online, interactive, collaborative, transmedia, and 360 degrees have also increasingly emerged over recent years. To put it as Peter Wintonick (2013, 376) would, animated documentary-makers too have been exploring and exploiting the "spectrum of possibilities" offered by the "new silicon-based technology." Indeed, as will be discussed in the concluding chapter, various online animated i-docs have been created since the 2010s. Yet, we have seen, for instance, also the emergence of a project like the web-based, collaborative autobiographical animated documentary *Bioscope*

(*Bioscopi: Una biografia collectiva animada*, 2021, dir. Pol Mallafré). This work edits together, in what is meant to be at the same time a collective biography and the autobiography of a place, short-form animated autoportrayals that web users of all ages made about their life and environment following guidelines and advice provided by the conceivers of the project on a namesake website. Moreover, we have been witnessing a flourishing of 360 degrees VR animated documentary pieces that tend to "position the viewer 'as-if' a witness to events" (Nash 2022, 110) and are often part of a larger transmedia project. Recent examples include *Accused #2: Walter Sisulu* (2018, dir. Nicolas Champeaux and Gilles Porte), *Ashe '68 VR Experience* (2019, dir. Brad Lichtenstein), and *12 Seconds of Gunfire: The True Story of a School Shooting* (2019, dir. Suzette Moyer and Seth Blanchard), which immerse their viewers respectively in the courtroom of the Rivonia Trial during Sisulu's hearing, in the 1968 US Open final that saw Arthur Ashe become the first Black man to win this tournament, and in the journey of trauma that first-grader Ava Gardner experienced after her friend Jacob Hall was killed in front of her during the 2016 Townville Elementary School shooting. We can recall also *Manic VR* (2018, dir. Kalina Bertin), wherein the director offers insight into manic depression by means of animating vocal messages that her siblings Felicia and François, who suffer from mental disorders, have left in her voicemail in a span of three years.

Elements of Continuity

At first sight, the classical and the contemporary animated documentary seem, thus, significantly different from each other. Nonetheless, if we set them against each other, it becomes apparent that the latter is an evolution of the former. Indeed, under their superficial differences lay several shared traits. First of all, it is possible to identify a good level of continuity between the pre- and post-1985 animated documentary in terms of the subcategories in which these works fall subject-wise. Indeed, if a significant number of classical animated documentaries are animated histories, the bulk of this form's contemporary production deals with a historical period or occurrence—showcasing in this also a connection with the docudrama, which frequently revisits historical events (e.g., see Ogunleye 2005; Lipkin 2011).[7] Only, to put it as Voci does, in the post-1985 works is added "the personal truth of the individual experience to the public truth of dramatical historical events" (Voci 2010, 61–2). Moreover, as in the classical era, in the current one also there are numerous animated documentaries on health-related issues. What has changed is simply the typology of diseases addressed, so as to respond to the new urgency of making visible the subjective. As anticipated, now the attention is posed on all those syndromes and disorders that involve a distorted perception of the real. Finally, similarly to what occurred during the classical era, also nowadays we can find an entire strand of animated documentaries dealing with sex and sexuality. To vary is the fact that, as already noted in relationship to *Naked*, the focus shifts from the biology to the sensations and emotions linked to them. In other words, instead of illustrating the functioning of the reproductive system or what happens in our body when a certain sexually transmitted disease is contracted, sex-related contemporary animated documentaries tend to deal with such topics as the first intercourse (*Never Like the First Time!* [*Aldrig som första gången!*, 2005, dir. Jonas Odell]), orgasm (*Little Deaths*), the difficulties couples can encounter in the bedroom (*The Trouble with Love and Sex* [2012, dir. Jonathan Hodgson]), the sex life of elderlies (*Backseat Bingo* [2003, dir. Liz Blazer]), and so on.

Second, the classical and the contemporary animated documentary have in common the fact of transcending the boundaries of a single animation technique. Certainly, if in the classical era hand-drawn animation was the most employed technique (in accordance with what at the time was commonplace for animation in general), nowadays CGI is the most adopted one in making these films. Nevertheless, all the range of animation techniques has been and keeps being used to create this typology of works. Indeed, one can find also animated documentaries employing rotoscope animation (*His Mother's Voice* or *Tower*), paint on glass (Sheila Sofian's *A Conversation with Harris* [2001] and *Truth Has Fallen*), hand-drawn animation (*Is the Man Who Is Tall Happy?*), and so on. Additionally, from time to time more than one technique can be combined within the same film. It is, for instance, the case of *It's Like That*, wherein, as Honess Roe (2013, 90) has highlighted, a series of techniques are combined, including "stop-motion puppet animation, computer 3-D animation, flash and hand-drawn on paper," which "reflect the input of the thirteen animators who worked on the project."

Third, like we have seen to occur for classical animated documentaries, also for contemporary ones the correctness and veracity of what is recounted are ensured by having an expert on the topic tackled offer his or her advice during the making of the film or, more frequently, through research on the subject conducted by the filmmakers themselves. In addition, whereas in the pre-1985 animated documentaries the fact that an expert was consulted in making the film was tendentially signposted in the opening credits in order to underline that these works were grounded in facts, in this form's contemporary works are similarly present opening captions claiming a direct link to reality.

Fourth, as already seen in Chapter 2, classical and contemporary animated documentaries have in common also the fact that their soundtracks carry out much of the burden of authenticating them as reality-related works. The sole difference is that during this form's classical era the informative and didactic voice-of-God commentary fulfilled this task, whereas nowadays audio-recordings of interviews do so, in line with the already mentioned increase in the usage of the direct testimony within the documentary realm. Furthermore, as observed for the voice-of-God narration in classical animated documentaries, these interview recordings also are made eccentric. In particular, nowadays, such effect is achieved by embodying these real-life declarations in one or more animated characters, or by anyhow submitting them to "the density of the body" of an onscreen actor (Doane 1980, 41). Moreover, exactly as it frequently happened with the voice-of-God of classical animated documentaries, the original grain of such interviews is manipulated via adding a sound carpet or extradiegetic music that confers pathos to the overall narration.

A further element of continuity between classical and contemporary animated documentaries is the presence also of some visual veridictive marks, although the codes and conventions used to this end change. Indeed, while, as seen in Chapter 5, in classical animated documentaries sober animation was employed to confer veridiction, it can hardly be found in post-1985 examples of the form. Nonetheless, live-action photographs, archival materials, and/or expressly shot documentarian scenes, which equally act as veridictive marks, are often present in contemporary animated documentaries. Also, always at the same end, via visually representing the interview situation, it is often highlighted that what is recounted is the result of testimonies from real-life people. Even in a film as *25 April*, which, unlike most contemporary animated documentaries, is based not on oral interviews but on written testimonies, the words contained in these documents have been transformed in declarations proffered by the animated actors during purported talking head interviews given in the aftermath of the Gallipoli conflict.

Other commonalities existing between classical and contemporary animated documentaries are that of being character-oriented, depicting issues of concern to national or international communities, and having as protagonists one or more figures that, by generalizing synecdoche, represent an entire category of people. In fact, although contemporary animated documentaries tend to revolve around the personal testimonies of specific individuals, the stories in them recounted are tackled due to their being a manifestation of a broader social or political issue that is felt as relevant by a more or less large community. In other words, those specific occurrences become a way to raise awareness on and stimulate discussion around a greater issue of which they are just one of many instances.[8] *Tower* makes explicit how the particular vicissitudes narrated in a contemporary animated documentary are a means to draw attention to the larger issue of which they are expression. Toward the end of this feature there is a sequence wherein, while we hear a declaration of a TV anchorman from the time of the University of Texas massacre on how violence had become a problem of US society, a montage of live-action images from news coverage of more recent mass shootings, such as the ones at Columbine High School, Virginia Tech, UMPQUA community college, or Louisiana Movie theater, is shown.

Through this montage it is, thus, made apparent how what occurred in Texas on that day of 1966 was only a manifestation of an issue that concerns the entire national territory.

Moreover, as anticipated, for contemporary animated documentaries also it is true that, for how much the stories narrated are personal and subjective, the characters at the center of these audiovisual works can be seen as representatives of a broader category of people. From the moment in which the bodies of the social actors are absented and replaced with animated ones—which generally do not even resemble their factual counterparts—universality is conferred to the vicissitudes narrated and, thus, a (latent) generalizing synecdoche is activated. In other words, the testimony of a certain person becomes by extension that of any man or woman who has lived that same trauma, suffered from that same disease, and so on. As Tupicoff highlights in discussing the genesis of his short *His Mother's Voice*, "[a]ny storyteller speaks with her own voice, but also speaks for others who may lack words, or the opportunity, or the audience" (Tupicoff 2005, 12). Moreover, Honess Roe explains how animation particularly facilitates this universalization since the simplified images that, in most cases, it offers of a body favor the identification of viewers with that set character. She writes: "Everyone can see himself or herself in a simplified cartoon face of a circle filled with two dots and a line, whereas arguably only a few (or just one) can identify with a photograph or, photorealistic image, of a face" (Honess Roe 2013, 111). As Satrapi puts it in talking about her feature *Persepolis*, the employment of animation itself grants universality to what is depicted, because it sets those events and declarations free from the specific body with definite racial traits that has experienced them (see Satrapi in Warren 2010). Also, bringing as examples the shorts *It's Like That*, *Hidden* (*Gömd*, 2002, dir. David Aronowitsch, Hanna Heilborn, and Mats Johansson) and *Backseat Bingo*, Honess Roe shows how "animation can complicate the relationship between visibility and testimony" even in interview documentaries, because, in hiding the identity of the speaker in order to protect it, it also prevents the body from being a visual carrier of situated and specific knowledge (Honess Roe 2013, 94). In sum, already simply through the act of having animated characters embody the personal experiences recounted, the vicissitudes narrated in animated documentaries become the possible occurrences of anybody who pertains to a set category of people, or even of any human being.

Additionally, in various cases, universality is further conferred to the testimonies offered by way of how they are related to an animated body as well as to which one they are connected. More often than not, the characters of these films do not resemble their factual counterparts and different techniques may be used in conceiving the animated actors to interpret them, which, however, have in common the fact of making that person into a spokesperson of a group of people. A first example of how this can be achieved is offered by

The Trouble with Love and Sex. In making this feature film for BBC, Jonathan Hodgson has chosen to develop the characters "searching . . . for archetypes that were easy to recognize from each demographic group" (Hodgson 2019, 198). In other words, he has created his characters so that each of them, by generalizing synecdoche, becomes representative of a different social class.

Sheila Sofian, instead, in *Survivors* universalizes the aural interviews with multiple victims of domestic violence offered in the soundtrack by avoiding to "illustrate each interviewee's voice with a specific consistent character design" (Sofian 2019, 227). Honess Roe (2013, 114) underlines that in visualizing the declarations of the victims of abuses, "Sofian animated multiple characters to represent each woman's point of view, thus no one animated figure is identified with any one voice heard on the soundtrack." In other words, excerpts from a same interview have been associated with the bodies of different animated actresses rather than to a same one, therefore explicitly suggesting that, even if it is a specific woman to talk about a set abuse, it could concern any female. Honess Roe adds: "The universality of the image is aided by the representation of different races and physical characteristics so that no one type becomes associated with domestic violence" (Honess Roe 2013, 114).

Similarly, in both *Centrefold* and *Sleepless*, Ellie Land achieves Sofian's same result of universalizing personal testimonies by operating, however, in reverse. Indeed, she conflates declarations from multiple people in a single body. More precisely, the soundtrack of *Centrefold* is composed of aural interviews with three different women who have undergone a labiaplasty. Yet, what these females narrate is visually enacted and dramatized by the same animated actress who, therefore, by generalizing synecdoche, ends up representing any woman who has had that surgical procedure. Even more interesting under this perspective of universalization of the subjective is *Sleepless*. This short film addresses an ungendered issue such as sleep disorders via offering the testimonies of four different people who suffer from them: three men—Bill, Samuel, and Steve—and a woman, Camille. Their declarations are associated with the same animated figure deprived of sex organs, hair, and any other element that could connote it as female or male (see Figure 10.2).

In sum, although the methods used differ, one can recognize a diffused tendency to liberating the testimonies offered from being the stories of a precise person and making them, instead, the vicissitudes of anybody who pertains to a more or less ample category of people.

Last but not least, obviously, in accordance with what we have seen to be a defining trait of the animated documentary in general, classical and contemporary examples of the form partake the employment of fabled animation. Indeed, also the personal vicissitudes recounted in post-1985 animated documentaries are visually reenacted and dramatized via recurring to animated actors as well as exploiting colors and all those magical devices

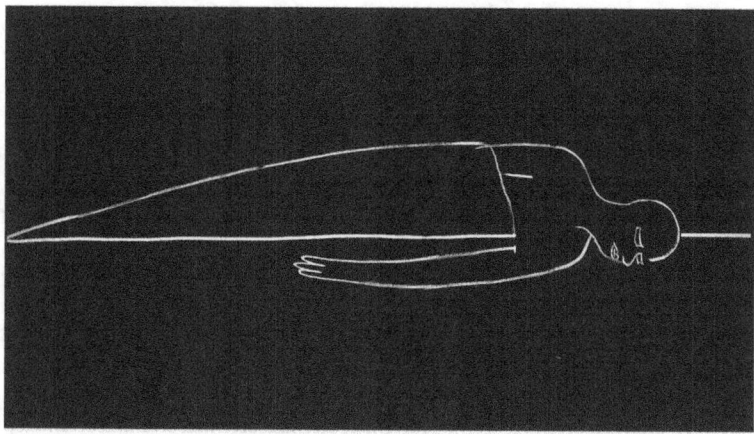

FIGURE 10.2 *The animated figure deprived of elements that could connote it as female or male associated with the testimonials of Bill, Samuel, Steve, and Camille in* Sleepless.

peculiar to animation's fictional language, such as the visual metaphor, the synecdoche, the metamorphosis, and so on. For instance, red flowers can take shape from a blood pool and start floating in the air (as it happens in *25 April*) or animated characters representing existing people can literally spread their arms and fly over a city (as it occurs in *Silence* or *Centrefold*). A cross, which metonymically stands for the Church, can push a man and a woman toward each other and then wrap itself around them, trapping them in a sort of cocoon. Subsequently, a pair of praying hands, which metonymically stand for worship, can smash the couple, like it is done in *Survivors* to visually return how religion can reveal itself as a source of oppression rather than support for an abused woman. In representing the loss of a tampon while swimming, a used sanitary pad floating in a pool can be visually compared to a shark, so as to emphasize the embarrassment of the situation for the character that has lost it and inject drama in the film, as it happens in "Ilham (13)".

This scene from Kamp's series is also an example of how moments of dramatic tension or irony are inserted within contemporary animated documentaries too. Only, while in classical titles such moments were purposely scripted, now, similarly to what is typical of the docudrama plot construction (see Paget [1998] 2011, 115), they are searched within the real-life events of which these works provide an account and are, then, highlighted.

In conclusion, a comparison of the classical and contemporary animated documentaries reveals that the works of these two periods share a series of macro commonalities. Undeniably, there are also many respects in which they differ. Still, these dissimilarities appear to be more variances determined by a desire to reflect the mutations that our conception of what a documentary is, and which are its markers of veridiction, has undergone over time and perhaps, in part, to mirror more the coeval docudrama production. The present-day animated documentary should, therefore, be seen as a new stage in the evolution of a long-standing form rather than something other than the classical production. Only in so doing, we can gain a full understanding of the form and the complex relationship it entertains with both documentary and docudrama.

Notes

1. At times, these films originate precisely from the need of their director to make sense of a set trauma, as it has been the case for *Waltz with Bashir* (see "Solo con l'animazione posso ricordare" 2008, 15). However, even when not expressly prompted by such urgency, these animated documentaries can end up proving therapeutic either for their director or, when not autobiographical, for their subject(s). For example, toward the end of *Tower*, one of the female survivors declares that participating in the film and revisiting the occurrences of that day for it has been "painful" but "very healing" for her.

2. As Honess Roe (2013, 13) highlights, in the late 1990s at DOK Leipzig, in Germany, the first festival strand devoted to the animated documentary emerged.

3. Examples of Australian animated documentaries are *His Mother's Voice, It's Like That, The Safe House* (2006, dir. Lee Withmore), *Revolving Door* (2007, dir. Alexandra and David Beesley), or the more recent *Nowhere Line: Voices from Manus Island* (2015, dir. Lukas Schrank).

4. For a treatise of the main Chinese animated documentaries, see Voci (2010, 61–71). On *Ketchup*, see Guo (2016), while on the Korean animated documentaries about comfort women, see Sung (2017, 107–18).

5. For a discussion of these and other contemporary African animated documentaries, see Callus (2015), Callus (2017).

6. It is, for instance, the case of *Medusa. Stories of Men on the Bottom* (*Medusa. Storia di uomini sul fondo*, 2009, dir. Fredo Valla), on the sinking of the Italian submarine *Medusa* during the Second World War, *The Dark Side of the Sun* (2011, dir. Carlo Shalom Hintermann), on the difficult life of children affected by that rare skin disease known as *xeroderma pigmentosum*, or *Girl with a Clenched Fist* (*Bimba col pugno chiuso*, 2013, dir. Claudio Di Mambro, Luca Madrile, and Umberto Migliaccio), on female partisan Giovanna Marturano.

7. Lipkin even goes as far as to state that "[d]ocudrama is not a kind or type of story, but rather ... a way of offering argument about the past" (Lipkin 2011, 2).

8. It is also not unusual for contemporary animated documentaries to be accompanied by a social media page or a website wherein viewers are offered

precise indications on how to actively take action in respect to the issue at the center of that set title or, at least, participate in the debate around it. For example, *Centrefold*'s website (i.e., http://thecentrefoldproject.virb.com) has a section entitled "Have Your Say," wherein internet users can discuss the issues raised by the film. Likewise, on the Facebook page for *Last Day of Freedom* (i.e., https://facebook.com/livingcobdition), aside from informing on the screenings of the film and the awards received, a discussion around the death penalty in the United States is encouraged.

11

The Persistence of the Classical Animated Documentary

In 2016 Montreal-based animator Lori Malépart-Traversy obtained great success in festivals all over the world with *The Clitoris* (*Le Clitoris*, 2016), a short expository animated documentary characterized by pink aesthetics that illustrates the anatomy and discovery of the clitoris as well as the numerous misinterpretations this organ has been the object of throughout history. Completed in eight months combining gouache on paper and 2D digital animation, this film shares with the dominant contemporary animated documentary production the fact of being a character-oriented, author-driven work made by a female animator and of resulting from research on the topic conducted by its director herself.[1] Additionally, Malépart-Traversy makes herself aurally present in the film by personally performing the voiceover commentary. Nevertheless, unlike what, in Chapter 10, we have seen to be peculiar of post-1985 animated documentaries, *The Clitoris* offers a purportedly objective and not a subjective treatment of the topic it addresses. It is not a first-person account, it does not have an autobiographical dimension of any kind, and it does not contain direct witness testimonies of what it describes. Indeed, the protagonist of this short is not Malépart-Traversy nor an animated character representing a real-life person. It is an anthropomorphic clitoris that, by generalizing synecdoche, stands for this female erogenous organ at large. Moreover, the film is a work shaped by "an informing logic," and Malépart-Traversy simply acts as its voice-of-God narrator (Nichols [2001] 2017, 122). Exactly as the visuals of a classical animated documentary, the ones of this short also are an imaginative dramatization of the informative, researched, and purportedly objective statements proffered by the voiceover. In brief, even if it showcases some of the traits proper of the dominant contemporary animated documentary production, *The Clitoris* is much closer to this form's classical production.

Although, as seen in the previous chapter, with the second half of the 1980s the bulk of the animated documentary production becomes personal and experiential, the purportedly objective, expository approach proper of the form's classical era is not completely divested. On the contrary, it withstands the form's overall subjective turn, exactly like in the realm of the documentary proper, the advent of the observational and the participatory modes of representation did not determine the abandonment of the prior dominant expository one (see Winston 2013). Indeed, in parallel to the creation of the experiential animated documentaries discussed in Chapter 10, a small number of titles developed according to the classical era's main approach kept being produced even after the mid-1980s.

This persistence of the classical animated documentary becomes particularly evident if one looks at the production of those animators and studios active both before and after the form's post-1985 evolution. Let us consider, for example, the works that have come out of the NFB from 1986 onward. Next to films like *Minoru, Ryan, Tying Your Own Shoes, I Was a Child of Holocaust Survivors* (2010, dir. Ann Marie Fleming), and the many other titles that are imbued with subjectivity, based in memories, and revolve around direct testimonies, one can also find expository works such as *Dreams of a Land* (1989, dir. Robert Doucet), *Mirrors of Time* (1991, dir. Jean-Jacques Leduc), and the series *Science Please!* (1998–2001) that are still built according to the modalities of the classical era. Indeed, Doucet's animated life story of Samuel de Champlain is based on the diaries of the French explorer who founded Quebec City. However, unlike it occurs, for instance, in *25 April*, which is similarly based on personal journals, the words written by Champlain in his diaries do not become the lines of the character. Quite the reverse, the animated actor interpreting Champlain has no lines and his vicissitudes are illustrated by a voice-of-God narrator external to the facts recounted. Certainly, here and there some excerpts of the explorer's journals are offered but always within the voice-of-God commentary and as quotes. Not dissimilarly, *Mirrors of Time*—which was made using the technique of computer animation and visually is an acquis of styles, since the eight animators involved in its making were let free of imprinting with their individual styles the sections of the film they worked on—is an expository work. More precisely, Leduc's film is an educational animated documentary that coalesces history and science. Employing both the fabled and, to a much lesser extent, the sober animation, *Mirrors of Time* illustrates and dramatizes the history of our time measurement systems, explaining, however, also the key scientific concepts behind it, such as how the various seasons are determined by the position of planet Earth in respect to the sun. As in classical animated documentaries, a voice-of-God commentary—which in this case is performed by a male and a female narrator who alternate themselves— is used to inform the viewer and the animation translates in visual terms what the two narrators state. *Science Please!*, instead, is a scientific educational series of twenty-six one-minute episodes targeted at children aged nine to twelve. Mixing fabled animation with some live-action archival materials, it offers a humorous but rigorous explanation of scientific discoveries and phenomena we encounter in our daily lives. The episodes are dissimilar in terms of visual styles as they were animated by different artists, but all showcase some common traits. Among the latter are: an extremely eccentric voice-of-God narration; the same scientific adviser, biologist Stéphane Durand; and a tendency to visually anthropomorphize molecules, atoms, and the other chemical elements represented in them. In brief, although *Dreams of a Land*, *Mirrors of Time*, and the *Science Please!* series are different in many respects (such as the topic addressed, the graphic style adopted, and so on), they all have in common the fact of having been developed according to the classical era's main approach. They are thus proof of how this typology of works continued to be produced at the NFB even after the form's post-1985 subjective turn.

This persistence of the classical animated documentary in the contemporaneity is evident if we look more generally at the work of those animators who started making animated documentaries during the classical period and have kept on creating titles falling in this form even after 1985. Undeniably, some of such filmmakers soon discarded the previously used expository mode in order to embrace the always more popular personal and experiential one proper of the form's contemporary era. A case in point is Joyce Borenstein. As we have seen in Chapter 8, in 1981 she authored *Five Billion Years*, which is fully an expression of the Canadian classical animated documentary. However, a little over a decade later, she became renowned worldwide for *The Colours of My Father*, a personal animated documentary grounded in direct testimonies and memories and traversed by some autobiographical elements. Plus, after the success obtained with this film, when creating animated documentaries, she continued making works fully aligned to the dominant post-1985 production, such as *One Divided by Two* (1998) and *Lida Moser Photographer. Odyssey in Black and White* (2017). Indeed, the former addresses the trauma of divorce from the perspective of kids who lived it and overcame it, while the latter animates the audio-recordings of recollections by New York photographer Lida Moser regarding the trip she made through Quebec in the summer of 1950 on assignment to magazines *Vogue* and *Look*.

Nonetheless, next to filmmakers, like Borenstein, who were fast in taking on the subjective approach illustrated in Chapter 10, there are others who, in creating their animated documentaries, continued to employ the expository mode of representation proper of the classical era. It is, for instance, the case of the Italian animator Bruno Bozzetto or the French one Jacques Rouxel. Indeed, as anticipated in Chapter 9, in 1981, and thus toward the end of the classical era, Bozzetto started working at a series of animated documentary shorts for the TV show *Quark* and went on to do so up to 1988 without any substantial change in the way he approached the chosen subject matters (see Mosconi 2003). In the course of the years, the length of these shorts varied, and the number of fields explored grew, for instance, to include economics as well, to which, in 1986, were dedicated thirteen shorts that aired as part of the show's "spin-off" *Quark Economy* (*Quark Economia*, 1986). However, the animated documentaries created by Bozzetto on commission of journalist Piero Angela kept being expository works grounded in research—normally they were written and developed together with "university scientists" (Ferrari 1986, 61; see also Angela 2017)—even after 1985. They also continued to have Angela himself perform the voice-of-God commentary and to be characterized by a tripartite structure (see Chapter 9), extensive use of analogy, and the blending of scientific rigor with moments of humor. In fact, if an evolution can be identified in the work of Bozzetto, it is a progressively greater attention toward avoiding his inventive approach to the subject matter and desire for comedy to get in the way of scientific accuracy. In other words, with the passing of years, he gradually stopped prioritizing humor over accuracy as instead he often did in early works like *Tapum!*. Paradoxically, he thus came to near that attention to offering rigorous accounts of the aspect of the real addressed proper of Halas' approach to the animated documentary form which he had found limiting when working with him on *History of Inventions* (see Chapter 9). However, the point of arrival of this evolution in Bozzetto's animated documentary filmmaking was reached at the beginning of his collaboration with Angela, and therefore under this respect, no significant change occurred between his pre- and post-1985 *Quark* animated documentaries.

Similarly, with his studio aaa Production, Jacques Rouxel continued to create short, expository animated documentaries for private and public companies and organizations even after 1985. Examples of these more contemporary works—which he mostly co-directed with Laurent Bounoure—are *Mercure* (1986) and *New Behaviors* (*Nouveaux comportements*, 1987), two industrial animated documentaries on the so-called Plan Mercure that were made for Citroën and targeted at this company's employees. In particular, the former short illustrates the principles on which this new system of production Citroën decided to implement is based, while the latter illustrates how Plan Mercure is destined to impact the company's organization of labor and explains which new behaviors the employees will be required to adopt. Other examples are the 1992 series *Pain* (*La douleur*), which, through its seven episodes, describes the mechanisms and functions of pain, or the two 1993 LFSM-sponsored shorts *Knowledge, the World and Me* (*Le savoir, le monde et moi*) and *The Small, Tragic Circus of So-and-so* (*Le petit cirque tragique des untels*) on violent families and their psychopathologies. All these titles share with Rouxel's pre-1985 animated documentaries the fact of being expository, sponsored works and more. Indeed, they also are equally characterized by plain or essential backgrounds, a simplified and stylized graphic representation, an employment of low-key humor for entertainment purpose, a voice-of-God narration, and bidimensional characters that do not have the power of speech (at best they can emit sounds)—since Rouxel believed that if they did talk, the film would acquire a "childish character" inappropriate for a nonfiction animation (Rouxel 1994, 203). Moreover, like the ones from the classical period, these post-1985 animated documentaries also are made using hand-drawn animation, a technique that Rouxel considered the most suitable for explaining the principles that govern our world to a general audience (Rouxel 1994, 200). In sum, Rouxel's approach to the form remains basically unchanged over time.

Emblematic of this persistence of the classical animated documentary approach after 1985 is also the work of Albert Barillé. Encouraged by the success obtained with *Once upon a Time . . . Man* (see Faviez 2010, 29), the French director and producer progressively transformed *Once upon a Time . . .* into a franchise that in the end will come to count among its installment other four animated documentary TV series. The titles in question are *Once upon a Time . . . Life* (*Il était une fois . . . la vie*, 1986), *Once upon a Time . . . The Americas* (*Il était une fois . . . les Amériques*, 1991), *Once upon a Time . . . The Discoverers* (*Il était une fois . . . les Découvreurs*, 1994), and *Once upon a Time . . . The Explorers* (*Il était une fois . . . les Explorateurs*, 1997). These series are independent of each other—as emphasized also by their having different theme songs—and focus on different aspects of the real. More precisely, *Once upon a Time . . . Life* explains in each episode the operating principles of an organ or apparatus of the human body. *Once upon a Time . . . The Americas* traces the history of the American continent by looking at its main settlements. *Once upon a Time . . . The Discoverers* illustrates the stories of the great inventions and the men and women who came up with them, while *Once upon a Time . . . The Explorers* focuses on the most important explorers. Nevertheless, similarly to what was noted for Bozzetto's and Rouxel's post-1985 productions, these four series have in common with *Once upon a Time . . . Man*, the adoption of an expository mode of representation and beyond. Indeed, they also share the same animated actors whom we can see interpret the same stereotypical ordinary characters impersonated in the 1978 series as well as other roles that are, however, always in line with that one. That is, The Pest and The Dwarf feature always in the role of villains, Maestro in that of an old sage, Jumbo in that of the strong young man, and so on. Yet, for instance, in *Once upon a Time . . . Life*, instead of appearing just as ordinary human villains, The Pest and The Dwarf feature also as bacteria and viruses. Similarly, in *Once upon a Time . . . The Discoverers* and *Once upon a Time . . . The Explorers*, Maestro, Peter, Jumbo, and the others perform also in the role of renowned figures. Let us consider, for instance, *Once upon a Time . . . The Discoverers*. Here, the franchise's recurrent animated actors interpret either a companion to the scientist on which the episode focuses or that set inventor himself. We thus see, for example, Maestro as Leonardo da Vinci; Peter as Lavoisier, Gutenberg, and Newton; or Jumbo as Mendel.

Moreover, *Once upon a Time . . . The Americas*, *Once upon a Time . . . The Discoverers*, and *Once upon a Time . . . The Explorers* share with *Once upon a Time . . . Man* the fact of being animated histories, tackling similar themes, and featuring in the left corner of the screen a personified squared clock with eyes and arms. This clock clarifies in which years the facts recounted took place and ensures that the characters adhere to the behaviors and lifestyle of the period addressed, lecturing them when they detach. Besides, in these three series, facts already illustrated in *Once upon a Time . . . Man* may be revisited from a different point of view or expanded upon. In fact, *Once upon a Time . . . The Americas* is even an out-and-out offshoot of *Man* since precisely the regret of not having been able to talk about indigenous American populations in the latter series prompted Barillé to produce the former one (see Elausti et al. 2016, 153).

Due to its scientific subject, *Once upon a Time . . . Life* may instead have fewer elements in common with *Man*. However, it is perfectly aligned to the health and medicine-related titles from the form's classical era. With them, it shares the representation of the human body as a series of interrelated factories (all organs except the brain) connected by busy streets (arteries and vessels) and coordinated by a central control station (the brain), the personification of the various smaller elements present in our organism (e.g., cells, antigens, neurotransmitters, and so on) and their portrayal as specialized workers, the dramatization of illness in the form of battles between bad and good, and the inclusion of advises on hygiene and nutrition. In fact, mainly just some futuristic choices made in representing the inside of the human body, such as, for instance, that of portraying the brain as a central control station that recalls more the cockpit of a spaceship than the telephone switchboard center of the classical era's titles, differentiate *Once upon a Time . . . Life* from similar animated documentaries produced before 1985.

Unquestionably, between *Once upon a Time . . . Man* and the four animated documentary series created at Procidis after 1985, it is possible to identify some differences at various levels. First, from one series to another the graphic style employed gradually becomes always less cartoonish and more realistic. Second, some changes in the production team take place. For instance, if for *Once upon a Time . . . Man* the research on the subject matter addressed is conducted by Barillé himself, from *Once upon a Time . . . Life* onward, this task is entrusted to a scientific journalist who worked for the magazine *Science et Vie*, Alexandre Dorozynski. Finally, with time, small changes occur also at the level of the narrative technique, such as the progressive abandonment of the voice-of-God narration in favor of a voice-of-authority one. The first instances of this transformation can be traced back to *Once upon a Time . . . Life*, where, from time to time an onscreen character—namely an old, personified red blood cell—takes on the duty of informing the viewer, otherwise carried out by the authoritative voiceover narrator. The definitive change from a voice-of-God narrator to a voice-of-authority one takes place with *Once upon a Time . . . The Discoverers*, where this role is clearly entrusted to the character of Maestro. Here, a narrative framework showing this old and wise figure surrounded by kids eager to hear what he has to recount to them on key inventions and their inventors is introduced, raising Maestro unmistakably to the status of voice-of-authority. And this approach is reiterated also in *Once upon a Time . . . The Explorers*. In short, unlike in the case of Rouxel's animated documentary production, with time Barillé's one does undergo some minor transformations. Yet, not only a strong continuity can be identified at multiple levels between his pre- and post-1985 animated documentary production but also none of the transformations that do occur are in the direction of nowadays' dominant personal and experiential approach.

On the basis of the examples discussed thus far, one could think that the classical animated documentary's main approach persists exclusively within the works of studios that were already active in the production of nonfiction animations before the beginning of the form's contemporary era or that it is adopted exclusively by the filmmakers who steer clear from today's dominant subjective and experiential approach. But it is not like that. For instance, Tim Haines starts a career in filmmaking only way after the end of the form's classical period, and yet in 1999, he directs for BBC what will become a staple expository animated documentary series of the contemporary era: *Walking with Dinosaurs*. There is no doubt that this six-part natural history series that has inaugurated a long-lasting franchise as well as kickstarted a significant wave of CGI paleontology-related titles is an out-and-out example of animated documentary. Even Annabelle Honess Roe discusses it in such terms in her monograph on the form (see Honess Roe 2013).[2] And yet this televisual product is undeniably closer to classical animated documentaries on prehistoric life like *The Age of Monsters*, *Woolly Mammoth*, and *64,000,000 Years Ago* than to contemporary films such as *Waltz with Bashir*, and not simply for the topic tackled. Its photorealistic CGI animated visuals are illustrative of what an omniscient voice-of-God narrator explains and not of the memories or feelings of a real-life person or of the director himself, as we have seen to be characteristic instead of today's subjectivity-imbued dominant production. In other words, like works such as *The Age of Monsters*, *Woolly Mammoth*, and *64,000,000 Years Ago*, this series is a purportedly objective, dramatic reconstruction of the life of dinosaurs that has been created consulting experts on the Mesozoic era (in this case over 100 people, including paleontologists, paleobotanists, paleo-entomologists, geologists, and the like have been consulted [see Scott and White 2003, 316]). Also, as scholar José van Dijck notes, *Walking with Dinosaurs* is characterized by a voice-of-God narration that "firmly anchors the series in the narrative mode of explanation, but more than that, it articulates the reconstructive mode ('this is what assumedly happened') . . . . Reconstruction and speculation hide behind an expository sheen of realistic visuals authenticated by a mixture of voice-over, 'real-time' (fabricated) sounds of animals, and background music to accentuate tense or romantic moments" (van Dijck 2006, 13). In short, if we look at *Walking with Dinosaurs* against previous televisual paleontology documentaries, with its shift away "from the paleontologist, the fossils and the lab, and onto the CG animations of extinct animals" (Campbell 2016, 97), this series has indisputably offered an innovative approach to its subject matter. Yet, it is far from groundbreaking if we compare it to the animated documentaries of the classical era on the same topic.

Likewise, consider Andy Glynne and his studio Mosaic Films. They are renowned for series such as *Animated Minds* and *Seeking Refuge* that are fully an expression of nowadays dominant animated documentary production. Nonetheless, among the films that they have created, we can also find titles such as *What's Blood Got to Do with It?* (2004) and the five shorts that form the Quick-fire series *BBC Learning: History* (2016). The former is a "'consciousness-raising' film" on blood and blood transfusions that asks viewers "to not only understand the issue, but to also take some positive action and give blood" (Ward 2005, 86). The latter instead is formed of four brief history lessons that are targeted at eight to eleven years old children and look each at a different era (and in particular at the Ancient Greeks, the Ancient Romans, the Vikings, and the Anglo-Saxons) plus a fifth short on the job of the historian. As Paul Ward highlights regarding *What's Blood Got to Do with It?* (see Ward 2005, 86), both these animated documentary projects are characterized by an expository mode of representation, heavy use of condensation, and an eccentric voice-of-God narrator, whose eccentricity is obtained through having a comedian perform it. In addition, they both are sponsored works. More precisely, Glynne made *What's Blood Got to Do with It?* on commission of the National Blood Service,[3] whereas *BBC Learning: History* was produced for the BBC Learning project.

In sum, while constituting a minority within the overall contemporary animated documentary filmography, purportedly objective, expository titles in continuity with the form's main production of the classical era not only have continued to be created worldwide even after 1985 but also are far from being a prerogative of a group of nostalgic directors and studios. On the contrary, this approach survives as an alternative mode of representation to the subjective one. All that remains is thus to understand in which cases it is favored and why.

Trends and Tendencies

Although there is no shortage of exceptions, it is possible to identify a few trends and tendencies in the use of this expository mode of representation after 1985. Indeed, if we look at the totality of contemporary animated documentary productions perpetrating the classical era's approach, we can notice that these works are mostly series and that television is the medium for which they are predominantly made. Also, this expository mode of representation is employed today primarily to create informational or informational-instructional audiovisual products. More in detail, it is used typically within science-related and, to a lesser extent, history-related titles.

As far as the former production is concerned, from anatomy to physics, from psychology to astronomy the range of scientific disciplines addressed within the post-1985 expository animated documentaries is vast. However, particularly rich in numbers are the paleontology-related titles. In the wake of *Walking with Dinosaurs*' success, an out-and-out sub-corpus of scientific, expository animated documentaries about dinosaurs has taken shape. The TV movie *March of the Dinosaurs* (2011, dir. Matthew Thompson), the 2011 series *Planet Dinosaur* and *Dinosaur Revolution*, and the feature film narrated by Werner Herzog in which the latter was recut, *Dinotasia* (2012), are only some of the titles that make up this subgroup of animated documentaries.[4]

Moreover, generally speaking, two macro typologies of expository, science-related animated documentaries have seen the light since the beginning of the form's contemporary era. On the one hand, there are works that focus on a precise subject within a specific scientific discipline, as is, for instance, the case of Studio Folimage's *The Joy of Life* (*Le Bonheur de la vie*, 1992). Targeted at elementary school children, this series, directed by Jacques-Rémy Girerd, tackles in each of its twenty episodes a different aspect of the anatomy and functioning of sexuality and procreation. On the other hand, there are titles that illustrate a selection of different science-related issues and that thus touch upon a variety of scientific disciplines. Examples are the first season of *Cosmos: A Spacetime Odyssey*, in whose episodes scientific theories and concepts ranging from natural selection to greenhouse effects to electromagnetism are discussed, and the Cuban series *For the Curious* (*Para Curiosos*, 2001–5) by Ernesto Padrón, which illustrates trivia concerning topics as diverse as the animal kingdom, natural phenomena, the human body, and technology.

As far as the history-related expository animated documentaries are concerned instead, they are basically animated reconstructions of past events, and, using the categorizations Steven Lipkin proposes for live-action docudramas, we could say that they tend to fall in the arena of representation of "noteworthy individuals" (Lipkin 2011, 3). Indeed, in line with the animated documentary's tendency to be character-driven, they often dramatize (a moment in) the life of one or more historical figures. Examples in this sense are the already mentioned *Once upon a Time . . . The Explorers* or *Dead Reckoning*, a Mountain Lake PBS TV movie on Champlain's years of exploration of North America that was created at Montreal-based Artifex Animation Studio.

Moreover, history and science may also be co-present in the same expository animated documentary, as it happens in works like *Once upon a Time . . . The Discoverers* and the first season of *Cosmos: A Spacetime Odyssey*, where the noteworthy individuals whose past is retraced are scientists. On the whole, thus, the majority of expository animated documentaries is about science, a fact that is unsurprising considering that most of such titles are created for the small screen and, as van Dijck notes, televisual nonfiction productions on science "are historically characterized as linear, expository, and didactic tales" (van Dijck 2006, 7).

A further tendency that traverses the contemporary expository animated documentary production is a preference for digital animation as the animation technique. According to what Vincent Campbell writes, if this is the case, it should be thanks to *Walking with Dinosaurs*. Indeed, in his view, it has been this series' "phenomenal success" that has "seriously kickstarted the extensive use of CGI in factual television across a huge range of subject areas" (Campbell 2016, 95). Consequently, since, as anticipated, the contemporary era's expository animated documentaries are mostly made for the small screen, it should be always in *Walking with Dinosaurs*' success that we should identify the initiator for the employment of this technique in making such works, and especially the science-related ones. Nevertheless, while there is no doubt that Tim Haines' series has contributed to making digital animation the preferred go-to technique when creating an expository animated documentary, it has hardly initiated its employment within such works. Just as a matter of example, almost ten years before *Walking with Dinosaurs*, Jean-Jacques Leduc, who has taken part in setting up the NFB's Computer Animation Center, "researched and wrote the script of *Mirrors of Time* with the idea of stretching the limits of computer animation."[5] Therefore, while perhaps it is effectively only with the new millennium that the "use of CGI" has become "a prevalent feature of ... science documentaries and factual entertainment programs" (Campbell 2016, 40), a draw toward it in making animated documentaries, and especially expository scientific ones, already existed early on in this form's contemporary era.

What Tim Haines' series has, instead, certainly stimulated is a greater adoption of a photorealistic style of animation in expository animated documentaries on paleontology, and more. As van Dijck (2006, 6) points out, *Walking with Dinosaurs* does "not negate realism; on the contrary, one of the series' most remarkable features is its adherence to the dominant realist paradigm, despite its abundant use of visual spectacle." And with the new millennium, it has become more commonplace for expository animated documentaries, in general, to showcase photorealism, even if just at background level as it occurs, for instance, in the animated portions of *Cosmos: A Spacetime Odyssey*'s first season. Indeed, for this series' animated segments a graphic novel-inspired style is mostly used. Nonetheless, the backgrounds of the animations are photorealistic and are obtained often through layering photographic images on top of each other (McLean 2014, 25), similarly to what is done for *Walking with Dinosaurs* itself, where the animation is superimposed on live-action shots of Chilean and New Caledonian forests or Californian landscapes (see Rampton 1999, 47; van Dijck 2006, 13).

Second, Tim Haines' series has also led the way to the employment of a "graphic vérité" CGI animation within paleontology animated documentaries (Hight 2008, 18; Campbell 2016, 101). That is, it has encouraged the practice of incorporating aesthetics immediately associable to fly-on-the-wall live-action documentaries within these CGI animated films on dinosaurs to generate a sense of immersion (Honess Roe 2013, 48–9). As a matter of fact, a last trend of the post-1985 expository animated documentary production is to adopt an updated version of the classical era's model obtained by way of operating small deviations from it. In a nutshell, the contemporary animated documentaries that embrace the purportedly objective, expository mode proper of the form's classical era tend to remain overall in close continuity with the latter period's dominant production. Yet, they may showcase one or more small differences from it, often aimed at making these works more the products of their times or at putting them in a clearer connection to a certain live-action production. And the adoption of fly-on-the-wall aesthetics borrowed from cinema vérité and Direct Cinema in *Walking with Dinosaurs* and the paleontology-related titles that followed is an example of this trend. Indeed, we can hardly find such aesthetics in the classical period's expository animated documentary, and not without reason, since they not only did not become a staple of the live-action documentary production until the 1960s (and thus when the animated documentary's classical era was well underway) but also are synonym of an observational mode of representation. "Proximity to natural animal behavior—so close you can almost reach out and touch the animals"—is, however, "a convention of natural history programmes," a "marker" of their "claims to authenticity" (Campbell 2016, 46). Recreating and including spittle or blood splatters on the lens, shaky movements, and the other aesthetics synonym of observational footage is thus a way to draw a visual link between these paleontology animated documentaries and the natural history live-action production.

Another example is the incorporation in *Dead Reckoning* of brief live-action interviews of some of the scholars and experts on Samuel de Champlain consulted to ensure the film's veracity. The insertion of live-action segments with experts per se is not unconventional in respect to the works of the classical era, where, especially when they were made for television, it was commonplace for real-life scientists or scholars to act as voices-of-authority. What is unusual in respect to classical era's animated documentaries is thus just the use of the interview format for bringing the experts onscreen. This technique, however, is in line with the evolutions that the nonfiction production has faced in the contemporaneity, since interviews with experts have become ubiquitous within today's live-action documentary production, including the expository one.

Such small deviations from the classical period's approach cannot be detected in all contemporary expository animated documentaries, a number of which remains highly adherent to it. Also, when limited detachments from the classical model are present, they do not necessarily concern a same aspect in all titles. There is, however, one quite recursive deviation from the classical model consisting in the reduction of the voice-of-God or voice-of-authority narration's presence in favor of an expansion of the dialog between the onscreen animated characters. Once again, per se, the fact that the characters are gifted with speech is not a novelty in respect to the classical era's production. However, when in the pre-1985 works there was a commentary, if the onscreen animated actors did have lines, they had only a few and, through them, they did not actually concur in enlightening or instructing the audience. Rather, they voiced the perplexities or questions that viewers may have had in respect to what the narrator was illustrating. In contemporary animated documentaries, instead, not only do the onscreen characters have an increasingly greater number of lines but also it is partly through the exchanges that occur between them that spectators learn about the topic addressed by the film. As such, the overall mode of representation is thus brought even closer to that of docudramas, where information is likewise conveyed partly diegetically through the words of the character and the mise-en-scène and partly through nondiegetic devices as captions or voiceover (see Paget [1998] 2011, 104–5).

In conclusion, not only, as seen in the previous chapter, today's subjective and experiential animated documentary production is an evolution of the classical one but also the latter's expository approach to illustrating the real has not been abandoned. It is still used nowadays with minor variations, which are mostly aimed at breathing new life into this consolidated way of recounting our world through animation. Incontrovertibly, today the classical era's purportedly objective, expository approach is employed for creating a narrower range of products than it occurred before 1985. But while titles like *Once upon a Time . . . Life*, *Walking with Dinosaurs*, and *Dead Reckoning* constitute only a minority of the overall contemporary animated documentary corpus of works, their very existence is further proof of how today's animated documentary production is strongly tied to the rich pre-1985 one and cannot be fully grasped without looking also at the latter.

Notes

1 In particular, the film has its main reference in the nonfiction monograph *La fabuleuse histoire du clitoris* by sexologist Jean-Claude Piquard. For a description of the film's genesis, see Linares (2016).

2. The Walking with … franchise includes other three expository, animated documentary series: *Walking with Beasts* (2001), *Walking with Caveman* (2003), and *Walking with Monsters—Life before Dinosaurs* (2005).
3. *What's Blood Got to Do with It?* is one of four films that make up the series *Blood Matters*. The other titles, which were produced each at a different studio, however, are not examples of the classical animated documentary's persistence.
4. For a discussion of these works, see Campbell 2016, 95–124. On *Planet Dinosaur,* see also Honess Roe (2013, 46–55).
5. NFB, "Mirrors of Time," in Folder *Mirrors of Time*, Academy Awards Reference collection, Margaret Herrick Library.

Toward a Post-Animated Documentary Age?

Among the novelties brought about in nonfiction filmmaking by the digital revolution and the technological advancements in the new millennium is the so-called interactive documentary (or i-doc), a new form of nonlinear, web-based documentary projects that make use of digital interactive technology in order to document the real (Aston and Gaudenzi 2012, 125). Over the last decade or so, the i-doc not only has rapidly grown in terms of scale and craft but also "has begun the process of developing an *industrial* base" (Dovey 2017, 273; see also O'Flynn 2016). Being the animated documentary, as we have seen, a form that tends to be responsive to the changes in live-action documentary filmmaking, and having the use of animation for tackling nonfiction subject matters peaked since the late 2000s, it did not take long for online animated i-docs to start being created as well.[1] The latter are generally part of a multi-platform project and adopt what Sandra Gaudenzi (2013) refers to as the "hitchhiking (or hypertext) model" of interaction. That is, users have only the possibility of choosing between a set of pre-determined options within a closed database, which in the case of animated i-docs tends to be particularly limited. In fact, animated i-docs are inclined to give users very little agency by maintaining a high level of control over their behavior. Also, they showcase greater linearity than most i-docs. Nonetheless, exactly as is the case for interactive documentaries in general, the animated ones also are characterized by a fragmented narration and require active fruition.

Like we have seen to occur for the majority of contemporary animated documentaries, most animated i-docs address political or social issues felt as relevant through first-person testimonies from individuals who have been touched by such matters. Indeed, animated i-docs also are often interview-driven accounts of real-life occurrences. However, unlike it normally is the case in animated documentaries, it is not infrequent for the visual and aural track of an animated i-doc to entertain only a feeble relationship, and more precisely one biased in favor of the latter. Indeed, there are animated i-docs wherein the sole sound is entrusted with the role of advancing the narration, while the animation is reduced to a mere visual filler. In other words, for how it is conceived and used here, the animation becomes a sort of visual equivalent of an ambient sound— that is, a sound that "envelops a scene and inhabits its space, without raising the question of the identification or visual embodiment of its source" (Chion 1994, 75). Indeed, in a similar way to an ambient sound, in some animated i-docs the animation "is present but unremarkable, a kind of unnoticed perceptual anchor" (Leonard and Strachan 2014, 166) that, if the components of these i-docs were to be "ordered hierarchically," would occupy the "lower rungs" (Chion 2009, 5).

This is what happens, for instance, in *The Next Day*, *Invisible Picture Show*, and *Last Hijack Interactive*—three animated i-docs that address respectively the issue of suicide, juvenile detention in immigration centers, and piracy.

Animation as Visual Territory

Co-produced by Pop Sandbox and the National Film Board of Canada, *The Next Day* revolves around the testimonies of Jenn, Ryan, Tina, and Chantal—four survivors of near-fatal suicide attempts, who were asked to answer the same twenty questions. The idea for this project originated from former social worker Paul Peterson in 2001, after having witnessed first-hand the destructive impact that suicide can have on a family (Scrivener 2011, IN.3). Peterson's initial intention was to create a traditional interview-driven live-action documentary. However, since a study conducted by the WHO showed that today young people are those at the highest risk of committing suicide, he opted for a medium more readily capable of speaking to them. The audio interviews, which were collected by Peterson himself, have thus been animated by Mathew den Boer in a childlike style close to that of cartoonist John Porcellino, on whose drawings the animation is based.

What distinguishes *The Next Day* is, however, that users are given the possibility to explore just an audio database and not an audiovisual one. Initially, the names of the four interviewees appear in black letters on a plain white screen one after the other, while the snippet of their testimony regarding the moment of the suicide attempt is heard. Immediately afterward, users are presented with four keywords, among which to choose, each of which corresponds to a fragment of Jenn, Ryan, Tina, or Chantal's testimony. Still, it is only after a selection is made that one discovers to which of the four stories each keyword pertains,[2] as only when the snippet starts playing, the indication is provided in the right-end corner of the screen. Moreover, users' choices are not reversible, and, once the fragment selected ends, they are presented with other four keywords between which to pick, and so on till the experience comes to an end. Anyhow, although more or less consciously, users have some agency over the soundtrack. As far as visuals are concerned, instead, regardless of the choices made, they are shown always the exact same animation of a storm progressively gathering around a house and then hitting it—which metaphorically evokes the hardship these persons have gone through. As a consequence, visually, the only difference between experiences is that, depending on the length of the sound excerpt selected, the following set of keywords among which to pick may appear in conjunction with an earlier or later moment of the animation. Most notably, the testimonies offered are not transposed into pictographs nor made into the lines of an animated actor. On the contrary, the animation even proceeds independently from what is heard. Indeed, it acts simply as a visual bed for the aural testimonies, as a symbolic visual territory for them to inhabit. Borrowing from sound studies, one could thus say that the animation of *The Next Day* is an ambient animation.

Phantasmatic Projections

Similar to *The Next Day*, *Invisible Picture Show* is based on the recordings of phone interviews conducted by the director himself with four youths aged between seven and sixteen, who at the time were in an asylum center of Australia, South Africa, Greece, or the United States. Created on commission of the International Detention Coalition and produced by Faction Films with a relatively low budget, this animated i-doc blends 2D animation and 3D environments. More specifically, the four aforementioned audio interviews have been animated in 2D using a distinct style for each of them. They have then been inserted in as many 3D virtual environments, each reimagining the interiors of a different asylum center. In this way, what Bryan Hawkins (2015, 30) defines "an un-natural yet illusionistic hybrid space between the architecture and illusion of surveillance and imprisonment and the virtual spaces of computer game and social media" has thus been created.

Invisible Picture Show gives users even less agency than *The Next Day*, since it only allows them to pick which of four environments to explore, or, in case one wants to visit them all, in which order to do so. That said, once inside the selected virtual asylum center, users are conducted through empty corridors to a space—which, depending on the environment chosen, might be a shower, a cell, a cafeteria, or a corner of the corridor itself—where a ringing phone is reached. By answering the call via clicking on the phone with the mouse, users activate the animated testimony of the child associated with that virtual environment. Unlike noted for *The Next Day*, per se the animations accompanying *Invisible Picture Show*'s audio interviews do entertain a linkage with the words spoken by the interviewees since often they visualize what is said. Therefore, potentially, in this case, the visual and the aural track could be on a more equal footing, if it was not for the fact that the interface is left in the foreground throughout the testimonies, reducing the animations to projections on the wall of the virtual environments that host them. At times, this even makes them unreadable, as in the case of the one accompanying the declarations of the kid held in the South African asylum center, whose color palette is close to that of the cell's walls on which it is projected.

Certainly, in treating as such the animation, on the one hand, the condition of invisibility in which these children, kept in inaccessible asylum centers, find themselves is symbolically conveyed also at the level of visuals. On the other hand, however, once again, the animation is declassed to a visual background, or better a visual ambient, for the sound to be hosted in.

Motionless, Recycled Animation

Last Hijack Interactive was produced by Submarine and, blending animation and live-action, retraces the phases of a hijack that took place in November 2008 a few miles off the Somali coast through the testimonies of both pirate Mohamed and Colin Darch, the captain of the assailed ship. More specifically, this animated i-doc is developed so that, in navigating it, the user can "experience a beginning, middle and end of a story, even when his experience will be different from the next person who watches" it (Wolting and Pallotta in Astle 2014). In fact, its interface is a timeline on which are located, respectively in the upper and in the lower part, the audiovisual snippets of the interviews to Mohamed and Darch.

As argued by Daniel Miller (2012) in regard to Ali Samadi Ahadi's *The Green Wave*, *Last Hijack Interactive*'s animations resemble "graphic novels or comics in motion." Indeed, they are formed of mostly static, framed images to which is conferred a sense of motion through slow virtual camera movements that leave the user with the impression that a camera is panning over the panels of a comic. Moreover, always in order to confer some movement to the shots, single elements of the frame are animated. For instance, there is a scene wherein Mohamed tells that, after having assaulted the ship, some pirates went by car to take food supplies. Visually, this recollection is accompanied by a shot portraying three cars traveling on the dirt road of a barren landscape. However, only one vehicle actually moves, while the other two are motionless. As a result, paradoxically the overall stillness of the shot is highlighted.

What is more, while here and there what is seen is linked to what is said by the interviewees, in *Last Hijack Interactive* the animations tend to be generic. That is, they frequently depict scenes broadly related to the topic at issue, but not precisely linked to what is said in the snippet of the interview they accompany. This occurs to the point that a same animated shot can be employed more than once. For instance, there is a shot of a ship's bow riving the waves used in conjunction with both Mohamed and the captain's recollections of the moment in which the chief pirate, Omar, has obliged the assaulted boat to dock off the coast of Eyl. Moreover, the same shot is also employed to illustrate the part of the interview wherein the captain talks about the sensations felt when told they were free to go. The same occurs for a wide shot portraying the ship stationing in the middle of the sea at night, illuminated only by the moonlight. Indeed, this shot is used to accompany both Darch's declaration on how he was sure that the company, in the end, would have paid the ransom that the pirates were asking for and his recollection of when one evening his chief engineer set down with one of the pirates and helped him identify more securable requests. As it emerges from this example, even in the case of *Last Hijack Interactive* the animation is thus treated almost as a mere visual filler.

In sum, although through adopting different approaches, in *The Next Day*, *Invisible Picture Show*, and *Last Hijack Interactive* the animation is reduced to an ambient animation. This has the effect of enhancing in them a trait that has long characterized the animated documentary as a form: the generalization of the experiences of single individuals attested. Indeed, this use of the animation confers to the oral testimonies an even greater universal character, indicating that what is narrated could be anybody's story. Therefore, in turn, it induces even more readily its users to put in place a fabled reading. If in this respect reducing the animation to a visual filler aligns these i-docs with the current animated documentary production, at the same time, however, it also differentiates them from it. Indeed, the ambientalization of the animation also suggests that, since there is already sound to authenticate as factual what recounted in these works, the animation can be freed from the unattainable goal of satisfying man's need to see a photographic image of a factual occurrence for believing an event to have taken place in our world (Jost 2003, 11).

A Glimpse into the Future?

So far, this ambientalization of the animation seems to be trackable just in animated i-docs. In fact, it must be noted that *The Next Day*, *Invisible Picture Show*, and *Last Hijack Interactive* are each a component of a larger multi-platform project. *The Next Day* is a companion piece to a documentary graphic novel of the same title, written by Paul Peterson and Jason Gilmore and illustrated by John Porcellino. *Invisible Picture Show* is part of a project that also includes a "traditional" animated documentary short and a live event combining performances from formerly detained children with the screening of the four aforementioned animated testimonies. Similarly, next to *Last Hijack Interactive* a "traditional" feature-length animated documentary entitled *Last Hijack* has been created.[3] However, the other texts forming the multi-platform projects of which these animated i-docs are part do not share their ambient visuals, making the latter for now a peculiarity of this relatively novel kind of animated documentary. Indeed, in the *Last Hijack* feature, not only the animated shots are not recycled but also the static graphic novel aesthetics are abandoned in favor of more traditional ones based on Hisko Hulsing's oil paintings. In the graphic novel *The Next Day*, each interviewee is assigned a drawn body from the outset, and although the metaphor of the house is present, only the first panel and the last page of each chapter are devoted to it, whereas the majority of the panels portray the happenings recounted by Chantal, Ryan, Tina, and Jenn. In the film *Invisible Picture Show*, we are presented with the same four animated testimonies among which users can choose in the i-doc. Still, here, the animation that accompanies the children's declarations is not faded into a projection on a wall. The virtual environments are wholly absent, and the equal footing between the aural and the visual track that generally characterizes the animated documentary is thus restored.

Undeniably, *The Next Day*, *Invisible Picture Show*, and *Last Hijack Interactive* are only three out of various online animated i-docs, among which we can encounter also works more in line with the current animated documentary production. It is the case of *My Grandmother's Lingo* (2016, dir. Jake Duczynski), an animated i-doc produced by the Australian public television network SBS, wherein the story of Angelina Joshua, a young aboriginal woman dedicated to preserving Marra, which is the disappearing language of her ancestors, is told through the oral testimony of Angelina herself. Here, a close relationship between sound and images can be found, since from time to time the animation is direct visualization of what is spoken. We can even find an animated i-doc like *A Short History of the Highrise* (2013, dir. Katerina Cizek), a global history of vertical living fully indebted to the expository approach characteristic of the classical animated documentary; or one such as *There Once Lived . . . Five Stories of Real People* (жили l были. Пять историй реальных людей, 2017), which, in talking about homelessness in Russia, coalesces elements of the classical approach with others proper of today's one imbued in memory and subjectivity.[4]

Nonetheless, in the face of the treatment that the animated visuals receive in *The Next Day*, *Invisible Picture Show*, and *Last Hijack Interactive* a question cannot but arises: Do they offer us a glimpse into the future of the animated documentary? That is, are they the germs of a post-animated documentary era wherein the animated visuals will be a mere visual filler? Only time will tell. As Jon Dovey underlines, to date the i-doc, in general, is "a very long way from becoming . . . part of everyday life and shedding its experimental nature" (Dovey 2017, 286). Therefore, in turn, the animated i-doc is still far from being the main face of the animated documentary. Consequently, it is too early to determine if the three animated i-docs at stake constitute the seeds of a further evolution of the animated documentary as a form. All we can say for now is that today the animated documentary proves to be in great shape, a fact that suggests it has a bright, long future to look forward to. However, in welcoming the works to come, we shall not forget this form's long and articulated past, as it is only by keeping it in mind that we will be able to understand fully the newcomers.

Notes

1 Animation today is highly used in i-docs to create interfaces. However, this is not sufficient for qualifying an i-doc as an animated documentary. Similar to what is suggested by Honess Roe (2013, 4–5) for the animated documentary in general, for animated i-docs, I here intend just those i-docs wherein the animation is fully integrated within the visual track and has a significant role in it.

2 Users may be able to know to whom the keyword selected pertains only if they have preemptively browsed the audio library section of the website, wherein all the keywords are listed under the name of each interviewee.

3 Only the *Last Hijack* project is an actual transmedia project in the sense proposed by Henry Jenkins, since it is the sole one whose texts effectively "make a distinctive and valuable contribution to the whole" (Jenkins 2006, 95–6). Indeed, Tommy Pallotta and Femke Wolting's filmic animated documentary can be viewed as a sequel of the interactive one, as it provides an account of Mohamed's decision to quit piracy, and of the hardship he encountered in standing by this position. The texts forming *The Next Day* and the *Invisible Picture Show* projects are instead simply adaptations of a same narrative, each providing only a minimal add-on to the general storyline.

4 Indeed, this i-doc animated by Viktoriya Spiryagina offers to the user the possibility of exploring the stories of five homeless people who died on the street: Lilya, Roma, Zhenya, Esma, and Raisa. The vicissitudes of these figures are told through expository captions that have, however, been written not out of research on them but from recollections of volunteers of the Friends on the Street Foundation, with which these people had interacted during their lifetime.

REFERENCES

7 Wise Dwarfs (1941), [Film] Dir. Richard Layford, Canada: NFB, Walt Disney Studios.
11 Steps to Survival (1973), [Film] Dir. Pierre L'Amare, Canada: NFB for Canada Emergency Measures Organization.
12 Seconds of Gunfire: The True Story of a School Shooting (2019), [Film] Dir. Suzette Moyer and Seth Blanchard, US: The Washington Post.
25 April (2015), [Film] Dir. Leanne Pooley, New Zealand: General Film Corporation.
90 Day Wondering? (1956), [Film] Dir. Chuck Jones, US: Warner Brothers for US Air Force.
600,000 Years on Earth (*600.000 anni sulla Terra*, 1966), [Film] Dir. Giuseppe Maria Bruscolini, Italy: Corona Cinematografica.
64,000,000 Years Ago (1981), [Film] Dir. Bill Maylone, Canada: NFB.
A Is for Architecture (1960), [Film] Dir. Gerald Budner and Robert Verrall, Canada: NFB.
A Is for Atom (1953), [Film] Dir. Carl Urbano, US: John Sutherland Productions for General Electric.
A Is for Autism (1992), [Film] Dir. Tim Webb, UK: Fine Take Productions, Channel 4.
The ABC of the Diesel Engine (1950), [Film] US: Film Graphics Inc. for General Motors.
The ABC of Hand Tools (1946), [Film] Dir. Bill Roberts, US: Walt Disney Studios for General Motors.
The ABC of Internal Combustion Engines (1948), [Film] US: Herb Lamb Productions for General Motors.
The ABC of Internal Combustion Engines. The Automobile Engine (1948), [Film] Dir. Gordon Sheehan, US: Sound Masters Inc. for General Motors.
The ABC of Jet Propulsion (1954), [Film] US: Sound Masters Inc. for General Motors.
Abductees (1995), [TV Short] Channel 4, June 14.
Abraham, A. (2012), *When Magoo Flew. The Rise and Fall of Animation Studio UPA*, Middletown: Wesleyan University Press.
Accused #2: Walter Sisulu (2018), [Film] Dir. Nicolas Champeaux and Gilles Porte, France: La Générale de Production.
Action of the Human Heart (1920), [Film] Dir. Francis Lyle Goldman, US: Bray Studios.
Adams, J. (2008), *Documentary Graphic Novels and Social Realism*, Bern: Peter Lang.

Adventure in the Cell (*Avventura nella cellula*, 1962), [Film] Dir. Gibba, Italy: Corona Cinematografica.
The Adventures of Junior Raindrop (1948), [Film] Dir. Carl S. Clancy, US: Department of Agriculture – Forest Service.
The Adventures of Tintin: Secret of the Unicorn (2011), [Film] Dir. Steven Spielberg, US: Columbia Pictures, Paramount Pictures.
The Age of Monsters (*L'età dei mostri*, 1966), [Film] Dir. Giuseppe Maria Bruscolini, Italy: Corona Cinematografica.
Agricultural Plot (*Il terreno agrario*, 1969), [Film] Dir. Giovanni Cecchinato, Italy: Montecatini.
Air Power American (1951), [Film] US: Raphael G. Wolff Studios for US Air Force.
Ajanovic-Ajanć, M. (2019), "Beyond Self-images. The Context and Development of Animated Documentaries, the Cornerstones of Modern Animation in Sweden," in F. Bruckner, N. Gilić, H. Lang, D. Šuljić, H. Turković (eds.), *Global Animation Theory. International Perspectives at Animafest Zagreb*, 99–113, New York/London: Bloomsbury.
Albert in Blunderland (1950), [Film] US: John Sutherland Productions for Alfred P. Sloan Foundation.
The Alcohol Cycle (*Le circuit de l'alcool*, 1919), [Film] Dir. O'Galop, France: Pathé.
An Alien in the Playground (2009), [Film] Dir. Mike and Tim Rauch, US: Rauch Brothers Animation Inc.
All About Polymorphics (1959), [Film] Dir. Bill Orr, US: Thompson Ramo Wooldridge Inc.
"All Set for the Academy's Winnahs Tomorrow. Certain Oscars Look 'In'" (1943), *Variety*, March 3: 2, 32.
All Together (1942), [Film] Dir. Jack King, Canada, US: NFB, Walt Disney Studios.
Alonge, G. (2000), *Il disegno armato. Cinema di animazione e propaganda bellica in Nord America e Gran Bretagna (1914–1945)*, Bologna: CLUEB.
Altman, R. (1999), *Film/Genre*, London: BFI.
Anatomy of Motion (*Anatomia del moto*, 1962), [Film] Dir. Elio Gagliardo, Italy: Corona Cinematografica.
Angela, P. (2017), *Il mio lungo viaggio. 90 anni di storie vissute*, Milan: Mondadori.
Animal, Vegetable, Mineral (1957), [Film] Dir. Louis Dahl, UK: Halas & Batchelor Cartoon Films for BP.
Animated Mathematics (*Mathematische Trickfilme*, 1912), [Film series] Germany: Lehrfilm.
Animated Minds (2003), [TV program] Channel 4.
Another Chance (1944), [Film] US: Walt Disney Studios.
Another Day of Life (2018), [Film] Dir. Raúl de la Fuente and Damian Nenow, Poland, Spain, Germany, Belgium, Hungary: Platige Films, Kanaki Films, Puppetworks Animation Studio, Animationsfabrik, Umedia, Walking The Dog, Wüste Film.
Antonini, A. and C. Tognolotti (2008), *Mondi possibili. Un viaggio nella storia del cinema d'animazione*, Milan: Il principe costante.
Approved for Adoption (*Couleur de peau: Miel*, 2012), [Film] Dir. Laurent Boileau and Jung Henin, France, Belgium: Artémis Productions, Belgacom, France 3 Cinéma, Mosaique Films, Panda Media.

Aprà, A. (2017), *Breve ma veridica storia del documentario. Dal cinema del reale alla nonfiction*, Alessandria: Falsopiano.

Arnold, G. B. (2017), *Animation and the American Imagination. A Brief History*, Santa Barbara: Praeger.

Art (1974), [Film] Dir. Bruce Petty, Australia.

The Art of Photography (*L'arte della fotografia*, 1962), [Film] Dir. Giampaolo Mercanti, Italy: Corona Cinematografica.

Artis, A. Q. ([2007] 2014), *The Shut Up and Shoot Documentary Guide. A Down & Dirty DV Production*, Burlington/Oxon: Focal Press.

As Old as the Hills (1950), [Film] Dir. John Halas and Alan Crick, UK: Halas & Batchelor Cartoon Films for BP.

Ashe '68 VR Experience (2019), [Film] Dir. Brad Lichtenstein, US: Custom Reality Services, Get Lifted, Oak Street Pictures, Rexpix Media, Sports Illustrated.

Astle, R. (2014), "Transmedia Is Still So Young: Femke Wolting and Tommy Pallotta on *Last Hijack Interactive*," *Filmmaker*, October 3. Available online: http://filmmakermagazine.com/87733-transmedia-is-still-so-young-femke-wolting-and-tommy-pallotta-on-last-hijack-interactive/#.Vtgw1JPhCqA (accessed July 19, 2019).

Aston, J. and S. Gaudenzi (2012), "Interactive Documentary: Setting the Field," *Studies in Documentary Film*, 6 (2): 125–39.

Atkinson, P. (2009), "Movements within Movements: Following the Line in Animation and Comic Books," *Animation: An Interdisciplinary Journal*, 4 (3): 265–81.

Atkinson, P. and S. Cooper (2012), "Untimely Narrations: *Waltz with Bashir* and the Incorporation of Historical Difference," *Screening the Past*, 34. Available online: http://www.screeningthepast.com/issue-34-untimely-cinema/untimely-animations-waltz-with-bashir-and-the-incorporation-of-historical-difference/ (accessed October 13, 2017).

The Atom in the Sea (*L'atomo in mare*, 1961), [Film] Dir. Virgilio Tosi, Italy: Comitato nazionale per l'Energia Nucleare.

Atoms and Electricity (*Des atomes et l'électricité*, 1975), [Film] Dir. Jacques Rouxel, France: aaa Production for EDF.

Avni, S. (2011), "Tying Your Own Shoes," *Journal on Developmental Disabilities*, 17 (1): 84–8.

Baby Story (1978), [Film] Dir. Bruno Bozzetto, Italy: Bruno Bozzetto Film.

Backseat Bingo (2003), [Film] Dir. Liz Blazer, US: University of Southern California.

Bailing Out (1949), [Film] US: UPA for Department of the Navy.

Balance 1950 (1951), [Film] Dir. Peter Sachs, UK: Larkins Studio for ICI.

Bandwidth (1960), [Film] Dir. René Jodoin, Canada: NFB.

Bashara, D. (2019), *Cartoon Vision. UPA Animation and Postwar Aesthetics*, Oakland: University of California Press.

The Basics of Einstein's Theory of Relativity (*Die Grundlagen der Einsteinschen Relativitäts-Theorie*, 1922), [Film] Dir. Hanns Walter Kornblum, Germany.

Bastiancich, A. (1998), "La diversità nella libertà. L'animazione del National Film Board of Canada," in B. Di Marino (ed.), *Animania. 100 anni di esperimenti nel cinema di animazione*, 47–53, Milan: Il Castoro.

The Battle of Austerlitz (La bataille d'Austerlitz 1909), [Film] Dir. Émile Cohl, France: Gaumont.
The Battle of the North Sea (1918), [Film] US: Signal Corps.
Baxter, J. (2014), *Disney During World War II. How the Walt Disney Studio Contributed to Victory in the War*, Glendale: Disney Editions.
Bazin, A. (1967), *What Is Cinema? Vol. 1*, trans. Hugh Gray, Berkeley: University of California Press.
BBC Learning: History (2016), [Web] UK: Mosaic Films for BBC Learning.
Be Said (On doit le dire, 1918), [Film] Dir. O'Galop, France: Pathé.
Beaudet, L. (1978), "L'Animation," in P. Véronneau (ed.), *Les Cinémas canadiens*, 71–86, Paris, Montreal: Lherminier, La Cinémathèque québéçoise.
Becattini, A. (2016), *Disney Comics. The Whole Story*, n. p.: Bob McLain Media.
The Beginning of the End (Il principio della fine, 1942), [Film] Dir. Liberio Pensuti, Italy: INCOM.
"Bell Shows *Hemo the Magnificent*" (1957), *Business Screen Magazine*, 18 (2): 12.
The Beloved Ones (2007), [Film] Dir. Samantha Moore, UK: UK Film Council, Screen West Midlands, Sapiens Productions.
Bendazzi, G. (2016a), *Animation. A World History*, vol. I, Boca Raton: CRC Press.
Bendazzi, G. (2016b), *Animation. A World History*, vol. II, Boca Raton: CRC Press.
Benson, G. S. (1951), "President's Comment," *Educational Screen*, 30 (7), September: 259–60.
Berlin: Symphony of a Great City (Berlin—Die Sinfonie der Großstadt, 1927), [Film] Dir. Walter Ruttman, Germany: Deutsche Vereins-Film, Les Productions Fox Europa.
Bertozzi, M. (2008), *Storia del documentario italiano. Immagini e culture dell'altro cinema*, Venice: Marsilio.
Beyond Freedom (2005), [Film] Dir. Jacquie Trowell, South Africa: Big World Cinema.
Biondi, T. (2010), "Sandro Pallavicini. Un produttore per tutte le stagioni," in E. G. Laura (ed.), *Storia del cinema italiano 1940/1944*, vol. VI, 386–7, Venice/Rome: Marsilio/Fondazione Centro Sperimentale di cinematografia.
Bioscope (Bioscopi: Una biografia collectiva animada, 2021), [Web] Dir. Pol Mallafré, Spain: Centre de Cultura Contemporàina de Barcelona.
The Birth of Earth (La nascita della Terra, 1962), [Film] Dir. Gibba, Italy: Corona Cinematografica.
Blind Justice (1987), [TV program] Channel 4.
Blitz on Bugs (1944), [Film] Dir. John Halas and Joy Batchelor, UK: Halas & Batchelor Cartoon Films for MOI.
Blood (C'était le sang, 1982), [Film] Dir. Jacques Rouxel, France: aaa Production for ECPA.
Blood Transfusion (1941), [Film] Dir. Hans M. Nieter, UK: Paul Rotha Productions for MOI.
Bones, Bones, Bones (1944), [Film] Dir. John Halas and Joy Batchelor, UK: Halas & Batchelor Cartoon Films for MOI.
Bongco, M. ([2000] 2013), *Reading Comics. Language, Culture and the Concept of Superhero in Comic Books*, Abingdon: Routledge.
Boon, T. (2008), *Films of Fact. A History of Science in Documentary Film and Television*, London: Wallflower.

"Book Reviews. How War Came" (1940), *Documentary News Letter*, 1 (3), March: 16.

Boschen, J. (2018), "A *Rhapsody of Steel* on Labor Day," *Cartoon Research*, September 3. Available online: https://cartoonresearch.com/index.php/a-rhapsody-of-steel-on-labor-day/ (accessed March 10, 2019).

Bottini, C. (2019), *Redesigning Animation. United Productions of America*, Boca Raton: CRC Press.

Bouldin, J. (2004), "Cadaver of the Real: Animation, Rotoscoping and the Politics of the Body," *Animation Journal*, 12: 7–31.

Boundary Lines (1946), [Film] Dir. Philip Stapp, US: Julien Bryan's International Film Foundation.

Bowling for Columbine (2002), [Film] Dir. Michael Moore, US, Canada, Germany: United Artists, Alliance Atlantis, Salter Street Films, VIF2, Dog Eat Dog Films, Iconolarty Productions Inc., TiMe Film- und TV Produktions GmbH.

Bozzetto, B. (2017), "Adagio, Accelerando," in D. Giurlando (ed.), *Fantasmagorie. Un secolo (e oltre) di cinema d'animazione*, 79–90, Venice: Marsilio.

Bristles and Brushes (1944), [Film] UK: Elwis Films for MOI.

Britain's Effort (1917), [Film] Dir. Lancelot Speed, UK: Lancelot Speed Films for MOI.

The Broadway Melody (1929), [Film] Dir. Harry Beaumont, US: Metro-Goldwyn-Mayer.

Broken Treaties (1941), [Film] Dir. Paul Fannell, US: Cartoon Films Ltd.

Brotherhood of Man (1945), [Film] Dir. Robert Cannon, US: UPA for UAW-CIO.

Buckland, W. (2000), *The Cognitive Semiotics of Film*, Cambridge: Cambridge University Press.

Burke, C. (2013), "Animated Isotype on Film, 1941–1947," in C. Burke, E. Kindle and S. Walker (eds.), *Isotype, Design and Contexts 1925–1971*, 366–89, London: Hyphen Press.

Burrows, E. (1986), "Live Action. A Brief History of British Animation," in C. Barr (ed.), *All Our Yesterdays. 90 Years of British Cinema*, 272–85, London: BFI.

By Word of Mouse (1954), [Film] Dir. Firz Freleng, US: Warner Brothers for Alfred P. Sloan Foundation.

Cain, V. (2012), ""An Indirect Influence upon Industry": Rockefeller Philantropies and the Development of Educational Film in the United States, 1935–1953," in D. Oregon, M. Oregon and D. Streible (eds.), *Learning with the Lights Off. Educational Film in the United States*, 230–48, New York: Oxford University Press.

Callus, P. (2015), "Animation, Fabrication, Photography. Reflections upon the Intersecting Practices of Sub-Saharan Artists within the Moving Image," *African Arts*, 48 (3): 58–69.

Callus, P. (2017), "Remediations of Nonfiction. Animation, Interactivity, and Documentary from Africa," *Critical Interventions. Journal of African Art History and Visual Culture*, 11 (3): 269–86.

Camouflage (1944), [Film] Dir. Frank Thomas, US: FMPU, Walt Disney Studios.

Campbell, V. (2016), *Science, Entertainment and Television Documentary*, Basingstoke: Palgrave MacMillan.

Canemaker, J. (1987), *Winsor McCay. His Life and Art*, New York: Abbeville Press.
Cantor, D. ([2007] 2008), "Uncertain Enthusiasm. The American Cancer Society Public Education and the Problem of the Movie, 1921–1960," in D. Cantor (ed.), *Cancer in the Twentieth Century*, 39–69, Baltimore: The Johns Hopkins University Press.
Cantor, D. (2020), "*Inside Magoo* (1960): Comedic Commentary on 1950s America and Cancer," in C. Bonah and A. Laukötter (eds.), *Body, Capital and Screens. Visual Media and the Healthy Self in the 20th Century*, 181–203, Amsterdam: Amsterdam University Press.
Carioti, G. R. (1972), "I venerdì degli autori. L'occhio perpetuo", *Il dramma*, 48 (7–8), July–August: 185–6.
Carousel (Carosello, 1957–77), [TV program] RAI, February 3–January 1.
The Case of the Metal Sheathed Elements (1973), [Film] Dir. Sid Mould, UK: Larkins Studio for the Electricity Council.
"Catching on Like Wildfire!" (1955), *The National Future Farmer*, 1 (1): 6.
"CBS Network Presents Colorful Case" (1952), *Business Screen Magazine*, 13 (6): 31.
Centrefold (2012), [Film] Dir. Ellie Land, UK: Lynchpin.
Chambers, C. A. (1958), "The Belief in Progress in Twentieth-Century America," *Journal of the History of Ideas*, 19 (2): 197–224.
"Channel 12 Highlights" (1964), *The News Journal*, March 11: 23.
Chapman, J. (2007), "Re-presenting War. British Television Drama-Documentary and the Second World War," *European Journal of Cultural Studies*, 10 (1): 13–33.
Chapman, J. (2015), *A New History of British Documentary*, Basingstoke: Palgrave MacMillan.
Charley in New Town (1946), [Film] Dir. John Halas and Joy Batchelor, UK: Halas & Batchelor Cartoon Films for COI.
Charley Junior's Schooldays (1948), [Film] Dir. John Halas and Joy Batchelor, UK: Halas & Batchelor Cartoon Films for COI.
"Charley Junior's School Days" (1950), *Monthly Film Bulletin*, 17 (193), January–February: 13.
Charley's Black Magic (1947), [Film] Dir. John Halas and Joy Batchelor, UK: Halas & Batchelor Cartoon Films for COI.
Charley's March of Time (1947), [Film] Dir. John Halas and Joy Batchelor, UK: Halas & Batchelor Cartoon Films for COI.
Chicago 10: Speak Your Peace (2007), [Film] Dir. Brett Morgen, US: Consolidate Documentaries, Participant Productions, River Road Entertainment.
Child Behavior Equals You (1972), [Film] Canada: Crawley Films for the Vanier Institute of the Family.
Children of the Sun (1960), [Film] Dir. Faith and John Hubley, US: Storyboard Productions for UNICEF.
Chion, M. (1994), *Audio-Vision*. Translated and edited by Claudia Gorbman. New York: Columbia University Press.
Chion, M. (2009), *Film, a Sound Art*, New York: Columbia University Press.
Chris the Swiss (2018), [Film] Dir. Anja Kofmel, Switzerland, Croatia, Germany, Finland: Dschoint Ventschr Filmproduktion, Nukleus Film, MA.JA.DE. Filmproduktion, IV Films.

Church, H. (1943), "War and Hollywood," *The Pittsburgh Press*, January 4: 17.
Cinderagella or Rags to Stitches (1944), [Film] Dir. John Halas and Joy Batchelor, UK: Halas & Batchelor Cartoon Films for MOI.
"Clay Ready for *Girl and River*" (1960), *The San Francisco Examiner*, April 5: 4.
Cleanliness Brings Health (1945), [Film] Dir. Jim Algar, US: Walt Disney Studios for OCIAA.
The Clitoris (*Le Clitoris*, 2016), [Film] Dir. Lori Malépart-Traversy, Canada.
Cold Comfort (1944), [Film] Dir. Joy Batchelor, UK: Halas & Batchelor Cartoon Films for MOI.
The Colombo Plan (1962), [Film] Dir. Joy Batchelor, UK: Halas & Batchelor Cartoon Films for COI.
The Colours of My Father: A Portrait of Sam Borenstein (1992), [Film] Dir. Joyce Borenstein, Canada: NFB.
Comet (1985), [Film] Dir. Sydney Goldsmith, Canada: NFB.
The Commonwealth (1962), [Film] Dir. Joy Batchelor, UK: Halas & Batchelor Cartoon Films for Nuffield Foundation and Commonwealth Institute.
Communication in the Workplace (*La communication dans l'enterprise*, 1972), [Film] Dir. Jacques Rouxel, France: aaa Production for CNPF.
Compost Heaps (1943), [Film] UK: Halas & Batchelor Cartoon Films for MOI.
Conde Aldana, J. A. (2018), "Little Voices and Big Spaces. Animated Documentary and Conceptual Blending Theory," in C. Brylla and M. Kramer (eds.), *Cognitive Theory and Documentary Film*, 39–58, Cham: Palgrave Macmillan.
Confessions of a Foyer Girl (1978), [TV program] BBC, July 13.
Conquest of the Sky, The (*La conquista del cielo*, 1968), [Film] Dir. Rodolfo Besesti, Italy: Corona Cinematografica.
Continental Drift (1968), [Film] Dir. Co Hoedeman, Canada: NFB.
Conversation Pieces (1982–3), [TV program] Channel 4.
A Conversation with Harris (2001), [Film] Dir. Sheila Sofian, US.
Cook, M and K. M. Thompson (2019), "Introduction to Animation and Advertising," in M. Cook and K. M. Thompson (eds.), *Animation and Advertising*, 1–51, Cham: Palgrave Macmillan.
Corner, J. (2002), "Sounds Real: Music and Documentary," *Popular Music*, 21 (3): 357–66.
Cosmos–A Personal Voyage (1980), [TV program] PBS, September 28–December 21.
Cote, G. L. (1956–7), "Animation Films in Canada," *The Journal of the British Film Academy*, Winter: 16–8.
Cosmos–A Spacetime Odyssey (2014), [TV program] FOX, March 9–June 8.
Council Matters (1984), [Film] UK: Leeds Animation Workshop for Sheffield City Court.
Coynik, D. (1972), *Real to Reel*, Winona: St Mary's College Press.
Crafton, D. (1982), *Before Mickey. The Animated Film, 1898-1928*, Cambridge: MIT Press.
Crafton, D. (2013), *Shadow of a Mouse. Performance, Belief, and World-Making in Animation*, Berkeley: University of California Press.
The Creation of the World (*Stvoření světa*, 1958), [Film] Dir. Eduard Hofman, Czechoslovakia, France: Krátky Film, Les Frères en Tricot.

Creature Comforts (1989), [Film] Dir. Nick Park, UK: Aardam Animations.
Creature Comforts (2003-11), [TV program] ITV1, June 4-December 11.
Cruz, B. (2011), "Paging Dr. Disney. Health Education Films, 1922-1973," in A. Bowdoin Van Riper (ed.), *Learning from Mickey, Donald and Walt. Essays on Disney's Edutainment Films*, 127-44, Jefferson: McFarland.
"Crystal Theatre" (1918), *The Ottawa Herald*, September 6: 3.
The Curious History of Money (1969), [Film] Dir. Anne Jolliffe and Beryl Stevens, UK: Larkins Studio for Barclays Bank.
Curlic: The Path to Beyond (*Crulic: Drumul spre dincolo*, 2011), [Film] Dir. Anca Damian, Romania, Poland: Aparte Film, Magellan Foundation.
DaCosta, C. and F. Hosseini-Shakib (2006), "Making Past Perfect Sense in Clay: Britishness/Englishness in the Works of Aardman Studios," *Cartoons. The International Journal of Animation*, 2 (1): 28-34.
Daddy's Little Bit of Dresden China (1988), [Film] Dir. Karen Watson, UK: West Surrey College of Art and Design.
Dagrada, E. ([1996] 2005), *Woody Allen. Manhattan*, Turin: Lindau.
Dam the Delta (1958), [Film] Dir. Joy Batchelor, UK: Halas & Batchelor Cartoon Films for Netherlands Government Information Service.
The Dark Side of the Sun (2011), [Film] Dir. Carlo Shalom Hintermann, Italy: Citrullo International, Rainbow.
"Davy Takes on River Pirates" (1956), *The San Bernardino County Sun*, July 20: 26.
Dead Reckoning: Champlain in America (2009), [TV program] Dir. Marc Hall, PBS, November 17.
Dear Uncle (1952), [Film] US: John Sutherland Productions for Alfred P. Sloan Foundation.
The Decline of an Empire (*Tramonto di un impero*, 1940), [Film] Dir. F.lli Amadoro, Italy: INCOM.
Defense Against Invasion (1943), [Film] Dir. Jack King, US: Walt Disney Studios for OCIAA.
Del Gaudio, S. (1997), "If Truth Be Told Can 'toons Tell It? Documentary and Animation," *Film History* 9 (2): 189-99.
Dessy, N. (1936), *Come si anima un cartone animato*, Cagliari: Edizione Sud Est.
The Devil and John Q. (1952), [Film] US: John Sutherland Productions for Alfred P. Sloan Foundation.
The Devil in the Bottle (*Il diavolo nella bottiglia*, 1968), [Film] Dir. Sergio Spina, Italy: Olivetti.
Diamond Head (1962), [Film] Dir. Guy Green, US: Jerry Bresler Productions.
Dinosaur Revolution (2011), [TV program] Discovery Channel, September 4-13.
Dinotasia (2012), [Film] Dir. David Krantz and Erik Nelson, US: Creative Differences for Discovery Channel.
Directivity (1960), [Film] Dir. René Jodoin, Canada: NFB.
Diseases Spread (*Byodoku no denpa*, 1926), [Film] Dir. Sanae Yamamoto, Japan: The Ministry of Education.
Disney, W. (1945), "Mickey as Professor," *The Public Opinion Quarterly*, 9 (2): 119-25.
Disney, W. (1949), "Disegni animati educativi," *Sequenze. Quaderni di cinema*, 1 (2): 23-4.

Disney, W. (1955), "Animated Cartoon," *Health Education Journal*, 13 (1): 70–7.
"Disney's War Effort", *The Age*, August 29: 8.
Disorientation Crashes (1946), [Film] US: UPA for US Navy.
Dive Bombing Crashes (1945), [Film] US: Warner Brothers for US Navy.
Dividend in Depth (1954), [Film] US: The Calvin Company for Carterpillar Tractor Co.
Doane, M. A. (1980), "The Voice in the Cinema: The Articulation of Body and Space," *Yale French Studies*, 60: 33–50.
Dobson, N. (2018), *Norman McLaren. Between the Frames*, New York/London: Bloomsbury.
Dollar Dance (1943), [Film] Dir. Norman McLaren, Canada: NFB.
Donald in Mathmagic Land (1959), [Film] Dir. Hamilton Luske, US: Walt Disney Studios.
Donald's Decision (1942), [Film] Dir. Ford Beebe, Canada, US: NFB, Walt Disney Studios.
Dovey, J. (2017), "Who Wants to Become Banal? The I-Doc from Experiment to Industry," in J. Aston, S. Gaudenzi and M. Rose (eds.), *I-Docs. The Evolving Practices of Interactive Documentary*, 272–88, New York/Chichester: Columbia University Press.
"Doug Fairbanks in *Say Young Fellow*" (1918), *Medford Mail Tribune*, September 6: 5.
Dow, C. (2003), "Private Snafu's Hidden War," *Bright Lights Film Journal*, 42. Available online: https://brightlightsfilm.com/private-snafus-hidden-war-historical-survey-and-analytical-perspective-historical-survey-and-analytical-perspective/#.YBykRGRKiYU (accessed July 5, 2019).
Down a Long Way. The Story of an Oil-Well (1954), [Film] Dir. Bob Privett, UK: Halas & Batchelor Cartoon Films for BP.
Down and Out (1979), [TV program] BBC, March 13.
Down the Gasoline Trail (1935), [Film] Dir. Rockwell Barnes, US: Jam Handy for the Chevrolet Division of General Motors.
Drafty, Isn't It (1957), [Film] Dir. Chuck Jones, US: Warner Brothers for the US Army.
Dreams of a Land (1989), [Film] Dir. Robert Doucet, Canada: NFB.
"Dunningcolor Puts Out New Picture" (1941), *Los Angeles Times*, July 26: 14.
Dustbin Parade (1942), [Film] Dir. John Halas and Joy Batchelor, UK: Realist Film, Halas & Batchelor Cartoon Films for MOI.
Dyer, R. and P. McDonald (1998), *Stars*, London: BFI.
The Dynamite Brothers (*I fratelli Dinamite*, 1949), [Film] Dir. Nino and Toni Pagot, Italy: Pagot Film.
Earth Is a Battlefield (1957), [Film] Dir. Richard Taylor and Roger MacDougall, UK: Larkins Studio for British Iron and Steel Federation.
"Earth Is Born Hits Screens This Autumn" (1957), *Fort Lauderdale News*, June 23: 10-F.
The Earth Is Born (1957), [Film] Dir. Zachary Schwartz, US: Transfilm, Dollywood for Life Magazine.
"Economic Facts for John Q. Public" (1957), *Business Screen Magazine*, 18 (4): 35.
The Einstein Theory of Relativity (1923), [Film] Dir. Max Fleischer, US: Premier Productions.

"The Einstein Theory of Relativity" (1924), *The Bioscope*, 61 (947), December 4: 56.
Ekinici, B. T. (2017), "A Hybrid Documentary Genre: Animated Documentary and the Analysis of *Waltz with Bashir* (2008) Movie," *CINEJ Cinema Journal*, 6 (1): 5-24.
Elausti, M., M. Soufflet and C. Lambert (2016), *Il était une fois... la belle histoire de Procidis*, Paris: Huginn & Muninn.
Elementary and Pylon Eights (1944), [Film] Dir. Gus Arriola, US: FMPU.
Emergency Landing on Land (1947), [Film] US: UPA for US Navy.
The Enemy Bacteria (1945), [Film] US: Walter Lantz Productions for U.S. Navy.
Energetically Yours (1957), [Film] Dir. David Hilberman, US: Transfilm Incorporated for Standard Oil Company (Esso).
Energy and Matter (1966), [Film] Dir. Robert Verrall, Canada: NFB.
The Energy Picture (1959), [Film] Dir. John Halas and Gerald Potterton, UK: Halas & Batchelor Cartoon Films for BP.
England vs Europe (Inghilterra vs Europa, 1940), [Film] Dir. Raoul Quattrocchi, Italy: INCOM.
Enterprise (1951), [Film] Dir. Peter Sachs, UK: Larkins Studio for ICI.
Environmental Sanitation (1946), [Film] Dir. Graham Heid, Earl Bench, and Ben Sharpsteen, US: Walt Disney Studios for OCIAA.
Ehrlich, N. (2021), *Animating Truth. Documentary and Visual Culture in 21st Century*, Edinburgh: Edinburgh University Press.
Eureka! (1980-1), [TV program] TVOntario.
Evolution (1923), [Film] Dir. Raymond Ditmars, US: Urban-Kineto.
Evolution (1925), [Film] Dir. Max Fleischer, US: Inkwell Studios.
Evans, G. (1991), *In the National Interest. A Chronicle of the National Film Board of Canada from 1949 to 1989*, Toronto/Buffalo/London: University of Toronto Press.
Evans, G., P. Véronneau and R. Todd (1991), "A Time-line of the National Film Board of Canada and the Canadian Film Industry from 1939 to 1989," in D. W. Bidd (ed.), *The NFB Film Guide. The Productions of the National Film Board of Canada from 1939 to 1989*, xxxi-lxxix, Montreal: NFB.
Everybody Rides the Carousel (1975), [Film] Dir. John and Faith Hubley, US: Storyboard Productions.
Expanding World Relationships (1946), [Film] Dir. David Hilberman, US: UPA for US State Department.
Export or Die (1946), [Film] Dir. John Halas, UK: Halas & Batchelor Cartoon Films for COI.
Extinction of the Dinosaurs (1976), [Film] Dir. Paul Bochner, Canada: NFB.
Eye's Magic (Magia dell'occhio, 1963), [Film] Dir. Gibba, Italy: Corona Cinematografica.
An Eyeful of Sound (2010), [Film] Dir. Samantha Moore, UK: Sapiens Production.
A Fable Retold (1965), [Film] Dir. Pramod Pati, India: Films Division of India.
Family Planning (1967), [Film] Dir. Les Clark, US: Walt Disney Productions for The Population Council.
Family Tree (1950), [Film] Dir. George Dunning and Evelyn Lambart, Canada: NFB.

Farmer Charley (1947), [Film] Dir. John Halas and Joy Batchelor, UK: Halas & Batchelor Cartoon Films for COI.
Faviez, P. (2010), *La Télé. Un destin animé*, Paris: Société des Écrivains.
Feinberg, S. (2015), "Oscars: This Year's Docs Are Breaking the Academy's Unwritten Rules in Unprecedented Numbers," *The Hollywood Reporter*, November 11. Available online: http://www.hollywoodreporter.com/race/oscars-years-docs-are-breaking-838150 (accessed April 19, 2018).
Ferrari, G. (1986), "Simple Words and Many Cartoons," *New Scientist*, 112 (1530), October 16: 61.
Fertilizers (*I concimi*, 1960), [Film] Dir. Giovanni Cecchinato, Italy: Montecatini.
A Few Quick Facts: About Fear (1945), [Film] Dir. Zack Schwartz, US: UPA.
A Few Quick Facts: Inflation (1944), [Film] Dir. Osmond Evans, US: UPA.
A Few Quick Facts: Japan (1945), [Film] US: UPA.
Fidotta, G. (2014), "Animated Maps and the Power of the Trace," *NECSUS*, 3 (1). Available online: http://www.necsus-ejms.org/animated-maps-power-trace/ (accessed April 15, 2019).
Fill 'Er Up! (1959), [Film] Dir. Carl Urbano, US: John Sutherland Productions for DuPont.
Filling the Gap (1942), [Film] Dir. John Halas and Joy Batchelor, UK: Realist Film, Halas & Batchelor Cartoon Films for MOI.
"Films for the Users" (1952), *Film User*, 6 (69), July: 335–6.
Final Fantasy: The Spirits Within (2001), [Film] Dir. Hironobu Sakaguchi and Motonori Sakakibara, US: Square Pictures.
Finding His Voice (1929), [Film] Dir. Francis Lyle Goldman and Max Fleischer, US: Western Electric.
First Line of Defence (1949), [Film] Dir. John Halas and Joy Batchelor, UK: Halas & Batchelor Cartoon Films for COI.
Fish Spoilage Control (1956), [Film] Dir. Gerald Potterton, Canada: NFB for Department of Fisheries Canada.
Fisher, M. (2018), "Capturing the Animated Soldier: Private Snafu and the Docile Body Assemblage," *Studies in Popular Culture*, 41 (1): 94–127.
Five Billion Years (1981), [Film] Dir. Joyce Borenstein, Canada: NFB.
Flat Hatting (1946), [Film] Dir. John Hubley, US: UPA for US Navy.
Flavours of Iraq (*Le Parfum d'Irak*, 2018), [Web] Dir. Léonard Cohen, France: ARTE.
Flight Safety and You (1976–7), [Film series] UK: World Wide Pictures for Royal Navy.
Flood of Memory (2008), [Film] Dir. Anitha Balachandran, UK, India.
The Fly (*La mouche*, 1919), [Film] Dir. O'Galop, France: Pathé.
Food Will Win the War (1942), [Film] Dir. Hamilton Luske, US: Walt Disney Studios for US Department of Agriculture.
Fog (1943), [Film] US: Walt Disney Studios.
For Better, For Worse (1961), [Film] Dir. John Halas and Peter Sachs, UK: Halas & Batchelor Cartoon Films for the Philips Company.
For Her (2017), [Film] Dir. Kim Junki, Korea.
For the Curious (*Para Curiosos*, 2001–5), [Film] Dir. Ernesto Padrón, Cuba: ICAIC.

Fore, S. (2011), "Reenacting Ryan: The Fantasmatic and the Animated Documentary," *Animation: An Interdisciplinary Journal* 6 (3): 277-92.

Formenti, C. (2014), "The Sincerest Form of Docudrama: Re-framing the Animated Documentary," *Studies in Documentary Film* 8 (2): 103-15.

Formenti, C. (2014), "Dal neorealismo al documentario animato scientifico: le animazioni "realiste" di Gibba," *Cabiria*, 44: 4-19.

Formenti, C. (2017), "Note sul documentario animato italiano e il suo periodo delle origini," *Immagine. Note di storia del cinema* 15: 65-8.

Four Methods of Flush Riveting (1942), [Film] Dir. James Algar, USA: Walt Disney Studios for Lockheed Aircraft Corporation.

Fresh Laid Plans (1951), [Film] Dir. George Gordon, US: John Sutherland Productions for Alfred P. Sloan Foundation.

Friedman, Y. (2017), "Beyond the Burden of Representation. Israeli Animation Between Escapism and Subversion," in S. Van De Peer (ed.), *Animation in the Middle East. Practice and Aesthetics from Baghdad to Casablanca*, 172-95, London/New York: I.B. Tauris.

From Space to Life (*Dallo spazio alla vita*, 1966), [Film] Dir. Giuseppe Maria Bruscolini, Italy: Corona Cinematografica.

Fundamental Fixed Gunnery Approaches (1943), [Film] US: Walt Disney Studios.

Furniss, M. ([1998] 2007), *Art in Motion. Animation Aesthetics*, New Barnet: John Libbey.

Furniss, M. (2017), *Animation. The Global History*, London: Thames & Hudson Ltd.

Gagnon, M. K. (2007), "Cinematic Imag(in)ings of the Japanese Canadian Internment," in E. Chang (ed.), *Reel Asian. Asian Canada on Screen*, 273-83, Toronto: Coach House Books.

Gardette, L. (1909), "Teaching History by Motography," *The Nickelodeon*, 2(4): 119-20.

Gas Naturally (1984), [Film] Dir. Clive Mitchell, UK: World Wide Pictures for BP.

Gasoline's Amazing Molecules/ The Inside Story of Modern Gasoline (1948a), [Film] US: Jerry Fairbanks Inc. for Standard Oil Company.

Gasoline's Amazing Molecules. The Inside Story of Modern Gasoline (1948b), Whiting: Standard Oil Company.

Gaudenzi, S. (2013), *The Living Documentary. From Representing Reality to Co-creating Reality in Digital Interactive Documentary*. Doctoral thesis, Goldsmiths, University of London.

Gaycken, O. (2012), "The Cinema of the Future: Visions of the Medium as Modern Educator, 1895-1910," in D. Oregon, M. Oregon and D. Streible (eds.), *Learning with the Lights Off. Educational Film in the United States*, 67-89, New York: Oxford University Press.

Gaycken, O. (2014a), ""A Living Developing Egg Is Present Before You": Animation, Scientific Visualization, Modeling," in K. Beckman (ed.), *Animating Film Theory*, 68-81, Durham: Duke University Press.

Gaycken, O. (2014b), "Early Cinema and Evolution," in B. Lightman and B. Zon (eds.), *Evolution and Victorian Culture*, 94-120, Cambridge: Cambridge University Press.

George Grosz' Interregnum (1960), [Film] Dir. Altina and Charles Carey, US: Educational Communications Corp.

Getting Warmer (1963), [Film] Dir. Henk Kabos, Netherlands, UK: Dollywood for Esso.

Geraghty, C. (2000), "Re-examining Stardom: Questions of Texts, Bodies and Performance," in C. Gledhill and L. Williams (eds.), *Reinventing Film Studies*, 183–201, London: Arnold.

Ghirardato, C. (1991), "Il cinema d'animazione a Milano 1945–1965," *Comunicazioni sociali*, 13 (1–2): 91–117.

The Ghost of Slumber Mountain (1918), [Film] Dir. Willis O'Brien, US: Herbert M. Dawley Productions.

Gill, A. (1964), "TV Tonight: Previews of Top Network Shows," *St. Cloud Daily Times*, April 18: 10.

Girl with a Clenched Fist (*Bimba col pugno chiuso*, 2013), [Film] Dir. Claudio Di Mambro, Luca Madrile, and Umberto Migliaccio, Italy: Todomodo.

Glassman, M. and W. Wise (1999), "A Filmmaker of Vision: *Take One*'s Interview with Colin Low, Part I," *Take One*, 23, Spring: 18–31.

Glynne, A. (2013), "Drawn from Life. The Animated Documentary," in B. Winston (ed.), *The Documentary Film Book*, 73–5, London: BFI.

Going Places (1948), [Film] US: John Sutherland Productions for Alfred P. Sloan Foundation.

Good Wrinkles. The Story of a Remarkable Fruit (1952), [Film] US: All-Scope Pictures for Sunsweet.

The Grain that Built a Hemisphere (1943), [Film] Dir. Bill Roberts, US: Walt Disney Studios for OCIAA.

The Grandchildren's Mother (*A Mãe Dos Netos*, 2008), [Film] Dir. Isabel Noronha and Vivian Altman, Mozambique: Ebano Multimedia.

Gray, J. (2010), *Show Sold Separately. Promos, Spoilers, and Other Media Paratexts*, New York: New York University Press.

The Great Cat Family (1956), [TV program] ABC, September 19.

"Great Cat Family Is Disney Offering" (1956), *The Coshocton Democrat*, September 15: 5.

Great Oaks from Small Acorns Grow (*Petites causes, grands effets!*, 1919), [Film] Dir. O' Gallop, France: Pathé.

A Great Problem (1960), [Film] Dir. Govind Saraiya and G. H. Saraiya, India: Films Division of India.

Great Synthesis (1964), [Film] Dir. Horst G. Koch, Germany: Atelier H. Koch K. G. for BP.

The Great Train Robbery (1903), [Film] Dir. Edwin S. Porter, US: Edison Manufacturing Company.

The Green Wave (2010), [Film] Dir. Ali Samadi Ahadi, Germany: ARTE, Dreamer Joint Venture Filmproduction, Westdeutscher Rundfunk, Wizard UG & Ko.

Grierson, J. (1933), "The Documentary Producer," *Cinema Quarterly*, 2 (1): 7–9.

Guido, F. M. (2008), *Gibba. Diario di un uomo di grande insuccesso*, Alassio: Editore Città di Alassio.

Gunter, M. C. (2012), *The Capra Touch. A Study of the Director's Hollywood Classics and War Documentaries, 1934–1945*, Jefferson and London: McFarland.

Guo, C. (2016), "The Archeology of Memory. The Exploration of Animated Documentary," *Cartoon and Animation Studies*, 45: 479–512.

Halas, J. (1956), "Not for Fun!," *Films & Filming*, 3 (2): 6, 13.
Halas, J. (1957), "The Art of Animation and Its Growing Application," *The Financial Times*, September 23: 15.
Halas, J. and J. Batchelor (1948), "Approach to Cartoon Film Scripting," *Impact*, December 1948: 11–3.
Halas, J. and R. Manvell ([1959] 1976), *The Technique of Film Animation*, New York: Hastings House.
Halas, V. and P. Wells (2006), *Halas & Batchelor Cartoons. An Animated History*, London: Southbank.
Handling, P. and M. Jean ([1999] 2000), "Film Animation," in J. H. Marsh (ed.), *The Canadian Encyclopedia*, Toronto: McClelland & Stewart Inc., 838.
Hangovers (1978), [TV program] BBC.
Harlem Wednesday (1958), [Film] Dir. John and Faith Hubley, US: Storyboard Productions.
Harness the Wind (1978), [Film] Dir. Sidney Goldsmith, Canada: NFB.
Harris, M. (2006), "Literary Len: *Trade Tatoo* and Len Lye's Link with the Literary Avant-Garde," in S. Buchan (ed.), *Animated Worlds*, 63–77, Eastleigh: John Libbey Publishing.
Haswell, H. (2014), "To Infinity and Back Again: Hand-drawn Aesthetic and Affection for the Past in Pixar's Pioneering Animation," *Alphaville: Journal of Film and Screen Media*, 8: 1–17. Available online: http://www.alphavillejournal.com/Issue8/HTML/ArticleHaswell.html (accessed March 15, 2018).
Hawkins, B. (2015), "Seeing in Dreams: The Shifting Landscapes of Drawn Animation," in C. Pallant (ed.), *Animated Landscapes. History, Form and Function*, 15–32, New York/London: Bloomsbury.
Healthy and Happy (*Swasthya Aur Sananda*, 1962), [Film] Dir. Pramod Pati, India: Films Division of India.
Heinrich, T. and B. Batchelor (2004), *Kotex, Kleenex, Huggies. Kimberly-Clark and the Consumer Revolution in American Business*, Columbus: The Ohio State University.
Heir-Conditioned (1955), [Film] Dir. Friz Freleng, US: Warner Brothers for Alfred P. Sloan Foundation.
Hemo the Magnificent (1957), [TV program] CBS, March 20.
Heredity (*Ereditarietà*, 1966), [Film] Dir. Rodolfo Besesti and Elio Gagliardo, Italy: Corona Cinematografica.
Herstory (*So-nyeo-i-ya-gi*, 2011), [Film] Dir. Jun Ki Kim, Korea: Chungkang College of Cultural Industries.
Hidden (*Gömd*, 2002), [Film] Dir. David Aronowitsch, Hanna Heilborn, and Mats Johansson, Sweden: Story AB, Kinotar.
Hight, C. (2008), "Primetime Digital Documentary Animation: The Photographic and Graphic within Play," *Studies in Documentary Film*, 2 (1): 9–31.
His Mother's Voice (1997), [Film] Dir. Dennis Tupicoff, Australia: Dennis Tupicoff Animation.
History (2016), [Web] UK: Mosaic Films for BBC Learning.
History of the Cinema (1956), [Film] Dir. John Halas, UK: Halas & Batchelor Cartoon Films.
History of Inventions (*La storia delle invenzioni*, 1959), [Film] Dir. Bruno Bozzetto, UK, Italy: Halas & Batchelor Cartoon Films, Bruno Bozzetto Film.

Hoare, F. A. (1952), "Modern Methods of Film-using by Industry," *Film User*, 6 (66), April: 175–8.
Hodgson, J. (2019), "Making *The Trouble with Love and Sex*," in J. Murray and N. Ehrlich (eds.), *Drawn from Life. Issues and Themes in Animated Documentary Cinema*, 191–205, Edinburgh: Edinburgh University Press.
Holiday Home (*Semesterhemmet*, 1981), [Film] Dir. Birgitta Jansson, Sweden: Filmverkstan.
Homo Technologicus (1981), [TV program] RAI.
Honess Roe, A. (2011), "The Canadian Shorts: Establishing Disney's Wartime Style," in A. Bowdoin Van Riper (ed.), *Learning from Mickey, Donald and Walt. Essays on Disney's Edutainment Films*, 15–26, Jefferson: McFarland.
Honess Roe, A. (2013), *Animated Documentary*, Basingstoke/New York: Palgrave Macmillan.
Honess Roe, A. (2016), "Animated Documentary," in D. Marcus and S. Kara (eds.), *Contemporary Documentary*, 42–56, Abingdon: Routledge.
Hookworm (1945), [Film] Dir. Jim Algar, US: Walt Disney Studios for OCIAA.
The Hope That Jack Built (1957), [Film] Dir. Gene Deitch, US: Garantray-Lawrence Animation Studio for the National Association of Investment Companies.
Horak, J.-C. (2014), *Saul Bass. Anatomy of Film Design*, Lexington: The University Press of Kentucky.
Horizons of Hope (1954), [Film] US: John Sutherland Productions for Alfred B. Sloan Foundation.
Horrocks, R. (2001), *Len Lye. A Biography*, Auckland: Auckland University Press.
How Disease Travels (1945), [Film] Dir. Bill Roberts, US: Walt Disney Studios for OCIAA.
How Man Learned to Fly (Jak se člověk naučil létat, 1958), [Film] Dir. Jirí Brdečka, Czechoslovakia.
How the Telephone Talks (1919), [Film] US: Bray Studios.
How to Catch a Cold (1951), [Film] Dir. Hamilton Luske, US: Walt Disney Studios for International Cellucotton Company.
How to Feed Plants (*Come si nutrono le piante*, 1960), [Film] Dir. Giovanni Cecchinato, Italy: Montecatini.
How to Have an Accident at Work (1959), [Film] Dir. Charles A. Nichols, US: Walt Disney Studios.
How to Have an Accident in the Home (1956), [Film] Dir. Charles A. Nichols, US: Walt Disney Studios.
How War Came (1941), [Film] Dir. Paul Fannell, US: Cartoon Films Ltd.
How We Hear (1920), [Film] Dir. Francis Lyle Goldman, US: Bray Studios.
How You See (1920), [Film] Dir. Jack Leventhal, US: Bray Studios.
Hubley, J. (1975), "Beyond Pigs and Bunnies: The New Animator's Art," *The American Scholar*, 44 (2): 213–23.
Hubley, J. and Z. Schwartz (1946), "Animation Learns a New Language," *Hollywood Quarterly*, 1 (4), July: 360–3.
Huff and Puff. A Story of Hyperventilation (1955), [Film] Dir. Grant Crabtree, Canada: NFB for Royal Canadian Airforce.
The Human Body (1945), [Film] Dir. Bill Roberts, US: Walt Disney Studios for OCIAA.
Human Growth (1947), [Film] Dir. Sy Wexler, US: Eddie Albert Productions for E.C. Brown Trust.

Huntley, J. (1956–7), "Animation in Britain," *The Journal of the British Film Academy*, Winter: 4–6.
Husbands, L. and C. Ruddell (2019), "Approaching Animation and Animation Studies," in N. Dobson, A. Honess Roe, A. Ratelle and C. Ruddell (eds.), *The Animation Studies Reader*, 5–16, New York/London: Bloomsbury.
I'm Glad You Asked That Question (1970), [Film] Dir. Nancy Hanna, Keith Learner, and Vera Linnecar, UK: Biographic Films for Gas Council.
I'm No Fool... (1955–6), [TV program] ABC, October 6–December 15.
I Was a Child of Holocaust Survivors (2010), [Film] Dir. Ann Marie Fleming, Canada: NFB.
In a Nutshell (1971), [Film] Dir. Les Drew and Michael Mills, Canada: NFB for Ministry of International Cooperation.
Infant Care (1945), [Film] Dir. Jim Algar, US: Walt Disney Studios for OCIAA.
Insects as Carriers of Disease (1945), [Film] Dir. Bill Roberts, US: Walt Disney Studios for OCIAA.
Inside Crackle Corner (1951), [Film] US: John Sutherland Productions for Alfred P. Sloan Foundation.
Inside Magoo (1960), [Film] Dir. Abe Levitow and John F. Becker, US: UPA for American Cancer Society.
Interview (1979), [Film] Dir. Caroline Leaf and Veronica Soul, Canada: NFB.
Introduction to Feedback (1960), [Film] Dir. Charles and Ray Eames, US: IBM.
The Invisible Moustache of Raoul Dufy (1955), [Film] Dir. Aurelius Battaglia, US: UPA for Museum of Modern Art.
Invisible Picture Show (2013), [Film] Dir. Tim Travers Hawkins, UK: Faction Films.
Invisible Picture Show (2013), [Web] Dir. Tim Travers Hawkins, UK: Faction Films.
Irinka & Sandrinka (*Irinka et Sandrinka*, 2007), [Film] Dir. Sandrine Stoïanov, France: Je Suis Bien Content, ARTE France.
It Makes You Think (1944), [Film] UK: Elwis Films for MOI.
It Must Be Said (*On doit le dire*, 1918), [Film] Dir. O'Galop, France: Pathé.
It Never Rains Oil (1953), [Film] Dir. Arnold Gillespie, US: John Sutherland Productions for Western Oil and Gas Association, Rocky Mountain Oil and Gas Association, and American Petroleum Institute.
It's Everybody's Business (1954), [Film] Dir. Carl Urbano, US: John Sutherland Productions in cooperation with E.I. du Pont de Nemours & Company for the Chamber of Commerce of the United States.
It's Like That (2003), [Film] Dir. Southern Ladies Animation Group, Australia: Southern Ladies Animation Group.
Jack, C. (2015), "Fun and Facts about American Business: Economic Education and Business Propaganda in an Early Cold War Cartoon Series," *Enterprise & Society*, 16 (3): 491–520.
Jenkins, B. (1956), "Television in Radio," *The Daily Reporter*, September 19: 15.
Jenkins, H. (2006), *Convergence Culture. Where Old and New Media Collide*, New York/London: New York University Press.
Join-Up Collisions (1946), [Film] US: UPA for US Navy.
Jones, D. B. (1996), *The Best Butler in the Business. Tom Daly of the National Film Board of Canada*, Toronto: University of Toronto Press.

Jost, F. (2003), *Realtà/Finzione*, Milan: Il Castoro.
Journey Through Electricity (*Voyage en électricité*, 1981–1983), [Film] Dir. Jacques Rouxel, France: aaa Production for EDF.
Journey Through Time: The Human Story (1983), [Film] Dir. George Geertsen, Canada: NFB.
The Joy of Life (*Le Bonheur de la vie*, 1992), [TV program] France 3.
"Junior Aides Allocate $1,200 for Obstetrical Table at Local Hospital" (1953), *The Daily Courier*, March 19: 4.
Karns, H. (1958), "A Hair-Raising Drama of the Lower Depths," *Independent Press-Telegram*, July 27: 14.
Kaufman, J. B. (2009), *South of the Border with Disney. Walt Disney and the Good Neighbor Program, 1941–1948*, New York: The Walt Disney Family Foundation Press.
Ketchup (2012), [Film] Dir. Chunning Guo and Baishen Yan, China.
The Keys of Heaven (1946), [Film] Dir. John Halas and Joy Batchelor, UK: Halas & Batchelor Cartoon Films for COI.
Kinshasa, September Noir (1992), [Film] Dir. Jean Michel Kibushi, Congo: Atelier Graphoui.
Kineto War Maps (1914–1916), [Film] Dir. Frank Percy Smith, UK: Kineto.
Kitson, C. (2008), *British Animation. The Channel 4 Factor*, Bloomington: Indiana University Press.
Klein, N. (1993), *7 Minutes. The Life and Death of the American Animated Cartoon*, London/New York: Verso.
Kleiner, D. (1982), "Professor Donald Duck. Learning with the Disney Characters," *The Index Journal*, July 3: 30.
Knowledge, the World and Me (*Le savoir, le monde et moi*, 1993), [Film] Dir. Laurent Bounoure and Jacques Rouxel, France: aaa Production for LFSM.
Kohn, A. and R. Weissbrod (2012), "*Waltz with Bashir* as a Case of Multidimensional Translation," in L. Raw (ed.), *Translation, Adaptation and Transformation*, 123–44, London/New York: Continuum.
Kornhaber, D. (2020), *Nightmares in the Dream Sanctuary. War and the Animated Film*, Chicago: The University of Chicago Press.
Kraemer, J. A. (2015), "*Waltz with Bashir* (2008): Trauma and Representation in the Animated Documentary," *Journal of Film and Video*, 67 (3–4): 57–68.
Kriger, J. (2012), *Animated Realism. A Behind-the-Scenes Look at the Animated Documentary Genre*, Waltham/Oxford: Focal Press.
Kroustallis, V. (2014), "Failure to Think, Failure to Move: Handicapped Reasoning in *Waltz with Bashir*," *Jewish Film & New Media*, 2 (2): 132–52.
Krows, A. E. (1944), "Motion Pictures. Not for Theatres," *Educational Screen*, 23 (2): 70.
Kunert-Graf, R. (2018), "Dehumanized Victims: Analogies and Animal Avatars for Palestinian Suffering in *Waltz with Bashir* and *War Rabbit*," *Humanities*, 7 (79): 1–12.
"La collaborazione di Walt Disney al Centro Cinematografico cattolico" (1946), *L'Osservatore romano*, February 7: 3.
La Luna (2011), [Film] Dir. Enrico Casarosa, US: Pixar.
Land Tilling (*Lavorazione dei terreni*) (1961), [Film] Dir. Giovanni Cecchinato, Italy: OPEC.

Landesman, O. and R. Bendor (2011), "Animated Recollections and Spectatorial Experience in *Waltz with Bashir*," *Animation: An Interdisciplinary Journal*, 6 (3): 1–18.
Landing Accidents (1946), [Film] US: UPA for US Navy.
Lant, A. ([1993] 2006), "Women's Independent Cinema. The Case of Leeds Animation Workshop," in L. Friedman (ed.), *Fires Were Started. British Cinema and Tatcherism*, 159–81, Minneapolis: University of Minnesota.
Last Day of Freedom (2015), [Film] Dir. Nomi Talisman and Dee Hibbert-Jones, US: Living Condition LLC.
Last Hijack (2014), [Film] Dir. Tommy Pallotta and Femke Wolting, Netherlands, Ireland, Germany, Belgium: Submarine, Still Films, Razor Film, Savage Film, Jamal Media, IKON, ZDF.
Last Hijack Interactive (2014), [Web] Dir. Tommy Pallotta and Femke Wolting, Netherlands: Submarine, IKON, Razor Film, ZDF.
Leab, D. J. (2007), *Orwell Subverted. The CIA and the Filming of Animal Farm*, University Park, Pennsylvania: The Pennsylvania State University Press.
Leather Must Last (1945), [Film] Dir. Henry J. Elwis, UK: Dufay-Chromex for MOI.
Lebow, A. (2012), "Introduction," in A. Lebow (ed.), *The Cinema of Me. The Self and Subjectivity in First Person Documentary*, 1–12, London: Wallflower Press.
Lefebvre, T. (2005), "Scientific Films: Europe," in R. Abel (ed.), *Encyclopedia of Early Cinema*, 566–9, Abingdon: Routledge.
Lefebvre, T. (2009), "Les films de propagande sanitaire de Lortac et O'Galop (1918–1919)," *1895. Mille huit cent quatre-vingt-quinze*, 59: 170–83. Available online: https://journals.openedition.org/1895/3925 (accessed March 12, 2019).
Lefèvre, P. (2019), "From Contextualisation to Categorisation of Animated Documentaries," in J. Murray and N. Ehrlich (eds.), *Drawn from Life. Issues and Themes in Animated Documentary Cinema*, 15–30, Edinburgh: Edinburgh University Press.
Lenburg, J. (2006), *Who's Who in Animated Cartoons. An International Guide to Film and Television's Award-Winning and Legendary Animators*, New York: Applause Theatre and Cinema Books.
Leon Schlesinger Presents "Bugs Bunny" (1942), [Film] Dir. Robert Clampett, US: Leon Schlesinger Studios for US Department of the Treasury.
Leonard, M. and R. Strachan (2014), "More than Background. Ambience and Sound-Design in Contemporary Art Documentary Film," in H. Rogers (ed.), *Music and Sound in Documentary Film*, 166–79, Abingdon/New York: Routledge.
Lesjak, D. (2014), *Service with Character. The Disney Studio & World War II*, n. p.: Theme Park Press.
Leskosky, R. J. (2011), "Cartoons Will Win War: World War II Propaganda Shorts," in A. Bowdoin Van Riper (ed.), *Learning from Mickey, Donald and Walt. Essays on Disney's Edutainment Films*, 40–62, Jefferson: McFarland.
Letter from Siberia (*Lettre de Sibérie*, 1958), [Film] Dir. Chris Marker, France: Agros Films, Procinex.
Liberti, F. (2007), "Nomen atque omen. Intervista a Bruno Bozzetto," *Cineforum*, 463: 43–6.

Lida Moser Photographer. Odyssey in Black and White (2017), [Film] Dir. Joyce Borenstein, Canada.
Light and Mankind (1954), [Film] Dir. Willem Van Otterloo, Netherlands: Dollywood for Philips.
Linares, O. (2016), "Interview: Lori Malépart-Traversy on Her Animated Short *Le Clitoris*," Grad/Aperture, October 29. Available online: http://gfmst.concordia.ca/interview-lori-malepart-traversy-on-her-animated-short-le-clitoris/ (accessed January 10, 2020).
Line of Fire (2002), [TV program] History Channel.
Lipkin, S. N. (1999), "Defining Docudrama: *In the Name of the Father*, *Schindler's List*, and *JFK*," in A. Rosenthal (ed.), *Why Docudrama? Fact-Fiction on Film and TV*, 370–83, Carbondale: Southern Illinois University Press.
Lipkin, S. N. (2002), *Real Emotional Logic. Film and Television Docudrama as Persuasive Practice*, Carbondale/Edwardsville: Southern Illinois University Press.
Lipkin, S. N. (2011), *Docudrama Performs the Past. Arenas of Argument in Films Based on True Stories*, Newcastle upon Tyne: Cambridge Scholars Publishing.
Lipkin, S. N., D. Paget, and J. Roscoe (2006), "Docudrama and Mock-Documentary: Defining Terms, Proposing Canons," in G. D. Rhodes and J. P. Springer (eds.), *Docufictions. Essay on the Intersection of Documentary and Fictional Filmmaking*, 11–26. Jefferson: Mc Farland.
Little Deaths (2010), [Film] Dir. Ruth Lingford, US.
Little Voices (*Pequeñas voces*, 2010), [Film] Dir. Jairo Eduardo Carrillo and Oscar Andrade, Colombia: ENNOVVA, RCN CINE, Cahupedillo Cine, Jaguar Taller Digital.
Live and Let Live (1947), [Film] US: for Ætna Casualty & Surety Company.
The Living Circle (1956), [Film] US: John Sutherland Productions for United Fruit Company.
Lloyd, F. (2019), "Making Animation Matter. Peter Sachs Comes to Britain," in M. Malet, R. Dickson, S. MacDougall and A. Nyburg (eds.), *Applied Arts in British Exile from 1933. Changing Visual and Material Culture*, 191–211, Amsterdam: Brill Rodopi.
Local Government. A History in Pictures (1949), [Film] Dir. Peter Sachs and Phil Windebank, UK: Larkins Studio for COI.
Look Who's Driving (1954), [Film] Dir. Bill Hurtz, US: UPA for Ætna Casualty & Surety Company.
Lorenzo Hernández, M. (2010), "A Film of One's Own: The Animated Self-Portraits of Young Contemporary Female Animators," *Animation: an interdisciplinary journal*, 5 (1): 73–90.
Low, R. (1950), *The History of British Film: 1914–1918*, London: Allen & Unwin.
Lubricating Oil's Amazing Molecules/The Inside Story of Lubricating Oil (1949), [Film] US: Jerry Fairbanks Inc. for Standard Oil Company.
Lutz, E. G. (1920), *Animated Cartoons. How They Are Made, Their Origin and Development*, New York: Charles Scribner's Sons.
m.g. (1936), "Dietro lo schermo," *La Stampa*, July 7: 3.
Magic Lab (*Laboratorio magico*, 1962), [Film] Dir. Elio Gagliardo, Italy: Corona Cinematografica.
Magna Carta. The Story of Man's Fight for Liberty (1946), [Film] UK: GB-Animation, GB-Instructional for The British Council.

Make Mine Freedom (1948), [Film] US: John Sutherland Productions for Alfred P. Sloan Foundation.

Maltin, L. ([1980] 1987), *Of Mice and Magic. A History of American Animated Cartoons*, New York: Plume.

Man Alive! (1952), [Film] Dir. William T. Hurtz, US: UPA for American Cancer Society.

Man and Space (*L'uomo e lo spazio*, 1965), [Film] Dir. Roberto and Gino Gavioli, Italy: Gamma Film.

Man and the Moon (1955), [Film] Dir. Ward Kimball, US: Walt Disney Studios.

Man in Flight (1957), [TV program] ABC, March 6.

Man in Space (1956), [Film] Dir. Ward Kimball, US: Walt Disney Studios.

Man on the Land (1951), [Film] Dir. Bill Hurtz, US: UPA for American Petroleum Institute.

The Man Who Is Tall Happy? An Animated Conversation with Noam Chomsky (2013), [Film] Dir. Michel Gondry, France: Partizan Films.

Man with a Movie Camera (*Chelovek s kino-apparatom*, 1929), [Film] Dir. Dziga Vertov, Soviet Union: Vseukrainske Foto Kino Upravlinnia.

Manhattan (1979), [Film] Dir. Woody Allen, US: Joffe Productions.

Manic VR (2018), [Film] Dir. Kalina Bertin, Canada: Eyesteelfilm.

Mansfield, N. J. (2010), "Loss and Mourning: Cinema's Language of Trauma in Waltz with Bashir," *Wide Screen*, 1 (2), June. Available online: http://widescreenjournal.org/index.php/journal/article/view/37/53 (accessed October 13, 2017).

Manvell, R. (1955), *The Film and the Public*, Harmondsworth: Penguin Books.

Manvell, R. (1980), *Art and Animation. The Story of Halas and Batchelor Animation Studio 1940–1980*, London: Tantivy Press.

The Map of Europe (*La carta d'Europa*, 1941), [Film] Dir. Domenico Paolella, Italy: INCOM.

March of the Dinosaurs (2011), [TV program] Dir. Matthew Thompson, ITV, April 25.

Mars and Beyond (1957), [Film] Dir. Ward Kimball, US: Walt Disney Studios.

Martinelli, L. T. (2012), *Il documentario animato. Un nuovo genere di racconto del reale e i suoi protagonisti*, Latina: Tunué.

The Masseuses (*Le massaggiatrici*, 1962), [Film] Dir. Lucio Fulci, Italy, France: Panda Film, Gallus Film.

Masson, E. (2012), *Watch and Learn. Rhetorical Devices in Classroom Films After 1940*, Amsterdam: Amsterdam University Press.

McGrain, E. L. (1956), "How Trade Groups Communicate," *Business Screen Magazine*, 17 (7): 35–45.

McGowan, D. (2019), *Animated Personalities. Cartoon Characters and Stardom in American Theatrical Shorts*, Austin: University of Texas Press.

McKernan, L. (2013), *Charles Urban. Pioneering the Non-Fiction Film in Britain and America, 1897–1925*, Exeter: University of Exeter Press.

McLane, B. A. ([2005] 2012), *A New History of Documentary Film*, New York/London: Continuum.

McLaren's Negatives (2006), [Film] Dir. Marie-Josée Saint-Pierre, Canada: MJSTP Films.

McLean, T. (2014), "Bending Time and Space," *Animation*, 28 (5): 24–6.

McLemore, H. (1964a), "Oscar Awards: Dullest Show on Earth," *Alexandria Daily Town Talk*, April 21: 7.
McLemore, H. (1964b), "Annual Academy Award Is Most Boring Show," *Valley Morning Star*, April 21: 4.
McLemore, H. (1964c), "Looking 'Em Over: He'd Rather See an Old Dog Movie," *Fort Myers News-Press*, April 21: 4-A.
Medusa. Stories of Men on the Bottom (*Medusa. Storia di uomini sul fondo*, 2009), [Film] Dir. Fredo Valla, Italy: Maxman Coop Società Cooperativa, Arealpina Associazione Culturale.
Meet King Joe (1949), [Film] US: John Sutherland Productions for Alfred P. Sloan Foundation.
Megumi (2008), [Film] Dir. Hidetoshi Ômori, Japan: Headquarters for the Abduction Issue.
Men of Merit (A Lantern Lecture) (1948), [Film] Dir. Peter Sachs, UK: Larkins Studio for COI.
Mengoni, A. (2011), "Restituire l'evento allo sguardo. Su *Valzer con Bashir* di Ari Folman," in D. Chimenti, M. Coviello, F. Zucconi (eds.), *Sguardi incrociati. Cinema, testimonianza, memoria nel lavoro teorico di Marco Dinoi*, Rome: Edizioni Fondazione Ente dello Spettacolo.
Mercure (1986), [Film] Dir. Jacques Rouxel and Laurent Bounoure, France: aaa Production for Citroën.
Meteorology (*Meteorologia*, 1965), [Film] Dir. Elio Gagliardo, Italy: Corona Cinematografica.
Metric System (Weights and Measures) (1958), [Film] Dir. G. H. Saraiya, India: Films Division of India.
Metz, C. (1974), *Film Language. A Semiotics of Cinema*, Chicago: Chicago University Press.
"Mickey Mouse and Donald Duck Have Gone to War Too" (1944), *The Daily Courier-Gazette*, July 7: 6.
Mickwitz, N. (2016), *Documentary Comics. Graphic Truth-telling in a Skeptical Age*, Basingstoke/New York: Palgrave Macmillan.
Midgley, C. (1999), "BBC Accused Over Dinosaur Series," *The Times*, October 6: 9.
Mihailova, M. (2019), "Before Sound, There Was Soul: The Role of Animation in Silent Nonfiction Cinema," in J. Murray and N. Ehrlich (eds.), *Drawn from Life. Issues and Themes in Animated Documentary Cinema*, 31–46, Edinburgh: Edinburgh University Press.
Miller, D. (2012), "Transnational Collaborations for Art and Impact in New Documentary Cinema," *Jump Cut. A Review of Contemporary Media*, 54, Fall. Available online: https://www.ejumpcut.org/archive/jc54.2012/DanMillerNewDocs/text.html (accessed May 6, 2018).
Miller, G. (2017), *Studying Waltz with Bashir*, Leighton Buzzard: Auteur Publishing.
Miller, S. (2018), "Real Life Takes Animated Shape," *Los Angeles Times*, November 20.
Minoru: Memory of Exile (1992), [Film] Dir. Michael Fukushima, Canada: NFB.
Mirrors of Time (1991), [Film] Dir. Jean-Jacques Leduc, Canada: NFB.
A Missile Named Mac (1962), [Film] Dir. Carl Urbano, US: John Sutherland Productions for AT&T/Bell System.

Mittell, J. (2001), "Cartoon Realism. Genre Mixing and the Cultural Life of *The Simpsons*," *The Velvet Light Trap*, 47: 15-28.
Model Sorter (1943), [Film] Dir. John Halas and Joy Batchelor, UK: Halas & Batchelor Cartoon Films for MOI.
Modern Guide to Health (1946), [Film] Dir. John Halas and Joy Batchelor, UK: Halas & Batchelor Cartoon Films for COI.
Mollet, T. (2017), *Cartoons in Hard Times. The Animated Shorts of Disney and Warner Brothers in Depression and War, 1932-1945*, London/New York: Bloomsbury.
Money and Steel (1959), [Film] Dir. Robin Cantelon, UK: Merton Park Studios for The British Iron and Steel Federation.
Moore, S. (2013), "Who Said That? The Dispensability of Original Sound in Animated Documentary," *animationstudies 2.0*, April 15. Available online: http://blog.animationstudies.org/?p=169 (accessed July 26, 2018).
Morag, R. (2013), *Waltzing with Bashir. Perpetrator Trauma and Cinema*, London/New York: I.B. Tauris.
More Exports (1947), [Film] Dir. John Halas and Joy Batchelor, UK: Halas & Batchelor Cartoon Films for COI.
More Hanky Panky (1945), [Film] Dir. Henry J. Elwis, UK: Dufay-Chromex for MOI.
More Pigs (1944), [Film] Dir. Laurence Hyde, Canada: NFB.
More Than Meets the Eye (1952), [Film] Dir. Bill Hurtz, US: UPA for CBS.
A Mortal Shock (1950), [Film] UK: Halas & Batchelor Cartoon Films for COI.
Mosconi, E. (1991), "Il film industriale," *Comunicazioni sociali*, 13 (1-2): 61-90.
Mosconi, E. (2003), "*Ludendo docere*. Gli educatori della leggerezza," in G. Bendazzi and R. De Berti (eds.), *La fabbrica dell'animazione. Bruno Bozzetto nell'industria culturale italiana*, 78-86, Milan: Il Castoro.
The Moving Spirit (1953), [Film] Dir. Bob Privett, UK: Halas & Batchelor Cartoon Films for BP.
Multiple Screening (1950), [Film] Dir. David Hilberman and William Tytla, US: Tempo Productions, Communication Materials Center of the Columbia University Press for Pennsylvania Department of Health, Commonwealth of Pennsylvania.
Murphy, M. (2014), "Coloring Real Life with Animation," *New York Times*, November 16: AR18.
Murrain, E. (1952), "Front and Center," *The New York Age*, June 14: 21.
Murray, J. (2019), "Memory Drawn into the Present. *Waltz with Bashir* and the Animated Documentary," in J. Murray and N. Ehrlich (eds.), *Drawn from Life. Issues and Themes in Animated Documentary Cinema*, 172-88, Edinburgh: Edinburgh University Press.
Murray, J. and N. Ehrlich (eds.) (2019), *Drawn from Life. Issues and Themes in Animated Documentary Cinema*, Edinburgh: Edinburgh University Press.
My Grandmother's Lingo (2016), [Web] Dir. Jake Duczynski, Australia: SBS.
My Universe Inside Out (1996), [Film] Dir. Faith Hubley, US: Hubley Studios.
Naked (Bloot, 2006), [TV program] Dir. Mischa Kamp, Netherlands: Submarine.
Nash, K. (2022), *Interactive Documentary. Theory and Debate*, Abingdon/New York: Routledge.

The Nature of Things (1956), [TV program] ABC, October 13–November 1.
Ned Wethered (1983), [Film] Dir. Lee Withmore, Australia: Women's Film Fund.
Neighbours (1952), [Film] Dir. Norman McLaren, Canada: NFB.
Neupert, R. (2011), *French Animation History*, Chicester: Wiley-Blackwell.
Neurath, M. (1946), "Isotype in Films," *Isotype Revisited*. Available online: http://isotyperevisited.org/1946/06/isotype-in-films.html (accessed March 2, 2018).
Never Ending Story (2014), [Film] Korea: M-Line Studio.
Never Like the First Time! (*Aldrig som första gången!*, 2005), [Film] Dir. Jonas Odell, Sweden: FilmTecknarna.
New Behaviors (*Nouveaux comportements*, 1987), [Film] Dir. Jacques Rouxel and Laurent Bounoure, France: aaa Production for Citroën.
"New Documentary Films" (1943), *Documentary News Letter*, 4 (2), February: 181–2, 184.
The New Spirit (1942), [Film] Dir. Wilfred Jackson and Ben Sharpsteen, US: Walt Disney Studios for US Department of Treasury.
The Next Day (2011), [Web] Dir. Jason Gilmore, Canada: NFB, Pop Sandbox.
Nichols, B. (1991), *Representing Reality. Issues and Concepts in Documentary*, Bloomington: Indiana University Press.
Nichols, B. (1994), *Blurred Boundaries. Questions of Meaning in Contemporary Culture*, Bloomington: Indiana University Press.
Nichols, B. ([2001] 2017), *Introduction to Documentary*, Bloomington: Indiana University Press.
Nichols, B. (2016), "Foreword," in D. Marcus and S. Kara (eds.), *Contemporary Documentary*, xi–xvii, Abingdon/New York: Routledge.
Niderost, E. (2014), *Sonnets to Sunspots. Dr. Research Baxter and the Belle Science Films*, Duncan: BearManor Media.
Norden, M. F. (2011), "A Journey Through the Wonderland of Mathematics: Donald in Mathmagic Land," in A. Bowdoin Van Riper (ed.), *Learning from Mickey, Donald and Walt. Essays on Disney's Edutainment Films*, 113–26, Jefferson: McFarland.
"Notes of the Month" (1943), *Documentary News Letter*, 4 (3), March: 186, 194.
Nowhere Line: Voices from Manus Island (2015), [Film] Dir. Lukas Schrank, Australia: Visitor Studio.
O'Flynn, S. (2016), "Designed Experiences in Interactive Documentaries," in D. Marcus and S. Kara (eds.), *Contemporary Documentary*, 72–86, Abingdon/New York: Routledge
O'Pray, M. (2003), *Avant-garde Film. Forms, Themes and Passions*, New York: Columbia University Press.
Oakes, B. (2010), "Building Films for Business. Jamison Handy and the Industrial Animation of the Jam Handy Organization," *Film History*, 22 (1): 95–107.
Odin, R. (1995), "A Semio-Pragmatic Approach to the Documentary Film," in W. Buckland (ed.), *The Film Spectator: Form Sign to Mind*, 227–35, Amsterdam: Amsterdam University Press.
Odin, R. (2004), *Della finzione*, trans. A. Masecchia, Milan: Vita e Pensiero.
Of Stars and Men (1964), [Film] Dir. John Hubley, US: Storyboard Productions.

Ogunleye, F. (2005), "Television Docudrama as Alternative Records of History," *History in Africa*, 32: 479–84.
"Ohio Outlaws and Crockett Mix in Film" (1956), *The Mason City Globe-Gazette*, August 23: 7.
On Your Doorstep (*Sottocasa*, 2010), [Film] Dir. Daniele Baiardini, Giulia Sara Bellunato, Mauro Ciocia, and Clyo Parecchini, Italy: CSC.
One Divided by Two (1998), [Film] Dir. Joyce Borenstein, Canada: NFB.
One of Sixteen Million (1968), [Film] Dir. R. Drew, US: Design Center Incorporated for The Arthritis Foundation.
One Pair of Nostrils (1944), [Film] Dir. Carl Giles, UK: Giles for MOI.
Once upon a Time... Life (*Il était une fois... la vie*, 1986), [TV program] Canal+, FR3.
Once upon a Time... Man (*Il était une fois... l'Homme*, 1978), [TV program] FR3.
Once upon a Time... The Americas (*Il était une fois... les Amériques*, 1991), [TV program] Canal+, FR3.
Once upon a Time... The Discoverers (*Il était une fois... les Découvreurs*, 1994), [TV program] Canal+, FR3.
Once upon a Time... The Explorers (*Il était une fois... les Explorateurs*, 1997), [TV program] Canal+, FR3.
Operation Quality (*Operazione qualità*, 1966), [Film] Dir. Virgilio Tosi, Italy: Clodio Cinematografica.
Origin of Life on Earth (1972), [Film] Dir. Kenneth Horn, Canada: NFB.
The Origins of Weather (1963), [Film] Dir. Joseph Koenig, Canada: NFB.
Orna, B. (1954), "Cartoons," *Films and Filming*, 1 (2), November: 29.
"The Orpheum Theatre" (1918), *Twin Falls Weekly News*, December 2: 5.
Ostherr, K. (2013), *Medical Visions. Producing the Patient through Film, Television, and Imaging Technologies*, New York: Oxford University Press.
Ostherr, K. (2018), "International Animation Aesthetics at the WHO. *To Your Health* (1956) and the Global Film Corpus," in C. Bonah, D. Cantor and A. Laukötter (eds.), *Health Education Films in the Twentieth Century*, 279–303, Rochester: University of Rochester Press.
Our Mr. Sun (1956), [TV program] CBS, November 19.
Our Friend the Atom (1957), [TV program] ABC, January 23.
Page, J. E. (1979), *Seeing Ourselves. Films for Canadian Studies*, Montreal: National Film Board of Canada.
Page, J. E. (1991), "L'Office national du film et les études canadiennes," in D. W. Bidd (ed.), *Le repertoire des films de l'ONF. La production de l'Office National du Canada de 1939 à 1989*, xcix–cxiii, Montreal: L'Office National du Film du Canada.
Paget, D. ([1998] 2011), *No Other Way to Tell It. Docudrama on Film and Television*, Manchester/New York: Manchester University Press.
Paget, D. (2000), "Disclaimers, Denials and Direct Address. Captioning in Docudrama," in J. Izod and R. Kilborn (eds.), *From Grierson to the Docu-soap. Breaking the Boundaries*, 197–208, Luton: University of Luton Press.
Pain (*La douleur*, 1992), [Film] Dir. Jacques Rouxel, France: aaa Production.
The Painters of Prehistory (*I pittori della preistoria*, 1962), [Film] Dir. Elio Gagliardo, Italy: Corona Cinematografica.

Palmer, C. (1990), *The Composer in Hollywood*, London/New York: Marion Boyars Publishers.
Pan-tele-tron (1957), [Film] Dir. Digby Turpin, UK: Pear & Dean for the Philips Company.
Paoletti, M. (2003), "Nota biografica," in G. Bendazzi and R. De Berti (eds.), *La fabbrica dell'animazione. Bruno Bozzetto nell'industria culturale italiana*, 151–2, Milan: Il Castoro.
Paperman (2012), [Film] Dir. John Kahrs, US: Pixar.
Patrick, E. (2004), "Representing Reality: Structural/Conceptual Design in Non-fiction Animation," *Animac Magazine*, 3: 36–47.
Pauwels, L. (2006), "Introduction. The Role of Visual Representation in the Production of Scientific Reality," in L. Pauwels (ed.), *Visual Culture of Science. Rethinking Representational Practices in Knowledge Building and Science Communication*, vii–xix, Hanover: Dartmouth College Press.
Pay Attention to the Label (*Occhio all'etichetta*, 1966), [Film] Dir. Giovanni Cecchinato, Italy: Gamma Film for Montecatini.
Peak Load (1944), [Film] Dir. G. M. Hollering, UK: Film Traders for MOI.
Peaslee, R. M. (2011), "'It's Fine as Long as You Draw, But Don't Film': *Waltz with Bashir* and the Postmodern Function of Animated Documentary," *Visual Communication Quarterly*, 18 (4): 223–35.
Perrett, R. W. (2016), "*Waltz with Bashir* and the Definition of Animated Documentary," *Film and Philosophy*, 20: 106–21.
Petra's Poem (2012), [Film] Dir. Shira Avni, Canada: NFB.
Pfeiffer, O. (2016), "Animating Gallipoli. Leanne Pooley and Matthew Metcalfe on 25 April," *Metro Magazine. Media and Education Magazine*, 188: 90–3.
Phosphorus. Life for the Plants (*Fosforo. Vita per le piante*, 1956), [Film] Dir. Giovanni Cecchinato, Italy: Montecatini.
Physical Fitness and Good Health (1969), [Film] Dir. Less Clark, US: Walt Disney Studios for Upjohn Pharmacy Company.
Picture in Your Mind (1948), [Film] Dir. Philip Stapp, US: Julien Bryan's International Film Foundation.
"Pictures: UAW's Successful Film Sours More Union Prod" (1948), *Variety*, May 12: 17.
Pikadon (1978), [Film] Dir. Renzō and Sayoko Kinoshita, Japan: Studio Lotus.
Pilling, J. (1992), "Introduction," in J. Pilling (ed.), *Women and Animation. A Compendium*, 5–8, London: BFI.
Pilling, J. (ed.) (1992), *Women & Animation: A Compendium*, London: BFI.
Pinocchio (1940), [Film] Dir. Hamilton Luske and Ben Sharpsteen, US: Walt Disney Studios.
The Pioneers (*I pionieri*, 1940), [Film] Dir. Gianni Franciolini, Italy: INCOM.
Piping Hot (1959), [Film] Dir. John Halas, UK: Halas & Batchelor Cartoon Films for Gas Council.
Planet Dinosaur (2011), [TV program] BBC, September 14–October 19.
Planning for Good Eating (1946), [Film] Dir. Gerry Geronimi, US: Walt Disney Studios for OCIAA.
The Plant of the Senses (*La centrale dei sensi*, 1961), [Film] Dir. Gibba, Italy: Corona Cinematografica.

"Platable Facts for Investors" (1957), *Business Screen Magazine*, 18 (5): 41.
Play Safe (1978), [Film] Dir. David Eady, UK: Antony Barrier Productions for the Electricity Council.
Point Rationing of Foods (1943), [Film] Dir. Chuck Jones, US: Leon Schlesinger Unit for Office of War Information.
The Polar Express (2004), [Film] Dir. Robert Zemeckis, US: Castle Rock Entertainment.
Pollone, M. and V. Sclaverani (2014), "Intervista a Bruno Bozzetto," *Mondo Niovo*, 49 (96).
Polonsky, B. (1969), "Animation NFB. An 'Inview' into the Animation Department of the National Film Board," *The Review*, November 7: 3–4.
Population Explosion (1968), [Film] Dir. Pierre Hébert, Canada: NFB.
Position Firing (1944), [Film] Dir. John Hubley and Chuck Jones, US: FMPU.
Posner, M. (2012), "Communicating Disease. Tuberculosis, Narrative, and Social Order in Thomas Edison's Red Cross Seal Films," in D. Oregon, M. Oregon and D. Streible (eds.), *Learning with the Lights Off. Educational Film in the United States*, 90–106, New York: Oxford University Press.
Power to Fly (1954), [Film] Dir. Bob Privett, UK: Halas & Batchelor Cartoon Films for BP.
Prelinger, R. (2006), *The Field Guide to Sponsored Films*, San Francisco: National Film Preservation Foundation.
Prelinger, R. (2009), "Eccentricity, Education and the Evolution of Corporate Speech. Jam Handy and His Organization," in V. Hediger and P. Vonderau (eds.), *Films That Work. Industrial Film and the Productivity of Media*, 211–20, Amsterdam: Amsterdam University Press.
Preserved Voices (*Liu sheng*, 2004), [Film] Dir. Zhou Tingting, China.
Price, H. (2019), ""A Very Flexible Medium": The Ministry of Information and Animated Propaganda Films on the Home Front," in M. Cook and K. Thompson (eds.), *Animation and Advertising*, 145–60, Cham: Palgrave Macmillan.
A Prison (*Una prigione*, 1940), [Film] Italy: INCOM.
Productivity (*Productivité*, 1951), [Film] Dir. Jacques Asséo, France: Les Gémeaux for US Economic Cooperation Administration.
"Progress Through Science" (1948), *Business Screen Magazine*, 9 (7): 35–6.
Propagation (1960), [Film] Dir. René Jodoin, Canada: NFB.
Providing Goods for You (1944), [Film] Dir. Philip Ragan, Canada: NFB.
Psychology of Color (*Psicologia del colore*, 1965), [Film] Dir. Rodolfo Besesti and Elio Gagliardo, Italy: Corona Cinematografica.
Public Threat n. 1. Life and Mishaps of the Koch Bacillus (*Il pericolo pubblico n. 1. Vita e misfatti del bacillo di Koch*, 1938), [Film] Dir. Liberio Pensuti and Ugo Amadoro, Italy: Istituto Luce for Federazione Italiana Nazionale Fascista per la Lotta alla Tubercolosi.
Pulling, J. (1972), "Animator's Cartoons Have Selling Power," *The Leader-Post*, July 24: 13.
Pump Trouble (1954), [Film] Dir. Gene Deitch, US: UPA for American Heart Association.
Q&A (2010), [Film] Dir. Mike and Tim Rauch, US: Rauch Brothers Animation Inc.
Quark (1981–94), [TV program] RAI.

Quark Economy (*Quark Economia*, 1986), [TV program] RAI.
Rampton, J. (1999), "The Missing Link," *The Independent*, October 8: 47.
Rastegar, K. (2015), "'Sawwaru Waynkum?" Human Rights and Social Trauma in *Waltz with Bashir*," *College Literature*, 40 (3), Summer: 60–80.
Reason and Emotion (1943), [Film] Dir. Bill Roberts, US: Walt Disney Studios.
Referee (1976), [Film] UK: World Wide Picture for COI.
Refining (1983), [Film] Dir. Denis Gilpin, UK: Larkins Studio for BP.
Refrigeration: Principles of Mechanical Refrigeration (1964), [Film] US: D4 Film Studios for US Air Force.
Renaissance Today (*Risorgimento oggi*, 1962), [Film] Dir. Michele Gandin and Giambattista Cavallaro, Italy: Comitato per le Celebrazioni bolognesi per l'Unità d'Italia.
Renov, M. (1993), "Towards a Poetics of Documentary," in M. Renov (ed.), *Theorizing Documentary*, 12–36, New York: Routledge.
Renov, M. (2002), "Animation: Documentary's Imaginary Signifier," Paper presented at Visible Evidence Conference X, Marseilles, France, December.
Renov, M. (2008), "First-person Films: Some Theses on Self-inscription," in T. Austin and W. De Jong (eds.), *Rethinking Documentary: New Perspectives, New Practices*, 39–50, Berkshire: Open University Press.
Revolving Door (2007), [Film] Dir. Alexandra and David Beesley, Australia: Beeworld Pyt Ltd.
Rhapsody of Steel (1959), [Film] Dir. Carl Urbano, US: John Sutherland Productions for US Steel.
Rhodes, G. D. and J. P. Springer (2006), "Introduction," in G. D. Rhodes and J. P. Springer (eds.), *Docufictions: Essay on the Intersection of Documentary and Fictional Filmmaking*, 1–9, Jefferson: Mc Farland & Company Publishers.
Riches of the Earth (1954), [Film] Dir. Colin Low, Canada: NFB.
River of Steel (1951), [Film] Dir. Peter Sachs, UK: Larkins Studio for British Iron and Steel Federation.
The Road Home (2013), [Film] Dir. Mike and Tim Rauch, US: Rauch Brothers Animation Inc.
The Road of Health (1936), [Film] Dir. Brian Salt, UK: Gaumont-British Instructional for The British Social Hygiene Council.
Robinson Charley (1948), [Film] Dir. John Halas and Joy Batchelor, UK: Halas & Batchelor Cartoon Films for COI.
Rodney (1950), [Film] Dir. Lu Guarnier, US: Film Graphic Inc. for the National Tuberculosis Association.
The Romance of Transportation in Canada (1952), [Film] Dir. Colin Low, Canada: NFB.
Rome and Carthage (*Roma e Cartagine*, 1941), [Film] Dir. Liberio Pensuti, Italy: INCOM.
Rondolino, G. (2003), *Storia del cinema d'animazione. Dalla lanterna magica a Walt Disney, da Tex Avery a Steven Spielberg*, Turin: UTET.
Roscoe, J. and C. Hight (2001), *Faking It. Mock-documentary and the Subversion of Factuality*, Manchester: Manchester University Press.
Rosenthal, N. (1966), "Disney, the Teacher," *The Age*, December 20: 4.
Ross, W. (1959), "Motion Pictures Worth 10,000 Lives. The Story of the Film Program of the American Cancer Society," *Business Screen Magazine*, 20 (2): 28–31.

Rosser, E. (1977), "Saul Bass," *Cinema Papers*, 11, January: 238-9.
Rotha, P. (1946), "The Film and Other Visual Techniques in Education," *The Museums Journal*, 46 (8): 141-5.
Rouxel, J. (1994), "Le cinéma d'animation," in A. Martinet (ed.), *Le cinéma et la science*, Paris: CNRS éditions.
Rowley, S. (2005), "Life Reproduced in Drawings. Preliminary Comments upon Realism in Animation," *Animation Journal*, 13: 65-85.
Rozenkrantz, J. (2011), "Colourful Claims. Towards a Theory of Animated Documentary," *Film International*, May 6. Available online: http://filmint.nu/?p=1809 (accessed September 5, 2017).
Ryan (2004), [Film] Dir. Chris Landreth, Canada: Copperheart Entertainment, NFB.
"*Ryan* and *Alter Egos*" (2005), *Cinema Scope*, 21, Winter: 50.
Rythmetic (1956), [Film] Dir. Norman McLaren and Evelyn Lambart, Canada: NFB.
Sachleben, M. and K. M. Yenerall (2004), *Seeing the Bigger Picture. Understanding Politics Through Film and Television*, New York: Peter Lang Publishing.
Safe as Houses (1983), [Film] Dir. David Eady, UK: Antony Barrier Productions for the Electricity Council.
The Safe House (2006), [Film] Dir. Lee Withmore, Australia: Film Australia.
"Safety Film Offers New Insight on Accidents" (1954), *Valley Times*, February 3: 15.
Sales Promotion. The Key to Efficiency (1953), [Film] Dir. Bob Privett and Digby Turpin, UK: Allan Crick Productions for BP.
Salvage Saves Shipping (1943), [Film] Dir. G. M. Hollering, UK: Film Traders for MOI.
Sammond, N. (2005), *Babes in Tomorrowland: Walt Disney and the Making of the American Child, 1930-1960*, Durham: Duke University Press.
Samouni Road (*La strada dei Samouni*, 2018), [Film] Dir. Stefano Savona, France, Italy: Dugon Production, Picofilms, Alter Ego Production.
Saludos Amigos (1942), [Film] Dir. Norman Ferguson, US: Walt Disney Studios.
Samuel de Champlain (1964), [Film] Dir. Denys Arcand, Canada: NFB.
Sappy Homiens (1956), [Film] Dir. Leo Salkin, US: UPA for American Cancer Society.
Satellites of the Sun (1974), [Film] Dir. Sidney Goldsmith, Canada: NFB.
Schlunke, K. (2011), "Animated Documentary and the Scene of Death. Experiencing *Waltz with Bashir*," *South Atlantic Quarterly*, 110 (4), Fall: 949-62.
Schneider, S. (1988), *That's All Folks! The Art of Warner Bros. Animation*, New York: Henry Holt and Company, Inc.
Science Please! (1998-2001), [Film] Canada: NFB.
Scott, K (2001), *The Moose that Roared. The Story of Jay Ward, Bill Scott, a Flying Squirrel and a Talking Moose*, New York: Thomas Dunne Books.
Scott, K. D. and A. M. White (2003), "Unnatural History? Deconstructing the *Walking with Dinosaurs* Phenomenon," *Media, Culture & Society*, 25 (3): 315-32.
Scrimitore, R. (2013), *Le origini dell'animazione italiana. La storia, gli autori e i film animati in Italia 1911-1949*, Latina: Tunué.

Scrivener, L. (2011), "Drawing Hope from Despair," *Toronto Star*, May 1: IN.3.
Seeking Refuge (2012), [TV program] BBC2, June 18–24.
Segrave, K. (2004), *Product Placement in Hollywood Films. A History*. Jefferson: McFarland.
Sexy Africa (*Africa Sexy*, 1963), [Film] Dir. Roberto Bianchi Montero, Italy: Cine-Produzioni Associate.
Shale, R. (1982), *Donald Duck Joins Up. The Walt Disney Studios During World War II*. Ann Arbor: UMI Research Press.
"The Short Parade" (1960), *Motion Picture Exhibitor*, 64 (3), June 8: 4711.
A Short History of the Highrise (2013), [Web] Dir. Katerina Cizek, US, Canada: NFB, *The New York Times*.
Shull, M. S. and D. E. Wilt, (2004) *Doing Their Bit. Wartime American Animated Short Films 1939-1945*, Jefferson: McFarland & Company, Inc.
Sibley, B. (1998), "The Medium," in B. Sibley and P. Lord, *Creating 3D Animation. The Aardman Book of Filmmaking*, 14–61, New York: Harry N. Abrams, Inc.
Silence (1998), [Film] Dir. Sylvie Bringas and Orly Yadin, UK: Halo Productions.
The Singing Princess (*La rosa di Bagdad*, 1949), [Film] Dir. Anton Gino Domeneghini, Italy: IMA Film.
The Sinking of the Lusitania (1918), [Film] Dir. Winsor McCay, US: Jewel Productions.
Skoller, J. (2011), "Making It (Un)real. Contemporary Theories and Practices in Documentary Animation," *Animation: An Interdisciplinary Journal*, 6 (3): 207–14.
Sleepless (2016), [Film] Dir. Ellie Land, UK: Silent Signal.
"Sloan Foundation Tells Cancer Research Progress" (1955), *Business Screen Magazine*, 16 (1): 122–23.
The Slum Has to Be Conquered (*Le taudis doit être vaincu*, 1918), [Film] Dir. Lortac, France: Pathé.
The Small, Tragic Circus of So-and-so (*Le petit cirque tragique des untels*, 1993), [Film] Dir. Laurent Bounoure and Jacques Rouxel, France: aaa Production for LFSM.
Smith, D. R. (2016), "They're Following Our Script. Disney's TV Trip to Tomorrowland," in D. Koihenschulte (ed.), *The Walt Disney Film Archives. The Animated Movies 1921-1968*, 486–98, Hohenzollernring: Taschen.
Smoodin, E. (1993), *Animating Culture. Hollywood Cartoons from the Sound Era*, New Brunswick: Rutgers University.
Snack and Drink (1999), [Film] Dir. Bob Sabiston, US: Flat Black Films.
Snow White and the Seven Dwarfs (1937), [Film] Dir. David Hand, US: Walt Disney Studios.
So Much for So Little (1949), [Film] Dir. Chuck Jones, US: Warner Brothers for the US Public Health Service.
The Social Side of Health (1969), [Film] Dir. Les Clark, US: Walt Disney Studios for Upjohn Pharmacy Company.
Sofian, S. M. (2019), "Creative Challenges in the Production of Documentary Animation," in J. Murray and N. Ehrlich (eds.), *Drawn from Life. Issues and Themes in Animated Documentary Cinema*, 221–34, Edinburgh: Edinburgh University Press.
The Soil Is Hungry (*La terra ha fame*, 1961), [Film] Dir. Giovanni Cecchinato, Italy: Montecatini.

Solbrig, H. (2012), "Dr. ERPI Finds His Voice. Electrical Research Products, Inc. and the Educational Film Market, 1927-1937," in D. Oregon, M. Oregon and D. Streible (eds.), *Learning with the Lights Off. Educational Film in the United States*, 193-214, New York: Oxford University Press.

"Solo con l'animazione posso ricordare l'orrore di Sabra e Shatila" (2008), *Liberazione*, May 16: 15.

Something You Didn't Eat (1945a), [Film] Dir. James Algar, US: Walt Disney Studios for US Department of Agriculture.

Something You Didn't Eat (1945b), *The Film Daily*, 87 (126), June 29: 11.

Sorlin, P. (2013), "Italy," in I. Aitken (ed.), *The Concise Routledge Encyclopedia of the Documentary Film*, 422-30, Abingdon/New York: Routledge.

Southall, J. (1999), "Cartoon Propaganda and the British School of Animation," *Animation Journal*, 8 (1): 74-87.

Spare a Thought (1978), [Film] UK: Doron Abrahami for Christian Aid and Oxfam.

A Spark in Time on the Firing Line (1962), [Film] US: Portafilms for Champion.

"Speaking to America. The Expanding Audiovisual Service Program of the Chamber of Commerce of the United States" (1957), *Business Screen Magazine*, 18 (2): 37-9, 63.

The Specific Gravity (Il peso specifico, 1966), [Film] Dir. Rodolfo Besesti, Italy: Corona Cinematografica.

Speed the Plough (1956), [Film] Dir. Bob Privett, UK: Halas & Batchelor Cartoon Films for BP.

"Standard Oil Movie Shows Manufacture of Lubricants" (1949), *The Hammond Times*, August 22: 12.

Stanley Takes a Trip (1947), [Film] Dir. Jim MacKay and Grant Murno, Canada: NFB for Department of National Health and Welfare.

Starlife (1983), [Film] Dir. Sidney Goldsmith, Canada: NFB.

Steps Towards Maturity and Health (1968), [Film] Dir. Les Clark, US: Walt Disney Studios for Upjohn Pharmacy Company.

Stewart, G. (2010), "Screen Memory in *Waltz with Bashir*," *Film Quarterly*, 63 (3): 58-62.

Stewart, J. (2014), "Artist, Writer and Animator," in V. Halas (ed.), *A Moving Image. Joy Batchelor 1914-91. Artist, Writer and Animator*, 7-21, London: Southbank Publishing.

Stitch and Save (1943), [Film] Dir. Jim MacKay, Canada: NFB.

Stop That Tank! (1942), [Film] Dir. Ub Iwerks, Canada, US: NFB, Walt Disney Studios.

A Story About Breadmaking in the Year 1255 A.D. (1948), [Film] Dir. Robert Verrall, Canada: NFB.

Story of a Rescue (Histoire d'un sauvetage, 1949), [Film] Dir. Jacques Asséo, France: Les Gémeaux for US Economic Cooperation Administration.

The Story of Creative Capital (1957), [Film] Dir. Carl Urbano, US: John Sutherland Productions in cooperation with E.I. du Pont de Nemours & Company for the Chamber of Commerce of the United States.

The Story of Light (1954), [Film] Dir. Joop Geesink, Netherlands, US: Dollywood, Transfilm for General Electric.

The Story of Menstruation (1946), [Film] Dir. Jack Kinney, US: Walt Disney Studios for International Cellucotton Company.

The Story of Oil (1955), [Film] Dir. Les Clark, US: Walt Disney Studios for Richfield Oil Corporation.
"Story of Oil. Richfield Shows Its Past and Future in Dramatic, Entertaining Exhibit" (1955), *Business Screen Magazine,* 16 (6): 5A–6A.
The Story of Time (1951), [Film] Dir. Michael Stainer-Hutchins, UK: Signal Films for Rolex.
The Strange Case of the Cosmic Rays (1957), [TV program] CBS, October 25.
Strøm, G. (2003), "The Animated Documentary," *Animation Journal,* 11: 46-63.
Strøm, G. (2015), "Animated Documentary," *Studies in Documentary Film,* 9 (1): 92–4.
The Structure of Unions (1955), [Film] Dir. Morten Parker, Canada: NFB for Canadian and Catholic Confederation of Labor, Canadian Congress of Labor, Trades and Labor Congress of Canada, Department of Labor.
Sung, K. (2017), "When Animation Meets Historical Taboo. Remembrance Through the Depiction of Comfort Women in Korean Animated Documentary," *Imago. Studi di cinema,* 16: 107-18.
Sunrise Over Tiananmen Square (1998), [Film] Dir. Shui-Bo Wang, Canada: NFB.
Super Natural Gas (1975), [Film] Dir. Nick Spargo, UK: Nicholas Cartoon Films Ltd. for the British Gas Corporation.
Survivors (1997), [Film] Dir. Sheila Sofian, US.
T for Teacher (1947), [Film] Dir. Peter Sachs, UK: Larkins Studio for Tea Bureau.
A Tale of Mail (1966), [Film] Dir. Donald Stearn and William Canning, Canada: NFB.
Tapum! The History of Arms (*La storia delle armi,* 1958), [Film] Dir. Bruno Bozzetto, Italy: Bruno Bozzetto Film.
The Tavern of Tuberculosis (*La taverna del tibbicì,* 1935), [Film] Dir. Lamberto Ristori, Italy: SICED for Federazione Italiana Nazionale Fascista per la Lotta alla Tuberculosi.
Tax: The Outcome of Income (1975), [Film] Dir. Veronika Soul, Canada: NFB.
Taylor, P. M. ([1990] 2003), *Munitions of the Mind. A History of Propaganda from the Ancient World to the Present Day,* Manchester/New York: Manchester University Press.
"Teacher Disney" (1942), *Time,* 40 (7), August 17.
Tear (2015), [Film] Korea.
Teeth Are to Keep (1949), [Film] Dir. Jim MacKay, Canada: NFB for Department of National Health and Welfare.
Ten: The Magic Number (1973), [Film] Dir. Barrie Nelson, Canada: NFB.
"The John Halas Story. Innovator in Animation" (1964), *Business Screen Magazine,* 25 (2): 42–3.
There Once Lived... Five Stories of Real People (жили I были. Пять историй реальных людей, 2017), [Web] Russia: Takie Dela.
Think of the Future (1956), [Film] Dir. John Halas, UK: Halas & Batchelor Cartoon Films for European Productivity Agency of O.E.E.C.
The Thinker? (1981), [Film] Dir. A. R. Sen, India: Films Division of India.
The Thinking Machine (1968), [Film] Dir. Henry R. Feinberg, US: Bell Telephone Laboratories.
A Thousand Million Years (1954), [Film] Dir. Colin Low, Canada: NFB.
Three Blind Mice (1945), [Film] Dir. George Dunning, Canada: NFB.
The Thrifty Pig (1941), [Film] Dir. Ford Beebe, Canada: NFB, Walt Disney Studios.

Time and Terrain (*Le temps et la Terre*, 1948), [Film] Dir. Colin Low, Canada: NFB.
Tinwell, A. (2015), *The Uncanny Valley in Games and Animation*, Boca Raton: CRC Press.
To Demonstrate How Spiders Fly (1909), [Film] Dir. Percy Smith, UK: Kineto.
To Resist Tuberculosis, Stay Strong (*Pour resister à la tuberculouse, soyons fort*, 1918), [Film] Dir. Lortac, France: Pathé.
To Save These Lives (1949), [Film] Dir. David Hilberman, US: Tempo Productions for the American Cancer Society.
To Your Health (1956), [Film] Dir. Philip Stapp, UK: Halas & Batchelor Cartoon Films for WHO.
Toccata for Toy Trains (1957), [Film] Dir. Charles and Ray Eames, US: Office of Charles & Ray Eames.
Tombolino's Hygiene (*L'igiene di Tombolino*, 1935 ca.), [Film] Dir. Luigi Liberio Pensuti, Italy: SICED.
Tombstone Canyon (1945), [Film] Dir. Henry J. Elwis, UK: Dufay-Chromex for MOI.
Toot, Whistle, Plunk and Boom (1953), [Film] Dir. Ward Kimball and Charles A. Nichols, US: Walt Disney Studios.
Torre, D. (2017), *Animation. Process, Cognition and Actuality*, New York/London: Bloomsbury.
Tower (2016), [Film] Dir. Keith Maitland, US: Go-Valley, ITVS.
The Trade Machine (1968), [Film] Dir. Gerald Potterton, Canada: Potterton Productions.
Trade Tatoo (1937), [Film] Dir. Len Lye, UK: GPO Film Unit.
"Traffic Safety Comic Strip Series Starts in This Issue" (1954), *The San Saba News and Star*, October 14: 8.
The Traitor Within (1946), [Film] Dir. George Gordon, US: John Sutherland Productions for The American Cancer Society.
The Trouble with Love and Sex (2012), [TV program] BBC, May 11.
The True Face of England. Facts and Mishaps of the English Domain in the World (*Il vero volto dell'Inghilterra. Fatti e misfatti del dominio inglese nel mondo*, 1940), [Film] Dir. Domenico Paolella, Italy: INCOM.
Truth Has Fallen (2013), [Film] Dir. Sheila Sofian, US.
Tuberculosis (1945), [Film] Dir. Jim Algar, US: Walt Disney Studios for OCIAA.
Tupicoff, D. (2005), "Radio with Pictures (Thousands of Them): *His Mother's Voice*," *Cartoons. The International Journal of Animation*, 1 (1): 11–3.
Turboglide (1958), [Film] US: Jam Hardy Organization for Chevrolet.
Two Breaths to... (1979), [Film] Dir. George Gordon, US: Hanna-Barbera Productions for US Department of Energy.
Two Populaces, a War (*Due popoli, una guerra*, 1941), [Film] Dir. Ugo Amadoro, Italy: INCOM.
Tying Your Own Shoes (2009), [Film] Dir. Shira Avni, Canada: NFB.
The Unchained Goddess (1958), [TV program] CBS, February 12.
Understanding Stress and Strains (1968), [Film] Dir. Hamilton S. Luske, US: Walt Disney Studios for Upjohn Pharmacy Company.
Understanding Alcohol. Use and Abuse (1979), [Film] Dir. John Ewing and Sam Harvey, US: Walt Disney Studios for Upjohn Pharmacy Company.

Universe (1960), [Film] Dir. Roman Kroitor and Colin Low, Canada: NFB.
The Unseen Enemy (1945), [Film] Dir. Bill Roberts, US: Walt Disney Studios for OCIAA.
van Dijck, J. (2006), "Picturizing Science. The Science Documentary as Multimedia Spectacle," *International Journal of Cultural Studies*, 9 (1): 5–24.
Van Riper, A. B. (2011), "The Promise of Things to Come. Disneyland and the Wonders of Technology, 1954–58," in A. Bowdoin Van Riper (ed.), *Learning from Mickey, Donald and Walt. Essays on Disney's Edutainment Films*, 84–102, Jefferson: McFarland.
VD Attack Plan (1973), [Film] Dir. Les Clark, US: Walt Disney Studios.
Velin, J. (2009), "A Growing Cross-Genre," *DOX. Documentary Film Magazine*, 81: 14–5.
Verger, M. (2010), "Le donne nell'animazione italiana," in M. Tortora (ed.), *Le donne nel cinema d'animazione*, 95–114, Latina: Tunué.
Veronesi, L. (1948), "Cinema a passo ridotto: il documentario," *Ferrania. Rivista mensile di fotografia, cinematografia e arti figurative*, 2 (12): 31.
Victory Through Air Power (1943), [Film] Dir. Henry C. Potter, Clyde Geronimi, Jack Kinney, and James Algar, US: Walt Disney Studios.
Viljoen, J.-M. (2013), "Representing the "Unrepresentable": The Unpredictable Life of Memory and Experience in *Waltz with Bashir*," *Scrutiny2*, 18 (2): 66–80.
Viljoen, J.-M. (2014), "*Waltz with Bashir*: Between Representation and Experience," *South-North Cultural and Media Studies*, 28 (1): 40–50.
Virus Tropical (2017), [Film] Dir. Santiago Caicedo, Colombia: Timbo Estudio, Ikki Films.
Voci, P. (2010), *China on Video. Smaller-screen Realities*, Oxon/New York: Routledge.
Voting for Servicemen Overseas (1944), [Film] US: Walt Disney Studios.
Waiting for Superman (2010), [Film] Dir. Davis Guggenheim, US: Electric Kinney.
Wald, M. (1957), "1956's Short Documentaries Indicate that Their Social Utility Is at Last Recognized in the US," *Film in Review*, 8 (4): 166–70.
Walking with Beasts (2001), [TV program] BBC, November 15–December 21.
Walking with Caveman (2003), [TV program] BBC, March 27–April 23.
Walking with Dinosaurs (1999), [TV program] BBC, October 4–November 8.
Walking with Monsters–Life Before Dinosaurs (2005), [TV program] BBC, November 5–December 19.
"Walt Disney Free Nature Movies at CI" (1959), *The Daily Republican*, March 16: 6.
"Walt Disney, Teacher of Tomorrow" (1945), *Look*, April 17: 23–7.
Waltz with Bashir (*Vals Im Bashir*, 2008), [Film] Dir. Ari Folman, Israel, France and Germany: Brigid Folman Film Gang, Les Films d'Ici, Razor Film Produktion Gmbh.
War Front (*Fronte di guerra*, 1940), [Film] Dir. Vittorio Gallo, Italy: INCOM.
The War Game (1965), [Film] Dir. Peter Watkins, UK: BBC.
The War that Never Ends (1949), [Film] Dir. Myna Johnson, India: Films Division of India.
Ward, P. (2005), *Documentary. The Margins of Reality*, London: Wallflower.
Ward, P. (2006), "Animated Interactions. Animation Aesthetics and the World of the "Interactive" Documentary," in S. Buchan (ed.), *Animated Worlds*, 113–29, Eastleigh: John Libbey.

Ward, P. (2008), "Animated Realities. The Animated Film, Documentary, Realism," *Reconstruction*, 8 (2). Available online: http://reconstruction.eserver.org/Issues/082/ward.shtml (accessed March 2, 2016).

Ward, P. (2011), "Animating with Facts. The Performative Process of Documentary Animation in *the ten mark* (2010)," *Animation: An Interdisciplinary Journal*, 6 (3): 293–305.

Warren, K. (2010), "Animation, Representation and the Power of the Personal Story: *Persepolis*," *Screen Education*, 58: 117–23.

Watch the Fuel Watcher (1946), [Film] UK: Halas & Batchelor Cartoon Films for COI.

Water, Friend or Enemy (1943), [Film] Dir. Norm Wright, US: Walt Disney Studios for OCIAA.

Water Hammers (*Colpi d'ariete*, 1940), [Film] Dir. Liberio Pensuti, Italy: INCOM for Federazione Italiana Nazionale Fascista per la Lotta alla Tubercolosi.

Weapon of War (1944), [Film] US: FMPU, MGM.

Wells, P. (1995), "Dustbins, Democracy and Defence. Halas and Batchelor and the Animated Film in Britain 1940–1947," in P. Kirkham and D. Thoms (eds.), *War Culture. Social Change and Changing Experience in World War Two*, 61–72, London: Lawrence & Wishart Ltd.

Wells, P. ([1996] 2011), "The Language of Animation," in J. Nelmes (ed.), *Introduction to Film Studies*, 229–60, London/New York: Routledge.

Wells, P. (1997), "The Beautiful Village and the True Village. A Consideration of Animation and Documentary Aesthetic," in P. Wells (ed.), *Art and Animation*, 40–5, London: Academy Editions.

Wells, P. (1998), *Understanding Animation*, London/New York: Routledge.

Wells, P. (2006), "From the Wildest Fantasy to the Coldest Fact," in V. Halas and P. Wells (eds.), *Halas & Batchelor Cartoons. An Animated History*, 157–79, London: Southbank Publishing.

Wells, P. (2014), "Joy, Britain Needs You," in V. Halas (ed.), *A Moving Image. Joy Batchelor 1914–91. Artist, Writer and Animator*, 59–78, London: Southbank Publishing.

Wells, P. (2016), "Writing Animated Documentary: A Theory of Practice," *International Journal of Film and Media Arts*, 1 (1): 6–18.

Wells, P. (2019), "Never Mind the Bollackers. Here's the Repositories, Sites and Archives in Nonfiction Animation," in J. Murray and N. Ehrlich (eds.), *Drawn from Life. Issues and Themes in Animated Documentary Cinema*, 106–25, Edinburgh: Edinburgh University Press.

We've Come a Long Way (1952), [Film] Dir. Allan Crick and Bob Privett, UK: Halas & Batchelor Cartoon Films for BP.

What Makes Us Tick (1952), [Film] Dir. Carl Urbano, US: John Sutherland Productions for New York Stock Exchange.

What's Blood Got to Do with It? (2004), [Film] Dir. Andy Glynne, UK: Mosaic Films for National Blood Service.

Why Man Creates (1968), [Film] Dir. Saul Bass, US: Saul Bass & Associates for Kaiser Aluminum.

Why Play Leap Frog? (1949), [Film] US: John Sutherland Productions for Alfred P. Sloan Foundation.

Williams, L. (1993), "Mirrors without Memories: Truth, History, and the New Documentary," *Film Quarterly*, 46 (3): 9–21.

The Winged Scourge (1943), [Film] Dir. Bill Roberts, US: Walt Disney Studios for OCIAA.
Winston, B. (2008), *Claiming the Real II. Documentary. Grierson and Beyond*, London: BFI.
Winston, B. (2013), "Introduction. The Documentary Film," in B. Winston (ed.), *The Documentary Film Book*, 1–29, London: BFI.
Wintonick, P. (2013), "New Platforms for Docmedia: 'Varient of a Manifesto'," in B. Winston (ed.), *The Documentary Film Book*, 376–82, London: BFI.
Without Fear (1952), [Film] Dir. Peter Sachs, UK: Larkins Studio for US Economic Cooperation Administration.
Wolfe, C. (1997), "Historicizing the "Voice-of-God": The Place of Vocal Narration in Classical Documentary," *Film History*, 9 (2): 149–67.
"The Woman's Viewpoint on Investments" (1963), *Business Screen Magazine*, 23 (8): 39–40.
Wood, A. (2007), *Digital Encounters*, Abingdon: Routledge.
Woodhead, L. (1999), "The Guardian Lecture. Dramatized Documentary," in A. Rosenthal (ed.), *Why Docudrama? Fact-Fiction on Film and TV*, 101–10, Carbondale: Southern Illinois University Press.
Woolly Mammoth (1979), [Film] Dir. Bill Maylone, Canada: NFB.
Wop May (1979), [Film] Dir. Blake James, Canada: NFB.
Working Dollars (1957), [Film] Dir. Carl Urbano, US: John Sutherland Productions for New York Stock Exchange.
A World Is Born (1955), [Film] US: Walt Disney Studios.
Wright, J. K. (2019), *They Shot, He Scored. The Life and Music of Eldon Rathburn*, Montreal: McGill-Queen's University Press.
Wurtzler, S. J. (2007), *Electric Sounds. Technological Change and the Rise of Corporate Mass Media*, New York: Columbia University Press.
Yankee Dood It (1956), [Film] Dir. Friz Freleng, US: Warner Brothers for Alfred P. Sloan Foundation.
Yosef, R. (2010), "War Fantasies. Memory, Trauma, and Ethics in Ari Folman's *Waltz with Bashir*," *Journal of Modern Jewish Studies*, 9 (3): 311–26.
You and Your... (1955–7), [TV program] ABC, October 20–October 3.
You and Your Health (1979), [Film] Dir. Harley Jones, UK: Welsh Association of Community Health Councils.
You Can Be Safe from X-Rays (1951), [Film] US: Communicable Disease Center for Federal Security Agency.
Your Very Good Health (1947), [Film] Dir. John Halas and Joy Batchelor, UK: Halas & Batchelor Cartoon Films for COI.
Zane, M. (1998), *Scatola a sorpresa. La Gamma Film di Roberto Gavioli e la comunicazione audiovisiva in Italia da Carosello ad oggi*, Milan: Jaca Book.
Zangrando, F. (1968), "Ombre italiane. Storia dei disegni e pupazzi animati," *Quaderni dell'Osservatore*, 2: 5–61.
Zanotto, P. and F. Zangrando (1973), *L'Italia di cartone*, Padova: Liviana.
Zimmermann, Y. (2009), ""What Hollywood Is to America, the Corporate Film Is to Switzerland." Remarks on Industrial Film as Utility Film," in V. Hediger and P. Vonderau (eds.), *Films that Work. Industrial Film and the Productivity of Media*, 101–17, Amsterdam: Amsterdam University Press.

INDEX

aaa Production 249
Aardman Animations 39, 120
ABC of Hand Tools, The (1946) 141, 153, 157
ABC of Internal Combustion, The (1948) 141, 145–6, 149
ABC of Internal Combustion Engines. The Automobile Engine, The (1948) 141, 145–6, 149
ABC of the Diesel Engine, The (1950) 141, 145–6, 149
ABC of Jet Propulsion, The (1954) 141, 145–6, 149
Academy Awards 52
   Best Animated Short Subject 60
   Best Documentary Feature 59–60, 62
   Best Documentary Short Subject 56–62, 118, 193
Academy of Motion Picture Arts and Sciences 35, 59–62. See also Academy Awards
actors 38, 173, 240–3
   animated 20, 28, 30, 35–6, 39–40, 50, 53, 79, 83, 100–1, 115–16, 144, 155, 179, 182, 196–7, 210, 247, 250, 257, 261
Adams, Jeff 69
adaptation 43, 69–70, 125, 149, 189, 212, 231–2
Adventure in the Cell (1962) 215–17
Adventures of Junior Raindrop, The (1948) 131–2
advertisement 62, 208–9, 212
   in animated documentaries 49, 51, 63, 79, 90, 113, 150–2, 169, 210
   of animated documentaries 49–50, 55, 148, 177

African animation 236
Age of Monsters, The (1966) 219–20, 252
Air Power American (1951) 98, 134
Alcohol Cycle, The (1919) 81–2, 84
Alfred P. Sloan Foundation 58, 141
All-Scope Pictures 58
Alonge, Giaime 154, 164
alternative scenario 105, 129
Altman, Rick 51, 64
ambient animation 260–5
ambient sound 194, 260
An Eyeful of Sound (2010) 91, 230
American Cancer Society 41, 57, 140
Analysis Films 162
Anatomy of Motion (1962) 102, 215, 217, 219–20
Andreotti Law 207–8, 214
Angela, Piero 213–14, 249
Animal, Vegetable, Mineral (1957) 109, 181
Animated Conversations film series (1978–81) 119–20, 176
animated documentary. See also classical animated documentary; contemporary animated documentary; early animated documentary
   agenda 16, 51, 63, 79, 85, 89–90, 111, 128, 140, 150, 169, 210
   definition 1–2, 5, 42, 44, 106–7, 126, 177, 236
   and eccentric sound 40–1, 53–5, 106–11, 118, 120, 144, 165, 173–5, 189, 216–17, 240, 248, 253

INDEX

feature-length 2, 7, 35, 46, 50, 70, 125, 149, 228–9, 231, 237, 240–2, 263–4
  and female animators 119, 175, 215, 234–5, 246
  and health 55, 58, 79–84, 97, 112–16, 125–6, 134–5, 140–1, 164, 172, 238–9, 251
  and music 84, 109, 136, 151, 199, 205, 207, 217, 240, 253
  of the origins (*see under* early animated documentary)
  periodization 6, 49–70
  and science 6, 49, 56, 62, 97, 114–16, 132, 137–42, 192–5, 206, 212–20, 247–51, 254–5
animated histories 7, 44, 50–1, 53, 55, 85, 97–8, 101–5, 115, 117–18, 131–2, 134, 142, 149, 151, 169–71, 178–83, 187, 191–5, 204, 209, 212–13, 216, 220, 238, 249–54, 264
animated i-doc (interactive animated documentary) 8, 237, 259–65
animated interjections 1–2, 20–3, 26, 28–9, 32, 209, 232, 237, 255–6
Animated Mathematics (1912) 25
animated memoir 36, 119. *See also* memory
Animated Minds film series (2003) 230, 253
animated segments. *See under* animated interjections
Another Chance (1944) 128–30
Another Day of Life (2018) 231, 237
anthropomorphism 16, 30, 35, 39, 51, 53–4, 58, 63, 81, 88–9, 99–102, 108, 111, 132, 134, 136, 145–6, 154, 163–6, 179, 189, 203, 206, 210, 213, 221, 246, 248
Antony Barrier Productions 166
Approved for Adoption (2012) 59, 231–2, 237
A Is for Architecture (1960) 194
archival footage 43, 61, 98, 240, 248
Art (1974) 118
Art of Photography, The (1962) 216, 220

As Old as the Hills (1950) 55, 109
A Is for Atom (1953) 57, 136, 145
Atoms and Electricity (1975) 115–16
audience 27–8, 30–1, 41–2, 46, 49, 53, 55, 79, 96, 103–4, 111–18, 126–7, 130, 132, 134–5, 137, 139, 149–52, 168, 172–82, 209, 220, 232, 234, 250, 257. *See also* spectatorship
audio recordings 37–40, 70, 120, 176, 230, 233, 239–40, 248, 261
Australian animation 95, 118–19, 235–6, 264
A Is for Autism (1992) 227, 230, 233
autobiography 61, 70, 119–20, 193, 231–8, 244, 246, 248
Avni, Shira 229–30, 233–4

Baby Story (1978) 97, 213
backgrounds 19, 25–7, 30, 67, 79, 81, 83, 86, 129, 175–6, 189, 204, 249, 255–6, 262
Bailing Out (1949) 133
Balance 1950 (1951) 114, 169, 172
Barillé, Albert 117, 250–2
Bass, Saul 61, 117–18
Batchelor, Joy 54, 94, 99, 163, 167, 169–73, 178, 234
Battle of Austerlitz, The (1909) 24–6, 28, 85
Battle of the North Sea, The (1918) 18–19, 22–4, 26
BBC Learning: History (2016) 253
Beginning of the End, The (1942) 204–5
Beloved Ones, The (2007) 38
Benson, George S. 158
Bergmann, Anna 234
Beyond Freedom (2005) 236
Bioscope (2021) 237–8
Birth of the Earth, The (1962) 215, 217
Blazer, Liz 234
Blitz on Bugs (1944) 164, 166
Blood (1982) 115–16
Blood Transfusion (1941) 16–19, 22–3, 26
Bones, Bones, Bones (1944) 164–6

INDEX

Boon, Timothy 167
Borenstein, Joyce 61, 234, 248
Boundary Lines (1946) 137–9
Bowling for Columbine (2002) 1–2
Bozzetto Film 214
Bozzetto, Bruno 115, 178, 212–14, 221, 248–50
Bray Studios 25
Bristles and Brushes (1944) 164–6
Britain's Effort (1917) 85–7
British animation 5–6, 28, 54–5, 58–9, 79, 83–9, 94, 107–9, 111, 113–14, 119, 162–83, 227, 234–6
Broken Treaties (1941) 123–4
Brotherhood of Man (1945) 35, 50, 56, 69, 80, 104, 137, 139, 143–4, 147, 149
Bruscolini, Giuseppe Maria 220
By Word of Mouse (1954) 141

Camouflage (1944) 35, 97, 99, 128–30
Campanelli, Antonietta 215
Canadian animation 5–7, 59, 61, 94, 185–202, 234, 236, 260–1
Capra, Frank 51, 99, 137, 139, 142, 145, 219
captions 21, 25, 42–3, 46, 69, 87, 97, 171, 180, 188, 207, 233, 239, 257
Carousel (1957–77) 209, 212
Carpenter, Ken 144
cartoon documentary 6, 38, 50–2, 214. See also animated documentary; documentary cartoon
Cartoon Films Ltd. 123
Case of the Metal Sheathed Elements, The (1973) 111, 169, 174
Catholic Cinematographic Center 158–9
Cecchinato, Giovanni 209–11
Centrefold (2012) 45, 242–3

CGI (computer generated imagery) 15, 31, 46, 239, 252, 255–6
Channel 4, 120, 227, 236
Chapman, Jane 167–8
Charley in New Town (1946) 35, 55, 167
Charley Junior's Schooldays (1948) 174, 179
Charley's Black Magic (1947) 167, 174, 180
Charley's March of Time (1947) 167, 173, 179–80, 183
Chicago 10: Speak Your Peace (2007) 1, 43–4
Children of the Sun (1960) 44–5, 58
Chinese animation 236
Chion, Michel 38
Chris the Swiss (2018) 235, 237
Cinderagella or Rags to Stitches (1944) 163
cinema verité 256
Ciucci, Rita 215
classical animated documentary 6–7, 41, 43, 67–9, 79, 94–221
 affirmation phase 6, 111–12, 115, 123–31, 137, 166
 consolidation phase 6, 111, 113–15, 134–44, 148, 152–3
 main narrative structures 102–5 (*see also* alternative scenario; animated histories; exemplar story)
 persistence 238–44, 246–57, 264
 precursors of 81, 85, 89, 91
 and print medium 147–9
 sponsors of 41, 50, 55, 57, 59, 94–6, 113, 117, 125, 131–42, 150–3, 162–72, 175, 178, 186, 192, 207–8
 transitional phase 6, 111, 115–21
Clitoris, The (2016) 246
Cohl, Émile 24–6, 28, 85
COI (Central Office of Information) 35, 54–5, 59, 167–8, 171
Cold Comfort (1944) 98, 112, 164–6

Colombo Plan, The
  (1962)   168, 178–9
color   30, 35–6, 55, 100, 145,
  189–90, 242, 262
*Colours of My Father: A Portrait
  of Sam Borenstein, The*
  (1992)   61, 248
Comet (1985)   60, 115, 193–4
comic antics   54, 175, 194, 213
comic books. *See also* graphic novel
  and adaptation   69–70, 147–8
  aesthetics   67–8, 262
  influences on animated
    documentary   67–9
Commonwealth, The (1962)
  170–1, 178
Communication in the Workplace
  (1972)   97
Compost Heaps (1943)   99, 164, 179
condensation   30, 51, 101, 104–5,
  175, 181–2, 253
Conquest of the Sky, The
  (1968)   216, 220
contemporary animated
  documentary   5–8, 35–6,
  40, 43–4, 65, 67, 70, 225–65.
  See also animated i-docs; VR
  animated documentary
  forerunners of   87, 91, 111,
    117–21, 176, 220
Conversation Pieces (1982–3)
  119–20, 176
Cook, Malcolm   151
Corona Cinematografica   7, 214–20
Cosmos–A Personal Voyage
  (1980)   29
Cosmos–A Spacetime Odyssey
  (2014)   29, 254–5
Council Matters (1984)   168, 174
Crafton, Donald   1, 30
Crawley Films   186
Creation of the World, The (1958)   7
Creature Comforts (2003–11)   39
Curious History of Money, The
  (1969)   169, 175
Curlic: The Path to Beyond
  (2011)   235, 237
Czech animation   7, 95, 97–8, 114

Daddy's Little Bit of Dresden China
  (1988)   230–1
Dam the Delta (1958)   168, 171, 178
*Dead Reckoning: Champlain in
  America* (2009)   1, 254, 256–7
Decline of an Empire, The
  (1940)   204
Defense Against Invasion (1943)
  16–19, 22–3, 53, 102, 109, 116,
  125, 158, 205
DelGaudio, Sybil   2, 34–5, 45
Dessy, Nicola   203
The Devil in the Bottle (1968)   209
D4 Film Studios Inc.   133–4
digital
  animation   23, 31–2, 246, 255
  revolution   4, 259
Direct Cinema   67, 120, 256
Diseases Spread (1926)   83
Disney, Walt   13, 21, 52–6, 59, 66,
  70, 96, 101, 113, 127, 152–9,
  177, 207
Disorientation Crashes (1946)   133
Dividend in Depth (1954)   142, 145,
  148, 151–2
docudrama   6, 8, 42–7, 62, 66, 97,
  144, 227, 238, 243–4, 254,
  257
docufiction   6, 41, 47, 62, 67, 237
documentary film   22, 61, 113, 177,
  237. *See also* nonfiction
documentary cartoon   6, 50, 54,
  96, 153. *See also* animated
  documentary; cartoon
  documentary
Dollar Dance (1943)   105,
  112, 188–9
Dollywood   7, 59
Donald Duck   56, 63, 101, 103,
  152, 155–6
Donald in Mathmagic Land
  (1959)   56, 61, 69, 97, 148,
  153, 155
Dopey   54, 106, 155
*Down a Long Way. The Story of an
  Oil-Well* (1954)   108–9
Down the Gasoline Trail
  (1935)   89–90

Drafty, Isn't It (1957)   134
drawn-on film animation   188
Dreams of a Land (1989)
   247–8
Dufay-Chromex   163–4
Dunning, George   187
Dustbin Parade (1942)   163
Dutch animation   7, 114, 237

Earle, Eyvind   158
early animated documentary   6, 65, 67, 77–91, 140, 228
Earth Is a Battlefield (1957)   169
Earth Is Born, The (1957)   59
educational film   6, 49, 51, 53, 55, 57–9, 62, 66, 87–9, 111–12, 129, 138–9, 151–2, 169, 204, 208–16, 247–8. *See also* visual education
Ehrlich, Nea   4
Elementary and Pylon Eights (1944)   128–30
Elwis Films   163
Emergency Landing on Land (1947)   133
Enemy Bacteria, The (1945)   128, 130
Energetically Yours (1957)   110, 142
Energy and Matter (1966)   193–4, 199
Enterprise (1951)   114, 169, 172
Eureka! (1980–1)   187
Everybody Rides the Carousel (1975)   118–19
exemplar story   41, 45, 57–8, 80–1, 102–5, 124, 126–7, 130, 132–6, 143, 152
Expanding World Relationships (1946)   131–2
experimentation   78, 84, 91, 139, 166, 173, 180–8, 201–4
expository mode   8, 34, 37, 53, 64, 98, 106
  in animation   25, 35, 37, 55, 65, 79–82, 95, 115–21, 123, 227–8, 246–57, 264

Extinction of the Dinosaurs (1976)   194
Eye's Magic (1963)   215

fabled animation   5–6, 23, 25, 28–32, 34–7, 51, 54–9, 62, 78–89, 124, 126, 129, 131, 136, 154, 163, 165–6, 171, 175–6, 186–7, 204–9, 216, 218, 235, 237, 242–3, 247–8
Fable Retold, A (1965)   95
Family Planning (1967)   101, 103, 106–7, 155
Family Tree (1950)   114, 197–8
Farmer Charley (1947)   167, 179
feminine aesthetic   235
Fertilizers (1960)   113, 209
Few Quick Facts: About Fear, A (1945)   128–30
Few Quick Facts: Inflation, A (1944)   112, 128–30
Few Quick Facts: Japan, A (1945)   127–8
Filling the Gap (1942)   163–4, 179, 181
Film Graphics Inc.   136, 149, 157
Film Traders   163, 166
Final Fantasy: The Spirit Within (2001)   13, 15
Finding His Voice (1929)   88–91
First Line of Defence (1949)   171, 178, 180–1
Fish Spoilage Control (1956)   192, 196, 199, 201
Five Billion Years (1981)   193, 196, 248
flashback   40, 133, 137
flashforward   133
Flat Hatting (1946)   56–7, 133
Flavours of Iraq (2018)   232
Fleischer, Max   79, 88–9
Fleming, Ann Marie   234
Fleming, Robert   199
Flight Safety and You (1976–7)   168, 172–3, 176
Flood of Memory (2008)   236
Fly, The (1919)   81–4

Food Will Win the War (1942) 125, 154
For Her (2017) 236
For the Curious (2001–5) 254
Four Methods of Flush Riveting (1942) 25–6, 124, 185–6
French animation 7, 28, 82, 95, 117, 132, 168, 236–7, 248–50
Fresh Laid Plans (1951) 57–8, 98–9, 136–7, 145
fun factor 101, 129, 141, 154
Furniss, Maureen 14–15, 100, 234

Gagliardo, Elio 102, 214, 217, 220
Gagliardo, Ezio 214, 217, 220
gags 55, 101, 129, 179. *See also* comic antics
Gamma Film 209, 212
Gas Naturally (1984) 169, 176
Gasoline's Amazing Molecules (1948) 100, 144–9
Gaudenzi, Sandra 259
generalizing synecdoche 79–83, 86, 89, 100–1, 103–6, 126–7, 164–5, 184, 189, 191, 222, 240–2, 246
German animation 25, 95, 98, 237
Gervasio, Raffaele 207
Gibba 214–16, 218
Glynne, Andy 63–4, 253
Goldsmith, Sidney 60, 115, 190, 193–4
Gomas, Guido 214, 220
Good Wrinkles. The Story of a Remarkable Fruit (1952) 58, 113, 150–1
Goss, Jacqueline 234
Grafilm Productions Inc. 187
Grain That Built a Hemisphere, The (1943) 53, 56, 61, 110, 125
Grampaw Pettibone 131, 133
Grandchildren's Mother, The (2008) 236
graphic novel 69–70, 231–2, 263
aesthetics 255, 262
graphic verité 220, 256
graphic vocabulary 2, 16, 19, 22, 25–7, 29–30, 54, 88, 175

Great Cat Family, The (1956) 50, 69, 137, 148, 153
Great Problem, A (1960) 95, 104, 106–7
Great Synthesis (1964) 98
Green Wave, The (2010) 43–4, 70, 237, 262
Grierson, John 41, 177, 185–6, 188–9, 201

Haines, Tim 46, 252–3, 255–6
Halas & Batchelor Cartoon Films 7, 35, 50, 54, 59, 64, 89, 108, 162, 166, 168–9, 173, 177–83, 201, 210, 220
Halas, John 29–31, 52, 54–6, 59, 70, 94, 99, 163–4, 167, 172–3, 177–83, 212–13, 249
hand-drawn animation 25, 31–2, 171, 217, 239, 250
Healthy and Happy (1962) 95, 114
Heilborn, Hanna 234, 241
Heir-Conditioned (1955) 141
Hemo the Magnificent (1957) 51, 102, 137, 139, 219
Heredity (1966) 215
Herstory (2011) 236
Hibbert-Jones, Dee 234–5
Hight, Craig 8, 23
His Mother's Voice (1997) 230, 239, 241
History of Inventions (1959) 178, 212–13, 249
History of the Cinema (1956) 101, 114, 178–9, 181
Holiday Home (1981) 119–20
Honess Roe, Annabelle 2, 4, 15, 26, 49, 62–3, 176, 230, 239, 241–2, 252
Hope That Jack Built, The (1957) 58, 138, 144
Horizons of Hope (1954) 57–8, 97, 136, 141
How Man Learned to Fly (1958) 7, 114
How to Catch a Cold (1951) 134, 145, 153, 157
How to Feed Plants (1960) 209–10

INDEX

How to Have an Accident at Work (1959)   96–7, 114, 153, 155
How to Have an Accident in the Home (1956)   114, 155
How War Came (1941)   123–4
Hubley, Faith   58, 118–19, 136, 149, 234
Hubley, John   58, 100, 111–12, 118–19, 136, 149, 157
Huff and Puff. A Story of Hyperventilation (1955)   192, 198, 200
humour   51, 89, 137, 139, 141, 154, 178, 248–50

i-doc (interactive documentary)   259, 264
I'm Glad You Asked That Question (1970)   111, 169, 174–5
I'm No Fool… (1955–6)   35–6, 98, 137, 154–5, 157
In a Nutshell (1971)   99, 192
indexicality   14, 26, 39–40, 42–3, 98, 176
Indian animation   95, 104, 106, 108, 114, 236
industrial film   89, 100, 117, 136, 141–4, 149–53, 169–72, 207–9, 212, 221, 249–50
informational film   19–20, 53, 96, 112–18, 125, 128–9, 150–2, 158–9, 163, 171, 254
Inside Magoo (1960)   57, 135, 141
Inside Story of Lubricating Oil, The (1949). *See under Lubricating Oil's Amazing Molecules*
Inside Story of Modern Gasoline, The (1948). *See under Gasoline's Amazing Molecules*
instructional film   52, 59, 61, 113, 115–16, 158, 163, 171–2, 192, 210, 254
Interview (1979)   119–20, 193–4, 201
interviews   37–40, 43, 228, 230, 233–4, 239–42, 256–7, 259–64
Invisible Picture Show (2013)   8, 260–4

Irinka & Sandrinka (2007)   232–3
Isotype   16–17, 181
Israeli animation   236
Is the Man Who Is Tall Happy? An Animated Conversation with Noam Chomsky (2013)   60, 232, 237, 239
It Must Be Said (1918)   80
It Never Rains Oil (1953)   143
It's Everybody's Business (1954)   138, 143
It's Like That (2003)   44–5, 235, 239, 241
Italian animation   7, 79, 95, 109, 113–15, 203–21, 237, 248–9

Japanese animation   83, 119, 236
Jiminy Cricket   35, 99, 155, 157
Jodoin, René   186–7
John Sutherland Productions   57, 136–8, 141, 143, 145, 149, 152, 157–8. *See also* Sutherland, John
Join-Up Collisions (1946)   133
Journey through Electricity (1981–3)   115–16
Journey through Time: The Human Story (1983)   193
Joy of Life, The (1992)   254

Kamp, Mischa   228, 235, 243
Ketchup (2012)   236
Kinshasa, September Noir (1992)   236
Kitson, Clare   227, 233
Knowledge, the World and Me (1993)   249
Koenig, Wolf   190
Kroitor, Roman   59

Lacey, Gillian   235
Lambart, Evelyn   187, 234
Land, Ellie   235, 242
Landing Accidents (1946)   133
Land Tilling (1961)   211
Larkins Studio   58, 132, 166, 168–9, 172–3, 175, 180
Last Day of Freedom (2015)   61

Last Hijack (2014)   60, 229, 235, 237, 264
Last Hijack Interactive (2014)   8, 260, 262–4
Lebow, Alisa   64
Leeds Animation Workshop   166, 235
Lefèvre, Pascal   34
Leon Schlesinger Presents "Bugs Bunny" (1942)   63
Les Gémeaux   132, 168
Letter from Siberia (1958)   28
Lida Moser Photographer. Odyssey in Black and White (2017)   248
lightning sketch   85, 87
limited animation   212, 217
Lingford, Ruth   91, 235
Little Deaths (2010)   91, 239
Little Voices (2010)   44, 233, 237
live-action   6–7, 13–14, 20–3, 26–32, 36–7, 43, 62–3, 81, 85, 87–91, 98, 102, 106, 123, 125, 131–2, 134, 142, 150, 167, 177, 185, 187, 205–6, 210, 214, 231–2, 235, 240, 248, 254, 256–7, 259–60, 262
   and animation   83, 89, 119, 168, 176, 209, 216, 237
   camera   67
   and docudramas   46–7
   prologue   87–8
Live and Let Live (1947)   151–2
Local Government. A History in Pictures (1949)   58–9, 171
Look Who's Driving (1954)   56–7, 67–9, 80, 148, 151–2
Lortac   79
Low, Colin   44, 59, 190, 193, 195, 201
Lubricating Oil's Amazing Molecules (1949)   100, 145, 148–50
Luce Institute   81
Lutz, Edwin George   77–8
Lye, Len   79, 90–1

McCay, Winsor   44, 65, 67, 79, 87–8
MacKay, Jim   187
McLaren, Norman   59, 185–8, 190, 193, 198

Magic Lab (1962)   102, 215
Magna Carta. The Story of Man's Fight for Liberty (1946)   168, 171, 176
Maitland, Keith   46
Make Mine Freedom (1948)   138
Malépart-Traversy, Lori   246
Man Alive! (1952)   41, 45, 50, 56–7, 61, 64, 141
Man and the Moon (1955)   153
Manhattan (1979)   198
Man in Space (1956)   56, 61, 137, 153
Man on the Land (1951)   56, 109, 136
Manvell, Roger   29, 31, 173
Man with a Movie Camera (1929)   28
map-film   19, 24, 83, 85–7, 204–5
Map of Europe, The (1941)   204
Mars and Beyond (1957)   153
Meet King Joe (1949)   138
Megumi (2008)   236
memory   3, 35–6, 44, 46, 154, 229–33, 247–8, 252, 264. See also animated memoir
Men of Merit (A Lantern Lecture) (1948)   98, 110, 171
Mercury (1986)   249
metamorphosis   30–1, 53, 101, 105, 182, 243
metaphor   16, 19–20, 30, 39, 53, 101–2, 109–10, 113–14, 127, 154, 207, 216, 243, 261, 264
Meteorology (1965)   218
metonymy   243
Metric System (1958)   95, 108
Metz, Christian   105
Mihailova, Mihaela   25
Minoru: Memory of Exile (1992)   227–8, 230–2, 247
Miracle of Blood, The (1962)   215, 218, 220
Mirrors of Time (1991)   247–8, 255
Missile Named Mac, A (1962)   136, 144–5, 150–1
mockumentary   39, 62
Model Sorter (1943)   99, 112, 163–6
Modern Guide to Health (1946)   114, 172
MOI (Ministry of Information)   162–3, 165–7

INDEX

Montecatini 89, 208–11, 221
Moore, Samantha 38, 91, 235
More Hanky Panky (1945) 164
More Than Meets the Eye (1952) 50, 150–1
Morgen, Brett 44, 67
Moving Spirit, The (1953) 55, 69, 169, 179, 181–2
Mukii, Ng'endo 235
Multiple Screening (1950) 131–2, 134–5
My Grandmother's Lingo (2016) 264
My Universe Inside Out (1996) 231

Naked (2006) 228, 239, 243
National Film Board of Canada 7, 60, 94, 115, 185–202, 227, 236, 247–8, 255
  Unit B 190, 201
Nature of Things, The (1956) 98, 137, 155
Ned Wethered (1983) 119–20
Neighbours (1952) 59, 61, 193–4, 198, 201
Neurath, Marie 16–17, 181
Neurath, Otto 16–17, 181
Never Ending Story (2014) 236
New Behaviors (1987) 249
New Spirit, The (1942) 56, 61, 63, 98, 112, 124–6, 155–6
Next Day, The (2011) 8, 260–1, 263–4
Nicholas Cartoon Films Ltd. 166
Nichols, Bill 3, 5, 8, 22, 34, 49, 53, 64, 90, 98, 102, 120
nonfiction 4, 14, 16, 22–3, 27–8, 37, 41–2, 47, 49, 56, 59, 64, 77, 106, 138, 164, 178, 204, 255–6, 259
  animation 2, 4–5, 17, 23–7, 34, 49, 52, 54, 62, 66, 78, 88–9, 98, 136–7, 139, 186, 204–5, 218, 250, 252 (*see also* sober animation)
  book 125, 212, 231
  comics 67–70
  and Disney 13, 21, 124, 158, 185

O'Gallop 79
observational mode 247, 256
OCIAA (Office of the Coordinator of Inter-American Affairs) 125–6
Odin, Roger 25, 27, 30–2, 100
Office of War Information 125
Of Stars and Men (1964) 109, 149
Once Upon a Time... franchise 250–7
Once Upon a Time... Man (1978) 117, 250–1
One Divided by Two (1998) 248
One Pair of Nostrils (1944) 112, 164–5
Origin of Life on Earth (1972) 193, 196
Ostherr, Kirsten 78, 112
Our Friend the Atom (1957) 97, 137, 145, 149, 153
Our Mr. Sun (1956) 43, 97, 99, 106, 137, 145
overture sequence 198–9, 201

Paget, Derek 42–4, 65–6
Pain (1992) 249–50
Painters of Prehistory, The (1962) 216–17
paint on glass 239
Pan-tele-tron (1957) 113, 169, 175
paratextuality 43, 49–52, 87, 151, 198
participatory mode 34, 120, 247
Paul Rotha Productions Ltd. 16–17
Pauwels, Luc 27
Pay Attention to the Label (1966) 89, 99, 110, 114, 209–10
Peak Load (1944) 164–6
Pearl & Dean 166, 169
Pensuti, Luigi Liberio 79–80, 204–5
performative mode 34
Persepolis (2007) 231, 237, 241
personification 51, 81–4, 88, 127, 136, 144–7, 173, 210, 251
Phosphorus. Life for the Plants (1956) 209–10
photography 14–15, 31–2, 43, 61, 78, 93, 98, 216, 240–1, 256, 263
  digital destruction of 4

Picture in Your Mind (1948)   137–9
Pikadon (1978)   119–20
Pinocchio (1940)   14, 99
Piping Hot (1959)   169, 179, 182
Planet Dinosaur (2011)   37, 254
Plant of the Senses, The (1961)   215–17, 220
Play Safe (1978)   116, 169, 172, 174, 176
poetic mode   34, 90–1
Portafilms   142, 144
Position Firing (1944)   128–30
Potterton, Gerald   187, 190, 192, 200–1
Potterton Productions   187
Power to Fly (1954)   50, 55, 169, 178, 181–2, 220
Primitive Pete   157
propaganda
 as agenda   63, 79, 85, 96, 111–12, 124–5, 127–9, 134, 204
 definition   96
 film   64, 113–14, 125–6, 152, 162–4, 180, 188, 204
psychorealism   230
public service film   6, 49–59, 62, 80–1, 84, 191–2, 205
Public Threat n. 1. Life and Mishaps of the Koch Bacillus (1938)   205–6
Pump Trouble (1954)   56–7, 135, 140

Quark (1981–94)   213–14, 248
Quark Economy (1986)   249

Ragan, Philip   187
Raphael G. Wolff Studios   133
Rathburn, Eldon   199
realism   5, 13–16, 21, 23, 194, 255
Reason and Emotion (1943)   125, 127
reenactment   36, 130, 168
 in live-action   29
Referee (1976)   168, 172
Refining (1983)   111, 169, 174–6
Refrigeration: Principles of Mechanical Refrigeration (1964)   134
Renov, Michael   2, 22–3, 231–2

Rhapsody of Steel (1959)   51, 57, 143, 151, 158
Riches of the Earth (1954)   193, 195
Rimminen, Marjut   235
River of Steel (1951)   105, 169
The Road of Health (1936)   83–4
Rodney (1950)   135, 140, 144–5
Romance of Transportation in Canada, The (1952)   44, 101, 109, 114, 192–5, 198–9
Rotha, Paul   17
rotoscope animation   46, 239
Rouxel, Jacques   115–16, 248–50, 252
Rowley, Stephen   14
Ruta, Carla   215
Ryan (2004)   39, 44, 229–30, 232–3, 247

Sabnani, Nina   235
Safe as Houses (1983)   116, 169, 172, 174, 176
safety film   57, 96–7, 114–16, 128, 132–3, 152, 155, 157, 164, 168, 172–3, 188–9
Saint-Pierre, Marie-Josée   235
Saludos Amigos (1942)   157
Samouni Road (2018)   237
Samuel de Champlain (1964)   194
Sappy Homiens (1956)   57, 135, 141
Satellites of the Sun (1974)   115, 193–4, 196, 198
Satrapi, Marjane   69, 231–2, 235, 241
Schwartz, Zachary   100, 111, 157
Science Please! (1998–2001)   247–8
Seeking Refuge (2012)   40, 253
Short History of the Highrise, A (2013)   264
Silence (1998)   35–6, 44, 231, 243
sincerity   45–7, 65
 lack of   54, 86
Sinking of the Lusitania, The (1918)   4, 18–19, 22–3, 28, 44, 65, 67, 85–7, 92
Sleepless (2016)   235, 242
Sleepy   155–6

Slum Has to Be Conquered, The (1918) 82
Small, Tragic Circus of So-and-so, The (1993) 249
Smoodin, Eric 137, 142
Snack and Drink (1999) 35, 230
Sneezy 155–6
Snow White and the Seven Dwarfs (1937) 14–15, 54, 156
sober animation 5, 23–8, 30, 34, 36–7, 44, 62, 78, 83–9, 98, 123–4, 126, 129, 131, 134, 139, 176, 179, 186, 203–6, 209, 218, 240, 247
  x-ray animation 200
sobriety 5, 16–23. *See also* sober animation
Sofian, Sheila 46, 235, 239, 242
Soil Is Hungry, The (1961) 114, 209–11
Something You Didn't Eat (1945) 50, 125, 131
So Much for So Little (1949) 58, 61, 68–9, 107, 131–2, 134–5, 141–3
Southern Ladies Animation Group 235
Spare a Thought (1978) 171
Spark in Time on the Firing Line, A (1962) 142, 144
Specific Gravity, The (1966) 215
spectatorship 13–15, 19, 25, 27–8, 31–2, 41, 46, 67–9, 79–80, 87, 98, 103–6, 114, 149, 156, 165, 171–2, 257. *See also* audience
Speed, Lancelot 79, 85–7
Speed the Plough (1956) 55, 99, 114, 169, 174, 181–2, 210
Stanley Takes a Trip (1947) 190–1
stardom 100, 155
Starlife (1983) 115, 193
Stevens, Beryl 175, 234
Stitch and Save (1943) 188
Stoïanov, Sandrine 233, 235
stop-motion 7, 19, 28, 58–9, 61, 151, 171, 194, 239
Story About Breadmaking in the Year 1255 A.D., A (1948) 190–1

Storyboard Productions 136
StoryCorps film series (2010–current)
  Q&A (2010) 230
  Road Home, The (2013) 40
Story of Menstruation, The (1946) 97, 134–5, 148, 151, 153–5
Story of Oil, The (1955) 50–1, 153
Strange Case of the Cosmic Rays, The (1957) 137
Strøm, Gunnar 1, 34, 190
Structure of Unions, The (1955) 194
Studio Folimage 254
subjectivity 7–8, 14, 37, 45, 64–5, 67, 117–20, 201, 227–9, 234, 238, 241–2, 246–8, 252–3, 257, 264
Sunrise Over Tiananmen Square (1998) 61, 231
Sutherland, John 51, 97, 157–8
Swedish animation 119, 236
symbolism 16, 19, 30–1, 53, 86, 101–2
synecdoche 16, 19, 30–1, 53, 154, 207, 243. *See also* generalizing synecdoche

Talisman, Nomi 235
Tapum! The History of Arms (1958) 212–14, 249
Tavern of Tuberculosis, The (1935) 205
Tax: The Outcome of Income (1975) 192–4
Tear (2015) 236
Teeth Are to Keep (1949) 190–2
Tempo Productions 132, 136, 140, 157
Ten: The Magic Number (1973) 193
T for Teacher (1947) 107–8, 110, 172
There Once Lived ... Five Stories of Real People (2017) 264
Thinker?, The (1981) 95
Think of the Future (1956) 181, 183
Thompson, Kirsten Moana 151
Thousand Million Years, A (1954) 193, 195

Three Blind Mice (1945) 96, 114, 188–9
Time and Terrain (1948) 190
Tiomkin, Dimitri 151
To Demonstrate How Spiders Fly (1909) 28, 65, 79
Tombolino's Hygiene (1935 ca.) 80
Toot, Whistle, Plunk and Boom (1953) 51, 98, 145, 153, 157–8, 212
To Resist Tuberculosis, Stay Strong (1918) 82
Torre, Dan 4
To Save These Lives (1949) 140
Tower (2016) 46, 60, 237, 239–41
To Your Health (1956) 59
Trade Tatoo (1937) 90–1
Traitor Within, The (1946) 100, 102, 135–6, 140
transmediality 237–8
trauma 7, 37, 40, 44, 65, 230, 233, 238, 241, 248
Trouble with Love and Sex, The (2012) 239, 242
Truth Has Fallen (2013) 235, 237, 239
Tying Your Own Shoes (2009) 230, 233–5, 247

uncanny 15
Unchained Goddess, The (1958) 137, 145
Universe (1960) 59, 61, 193, 201
Unseen Enemy, The (1945) 126
UPA (United Productions of America) 41, 50, 56–7, 64, 69, 80, 104, 129, 132, 136, 140–1, 143, 152, 157, 217
Upjohn's Triangle of Health film series (1968–9, 1979) 116
Urbano, Carl 136, 138, 145
US animation 5–6, 94, 98, 123–61, 234, 236

van Dijck, José 252–3, 255
veridiction 41–3, 106, 189

markers of 23, 36–7, 64, 87, 98, 240, 244
Veronesi, Luigi 207
Verrall, Robert 190, 199
Victory Through Air Power (1943) 50–1, 125
visual education 17, 54, 95–6, 153–4, 158
voice of animated documentary 37–41, 84, 228, 241–2
voice-in 144
voice-of-authority (*see under* voice-of-God)
voice-of-God 6, 26–7, 30, 35, 37, 41, 46, 50–1, 53–5, 62–4, 68–9, 80, 97–9, 101, 103–11, 116–18, 123, 125, 129–37, 142–5, 149–57, 163–5, 173–90, 195, 198–217, 240, 246–52, 256–7
voice-off 41
voiceover 40, 42–3, 253 (*see also* voice-of-God)
Voting for Servicemen Overseas (1944) 128–30
VR animated documentary 238

Waiting for Superman (2010) 1–2, 20–3
Walking with Dinosaurs (1999) 37, 46, 220, 252–7
Walt Disney Studios 7, 14–16, 25, 50–1, 61, 64, 69, 97–9, 106, 116, 124–6, 129, 131–2, 134–7, 145, 149, 151–9, 185–7, 205, 212
Waltz with Bashir (2008) 3–4, 35, 44, 231, 235–7, 262
Ward, Paul 36, 45, 91, 253
War Front (1940) 204
Warner Brothers 58, 129–34, 136–7, 141
War that Never Ends, The (1949) 95
Water, Friend or Enemy (1943) 53, 107–8, 125, 158
Water Hammers (1940) 205–6
Watson, Karen 231, 235

We've Come a Long Way (1952) 107, 169, 181
Weapon of War (1944) 127, 129
Wells, Paul 2, 21, 23, 30, 46, 54, 178, 180–1, 235
What Makes Us Tick (1952) 138
What's Blood Got to Do with It? (2004) 253
Why Man Creates (1968) 61, 117–18
Williams, Chester 140
Williams, Kenneth 173
Williams, Linda 8
Winged Scourge, The (1943) 35–6, 44, 53–4, 64, 81, 106, 112, 125–7, 155–6, 158–9
Winston, Brian 4, 38, 227
Withmore, Lee 119, 235
Without Fear (1951) 115, 132, 168
Wolting, Femke 229, 235
Woolly Mammoth (1979) 193–6, 252
Wop May (1979) 194
Working Dollars (1957) 136, 138
World Is Born, A (1955) 153
World Wide Pictures 166, 168–9

Yadin, Orly 235
Yamamoto, Sanae 79
Yankee Dood It (1956) 141
You and Your... (1955–7) 35–6, 98–9, 155
You and Your Health (1979) 168, 180
You Can Be Safe from X-Rays (1952) 131–2, 134
Your Very Good Health (1947) 55, 167, 173, 176

Zangrando, Fiorello 209–10
Zimmermann, Yvonne 209–10
zoomorphism 30

2D animation 246, 261
3D animation 239, 261
11 Steps to Survival (1973) 116, 192, 197, 199
25 April (2015) 70, 228–9, 237, 240, 243, 247
90 Day Wondering? (1956) 58, 134
64,000,000 Years Ago (1981) 193–5, 198, 252

www.ingramcontent.com/pod-product-compliance
Lightning Source LLC
Chambersburg PA
CBHW052148300426
44115CB00011B/1568